A Corpus-driven Study of Discourse Intonation

Studies in Corpus Linguistics (SCL)

SCL focuses on the use of corpora throughout language study, the development of a quantitative approach to linguistics, the design and use of new tools for processing language texts, and the theoretical implications of a data-rich discipline.

Volume 32

A Corpus-driven Study of Discourse Intonation. The Hong Kong Corpus of Spoken English (Prosodic)
by Winnie Cheng, Chris Greaves and Martin Warren

A Corpus-driven Study
of Discourse Intonation

The Hong Kong Corpus of Spoken English
(Prosodic)

Winnie Cheng

Chris Greaves

Martin Warren

The Hong Kong Polytechnic University

John Benjamins Publishing Company

Amsterdam / Philadelphia

™ The paper used in this publication meets the minimum requirements of American National Standard for Information Sciences – Permanence of Paper for Printed Library Materials, ANSI z39.48-1984.

Library of Congress Cataloging-in-Publication Data

Cheng, Winnie.
 A corpus-driven study of discourse intonation : the Hong Kong corpus of spoken
     English (prosodic) / by Winnie Cheng, Chris Greaves, and Martin Warren.
   p. cm. (Studies in Corpus Linguistics, ISSN 1388-0373 ; v. 32)
 Includes bibliographical references and index.
     1. English language--Intonation. 2. English language--Phonology, Comparative--
     Chinese. 3. Intercultural communication--China--Hong Kong. 4. Cantonese
     dialects. I. Greaves, Chris. II. Warren, Martin, 1962- III. Title. IV. Series.
   PE1139.5.C445   2008
 421'.6--dc22   2008037432
 ISBN 978 90 272 2306 7 (Hb; alk. paper)

John Benjamins Publishing Co. · P.O. Box 36224 · 1020 ME Amsterdam · The Netherlands
John Benjamins North America · P.O. Box 27519 · Philadelphia PA 19118-0519 · USA

Respectfully dedicated to the memory of
David Brazil and John McHardy Sinclair

Table of contents

Acknowledgement

The study reported in this book spans many years of work and the authors owe a debt of gratitude to many individuals; from those who so generously allowed us to record them to the many research assistants and student assistants who helped us to collect and transcribe the data. Among these, some deserve special mention because of the time and effort which they devoted to the project. Alice Lo was a great help to us in collecting and orthographically transcribing the Hong Kong Corpus of Spoken English (HKSCE) and Sharon Chu was the key figure in the monumental task of prosodically transcribing the HKCSE (prosodic). Esther Ho and Phoenix Lam were heavily involved in the process of checking the accuracy of the transcripts and never complained about the tedious nature of such work. Richard Cauldwell was outstanding in his role as project consultant and his advice was crucial to the success of the project. John Sinclair and Elena Tognini-Bonelli were very supportive of our work and provided invaluable opportunities for us to present the corpus, iConc software and some of our findings at their Tuscan Word Centre Workshops in 2005 and 2006. As editor of the series Studies in Corpus Linguistics, Elena made available to us her editorial expertise throughout the editorial process as did her colleague Kees Vaes. Many other colleagues have also supported our work over the years and given us useful critical feedback and so we would like here to thank Annelie Ädel, Julia Bamford, Francesca Bargiela, Marina Bondi, Ulla Connor, Joan Cutting, Fiona Farr, John Flowerdew, Mauricio Gotti, Michaela Mahlberg, Michael McCarthy, Anne O'Keeffe, Randi Reppen, Jane Setter, Thom Upton and Steve Walsh. Finally, we would like to thank Martin Hewings for his very thorough and insightful comments on the manuscript.

The work described in this book was substantially supported by a grant from the Research Grants Council of the Hong Kong Special Administrative Region (Project No. BQ 396 [PolyU 5270/00H]).

CHAPTER 1

Introduction

Background

This study represents the first attempt that has ever been made to provide a description of the communicative role of discourse intonation (Brazil 1985, 1997) manifested in a corpus of naturally-occurring discourses. The corpus is the 0.9-million-word Hong Kong Corpus of Spoken English (HKCSE) (prosodic), comprised of four sub-corpora (academic, business, conversation and public), which was compiled in Hong Kong between 1997 and 2002.

The HKCSE (prosodic) has been of great value for teaching and learning, serving as a resource bank for such subjects as discourse intonation, discourse analysis, intercultural communication, pragmatics, and, obviously, corpus linguistics. Its value in research is equally great, particularly since the computer-mediated software, iConc, designed by Chris Greaves, has become available for performing searches for the discourse intonation systems and choices in the HKCSE (prosodic) (Cheng, Greaves and Warren 2005) (see Chapter 3 for a description of iConc). Since 2002, about thirty research studies[1] have been published or presented to different audiences, including interested academics and researchers in the Tuscan Word Centre international workshops in 2005 and 2006. Examples of these research studies are those on the intonation of indirect speech acts (Cheng 2002), the intonation of declarative-mood questions (Cheng and Warren 2002), speakers making tone choices (i.e. rise and rise-fall tones) to exert dominance and control (Warren 2004), the intonation of 'yes/no' questions, *wh*-questions, and declarative questions (Cheng 2004b), the intonation of extended collocations (Cheng and Warren 2008), the intonation of disagreement (Cheng and Warren 2005), and discourse intonation and vague language (Warren 2007). Investigations into discourse intonation in the HKCSE (prosodic) have examined an array of topics of interest to individual academics, researchers and students, and contributed to an informed understanding of the communicative value of discourse intonation.

The HKCSE (prosodic), therefore, has proven to serve as a rich resource in providing a large volume of authentic data, situated in a wide range of intercultural communicative contexts fulfilling different communicative purposes, the patterns

---

1. A full list of HKCSE (prosodic) related publications is in Appendix 1.

and associated meanings of which are readily analyzable. It is not only the size of the HKCSE that makes it so invaluable, but, most important of all, the framework adopted to transcribe it, which essentially focuses on meaning making by speakers in the moment-by-moment real-time interaction. This chapter describes the HKCSE (prosodic) with respect to contents, collection of data, and distribution of speaker groups and gender. The discourse intonation systems (Brazil 1997) are described in Chapter two.

The Hong Kong Corpus of Spoken English (HKCSE)

The work to compile the Hong Kong Corpus of Spoken English (HKCSE) began in the mid-1990s with the collection of half-a-million words of authentic, naturally occurring conversations (Cheng and Warren 1999b), and has grown to include a total of four sub-corpora, each consisting of 50 hours of naturally occurring talk (i.e. approximately two million words in total). The four sub-corpora were chosen to represent the main overarching domains of spoken discourses found in the Hong Kong context, namely academic, business, conversation, and public. Fishman (1972) categorises day-to-day language use into 'domains': family, friendship, religion, education, and employment, and defines 'domains' in terms of "institutional contexts or socio-ecological co-occurrences" which "enable us to understand that language choice and topic, appropriate though they may be for analysis of individual behavior at the level of face-to-face verbal encounters, are related to widespread socio-cultural norms and expectations" (ibid.: 441). In cross-cultural pragmatics studies, Boxer (2002: 153) considers the three most relevant domains to be "the spheres of social interaction, educational encounters, and work life".

In the HKSCE, each of the four sub-corpora consists of a variety of discourse types and speakers, with the speakers engaging in different communicative or discursive events and practices, and for different communicative purposes. Briefly, the four sub-corpora are, in the sequence in which they were compiled from 1997 to 2002, conversations, academic discourses, business discourses and public discourses. The two-million-word HKCSE is the largest corpus of authentic, naturally-occurring spoken English discourses compiled in Hong Kong to date.

In 2000, it was decided to further enrich the HKCSE as a research, learning and teaching resource by adding a prosodic transcription to the orthographic transcription. A combination of financial constraints and quality of data issues resulting from working with naturally occurring data has meant that it has not been possible to prosodically transcribe all of the two-million-word HKCSE, and so 900,214 words have been prosodically transcribed. Prosodically transcribing the HKCSE was a major task rarely undertaken with a corpus of this size.

The model adopted for the prosodic transcription is the systems of discourse intonation originated by David Brazil (1925-1995) described in *The Communicative Value of Intonation in English* (1985, 1997). In his description and illustration of the discourse intonation framework, Brazil uses "minimally contrasted pairs" to advance the proposition, invented examples to pre-empt questions about "what (in terms of the evolving description) might *alternatively have* happened", and rather short examples to focus on specific contextual implications of the text being examined (Brazil 1997: x). The present study is not suggesting that Brazil always relied on constructed examples because elsewhere he uses examples drawn from naturally-occurring data (see for example, Brazil, Coulthard and Johns, 1980). Others (see, for example, Goh 1998, 2000, Chun 2002, Hewings 1986, 1990, Cauldwell 2007) have used discourse intonation across a range of discourse types, and across different languages, and it has proved to be successful in English language teaching (for example, Cauldwell 2003a, 2003b).

The HKCSE (prosodic) is the first large-scale attempt to use the categories and conventions of discourse intonation in its transcription. Forty-five percent of the 2-million-word HKCSE has been prosodically transcribed, and has become the HKCSE (prosodic). It is this HKCSE (prosodic) that is examined and described in this book. The HKCSE (prosodic), however, is not the first corpus to have added a prosodic transcription. The 500,000-word London-Lund Corpus (LLC) (Svartvik 1990: 15), for instance, has prosodic transcriptions that show tone units, onsets, location of nuclei, direction of nuclear tones and two degrees of stress. The 170,000-word Survey of English Usage corpus (Svartvik 1990: 15) has a fuller marking of prosodic features which includes degrees of loudness and tempo, modifications in voice quality and other paralinguistic features, in addition to the features in the London-Lund Corpus. The 50,000-word Lancaster/IBM Spoken English Corpus (SEC) (see, for example, Knowles *et al.* 1996; Wichmann 2000) represents the following prosodic features: tone groups, stressed and accented syllables, pitch direction, simple and complex tones, high and low tones, and significant changes of pitch not covered by the tone markings (Taylor 1996: 28-29). SEC which was compiled during 1984-87, amounts to 52,637 words, or 339 minutes of recording time (Leech 1996: ix). The C-ORAL-ROM Corpus for Spoken Romance Languages (300,000 words for each of the languages Italian, French, Spanish and Portuguese) (Cresti and Moneglia 2005) is prosodically tagged for terminal and non-terminal breaks, with a terminal break marking an utterance and a non-terminal break marking "the internal prosodic parsing of a textual string which ends with a terminal break" (Cresti and Moneglia 2005: 25-26). A representative sample of 150,000 words of the 0.5 million-word Bergen Corpus of London Teenage Language (COLT) has been prosodically marked. The prosodic features are nucleus, tones (fall, rise, fall-rise, rise-fall, level), and tone unit boundary (COLT website, 2007). In the Intonation

Variation in English (IViE) Corpus, about 12 hours of speech data are transcribed in terms of rhythmic structure, acoustic-phonetic structure, and phonological structure (Grabe and Post 2002).

Collection of data for HKCSE

All the data in the HKCSE were audio-recorded with the prior knowledge and consent of the speakers concerned as far as possible. To comply with ethical standards for research studies involving human subjects, certain safeguards were built in. As far as possible, speakers were asked to sign a consent form, which states the purpose of the research. The consent form was also a means of acquiring demographic details about the speakers, namely age, sex, place of birth, first language, educational background, residence patterns and occupation. Educational background is an important social parameter because in Hong Kong "English is almost entirely a 'learnt' language" (Bolt and Bolton 1996: 3), and Hong Kong people mainly learn the language at school. It was thought that educational experience in an English-speaking country is likely to affect the nature of the language used, the ways in which it is used, and possibly the linguistic competence of the speaker.

When the data for the academic and conversational sub-corpora and part of the business sub-corpus were collected, the researcher was not present in any of the spoken discourses recorded. The recording equipment was a Sony MD recorder and a Sony microphone which provided maximal sound recordings and minimal intrusion. In some cases, individual speakers were given the recording equipment and mini-discs, and then told how to operate the equipment. The speakers were instructed to place the mini-disc recorder and the microphone in the immediate vicinity of the spoken discourses. In other cases, research assistants were responsible for placing the recording machine in the vicinity of the spoken discourses, and turning on and off the machine.

The physical contexts, all in Hong Kong, in which different spoken discourses were recorded or retrieved, vary a great deal. In the case of academic discourses, the physical settings are lecture theatres, classrooms and staff offices in a university in Hong Kong. As the speakers in the business sub-corpus came from a range of organizations, the physical contexts include meeting rooms in business organizations and government and university offices, hotel and airport reception or information desks, convention and conference rooms where presentations related to business and financial services were given. Across the four sub-corpora, compilation of the business sub-corpus has proved to be the most challenging. It has proved to be very difficult to obtain consent from companies to allow the research team access to their meetings and negotiations, due to the confidential nature of the subject matter. As a result, some audio recordings of presentations on the topics of business and financial services were downloaded from the websites of different organizations. Regarding the conversations, they were recorded in places including private homes and places where groups of HKC and NES would be expected to gather, such as social areas in the workplace, the common room in a church, in a private car, in a school playground, in restaurants, cafeterias, food courts, sandwich shops and exclusive clubs and societies in Hong Kong. The public sub-corpus captures speakers from the government of the Hong Kong SAR, banks, public utilities, public forum, conference and event organisers, and interviews or forum discussions broadcast on television and radio. Examples of such events and occasions are the Global Summit of Women 2001, Asian Society Luncheon 2001, an interview of the Secretary for the Environment, Transport and Works, a radio announcement by the Director of Health on the Prevention of SARS (severe acute respiratory syndrome) in 2003, and an interview of the Hong Kong Chief Executive about the implementation of the "one-country two-systems" policy in Hong Kong.

Composition of HKCSE (prosodic)

The HKCSE (prosodic) consists of 900,214 words in 311 word files (Table 1.1). The business sub-corpus is the largest (27.42%) and the academic sub-corpus is the smallest (22.97%).

While the conversation sub-corpus contains 71 two-party and multi-party conversations, the other three sub-corpora are made up of various discourse types. Tables 1.2-1.4 describe the respective composition of the academic, business and public sub-corpora, the relative proportion of individual discourse types, and the number of recordings for each type. For instance, the academic sub-corpus comprises 42.72% of university students giving oral presentations followed by Q&A sessions; the business sub-corpus has the highest proportion (31%) of job and hotel internship placement interviews; and the public sub-corpus has an equal distribution of speeches (40.50%) and interviews (39.90%).

Table 1.1 Composition of HKCSE (prosodic)

Sub-corpus	Number of words	Proportion	Number of recordings
Academic	206,750	22.97 %	29
Business	246,816	27.42 %	112
Conversation	229,568	25.50 %	71
Public	217,080	24.11 %	99
Total	900,214	100.00 %	311

Table 1.2 shows that there are five discourse types in the academic sub-corpus of the HKCSE (prosodic), all of which were recorded in a university in Hong Kong. The discourse types are student presentations and Q&A sessions, lectures, seminars and tutorials, consultation sessions in the Writing Assistance Programme offered by the English Department where a student seeks advice from an academic staff about academic writing, and workshops for academic and research staff and postgraduate research students also offered by the English Department. Recordings of lectures, seminars and tutorials are made up of a range of disciplines including Applied Biology and Chemical Technology, Applied Linguistics, Building and Services Engineering, Construction and Land Use, Manufacturing Engineering, Rehabilitation Science, Social Work, Textiles and Clothing, and Hotel and Tourism Management.

Table 1.3 lists the nine discourse types in the business sub-corpus of the HKCSE (prosodic): job and placement interviews, presentations and Q&A sessions, company meetings, informal office talk, announcements followed by Q&A sessions, presentations without any Q&A sessions, service encounters, conference calls and video conferencing, and workplace telephone talk.

Table 1.4 shows the seven discourse types in the public sub-corpus of the HKCSE (prosodic). They are speeches without any Q&A sessions, interviews, speeches followed by Q&A sessions, press briefings followed by Q&A sessions, discussion forums, press briefings without Q&A sessions, and announcements on the radio.

Table 1.2 Composition of academic sub-corpus in HKCSE (prosodic)

Academic sub-corpus	Proportion	Number of recordings
Student presentation and Q&A	42.72 %	8
Lecture	29.23 %	9
Seminar and tutorial	18.11 %	6
Writing Assistance Programme (WAP) consultation	8.35 %	5
Workshop for academic and research staff and postgraduate research students	1.59 %	1
Total	100.00 %	29

Table 1.3 Composition of business sub-corpus in HKCSE (prosodic)

Business sub-corpus	Proportion	Number of recordings
Job and placement interview	31.00 %	25
Presentation and Q&A	19.74 %	4
Meeting	13.98 %	9
Informal office talk	10.54 %	4
Announcement and Q&A	8.52 %	3
Presentation	7.75 %	10
Service encounter	5.57 %	52
Conference call/ video conferencing	2.32 %	2
Workplace telephone talk	0.58 %	3
Total	100.00 %	112

Table 1.4 Composition of public sub-corpus in HKCSE (prosodic)

Public sub-corpus	Proportion	Number of recordings
Speech	40.50 %	57
Interview	39.90 %	25
Speech and Q&A	10.14 %	5
Press briefing and Q&A	4.63 %	2
Discussion forum	3.07 %	2
Press briefing	1.73 %	7
Radio announcement	0.04 %	1
Total	100.00 %	99

Speaker characteristics

The HKCSE (prosodic) is an intercultural corpus. The term 'intercultural', as defined by Spencer-Oatey (2000: 4), refers to "interactional data ... data obtained when people from two different cultural groups interact with each other". Intercultural communication involves a comparison of the discourse of people of different cultural and linguistic backgrounds interacting either in a lingua franca or in one of the participants' native language (Bargiela-Chiappini and Harris 1997, Lustig and Koester 2006). In the HKCSE (prosodic), speakers are classified in terms of their cultural backgrounds (defined by national, racial, ethnicity and first language) and sex (male and female). The two main different cultural groups are Hong Kong Chinese (HKC) and native English speakers (NES). NES are not distinguished into different national groups, but they mainly come from Britain, the United States of America and Australia. A third and very small group of speakers, Other Speakers, consists of primarily mainland Chinese, Indian and Japanese speakers. Tables 1.5-1.7 show the number of words spoken by respective speaker groups in the HKCSE (prosodic), and Table 1.5 shows the distribution of the speaker groups.

In the 0.9-million-word HKCSE (prosodic), the majority (71.46%) of the words are spoken by HKC, with 25.32% by NES, and 3.22% by other speakers. Except for the conversation sub-corpus, all other sub-corpora have a lot more words spoken by HKC than NES. This reflects the fact that in the context of Hong Kong, there is a much greater frequency of occurrence of English discourses produced by HKC, compared to non-HKC, in tertiary education and in business and public communication. On 1 July 1997, Hong Kong stopped being a British colony and became a Special Administrative Region (SAR) under Chinese sovereignty and the Government of the HKSAR initiated a change in language policy. Specifically, after the handover in 1997, both Chinese and English have become the official languages of the HKSAR. In fact, the government began to promote a wider use of Chinese within the civil service from 1996 (Lee 2005), and there was a noticeable shift from English to Cantonese in Legislative Council[2] meetings (Yau 1997).

Turning to the third Millennium, Hong Kong has become a trilingual (Cantonese, Putonhgua and spoken English) and biliterate (Standard Written Chinese and English) society (Bolton 2002). The importance of English in business and professional communication is evidenced in the financial support rendered by the Hong Kong Workplace English Campaign (WEC) that was launched by the Government of the HKSAR in 2000. The WEC has the objective to increase people's awareness of the importance of English proficiency in the workplace, and enhance business English skills among personnel working in key sectors of the local economy (SCOLAR 2005).

Table 1.6 summarises the distribution of male speakers in the HKCSE (prosodic). Over 60% of the words are spoken by HKC males. Across the four sub-corpora, there are more HKC males in the public (88.07%) and academic (79.23%), and far fewer in the conversation (33.86%) sub-corpus. In the business sub-corpus, the proportion of talk by HKC males and NES males is the same at about 48%. The percentage of talk by other male speakers is greater in conversation (6.68%) than in the other corpora; their talk was captured in multi-party conversations involving both HKC and NES speakers.

---

2.   The Legislative Council is Hong Kong's equivalent to an elected parliament.

Table 1.5 Distribution of speaker groups by first language in HKCSE (prosodic)

	HKC	NES	Other Speakers	Unidentified Speakers	All Speakers
HKCSE (prosodic)	643,286 (71.46%)	227,894 (25.32%)	28,682 (3.19%)	382 (0.04%)	900,214 (100%)
Academic sub-corpus	168,784 (81.64%)	30,526 (14.76%)	7,421 (3.59%)	31 (0.01%)	206,750 (100%)
Business sub-corpus	174,135 (70.54%)	68,807 (27.88%)	3,849 (1.56%)	45 (0.02%)	246,816 (100%)
Conversation sub-corpus	107,825 (46.97%)	107,851 (46.98%)	13,584 (5.92%)	306 (0.13%)	229,568 (100%)
Public sub-corpus	192,542 (88.7%)	20,710 (9.54%)	3,828 (1.76%)	0 (0%)	217,080 (100%)

Table 1.6 Distribution of male speakers in HKCSE (prosodic)

	HKC Males	NES Males	Other Speakers Males	All Males
HKCSE (prosodic)	337,927 (63.11%)	183,150 (34.2%)	14,406 (2.69%)	535,483 (100%)
Academic sub-corpus	88,708 (79.23%)	23,265 (20.78%)	0 (0%)	111,973 (100%)
Business sub-corpus	59,060 (48.18%)	59,875 (48.85%)	3,660 (2.99%)	122,598 (100%)
Conversation sub-corpus	46,682 (33.83%)	82,104 (59.49%)	9,216 (6.68%)	138,002 (100%)
Public sub-corpus	143,477 (88.07%)	17,906 (10.99%)	1,526 (0.94%)	162,909 (100%)

Table 1.7 Distribution of female speakers in HKCSE (prosodic)

	HKC Females	NES Females	Other Speakers Females	All Females
HKCSE (prosodic)	305,371 (83.8%)	44,756 (12.28%)	14,288 (3.92%)	364,415 (100%)
Academic sub-corpus	80,080 (84.51%)	7,265 (7.67%)	7,421 (7.83%)	94,766 (100%)
Business sub-corpus	115,083 (92.57%)	9,034 (7.27%)	197 (0.16%)	124,314 (100%)
Conversation sub-corpus	61,143 (67%)	25,747 (28.21%)	4,368 (4.79%)	91,258 (100%)
Public sub-corpus	49,065 (90.57%)	2,804 (5.18%)	2,302 (4.25%)	54,171 (100%)

Table 1.7 shows that across the female speakers in the corpus, HKC females pre-dominate (83.8%), and NES females speak only 12.28%, followed by Other Speaker females (3.92%). Except for conversation, HKC females dominate in all discourse types, with the amount of talk as high as 90.57% in the public sub-corpus.

Structure of the book

Chapter two explains the systems and choices of discourse intonation (Brazil 1997). Chapter three describes the procedure for prosodically transcribing the 0.9-million-word HKCSE (prosodic), and the annotation system. It also discusses the main problems encountered during prosodic transcription, and how these prob-lems were resolved. Chapter four is a description of the design and implementa-tion of the software (iConc) used to interrogate the HKCSE (prosodic). This is followed by four chapters, each of which discusses one of the four systems: tone units (Chapter five), prominence (Chapter six), tones (Chapter seven), and key and termination (Chapter eight). These chapters examine how the discourse into-nation systems work, and how the systems are manifested in the HKCSE (pro-sodic), both across the sub-corpora and across speaker groups in the corpus. Both quantitative and qualitative findings are discussed. Chapter six focuses on some of the major uses of prominence observed in the HKCSE (prosodic). In Chapter sev-en, the communicative role of tones, particularly the level tone, is revisited. Chapter eight explores the notion of predictability, examines points in the discourse that tend to attract high or low key and termination choices, and also revisits the no-tion of pitch concord. The final chapter (nine) discusses the implications of the findings for the study of discourse intonation, discourse, pragmatics, intercultural communication, English language learning, and future directions for research. It needs to be pointed out that the book, while dealing in detail with some important aspects and patterns of discourse intonation, does not, in any sense, claim to offer an exhaustive description of discourse intonation in the HKCSE (prosodic).

CHAPTER 2

Discourse intonation systems

Introduction

This chapter describes the systems of discourse intonation (Brazil 1985, 1997) which are used for transcribing and analyzing the HKCSE (prosodic).

Discourse intonation framework

The descriptive framework of discourse intonation developed by Brazil (1985, 1995, 1997), and adopted by others (Coulthard and Brazil 1981; Coulthard and Montgomery 1981; Sinclair and Brazil 1982; Hewings 1990; Cauldwell 2002), was chosen to prosodically transcribe the HKCSE. Discourse intonation is based on the view that spontaneous speech is purpose-driven rather than sentence-oriented. It is speaker controlled, interactive, co-operative, context-referenced, and context-changing (Brazil 1995: 26-39). The communicative value of intonation is concerned with the choices that speakers make, and their reactions to the ongoing task of making sense to their hearers in context in real-time (Cauldwell 2002). The choices of discourse intonation are in line with those (see, for example, Couper-Kuhlen and Selting 1996: 12-13) who call for the examination of intonational meaning and the way intonation affects the communicative value of English utterances as part of a communicative event to better determine their pragmatic and situated meanings (Brazil 1997: ix). Discourse intonation is, therefore, of particular relevance to the researchers working with the HKCSE (prosodic) to further the understanding of the way speech functions in interactive discourse through careful examination of naturally-occurring data (see, for example, Cheng and Warren 1999a, 2001a, 2001b, 2001c).

The discourse intonation systems (Brazil 1997) view intonation as discoursal and pragmatic in function. As noted by Brazil (1994: 46), "The significance of intonation is related to the function of the utterance as an existentially appropriate contribution to an interactive discourse". Discourse intonation systems are motivated by real-time, situation-specific decisions by speakers to add extra layers of interpersonal meaning to words as they are spoken. They are concerned with "the speakers' moment-by-moment context-referenced choices" (Cauldwell 2007).

Traditionally, intonation is perceived as a speaker's pitch variations on a continuous scale. Brazil's conceptual framework of discourse intonation is characterised by a finite set of meaningful intonational oppositions, each of which is regarded as "an occasion for setting up *ad hoc* categories in the light of the speaker's apprehensions of how things presently stand between them and a putative hearer" (Brazil 1997: xii). In other words, the communicative value of the utterance is affected by intonational variations on the basis of "a small set of either/or choices" which relates to "a set of meaningful oppositions that together constitute a distinctive subcomponent of the meaning-potential of English" (ibid.: 2).

Discourse intonation can in part be traced back to the work of Halliday (1963, 1967, 1970; see also Halliday and Greaves 2008) who was concerned with developing a phonological typology based on meaning-making grammatical choices (Cauldwell 1997). Halliday views intonation as highly structured, consisting of three hierarchical systems: tonality, tonicity and tone. Tonality refers to the division of speech into intonation/tone groups. Each tone group contains a single unit of information and represents the speaker's perception and management of the whole message. Tonicity refers to the placement of accents, that is, the assignment and realization of the most prominent word in a tone group, indicating the focus of information. Tone, the contrasting pitch movements in each tone group, expresses different speech functions and the status of information (Halliday 1994: 36).

In her study of the various approaches to intonation, Chun (2002: 15-45) points out that discourse intonation offers a different description of intonation to the grammatical (see, for example, Chomsky and Halle 1968; Liberman and Prince 1977; Pierrehumbert 1980; Pierrehumbert and Hirschberg 1990) and the attitudinal (see, for example, O'Connor and Arnold 1973; Crystal 1975, 1995). Discourse intonation is different to those (see, for example, Chomsky and Halle 1968; Liberman and Prince 1977; Pierrehumbert 1980) who saw rule-driven generative phonology as a natural follow-on to their work in generative grammar. Sentence-based models which view intonation as grammatical regard tones as typically chosen with particular syntactic structures, such as rise tone with yes/no questions, and fall tone with *wh-* questions, statements and commands. Sentence-based models suggest that even when the conventional structure is not employed, the meanings conventionally associated with them will also be spoken with these same tones. Later research by the generative phonologists (see, for example, Pierrehumbert and Hirschberg 1990) has tried to assign meaning to intonation, but the data used have been experimentally acquired for the most part.

Harris (1988: 59) remarks that "There are other meanings expressed in speech – by intonation, by pauses, by the loudness and the rate of speech: but these do not combine in any regular way with the rest of language, and cannot be fitted into the structural system". This position differs from that of discourse intonation (Brazil 1997). As stated by Brazil (1995), in purpose-driven talk, although syntax and intonation have a relationship, syntax and intonation are considered "separate areas of choice", and "there is no 'normal' relationship between tone units and clauses" (Cauldwell 2007). In fact, discourse intonation moves beyond the context of the single sentence, and describes the rules which govern the pitch movement beyond and between the borders of tone units, rather than sentences. Brazil (1985: 238) argues for a "need for stating the communicative value of intonation in terms of the projected contextual implications of the tone unit: only if we regard intonation as a 'situation-creating' device, … can we give proper recognition to its ability to carry independent meanings".

Discourse intonation (Brazil 1997) is also different from descriptions of intonation which view the attitudinal or function of intonation as primary and central (O'Connor and Arnold 1973; Crystal 1975, 1995; Cruttenden 1997). In their description of the intonation of colloquial English, O'Connor and Arnold (1973: 4) remark that "a major function of intonation is to express the speaker's attitude, at the moment of speaking, to the situation in which he or she is placed". O'Connor and Arnold attach attitudinal meanings to each of ten tone groups combined with each of four sentence types: statement, question (*wh-* and yes/no), command, and interjection. For Cruttenden (1997: 97-99), for instance, the rise tone is described as having the attitudinal meaning of "reassuring" with *wh-* questions, and "non-committal" or "grumbling" with declaratives. The rise-fall tone can mean "impressed" with yes/no question and declaratives, or "challenging" with "clauses of any syntactic type" (ibid.: 92-93).

While O'Connor and Arnold (1973) and others highlight the role of intonation in expressing a speaker's attitude at the moment of speaking about the current situation, discourse intonation (Brazil 1997) highlights the role of intonation in communicative interaction and meaning contrasts. It views the description of intonation as "one aspect of the description of interaction", and argues that "intonational choices carry information about the structure of the interaction, the relationships between the discourse function of individual utterances, the interactional "givenness" and "newness" of information, and the state of convergence and divergence of the participants" (Brazil, Coulthard and Johns 1980: 11), implying that "when intonation seems to fulfill different functions, this is because of other factors in the situation and not because of intonation at all" (Brazil, Coulthard and Johns 1980: 98). Cauldwell and Hewings (1996: 51) contend that meanings like surprise, irony, sarcasm, grumpiness are features of particular contexts of interaction, but not directly attributable to any tone choice.

Having said this, discourse intonation does not discount an association be-tween intonation and attitudinal meanings. Cruttenden (1997) observes that some parts of the local meanings of almost all of the five tones in discourse into-nation (rise, fall-rise, fall, rise-fall, and level) are attitudinal. In specific contexts of interaction the association between discourse intonation and the speaker's at-titude can be observed in Brazil's studies, for example, "to imply a willingness to voice the proclaimed agreement that A evidently wishes to elicit" (Brazil 1997: 76). More examples are provided: "Choice of r+ tone ... heard as a warmer offer", "the r+ version is more pressing and cordial", "over dominance introduces a su-perimposed note of irritation or exasperation into the relationship", and "some-thing we might perhaps characterize locally as 'forcefulness' or 'insistence' can be traced" (The University of Ljubljana, 1998). Nevertheless, in discourse intonation (Brazil 1997), any attitudes associated with a tone choice are determined locally and are not fixed.

Four systems of speaker intonational choices

Discourse intonation comprises four systems of speaker choice (prominence, tone, key, and termination), each of which has a general meaning which takes on a local meaning within a particular context (Brazil 1997: xi), by which Brazil seeks to underline that these are moment-by-moment judgments made by speakers based on their assessment of the current state of understanding operating between the participants (see Table 2.1 below).

Brazil (1995) sums up the essential descriptive categories of the discourse in-tonation framework as follows:

1. Used language is divided into 'tone units'.
2   The tone units of used speech normally have either one or two 'prominent syllables'.
3   The last prominent syllable in each tone unit is the 'tonic syllable' and it carries one of the five tones.
4   At all prominent syllables, there is a possibility of choice in a three-term sys-tem of pitch level: high, mid, or low. The pitch level of the first prominent syl-lable in a tone unit establishes key and the pitch level on the last prominent syllable establishes termination. In a tone unit with only one prominent sylla-ble, key and termination are selected simultaneously.

(Brazil 1995: 240-246)

Table 2.1 Discourse intonation choices available to speakers

System	Choice
Prominence	prominent/non-prominent syllables
Tone	rise-fall, fall, rise, fall-rise, level
Key	high, mid, low
Termination	high, mid, low

(Adapted from Hewings and Cauldwell 1997: vii, in Brazil 1997)

Tone unit

All of these intonation choices, and there are thirteen in all, from the four systems (Hewings and Cauldwell 1997: vii), occur within the boundaries of a tone unit. In discourse intonation, a tone unit refers to "the stretch of language that carries the systematically-opposed features of intonation" (Brazil 1997: 3). This is different from other descriptive models using "'sense groups', 'breath groups' and 'tone groups'" which suggest "semantic, physiological and formal considerations" (ibid.: 5). The internal organization of the tone unit in discourse intonation can be described in terms of three parts: non-prominent optional stretches (proclitic and enclitic segments) and the mandatory tonic segment delimited by the first and last prominent syllables in which all the significant speaker-decisions are made (ibid.: 15) (Table 2.2):

A tonic segment therefore typically comprises one or two prominent syllables, any of the five tones or pitch movements (fall, rise, fall-rise, rise-fall, and level) carried by the final prominent tonic syllable, the three-term pitch-level system (high, mid and low) associated with the tonic syllable, and the three-term pitch-level system (high, mid and low) associated with the onset syllable.

Table 2.2 The three-part structure of the tone unit

(Proclitic segment)	Tonic segment	(Enclitic segment)
without prominent syllables	minimal tonic segment in minimal tone unit with one prominent syllable (tonic syllable)	without prominent syllables
	extended tonic segment in extended tone unit typically with two prominent syllables (onset and tonic)	

In discourse intonation, both internal and external criteria are applied to define tone unit boundaries. Internally, as discussed above, once a tonic prominence has occurred, the identification of the tone is complete. Any subsequent prominences occur in a new tone-unit. Thus a tone unit is complete when a tone has occurred, and there can only be one tone per tone unit. The external criterion is the pause. Wherever they occur, pauses are considered to be marking the end of tone units, even if the result is an incomplete, or truncated, tone unit. The result is that wherever there is a pause, even a very short encoding pause, there is a tone unit boundary. However, the reverse is not true. In other words, tone unit boundaries can occur where there is no pause. In these cases, they occur between the tonic prominence and any subsequent prominence.

Prominence, key and termination

In discourse intonation (Brazil 1997), each prominent syllable gives prominence to a word. The finite set of opposition, or either/or choice, available to a speaker is "a binary prominent/non-prominent choice" (ibid.: 9). A prominent syllable is one that a hearer recognises as being in some sense more emphatic than the others in the tone unit. The first (onset) and the last (tonic) prominent syllables in the tone unit constitute sub-sets of prominent syllables. Specifically, prominence determines the beginning and end of the tonic segment.

Prominent words, which contain prominent syllables, realise existential sense selections. Unlike in other descriptive models, prominent syllables in discourse intonation are not seen as necessarily and automatically determined by the lexis and grammar of the utterances; rather they are "a feature which speakers can vary voluntarily" (ibid.: 7). Despite the fact that prominence is "an independent variable" (ibid.: 8), the speaker's voluntary meaningful choice is constrained by the communicative context which may allow or remove the possibility of the speaker making any kind of selection. A prominent word is presented as "a selection from a set of possibilities defined by the context of situation" (ibid.: 41). More correctly, a speaker's intonation projects a certain context of interaction, or projects the assumption that a particular word in the tone unit is selected, with the assumption being understood as "part of the communicative value of the utterance" (ibid.: 27). In other words, a speaker exploits the prominence system to project a context of interaction which suits his/her current conversational purposes.

In making a selection between prominence and non-prominence, speakers have available to them two paradigms: existential and general. The existential paradigm is "the set of possibilities that a speaker regard as actually available in a given situation", and the general paradigm is the set of possibilities that is "inherent in the language system" (ibid.: 23), with the words comprising the existential paradigm being a sub-set of those comprising the general one. The selection of prominence is "what a speaker does when he chooses from an existential paradigm" (ibid.: 45). Brazil (1997: 22-23) exemplifies the two paradigms with his well-known *queen of hearts* said in response to *which card did you play*. In this utterance, *of* is a product of the general paradigm because the speaker is limited in this context to this word by the language system. Conversely, *queen* and *hearts* are choices limited by the contents of the pack of cards rather than the language system, and are therefore part of an existential paradigm as opposed to a general paradigm. The word *queen* is a selection from an existential paradigm of thirteen members, and *hearts* of four members.

(23)   Q: What heart did you play?   R: // the <u>*QUEEN*</u> of hearts //

(24)   Q: What queen did you play?   R: // the queen of <u>*HEARTS*</u> //

(Brazil 1997: 23)

Non-prominent words or non-selection are due to shared extralinguistic factors which have "a very wide currency", and "shared experience of the immediate conversational environment of the response" which have a circumscribed currency (ibid.: 25).

Whereas prominence is considered to be an attribute of the word, "each of the other three features (key, termination and tone) is an attribute of the larger unit *considered as a whole*", that is, the tonic segment (ibid.: 39). It is therefore important to relate speaker choices to both the sense unit realised by the word and the sense unit realised by the tonic segment. In cases when a tonic segment has more than one prominent syllable which constitutes a single selection, the tonic segment becomes a sense unit and enters "*as a syntagm* into the speaker's selective procedures when selection involves contrast" (ibid.: 45). For example, in

JOHN'S new SECretary
// LOOK // it's   //

it is the whole of the tonic segment 'JOHN'S new SECretary' that is presented as one side of a binary opposition and so excludes an implied alternative (ibid.: 46).

The two-prominence pattern of an extended tone unit is considered the typical case; nevertheless, Brazil (1997: 14) observes rare instances in spontaneous discourse of additional, intermediate prominent syllables between onset and tonic. Such instances may reflect the speaker's selection of orientation towards hearer-insensitive, non-interactive, oblique discourse, "temporarily withdrawing from involvement in the convergence process" (ibid.: 145), as in the act of quotation of some previous words. In other words, the speaker is engaged with the language system, choosing to emphasise "This is the word I use", and not "This is the sense I select" (ibid.: 144). An example is given in Brazil (1997) to explain "at least some of the cases where tone units have more than the expected two prominent sylla-bles" (ibid.: 145):

> Speaker A: Why hasn't John finished his project?

(290)   Speaker B: // *p* he HASn't been very <u>WELL</u> //

(291)   Speaker B: // *p* he HASn't BEEN very <u>WELL</u> //

(292)   Speaker B: // *p* he HASn't BEEN VEry <u>WELL</u> //

The two prominent tone units in (290) is a "directly-oriented response to the en-quiries", and the additional, i.e. three (291) and four (292), prominences, shows that Speaker B declares no responsibility for the assertion made in the response, and that the response is "merely a disengaged quotation of what has been said to be the reason" (ibid.: 145). It needs to be pointed out that the present study of the HKCSE (prosodic) finds instances of up to four prominent syllables in a tone unit. This is also the case in Cauldwell's (2003a, 2003b) data where four is found to be the maximum number of prominent syllables in a tone unit. However, as discussed in Chapter 6, the occurrences of triple and quadruple prominence tone units in the HKCSE (prosodic) are relatively rare, 6.76% and 1.51% respectively.

The prominent syllable is defined as "a decision point in that part of the total pitch treatment of the tone unit that serves to define one or more of the three speaker options", namely key, termination and tone (Cauldwell 1997: 12). Key and termination refer to pitch-level choices available to speakers. Key is the pitch-level choice associated with the first prominent syllable (onset) in the tone unit. The high, mid, and low pitch levels at which the onset is pitched are recognised in rela-tion to the onset syllable of the previous tone unit. Termination is the pitch-level choice associated with the last prominent syllable in the tone unit. The high, mid and low levels at which the tonic is pitched are recognised in relation to the pitch level of the preceding prominent syllable in the same tone unit (i.e. the onset), or prior tone unit in the case of minimal tone units. Key and termination are there-fore two systems with independent speaker choices for different meaning realiza-tions. Key and termination choice in a particular tonic segment is "never more than one 'level' in the three-term system" (ibid.: 62), namely one step above or one step below. The determination of high, mid or low key and termination is a par-ticularly difficult skill to acquire. The input of the project's consultant, Dr Richard Cauldwell, was invaluable during the period devoted to transcriber training. According to him, determining mid-key at the beginning of a turn at speech is problematic for transcribers of all levels of experience. For any speaker, the pitch levels associated with mid, high, and low key and termination are relative, not ab-solute. It was therefore necessary to do a quick play of a substantial portion of the turn to be transcribed in order to determine what counts as mid, high, and low for that speaker during the turn in question.

Brazil (1997) distinguishes between minimal and extended tonic segments, depending on whether the tonic segment contains one or more than one prominence. In tone units of both the minimal and extended types, pitch-level choices serve to determine the key and termination of the whole tonic segment. In the case of minimal tonic segments, however, it is not possible to make the selection of key and termination independently. In single prominence tone units without an onset syllable, "the first prominent syllable is also the last, so there can be no independent choices in the two systems" (ibid.: 12), representing a simultaneous selection of key + termination. This method of analysis needs to be justified by showing that "the meaning increments derived from the two choices are compatible and both appropriate to the situation" (ibid.: 12). The hearer then assigns communicative value to either key or termination in the local context. Nevertheless, there are conditions where a syllable in a tone unit which is not intended to realise a sense selection can be made prominent, simply in order to achieve a choice of key or termination since "an intonation choice can be associated with a syllable only if it is prominent" (ibid.: 65).

Key, defined as the pitch choice on the first prominence syllable, "affects the communicative value of the whole tonic segment" (ibid.: 50). The selection of key projects the speaker's assumption about the hearer's expectations as the talk unfolds. High key, for example, has contrastive implications, and may show surprise, pleasure, annoyance, alarm, and so on in the local context. 'Contrasting' here refers to a selection which "projects a binary opposition upon the existential paradigm and explicitly denies an alternative" (ibid.: 45). High key adds an increment of meaning that "this tone unit has a denial of expectation relations to what has preceded" (Brazil 1997: 75-84; Cauldwell 2007). In the second tone unit in the example, // look // it's John //, the selection of high key on John is associated with a binary opposition in which one might have expected // it's Peter //. In addition, the contrasting can involve an existential opposition "between one item and all other available items", that is, // its John // not // it's x, y, z, etc. // (Brazil 1997: 45). The latter is a special kind of contrasting called "particularizing", which refers to instances of contrasting which "reject all the existentially possible alternatives rather than rejecting one of a notionally symmetrical pair" (ibid.: 45).

The selection of low key in a tonic segment projects existential equivalence to the previous topic segment. Low key has equative value, adding an increment of meaning that "This tone unit has an equative relationship with what has gone before" (Brazil 1997: 75-84; Cauldwell 2007). In other words, low key assumes that the hearer will perceive the content as following naturally upon what has gone before, and as "being entirely in line with what the hearer would expect" (Brazil 1995: 245).

Mid key attributes no special expectations to the hearer. It only has additive value, that is, "merely adding its content to what has gone before" (Brazil 1995: 245). For example, in minimal response utterances 'yes' and 'no', mid key has a "concurring" function (ibid.: 49), associating the speaker with the expected endorsement of either positive or negative polarity in the preceding speaker's utterance, whereas high key has an "adjudicating" function, with "the speaker in an *independent* assignment of polarity" (ibid.: 49), going against the polarity expectations of the preceding utterance. Another example that involves a polarity choice is // *it was John* // (Brazil 1997: 42), where only *was* is selected prominence. Here the existential paradigm consists of either // *it was John* // or // *it wasn't John* //. For the mid key version of // *it was John* //, *was* is a selection from two possibilities, namely "*asserting that something was* the case", but it does not imply that it could be otherwise. Whereas the high key version "expressly contradicts a recent assertion, or a projected belief or assumption, that it wasn't", that is, "*denying that it wasn't*" (ibid.: 42).

When responding to a question, the speaker's high or mid key choice is viewed as being constrained by the previous speaker's termination choice. In other words, the selection of termination constrains the next speaker in his/her selection of key. This phenomenon is termed "pitch concord" (ibid.: 86). A speaker who conforms to pitch concord is likely to be giving a preferred response, and a speaker who does not is likely to be giving a dispreferred response (ibid.: 53-58).

TERMINATION

HIGH anticipates HIGH KEY response (i.e. adjudication)
MID anticipates MID KEY response (i.e. concurrence)
LOW sets up no particular expectations, and permits choice of high key, mid key or low key

(Brazil 1995: 246, 1997: 119)

In interrogatives, mid termination imposes no constraint, and low termination does not predict a response, and thus leaving the next speaker to initiate a new topic or for the discourse to come to a close (Brazil 1997: 58). In the case of yes/no questions, the selection of high termination carries the meaning that adjudication is invited from the hearer while mid termination seeks concurrence (ibid..: 54-55). In *wh*-type questions, high termination carries the meaning that "an improbable answer is expected", and mid termination is a "straightforward request for information" (ibid.: 58).

In questions, termination choices are linked to question types in that the local meaning of selecting high or mid termination varies according to the functional value of what is being said. First, in *wh*- questions that elicit non-polar information, mid termination projects "expectation of concurrence", and high termination projects "invitation to adjudicate" (ibid.: 56), adding an increment of meaning "This is something I want you to give judgment on" (Cauldwell 2007). Second, in *wh*-questions that elicit an informational response, mid termination projects "making a straightforward request for information" (Brazil 1997: 56), and high termination projects that "an improbable answer is expected" (ibid.: 56). Third, in yes/no questions, high termination projects the meaning that adjudication is invited from the hearer, while mid termination seeks concurrence.

In declaratives, when a speaker provides factual information that the second speaker does not yet possess, the "concord rule" does not apply, and "concord-breaking" is expected to occur (ibid.: 54). In declaratives, the selection of high termination denotes the meaning "this will surprise you" and mid termination the meaning "this will not surprise you" (ibid.: 58). The selection of mid termination projects that the information provided will be received in the way being presented; whereas high termination anticipates a contrastive response and sets up the expectation of a further high-key contribution from the hearer. The choice of low termination can add an increment of meaning "this is discourse-final" (Cauldwell 2007).

When instructions are made, mid termination is perceived as the normal choice because people making them do not usually see themselves as inviting the hearer to adjudicate in any way. However, when the hearer does not follow the instruction, high termination to project "crossness or exasperation" (ibid.: 59) may be chosen. When there is no change of speaker in a monologue, supportive and verbal response, such as a murmured 'yes', is expected to obey the same pitch-concord rule that operates between discrete utterances. Brazil (1997: 60) also discusses the use of a rhetorical device, where a speaker uses high termination in the first tone unit (the addressee is asked to adjudicate) and mid termination in the second (takes concurrence for granted).

Tone

In discourse intonation, the tone or pitch movement in the tone unit is associated with the final prominent syllable (the tonic syllable) in the tone unit, and so tone choices "attach additional meaning increments to tonic segments" (ibid.: 20). There are five tones that speakers may choose from: the rise, fall-rise, fall, fall-rise, and level tones.

Tone choice: proclaiming and referring

Four of the tones are used to distinguish between information that is common ground, i.e. referring tones (R): rise (*r+*) and fall-rise (*r*), and information that is new, i.e. proclaiming tones (P): fall (*p*) and rise-fall (*p+*) (Figure 2.1).

Any spoken discourse proceeds on the basis of a considerable amount of shared knowledge between discourse participants (ibid.: 109), and it is for the speaker to decide moment-by-moment whether what he/she is saying is shared or not. Table 2.3 describes the communicative functions of the proclaiming and referring tones (ibid.: 82-98).

Examples of proclaiming and referring tones:

(125)   Speaker A: // p WHERE does he <u>COME</u> from //
        Speaker B: (i) // p SOMEwhere in <u>SCOT</u>land //
                       (ii) // r SOMEwhere in <u>SCOT</u>land //

(Brazil 1997: 76)

In (125), speaker B's response to speaker A's enquiry with a proclaiming tone (p) in (i) tells A what A wants to know by furthering ongoing business, but that with a referring tone (r) in (ii) can be interpreted as "an excursion into assumed common ground rather than as a step towards the greater convergence that A evidently desires" (ibid.: 1997: 74). In other words, the use of referring tone (r) by B is heard to mean "Instead of taking matters further in the way I know you want me to, I can only reiterate what I assume you already know" (ibid.: 75).

Tone selections are also accorded social significance. Adverbials such as 'actually', 'frankly' and so on tend to be non-prominent as "they seldom constitute selections in a sense paradigm" (ibid.: 77). In contexts where adverbials are assigned prominence in a tone unit with referring tone, they carry "two simultaneous selections": "both a sense selection and a social connotation", with the connotation referring to an assumption of solidarity or intimacy between speaker and hearer (ibid.: 79). Items such as 'personally', 'really' and 'to tell you the truth' may suggest confidentiality or conspiracy (ibid.: 79) in the local context.

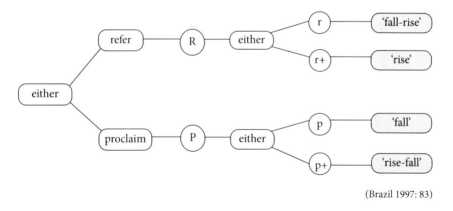

(Brazil 1997: 83)

Figure 2.1 The referring and proclaiming tone choices available to speakers

Table 2.3 Functions of proclaiming and referring tones

Tone	Functions
Referring tone: rise tone (r+)	To reactivate something which is part of the common ground
Referring tone: fall-rise tone (r)	To indicate that this part of the discourse is already present in the common ground, and therefore will not enlarge the common ground assumed to exist between the participants
Proclaiming tone: fall tone (p)	To indicate that this part of the discourse is not yet present in the common ground, and so will be news and world-changing. The area of speaker-hearer convergence is being enlarged
Proclaiming tone: rise-fall tone (p+)	– To indicate addition to the common ground and to the speaker's own knowledge at one and the same time – To indicate to the hearer that no feedback of either an adjudication or concurring kind is expected – To indicate that the speaker intends to continue to speak and so asserts control of the progress of the discourse

Tone choice: dominance and control

As described earlier, the proclaiming/referring opposition and the choices in the referring tone system contribute implications of common ground information or new information to the tonic segment. The selection of tones, as with other linguistic options, rests with the speaker, and the decision to present information as shared or new is based on a subjective assessment of the state of shared knowledge between the participants, and is also open to exploitation should the speaker choose to do so. There are tone selections which may be characterised as being participant-specific in specialised discourse types (i.e. discourse types other than conversation), and implies a certain role relationship pertaining between the participants in a discourse (ibid.: 82-98). These participant-specific tones are the rise tone and the rise-fall tone. If a speaker selects a rise-fall (instead of a fall) in proclaiming something, or a rise (instead of a fall-rise) in referring to something, the speaker is considered to be exerting dominance and control additionally (Brazil 1995: 243).

In discourse types where one speaker is dominant, in the sense of having greater responsibility for the discourse and greater freedom in making linguistic choices, that designated dominant speaker monopolises the fall-rise/rise choice.

This observation would apply to the teacher in classroom talk, the interviewer in an interview, the doctor in a doctor/patient consultation, and so on.

The continuative use of rise tone serves to project to the hearer the speaker's expectation that he/she will be allowed to continue to speak. In addition, the speaker can choose the rise tone in certain contexts to put pressure on the hearer to respond to what he/she has said. For example, when a service provider says *may I help you* with rise tone to a customer, this has the effect of making the offer of assistance sound "warmer" (Brazil 1997: 95). The dominant speaker in a discourse can also choose to assert dominance through the use of the rise tone to openly assert that the hearer needs to be reminded of something that is common ground between the participants.

The rise-fall tone is the least prevalent of the tones, according to Brazil (1997), and he claims that in a discourse in which the participants are of unequal status, it tends to be the dominant speaker who alone makes this selection. The types of discourse in which one participant is dominant, and thus is designated "all-knowing" by the institutionalised relationships in force, would limit the selection of the rise-fall tone to that participant. In other words, in the same kinds of discourse in which one finds the use of the rise tone the preserve of a particular participant, one can expect to find that the selection of the rise-fall tone is similarly restricted.

In conversations, however, the selection of the rise and rise-fall tones is not restricted by the existence of institutionalised inequalities between the participants. If a speaker, for whatever reason, wishes to assert dominance and control through the selection of these tones, he/she has the option to do so. Consequently, in conversation these tones are selected by all, some or none of the participants depending on the moment-by-moment decisions of those involved and not on the basis of a restrictive set of conventions. Brazil (1985: 131) argues that in conversation there is "an ongoing, albeit incipient, competition for dominance". However, he adds that this does not necessarily imply aggressiveness or rudeness on the part of speakers, rather it can be characterised as "to remind, underline, emphasize, insist or convey forcefulness" (Brazil 1997: 98) when a speaker selects the rise or rise-fall tone, and so overtly assumes the status of the dominant speaker. The important point is that dominant speaker status is neither predetermined nor fixed in conversation, and is typically interchangeable among the participants as the discourse unfolds.

It needs to be made clear that while the words "dominance and control" have a generally negative "semantic environment" or "semantic prosody" (see, for example, Sinclair 1991: 112; Louw 1993: 158-159), the fact that speakers select the rise and rise-fall tones to exert dominance and control locally in a discourse is not an inherently negative behaviour. While it is possible that the overuse of these tones by a participant not deemed to be in an institutionalised dominant role might be heard to be usurping the designated dominant speaker, this would require repeated rather than isolated use of these tones by the speaker.

Orientation

The fifth tone, level tone, is discussed in the context of the orientation or stance the speaker takes. The use of level tone neither projects a certain context of interaction nor projects any communicative value of the utterance. In fact, it is used when the speaker does not intend to either proclaim or refer, and in so doing disengages from the immediate interpersonal, interactive context of interaction. In other words, the speaker does not make "either/or" choices of any kind, and presents the language with neutral projections as to the assumption made about the current state of understanding between the speaker and a hearer (Brazil 1997: 132). The choice focuses on the linguistic properties or message organization of the utterance, rather than the truth of the assertion made in the utterance. Brazil (1997: 133-139) provides a detailed description of the two main contexts when speakers select the level tone. The first is when a speaker is adopting an "oblique presentation" (ibid.: 133), or when a speaker is saying something, on paper or in the speaker's memory, that is either pre-coded or partially coded information (ibid.: 136-139). Examples of hearer-insensitive oblique discourse are ritualised or precoded speech, such as the oblique reading out of a piece of text, "the public recitation of prayers and other liturgical material" (ibid.: 137), parade-ground commands, and the teaching of languages in classrooms where linguistic specimens are presented and repeated.

The second context is when encoding has not yet been achieved, or when encoding presents some kind of difficulty for the speaker (ibid.: 139), which is likely to happen when the speaker is telling a story (ibid.: 140). Brazil (1995: 244) describes another context where the level tone is used. It is not related to encoding problems, but is found when a speaker says "incremental elements" which form part of a "telling increment". These elements are message fragments which have not yet reached the "target state" (Brazil 1995: 165), namely the end of a discrete information unit. Typically, the incremental elements are said with level tones until the final tone unit which is said with the fall tone. In Cauldwell's (2003b: 107) data, the level tone is ranked second in frequency among the five tones, and he suggests that elsewhere the level tones in similar contexts are wrongly categorised as rising tones. Brazil states that a speaker's selection of tone signals her/his orientation to the ongoing talk at that moment in time. Figure 2.2 below shows the decisions the speaker has to make for each tone unit:

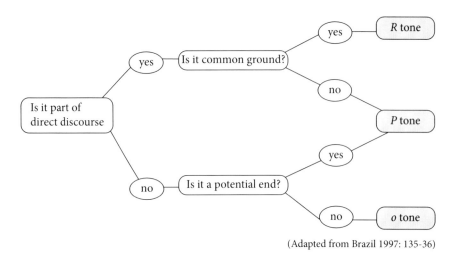

(Adapted from Brazil 1997: 135-36)

Figure 2.2 Tone choices available to speakers

Tone: questions and social elicitation

The uses of proclaiming and referring tones are also discussed with respect to "interrogative function" (Brazil 1997: 99). Brazil outlines the communicative value of different intonation choices with three types of questions: declarative-mood question, yes/no question, and information questions.

Declarative-mood questions

In the discourse intonation model, the use of intonation can no longer tell the hearer whether the utterance is a statement or a question, as it is unrelated to the grammatical structure of the utterance. Instead, the discourse function of an utterance depends crucially on the state of understanding existing between the speaker and the hearer (Brazil 1997). In other words, whether the utterance is a declarative or an interrogative depends on who holds the information. An example by Brazil (1997: 100):

[103]   John prefers that one (?)

In utterance [103], the appropriacy or inappropriacy of the question mark will depend on whether it is the speaker or the hearer who is privy to John's preference. In other words, [103] is regarded as a declarative question when the hearer holds the information that John prefers. Thus, if [103] is produced with a fall tone (which is one of the two proclaiming tones), the speaker either offers to change the hearer's world view or articulates an assumption that the

latter will change his/her world view, depending on the existing context of in
teraction (ibid.: 101). If the utterance is produced with a fall-rise tone (*r*) or rise
tone (*r+*) (which are both referring tones), they project a context of common
ground. However, in the case of a rise tone, this is heard as more tentative and asking the hearer to concur with, or adjudicate with respect to its validity (ibid.: 101).

Table 2.4 summarises the communicative value of the use of different tone
choices in declarative questions and the types of responses that they expect (ibid:
104). For declarative-mood questions, different meanings are discussed when referring and proclaiming tones combine with high and mid termination:

Table 2.4 Communicative value of tones in questions

	Mid termination	High termination
Referring tone	This is what I infer, or think I heard. Please confirm that I am right.	This is what I infer, or think I heard. Please tell me whether I am right or not.
Proclaiming tone	Can I infer, or did you say (mean), this or something else? Please confirm that it was *this*.	Can I infer, or did you say (mean), this or something else? Please tell me whether *this* is right or not.

Yes-no questions

The grammatical form of yes-no questions marks the utterance as interrogative
even in the absence of any relevant features of speaker/hearer understanding (as
compared to the case of declarative question). This can be illustrated with an example in Brazil (1997: 105):

[104]   Do you prefer that one?

[104] is unambiguously interrogative in situations where the value of "He prefers
that one" might well be in doubt, and this unambiguity is a product of the grammatical form of this type of questions (ibid.: 105). If the utterance is produced with
a fall (*p*) tone, the speaker means "I don't know whether you do or not – please tell
me", while he/she means "Am I right in assuming you do?" when the question is
produced with a fall-rise (*r*) tone (ibid.: 106).

As Brazil (1997) suggests, in producing an utterance such as [104], the speaker
is projecting two sense selections; that is, two matters with respect to which the
speaker might be declaring his uncertainty. He further illustrates this point with
an example which can be commonly identified in guessing games (ibid.: 106):

[105]   // *p* IS it an <u>E</u>lephant//

[106]				elephant
		is		
	It		an	alligator
		isn't		
				armadillo

[106] shows that the utterance may seek to determine (i) whether it is or is not an elephant, or he/she may want to know (ii) whether it is an elephant or something else by producing [105]. Thus a concurring 'yes' as a response to (i) and (ii) will have the meaning of 'Yes, it is' or 'Yes, an elephant' respectively. In other words, a yes-no question produced in a guessing game with a fall (*p*) tone is genuine guessing with selections from a set, and this is usually used in the beginning round of the game. At a later stage of the game, having gone through the process of genuine guessing for some time, the possibilities may have narrowed and items are now put forward as "likely winners not just hopeful selections" and such yes-no questions are more likely to be produced with a fall-rise (*r*) tone and, in effect, the hearer is asked to concur. If the player is unsuccessful in getting the right answer, he/she may return to guessing by reverting to the proclaiming tone.

As Brazil (1997) states, the communicative value of discourse intonation in yes-no questions is generally of two groups:

> With proclaiming tone, the speaker asks for the removal of uncertainty with respect to one of a number of existentially possible options: s/he projects a context in which the response is so far unnegotiated and, trying out one of the options, offers it for the hearer to concur with or reject. With referring tone, the speaker tentatively projects a context in which the response has been negotiated: all s/he asks of a respondent is confirmation (or denial) that the assumption s/he is making about the common ground is the proper one.
>
> (Brazil 1997: 107)

In addition, an expectation of a concurring 'yes' is signalled simultaneously with a mid-termination choice in a yes-no question with a referring tone. Given the different communicative values of discourse intonation in yes-no questions, it can be observed that we use yes/no questions more often to direct enquiry to a yes/no choice in circumstances where the speaker has some reason for projecting an assumption that they know the answer (in this case with a referring tone) than representing elicitation in unnegotiated situations (in this case with a proclaiming tone) (ibid.: 109). This can explain why it is so often (and wrongly, see Chapter 7 on tones) asserted that it is more common to produce yes-no questions with rising intonation. Table 2.5 summarises the communicative value of discourse intonation in yes-no questions.

Table 2.5 The communicative value of tone choice in yes-no questions and their responses

	Referring tone	Proclaiming tone
yes-no question	– asks for confirmation (or denial) and asks for approval of modification of world view that is submitted (negotiated) – expects a concurring yes when produced with mid termination	– asks for the removal of uncertainty, asks the hearer to concur with or reject the options that are offered (unnegotiated)

Information questions

Brazil (1985, 1997) argues that information questions can be produced with either proclaiming or referring tone. Consider the following example which is quoted from Brazil (1997: 111):

[107]   A: I can't find my book.
        B: // p WHAT'S it <u>CALLED</u> //

With the selection of fall tone, the existential paradigm for the item in the prospected response might have a considerable number of members. Therefore, in the case of [107], there is an implication of openness in respect to the title of the book with the selection of fall tone.

[108]   A: I can't find my book.
        B: // r WHAT'S it <u>CALLED</u> //

On the other hand, if the information question is produced with fall-rise tone, the utterance is then heard as whether it is the book he/she recently saw in the bathroom or elsewhere instead of which of the many titles the book might have. With the communicative value of referring tone, the speaker makes a provisional assumption, and the question then has a function similar to a yes-no question with referring tone.

   Brazil (1997) offers a rationale for the assertion that *wh*-interrogatives have some natural affinity with falling intonation with a similar explanation. He states that requests for information with *wh*-elements may well occur most frequently in situations where the information is unnegotiated, indicating that 'I don't know the answer, please tell me' (ibid.: 113). Below, Table 2.6 summarises the communicative value of discourse intonation in information questions.

Table 2.6 The communicative value of discourse intonation in information questions

	Referring tone	Proclaiming tone
Information question	– asks for confirmation of assumption, rather than information (negotiated)	– asks for information, an implication of openness (implies an absence of prediction; unnegotiated)

Conclusion

This chapter has presented a short overview of the discourse intonation systems and choices, and how they function in local contexts to add communicative value to what is said. There is more that can be written about discourse intonation and the reader is directed to Brazil's 1997 book, *The Communicative Value of Intonation in English*, for the most detailed description. Discourse intonation also plays a significant role in Brazil's 1995 book, *A Grammar of Speech*, and further insights into the systems can be gleaned from this work. There is a very good summary of all of the systems in the Appendix of this book.

In the chapters that follow, the communicative role and value of discourse intonation in the HKCSE (prosodic) is examined both quantitatively and qualitatively. It is shown that while Brazil's claims that the systems are not pre-determined with regard to speakers' selections, there are, nonetheless, patterns of usage which can be identified and described.

CHAPTER 3

Transcribing the Hong Kong Corpus of Spoken English (HKCSE)

Introduction

This chapter describes the orthographic and prosodic transcription methodologies and notation systems for the HKCSE (prosodic). It also discusses the problems encountered in the transcription process, and how these were resolved.

Transcribing the HKCSE (prosodic)

The procedure for orthographically transcribing the two-million-word HKCSE is described in Cheng and Warren (1999b). The following is about how 45% of the HKCSE was turned into the HKCSE (prosodic). The prosodic transcribing task underwent several stages.

Cauldwell (2007) describes Brazil's discourse intonation framework as an approach to the analysis and teaching of real, everyday speech, as consisting of four components: "a theory, a set of categories & realisations, a notation, and transcription practice" (Cauldwell 2007). Pickering (2001, 2004) considers Brazil's discourse intonation, among all the systems of transcribing and explaining prosodic choices, "the most usable system of transcription, and the most insightful metalanguage for commentary on the choices speakers made".

The application of the discourse intonation framework has not been confined to British English. Other varieties of English such as Malaysian English (Hewings 1986) and Singaporean English (Goh 1998, 2000) have been analysed using discourse intonation and also other languages such as Italian, German and Swedish (Hewings 1990). Such studies suggest that the communicative role of intonation described by Brazil (1985 and 1997) has wider applications. Therefore while this project is breaking new ground in applying the discourse intonation framework to the English spoken by Hong Kong Chinese (HKC) and native speakers of English (NES), it is by no means the first attempt to apply it to data that are not "standard" British English.

From a logistical perspective, transcribing naturally-occurring data prosodically by human ears and judgment has proven to be both time-consuming and difficult. It requires inter-transcriber reliability measures to ensure the quality of the transcription. The prosodic transcriptions of the HKCSE (prosodic) were subjected to cross-checking, involving three individual researchers. Further quality assurance was provided by a consultant to the project, Dr. Richard Cauldwell, SpeechinAction Research Centre (SPARC), who has had 25 years of research and teaching experience, working with the systems of discourse intonation, much of which was with David Brazil and Martin Hewings at the University of Birmingham.

Prosodic transcription of the HKCSE, using discourse intonation systems (Brazil 1997), was carried out by a research associate (Chu 2002). By the end of three years, about 0.9 million words of the HKCSE had been prosodically transcribed. The bulk of the work involved the research associate listening to recorded tracks of spoken discourse via an MD recorder and headphones. By means of careful and repeated listening to the recordings, the research associate determined the prosodic features (tone unit, tone, prominence, key and termination) and annotated them on a hard copy of the orthographic transcription. The same utterance, the same tone unit, and even the same word would need to be listened to several times for a complete transcription to be made. During the first stage of transcribing the prosodic features of the HKCSE, cross-checking of sample transcriptions was carried out at regular intervals by the project consultant to establish inter-transcriber reliability.

As described by Cauldwell (2007) in the website of his Speechinaction Research Centre, the notation of discourse intonations began in the 1970s as a type-writer friendly notation, using UPPER CASE letters for prominent syllables, lower case letters for non-prominent syllables, underlying for the tonic syllables, upward and downward lines for respectively high and low key and termination, and letters for tone symbols (for example, 'r' for referring (rising) tones and 'p' for proclaiming (falling) tones). When the word processor became available, more use was made of arrows (Cauldwell 2007).

The notation used in the HKCSE (prosodic) project underwent a few stages of development, all of which were based on Brazil's systems of discourse intonation, namely tone units, tones, prominence, key and termination. The following describes and exemplifies, with a service encounter at the Hong Kong airport (B025), the various stages of the notation used in HKCSE (prosodic). Figure 3.1 describes the notation for the orthographic transcription of the HKCSE, and Figure 3.2 the orthographic transcription of B025.

Simultaneous utterances	[
Non-linguistic features	((pause)), ((cough)), ((telephone rings)), etc.
Indecipherable utterances	((inaudible))
A short, untimed pause	(.)
Speakers identified by letters	'a' and 'A' for females; 'b' and 'B' for males;
	'x' for female and 'y' for male 'Other Speakers'
Lower case letters	Hong Kong Chinese speakers of English (HKC)
Upper case letters	Native speakers of English (NES)

Figure 3.1 Orthographic transcription adopted by the HKCSE

B025

1   a: [yes can i help you
2   B: [i've already i've already got my boarding pass actually i need to pay my
3   airport tax
4   a: oh you are a transit passengers [right
5   B: [well yeah
6   a: okay so since you have the boarding card already [you can pay the tax at the
7   B: [yeah
8   opposite check in counter

Figure 3.2 Orthographic transcription of B025

The notation used by the research associate to manually annotate prosodic features is shown in Figure 3.3 below, and Figure 3.4 shows the handwritten prosodic transcription of B025.

Tone unit:	// ... //
Prominent syllable:	|____|
Non-prominent syllable:	(Not annotated)
Tone:	*r*+ (fall rise); *r* (rise); *p* (fall); *p*+ (rise fall);
	o (level); *u* (unidentified)
Key:	*hl* (high key)
	(Mid key is not annotated)
	ll (low key)
Termination:	*hl* (high termination)
	(Mid termination is not annotated)
	ll (low termination)
Simultaneous talk:	[

Figure 3.3 Prosodic transcription notation

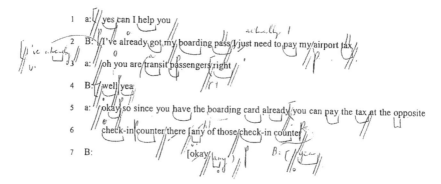

Figure 3.4 Handwritten prosodic transcription of B025

In B025, both 'pass' in 'boarding pass' (line 2) and 'tax' in 'airport tax' (line 2) are uttered with low pitch-level, annotated by the symbol 'll'. In the tone unit 'boarding pass', both 'board' and 'pass' are prominent syllables, and they are indicated as '|board|ing |pass|'. Tones are annotated by having the symbols (*p*, *o*, *r+*, *u*, etc.) written underneath the line at the beginning of the tone units.

After the recordings had been manually transcribed, the transcriptions had to be typed up. A literature search was then performed for a widely-used format for typewritten notation symbols for intonational features, but no such format was found to exist. Reference, however, was made to the notation used by Brazil (1997) when creating a set of computer keyboard-friendly symbols for representing the discourse intonation systems in the HKCSE (prosodic). Figure 3.5 shows the typed up version of B025. The second prominent syllable 'pass' in 'boarding pass' (line 2) is both underlined and written below the line, indicating that it is prominent and said with low termination in the tone unit. The word 'tax' in 'airport tax' (line 3) is underlined and written below the line, indicating that it is low key + termination in the tone unit.

B025

1　a: // ⟍ YES // → can i HELP you //
2　B: // ? i've already // → i've already <u>GOT</u> my // ⟍ BOARding　　　　// →
　　　　　　　　　　　　　　　　　　　　　　　　　　　　　PASS
3　actually i need to <u>PAY</u> my // ⟍ airport　　　　　//
　　　　　　　　　　　　　　　　　　　TAX
4　a: // ⟍ oh you are a TRANsit <u>PAS</u>sengers // ⟍↗ <u>RIGHT</u> //
5　B:　　　　　　　　　　　　　　　　// → <u>WELL</u> // ⟍ <u>YEAH</u> //
6　a: // → o<u>KAY</u> // ⟍ so since you HAVE the boarding CARD al<u>REA</u>dy //
7　　// ⟍ you can PAY the <u>TAX</u> //? at the OPposite CHECK in <u>COUN</u>ter //
8　B: // → <u>YEAH</u> //

Figure 3.5 Typed up version of B025 with the notation system of Brazil (1997)

B025

1. a: * { \ [< YES >] } { = can i [< HELP >] you }
2. B: ** {?< I'VE> [< alREAdy >] } } { = i've already [< GOT >] my } { \ [BOARding]
3.   < _ PASS > } { = actually i need to [< PAY >] my } { \ airport [< _ TAX >] }
4. a: { \ oh you are a [TRANsit] < PASsengers > } * { \/ [< RIGHT >] }
5. B: ** { = [< WELL >] } { \ [<
6.   YEAH >] }
7. a: { = [< oKAY >] } { \ so since you [HAVE] the boarding CARD < alREAdy > }
8.   * { \ you can [PAY] the < TAX > } {? at the [OPposite] CHECK in <
9. B: ** { = [< YEAH >] }
10.   COUNter > }

Figure 3.6 The transcription of B025 typed up using the iConc notation system

The notation described above was both computer keyboard- and reader-friendly. However, it was quickly found that these transcription conventions were not computer-friendly, and so a completely different set of transcription conventions that are computer readable had to be devised. A search engine, iConc, was then designed by Chris Greaves (Cheng, Greaves and Warren 2005), specifically for reading the systems of discourse intonation in the HKCSE (prosodic) (see Chapter 4 for a detailed description). The main features of the iConc computer readable notation include distinguishing each tone unit, and indicating key and termination in tone units with more than one prominence. Modification was then made to the notation so that single prominences are represented as key + termination by means of a combination of the symbols used for each, [< … >], to reflect the status of single prominences. In addition, it was found necessary to include symbols to clearly distinguish simultaneous talk in order to facilitate computer searches. Points in the discourses where simultaneous talk occurs are annotated with a single '*' in the utterance of the current speaker, and '**' in the utterance of the speaker who initiates simultaneous talk. Figure 3.6 shows the iConc readable notation described above.

Table 3.1 below outlines the comparison of the various notation systems developed and used during the different stages of transcribing the HKCSE (prosodic), with each version representing a proactive attempt to resolve difficulties encountered.

Table 3.1 Comparison of notation systems

Discourse intonation systems	Brazil (1997)	HKCSE (prosodic)	iConc prosodic notation system
Tone unit	// ... //	// ... //	{ ... }
Prominent syllable	UPPER CASE letters	UPPER CASE letters	UPPER CASE letters
Non-prominent syllable	lower case letters	lower case letters	lower case letters
Tone	r+ (fall rise)	↘↗ (fall rise)	\/ (fall-rise)
	r (rise)	↗ (rise)	/ (rise)
	p (fall)	↘ (fall)	\ (fall)
	p+ (rise fall)	↗↘ (rise fall)	/\ (rise-fall)
	o (level tone)	→ (level)	= (level)
		? (unidentified)	? (unclassifiable)
Key	high – in the case of a tone unit with more than one prominence, the first prominent word and all the following words in the tone units are above the line; mid – all the words are on the same line; low – in the case of a tone unit with more than one prominence, the first prominent word and all the following words in the tone units are below the line	high – typewritten above the line; mid – typewritten on the line; low – typewritten below the line	[^...] (high) [...] (mid) [_...] (low)
Termination	high – in the case of a tone unit with more than one prominence, the last prominent words in the tone units is above the line; mid – all the words are on the same line; low – in the case of a tone unit with more than one prominence, the last prominent words in the tone units is below the line	high – typewritten above the line and underlined; mid – typewritten on the line and underlined low – typewritten below the line and underlined;	< ^... > (high) < ... > (mid) < _... > (low)
Key + termination simultaneously selected	No special symbols	No special symbols	[< ^ ... >] (high) [< ... >] (mid) [< _ ... >] (low)
Simultaneous talk	No symbols used; lines aligned	[(current speaker) [(initiator of simultaneous talk)	* (current speaker) ** (initiator of simultaneous talk)

Problems encountered in transcribing HKCSE (prosodic)

The initial training of the research associate responsible for the transcription was conducted by Dr Jane Setter, who was also a member of the original proposed project team. Further, and more extensive, training was then conducted by Dr Richard Cauldwell because of his expertise in the specific prosodic transcription conventions required for fully transcribing the four systems of discourse intonation (i.e. prominence, tone, key and termination). The training provided by Dr Cauldwell to the transcriber of the HKCSE (prosodic) is best summarized by Dr Cauldwell himself: "Transcribers are trained through a process of standardization with recordings and with other transcribers. There is a simple notation to learn: but the main task is to learn to relate the categories of DI to the particular characteristics of the recordings being transcribed" (Cauldwell 2007). The training provided by Dr Cauldwell also included the discussion, and usually the resolution, of problems encountered by the transcriber when working with the naturally-occurring data of the HKCSE, with all of its issues of sound quality, speaker overlap, background noises, a wide variety of speakers, identifying participants in multi-party discourse, and so on. The two main problems were assigning tone unit boundaries and assigning tones. These problems and their solutions are briefly described below.

Tone-unit boundaries are difficult to define (Brown, Currie and Kenworthy 1980, Knowles 1991). Chu (2002) discusses a tendency for any transcriber to adhere to the traditional approach, namely that tone unit boundaries coincide with boundaries of clausal or sentential elements. The training that the project consultant Dr Richard Cauldwell gave to the transcriber in transcription with respect to tone units included the following considerations. Determining where a tone unit begins and ends was done auditorially, and was done by attending to the sound substance of the recording, and not to syntactic patterning. The transcriber was trained to identify sound packets/sound envelopes/tone-units which have their own internal rhythm that sets them apart from surrounding tone-units. Units have their own distinctive rhythm, have only one tone, and may have between one and four prominences. Incomplete tone-units also occur with no prominences. Non-prominent syllables may occur preceding, in between, and after any prominence. If and when a pause occurs, this is a break in rhythm, and therefore pauses mark some unit boundaries, but not all. Rhythm changes and other factors internal to the tone-unit may require the recognition that a unit has ended and another has begun. Because of the requirement to have only one tone, and for the tone to occur on the final prominence, a boundary must occur between the tone of one unit and the first prominence of the following unit – but the precise location of the boundary will vary in context. Thus tone units are identified, using the properties of the sound substance of the recording which are internal to the tone unit (rhythm, prominence, tone, key, termination). There are no properties of the sound substance which can uniquely identify a tone unit boundary.

Tones tend to be presented as very neatly circumscribed and readily identifiable in the representations of tones found in much of the literature. However, the reality of naturally-occurring data makes assigning tones harder in practice. For example, sometimes when the word that carries the tonic is followed by another word, a fall tone does not sound like a smooth slope sliding downwards confined to the word made prominent. The transcriber might be inclined to put the prominence on the last word in the tone unit, but such instances are examples of final-lengthening on the last word, and it is not prominent. Related to the fall tone is the determination of where a fall begins and, again, this needs to be driven by the speaker's selection of prominence.

When the tonic in a tone unit is preceded by a non-prominent word which appears to have the start of a fall, determining the tone can also be problematic. In such cases, since the preceding word does not carry prominence, it is not appropriate to consider it a point at which a pitch change begins (i.e. a point where a selection is being made) and, since it is non-prominent and sounds sufficiently level, a level tone is assigned. Deciding between level and fall tone is also difficult when final lengthening occurs on the last word in the tone, when it is preceded by a prominence which exhibits a slight fall. In such cases, the transcriber needs to listen carefully to determine whether the final word is an instance of final lengthening of the fall or whether the final word is also prominent and assign a level tone.

The distinction between rise and fall-rise is sometimes hard to make, and the solution was to assign a fall-rise tone, based on its characteristic that the fall has to be reasonably perceptible, beginning on the centre of the syllable concerned. Sometimes a fall-rise is accompanied by a slight rise at the beginning, making it sound like a rise-fall-rise tone. Given that there is usually a step up in anticipation of a tone which is of a falling direction, in this case the tone is still perceived as a fall-rise, while the slight rise beforehand is designated a non-criterial movement.

Most of the unclassifiable tones are found in truncated tone units, whether due to encoding problems or message fragments. Very often these are parts of an utterance that is cut short, and the movement is often hard to be confidently labelled as a step up or a step down, but a level tone seems problematic, due to the transcriber's detection of movement. In such doubtful cases, the solution is to label the tone unit 'unclassified' in terms of tone, using a question mark ('?').

Conclusion

This chapter has described the methods employed for transcribing the data and the changes made to the transcription conventions to enable iConc to search for the features of discourse intonation in the corpus. The training required for the transcription of discourse intonation has also been outlined along with some of the main problems encountered when transcribing the data and the solutions adopted.

CHAPTER 4

The iConc concordancing program

Introduction

The iConc program is written specially to provide customised searches and statistical data for the HKCSE (prosodic) of the discourse intonation systems described in Chapter 2. Since the prosodic corpus uses a number of symbols to represent Discourse Intonation, the program features a number of functions which search for these symbols and provide the intonation data accordingly.

There are several menus which are specific to iConc, namely the Corpus, Intonation and Special Searches menus, as well as the Concordance and Statistics menus which are specific to iConc and other concordancing programs, such as ConcApp and ConcGram. All these menu functions are described in this chapter, starting first with those functions which are specific to iConc and dealing with the other concordancing and statistics functions later. The remaining functions (File, Edit, View, Window, Format and Help menus) are all standard Windows functions and not described here.

The corpus menu

Before performing any of the search functions listed under the Intonation, Special Searches and Concordance menus, one of the corpus files listed under the Corpus Menu (Figure 4.1) must first be loaded to serve as the data to operate on. The items listed under this menu are therefore described first.

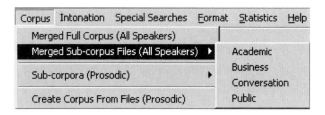

Figure 4.1 The basic corpus and sub-corpus files listed under Corpus Menu

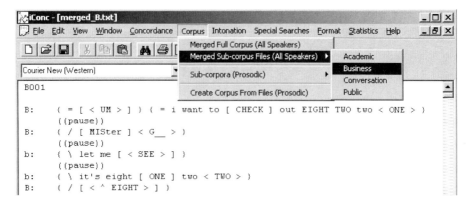

Figure 4.2 The business sub-corpus loaded by selecting from the second Corpus Menu item

The HKCSE (prosodic) consists of four basic text types: academic, business, conversation, and public discourses (see Chapter 1 for a detailed description of these text types and the differences between them). All of these sub-corpus files are available as merged files in text format, and the full corpus itself (created by merging the academic, business, conversation, and public sub-corpora) can be loaded by selecting the first Merged Full Corpus menu item. The individual sub-corpus files can be loaded by selecting from the second menu item Merged Sub-corpus Files (All speakers) (Figure 4.2).

All of the corpus and sub-corpus files selected under the first two items under the Corpus Menu feature all speakers involved in the discourses. However, it is also possible to select from the third item in the menu to choose whether the sub-corpus should comprise only speakers of a particular type. As described elsewhere (see for example, Chapter 2), speakers are recorded as being male, female, NES, HKC, etc, and there are individual sub-corpora for these speakers only. For example, if a user is interested only in female HKC speakers, he/she can select the relevant sub-corpus file from item three of the Corpus Menu (Figure 4.3).

Item four of the menu allows users to create their own customized prosodic corpus by selecting from the index file of all the individual corpus files. For example, if a user wants to create a sub-corpus from the academic and business files only, these files are listed in the index of all corpus files with a code number for the file together with information about participants and word count. The index and sample customized sub-corpus file can be seen in Figures 4.4 and 4.5.

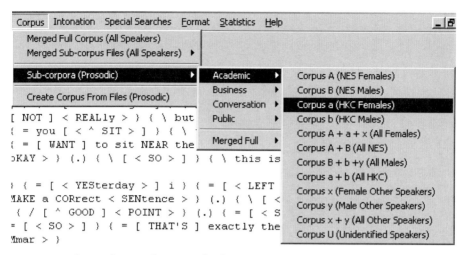

Figure 4.3 The academic sub-corpus for female HKC speakers loaded by selecting from the third Corpus Menu item

CODE	-- DISCOURSE TYPE --	DURATION	---- PARTICIPANTS ----	WORDS	
B123	Speech	108m 6s	A; a1-a16; B; b1-b13;...	15,235	
B125	Speech	109m 30s	A; a1-a7; b1-b4; ...	15,708	
B146	Informal office talk	56m 28s	a; B1-B2;	9,250	
B147	Video conference	10m 22s	A; a;	2,015	
B148	Informal office talk	44m 36s	a1-a2;	8,172	
B150	Speech	13m 49s	b;	1,638	
B151	Announcement	2m 22s	b;	308	
B154	Speech	29m 11s	b;	3,859	
B155	Announcement	58m 10s	a1-a3; B; b1-b9; ...	7,908	
B156	Announcement	32m 48s	a1-a3; B; b1-b6; ...	5,120	

Figure 4.4 The fourth Corpus Menu item allows users to create their own customized corpus by selecting from the index file of all individual corpus files

```
█ PersonalCorpus.txt                                                    _ |□| x |
 B011                                                                          ▲

   b:      { = good [ < AFternoon > ] }
   B:      { ? my name } ((clear throat)) { ? [ < SORry > ] }
   b:       { ? [ < CHECK > ] in sir }
   B:      { = [ YEAH ] i'm mister < ^ F__ > }
   b:      { = [ < _ Okay > ] } { = mister [ < F__ > ] }
 ((pause))
   b:      { ? [ < MISter > ] } { ? mister [ < F__ > ] } { \ when you [ MA
   B:      { ? about a about a week }
   b:      { \ i could not [ FIND ] it from the < comPUter > }
 ((pause))
   B:      { = regal [ < HONG > ] kong hotel }
   b:      { \ [ < _ OH > ] } { \ regal [ HONG ] kong < ^ hoTEL > } { \ th ▼
   B:      { \ [ <   OH > ] }
 ◄                                                                        ► //
```

Figure 4.5 A customized sub-corpus file created from the index file opened in its own window

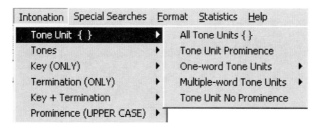

Figure 4.6 The sub-menu for Tone Unit { }

The intonation menu: tone units

All the items in the Intonation Menu have sub-menus, which will be discussed individually. The statistics (see Chapters 5-8) given for the corpus and sub-corpus files were created using these functions. The sub-menu for the first item is shown in Figure 4.6.

Tone Units are delineated by curly brackets { } which mark the beginning and end of each tone unit (see Chapter 5). Selecting the first item in the sub-menu lists all tone units in the corpus or sub-corpus file which has been loaded (Figure 4.7).

As shown in Figure 4.7, each tone unit is displayed on the left. All tone units are listed in the order in which they occur, regardless of the number of words or prominences in the tone unit. In the academic sub-corpus for all HKC, for instance, there are 65,777 tone units listed. In this sub-corpus, the number of words in a tone unit ranges from one to eighteen words, and the number of prominences one to four. There is a diminishing number of tone units, according to whether word counts or prominence counts is used as the criterion, so that the largest number of tone units is found for single word tone units with one prominence, and the smallest number of tone units is found for tone units with four prominences and/or a large word count. Some of the functions shown in the Tone Units sub-menu above allow us to list the tone units according to how many prominences or words there are in each tone unit.

Figure 4.8 shows the display for tone units in the academic sub-corpus for all NES which contain two prominences.

Corpus_A_all_HKC.txt

Concordances for / TONE UNIT { (}) /

```
 2      { = [ < TESting > ] } { / [ < TESting > ] } { = [ < PROject > ] } { = [ < UM > ]
 3      { / [ < TESting > ] } { = [ < PROject > ] } { = [ < UM > ] } { \ and [ < SO > ]
 4      { = [ < PROject > ] } { = [ < UM > ] } { \ and [ < SO > ] she's } { \ [ HERE ] t
 5      { = [ < UM > ] } { \ and [ < SO > ] she's } { \ [ HERE ] to VIdeo < _ TAPE > } {
 6      { \ and [ < SO > ] she's } { \ [ HERE ] to VIdeo < _ TAPE > } { \ my [ < LECture
 7      { \ [ HERE ] to VIdeo < _ TAPE > } { \ my [ < LECture > ] } { \ [ < toDAY > ] }
 8      { \ my [ < LECture > ] } { \ [ < toDAY > ] } { = [ < SO > ] } (.) { \ [ < ^ TOO
 9      { \ [ < toDAY > ] } { = [ < SO > ] } (.) { \ [ < ^ TOO > ] bad } { = [ < YOU > ]
10      { = [ < SO > ] } (.) { \ [ < ^ TOO > ] bad } { = [ < YOU > ] } { = you'll [ NOT
11      { \ [ < ^ TOO > ] bad } { = [ < YOU > ] } { = you'll [ NOT ] able to be < ON > }
12      { = [ < YOU > ] } { = you'll [ NOT ] able to be < ON > } { \ [ ON ] this < CAMer
13      { = you'll [ NOT ] able to be < ON > } { \ [ ON ] this < CAMera > } { \ [ JUST ]
14      { \ [ ON ] this < CAMera > } { \ [ JUST ] < ME > } { \ [ < ME > ] } { \ [ < _ ME
15      { \ [ JUST ] < ME > } { \ [ < ME > ] } { \ [ < _ ME > ] } { \/ but [ < toMORrow
16      { \ [ < ME > ] } { \ [ < _ ME > ] } { \/ but [ < toMORrow > ] } { = we'll [ < HA
```

Figure 4.7 The display for all tone units

Corpus_A_all_NES.txt

Concordances for / TONE UNIT PROMINENCE ( ) /

```
 1      { = and [ CAN ] i < ASK > you } ((inaudible)) { \ [ KEEping ] the < CLASS > } { =
 2      { \ [ KEEping ] the < CLASS > } { = [ < THIS > ] } { / [ < AFterNOON > ] } { \/ t
 3      { / [ < AFterNOON > ] } { \/ to [ KEEP ] as QUIET as < POSsible > } { \/ [ BEcause
 4      { \/ [ ^ MIcrophone ] < HERE > } { = [ < AND > ] i } { \ [ MY ] VOICE WON'T last  t
 5      { \ [ aBOVE ] everybody else < TALking > } { / [ < oKAY > ] } { = [ < WELL > ] er
 6      { / you are all [ aWARE ] of who i < AM > } { = [ < THE > ] } { \/ the [ COURSE ]
 7      { \/ the [ COURSE ] < LEAder > } { = of [ < THIS > ] } { ? of [ < THE > ] } { / [
 8      { = [ I'LL ] be < HERE > } { / to [ TAKE ] you for this < SUBject > } { \/ [ MAnu
 9      { / to [ TAKE ] you for this < SUBject > } { \/ [ MAnuFACturing ] MAnagement < TWO
10      { / it is [ ^ VEry ] < MUCH > } { \/ a [ < conTINuAtion > ] } { \ [ OF ] what you
11      { \/ a [ < conTINuAtion > ] } { \ [ OF ] what you were DOing LAST < ^ YEAR > } { \
12      { \/ [ VArious ] < TOpics > } { = that [ WILL ] be < DEALT > with } { \ [ IN ] thi
13      { = that [ WILL ] be < DEALT > with } { \ [ IN ] this < SUBject > } { = i [ THINK
```

Figure 4.8 The display for tone units with two prominences

Tone units with two prominences are displayed on the left, again in the order in which they occur. For the academic sub-corpus for all NES the total is 2,715, fewer than the 3,953 listed with one prominence, but more than the 1,187 listed for three prominence tone units (totals appear in the Status Bar at the bottom right-hand corner of the program 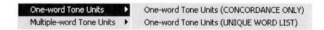). The number of words is variable, but the largest single group of tone units occurs with one prominence only (206,493 out of a total of 323,703 tone units in the HKCSE), and of these tone units with one word form more than half (107,003). The third sub-menu item thus lists only tone units which have one word. Since all tone units must have at least one prominence, these are mainly tone units which have one prominence and one word. The user can choose to ignore prominences, but since all tone units should have at least one prominence, those without a prominence are the result of the transcriber not being able to determine where the prominence fell, and are very few. The menu item for One-Word Tone Units has two options shown in Figure 4.9:

Figure 4.9 The options for tone units sub-menu item three (one-word tone units)

These two options are:

– One-word tone units in concordances only
– One-word tone units with a Unique Word List showing the words which occur in one-word tone units

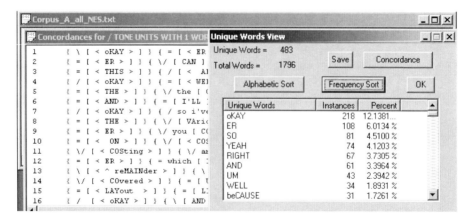

Figure 4.10 The display for tone units with one word (tone units sub-menu item three, with UW list)

Figure 4.10 shows what words are most often used in one-word tone units, when sorted by frequency.

Single word tone units are listed as 1,796 for the academic sub-corpus for all NES. The option has been selected for a Unique Word List to be displayed together with the concordances. For the display in Figure 4.10, both options have been selected to get the Unique Words List displayed with the Concordance View. The Unique Words have been sorted according to their frequency, so showing the words that are used most often in one-word tone units.

The fourth sub-menu item Multiple-Word Tone Units also provides for two options from the Tone Units sub-menu, which are the same as those for One-Word Tone Units (Figure 4.11):

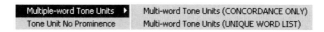

Figure 4.11 The options for tone units sub-menu item four (multiple-word tone units)

As the third sub-menu lists the tone units which have only a single word, so the fourth sub-menu item provides a function which lists the tone units according to the number of words specified by the user in the tone unit. A dialog provides the option to specify or ignore the number of prominences, and Figure 4.12 shows the display for four-word tone units with the number of prominences ignored.

There are 1,181 four-word tone units listed for the academic sub-corpus for all NES. The Unique Word List, when sorted by frequency, for four-word tone units is very different from that for one-word tone units. The words for one-word tone units are most frequently interactive words such as 'OKAY' or fillers such as 'ER', whereas the most frequent words found for four-word tone units are grammatical words such as 'the', 'you' and 'of'.

Figure 4.12 The display for tone units with four words (tone units sub-menu item four, with UW list)

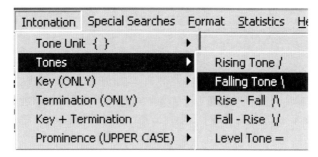

Figure 4.13 The sub-menu for tones with falling tone (\ ) selected

```
Corpus_A_all_Males.txt                                              _ □ ×
b6: { \ i [ < DON'T > ] hear }                                           ▲
Concordances for / FALLING TONE ( \ ) /                            _ □ ×
   1                           A001 b:   { \ to [ HELP ] you to MAKE a CORrect < S ▲
   2     t < SENtence > } b:   { = [ < beCAUSE > ] } { \ if you [ KNOW ] the word < _ CLASS >
   3     LASS > } (.) { = [ YOU'LL ] know < THE > } { \ [ THE ] universal < ^ RULE > } { = to
   4     rsal < ^ RULE > } { = to [ WRITE ] < A > } { \ [ GRAMmatically ] CORrect < _ SENtenc
   5     ] } { = is [ < A > ] } { / [ < NOUN > ] } { \ [ AND ] is a < _ VERB > } { / and a [
   6     is a < _ VERB > } { / and a [ < BOY > ] } { \ [ < YOU > ] can say } { = a [ < obJEC
   7     (.) { / [ < SO > ] } { = you [ < CAN > ] } { \ [ < ^ SUBstitute > ] } { \ with [ Oth
   8     u [ < CAN > ] } { \ [ < ^ SUBstitute > ] } { \ with [ Other ] SAME kind of word < _
   9     [ Other ] SAME kind of word < _ CLASS > } { \ in a [ < _ SENtence > ] } b:   { = you
  10     > ] is } { / [ < NICE > ] } ((laugh)) b:   { \ [ < rePUblic > ] }   b:   { = generatio
  11     > ] } b:   { ? [ < ^ SOMEbody > ] should } { \ have [ < TOLD > ] me } b:   { = [ THE ]
  12     ] me } b:   { = [ THE ] < morphoLOgical > } { \ [ OF ] < EACH > verb } ((inaudible))
  13     ] } b:   { = because we learn [ < THE > ] } { \ [ (DEScriptive) ] [ < GRAMmar > ] } (
  14     { = [ < _ MM > ] } { = [ SOME ] < FOOD > } { \ are [ < deLIcious > ] } b:   { \ [ <   ▼
```

Figure 4.14 The display for falling tone (\ )

The intonation menu: tones

The tones sub-menu has five items: rising tone /, falling tone \, rise – fall /\, fall – rise \/, and level tone = (Figure 4.13).

Figure 4.14 shows the display for falling tones for the academic sub-corpus for all males, with 14,496 instances listed. Tones are centred when listed.

The intonation menu: key (ONLY)

Key (ONLY) is shown by square brackets [ ], and occurs in tone units with at least two prominences, and indicates the syllable which has the first prominence in the tone unit. The Key sub-menu has four items: High [^], Mid [ ], Low [_] and ALL [***] (Figure 4.15).

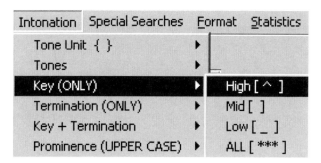

Figure 4.15 The sub-menu for key with high key [^] selected

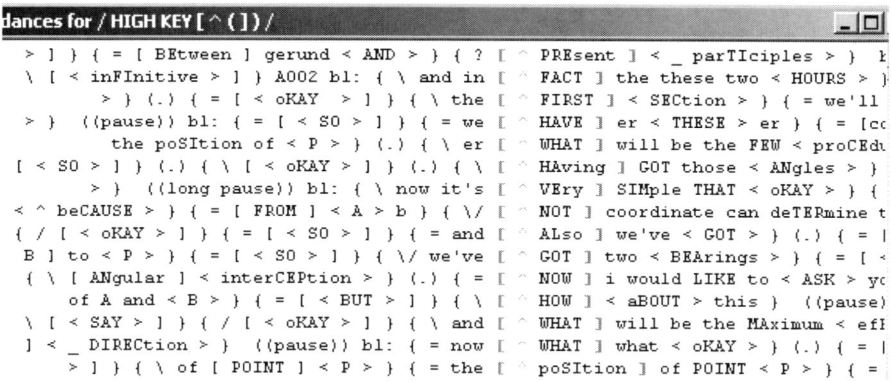

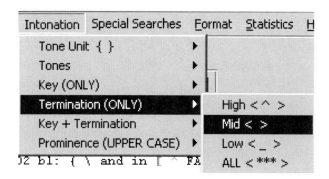

Figure 4.16 The display for high key [^]

Figure 4.16 shows the display for High Key [^] for the academic sub-corpus for all males, with 1,217 listed. Key is centred when listed.

Figure 4.17 The sub-menu for termination with mid termination selected

```
dances for / MID TERMINATION ONLY < { > ) /                    _ □
    b:   { \ to [ HELP ] you to MAKE a CORrect < SENtence > } b:   { = [ < beCAUSE >
 word < _ CLASS > } (.) { = [ YOU'LL ] know < THE > } { \ [ THE ] universal < ^
   ] universal < ^ RULE > } { = to [ WRITE ] < A > } { \ [ GRAMmatically ] CORrec
     > } b:   { = [ < UM > ] } { = [ JUST ] < LIKE > } { / [ I ] am a < BOY > }
   ] } { = [ JUST ] < LIKE > } { / [ I ] am a < BOY > } (.) { / [ < I > ] } { = is
   > ] } { = [ < OR > ] a } { / [ OBjective ] < PHRASE > } (.) { / [ < SO > ] } {
 } { \ have [ < TOLD > ] me } b:   { = [ THE ] < morphoLOgical > } { \ [ OF ] < EAC
   { = [ THE ] < morphoLOgical > } { \ [ OF ] < EACH > verb } ((inaudible))   b:   {
 GRAMmar > ] } ((laugh)) { = we [ KNOW ] the < FACT > } { = [ < BUT > ] } { = we
   > } { = [ < BUT > ] } { = we [ DON'T ] know < WHY > } b:   { = [ < _ MM > ] } { =
 WHY > } b:   { = [ < _ MM > ] } { = [ SOME ] < FOOD > } { \ are [ < deLIcious > ]
```

Figure 4.18 The display for mid termination < >

The intonation menu: termination (ONLY)

The fourth item in the Intonation Menu is Termination (ONLY), which is shown by the arrow brackets < >, and as with key, occurs in tone units with at least two prominences.. The Termination sub-menu also has four items, the same as those for Key (Figure 4.17).

Figure 4.18 shows the display for mid termination for the academic sub-corpus for all females, with 11,542 listed. Termination is centred when listed.

The intonation menu: key + termination

The fifth item in the Intonation Menu is Key + Termination, which is shown by both the square and arrow brackets [< >] (Figure 4.19).

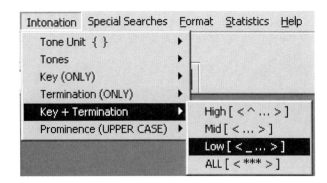

Figure 4.19 The sub-menu for Key + Termination with low key +termination selected

```
ances for / LOW KEY+TERMINATION [ < _ ( > ] ) /                              _ □
] SAME kind of word <  _  CLASS > } { \ in a [ <  _  SENtence > ] } b:   { = your [ < MOne
] } { = we [ DON'T ] know < WHY > } b:   { = [ <  _  MM > ] } { = [ SOME ] < FOOD > } { \
    > } { \ are [ < deLIcious > ] } b:   { \ [ <  _  YES > ] } b:   { = [ < FOODS > ] } {
[ <  _  YES > ] } b:   { = [ < FOODS > ] } { ? [ <  _  D > ] }    ((laugh)) b:   { = [ < oKA
  < BOring > } ((laugh)) ((laugh)) b:   { = a [ <  _  BORED > ] } { = a [ < BORED > ] } {
the GOOD angular < interSECtion > } (.) { \ [ <  _  NOW > ] } { = can [ Anybody ] TELL m
deTERmine ] the poSItion of < P > } (.) { \ [ <  _  NOW > ] } { = can i [ < ASK > ] some
} (.) { \ [ MALE ] or < FEmale > } (.) { \ [ <  _  oKAY > ] } (.) { \ give me the [ <
at } { \ [ < P > ] } ((inaudible)) b1:   { \ [ <  _  oKAY > ] } { = [ < SO > ] } { = you
HOW ] < aBOUT > this } ((pause))   b1:   { \ [ <  _  NOW > ] } { = if i [ asSUME ] < ^ TH
] } { \ for the [ ANgle ] a and < B > } { \ [ <  _  NOW > ] } { \/ in [ < ^ CASE > ] } (
    > } { \ [ WHAT ] are < THEY > } b3:   { = [ <  _  ER > ] } (.) { = [ ANgle ] < B > a }
```

Figure 4.20 The display for low key + termination

It has been reported that tone units with one prominence form the largest single group of tone units, and in this case the syllable which has the prominence has both key and termination in the tone unit. The Key + Termination sub-menu also has four items, which are the same as those for the Key and Termination sub-menus. Figure 4.20 shows the display for Low Key + Termination for the academic sub-corpus for all females, with 1,092 listed. Key + Termination is centred when listed.

The intonation menu: prominence

The last item in the intonation menu is prominence, which is denoted by upper case (Figure 4.21).

Figure 4.22 shows the display for all prominence for the academic sub-corpus for all females, for which there are 51,810 instances. Prominence is centred when displayed.

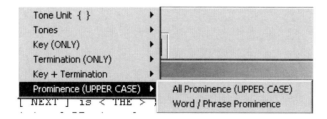

Figure 4.21 The intonation menu for prominence with its two-item sub-menu

```
Corpus_A_all_Females.txt                                                    _ □ x
Concordances for / PROMINENCE (UPPER CASE) /
1                           A001 al:   { = shall i [ < SAY > ] } { = [ < TESting
2                A001 al:   { = shall i [ < SAY > ] } { = [ < TESting > ] } { / [ < TESt
3      all i [ < SAY > ] } { = [ < TESting > ] } { / [ < TESting > ] } { = [ < PRO: 
4      = [ < TESting > ] } { / [ < TESting > ] } { = [ < PROject > ] } { = [ < UM > 
5      / [ < TESting > ] } { = [ < PROject > ] } { = [ < UM > ] } { \ and [ < SO > 
6         = [ < PROject > ] } { = [ < UM > ] } { \ and [ < SO > ] she's } { \ [ HERE
7      { = [ < UM > ] } { \ and [ < SO > ] she's } { \ [ HERE ] to VIdeo < _ TAPE > 
8         > ] } { \ and [ < SO > ] she's } { \ [ HERE ] to VIdeo < _ TAPE > } { \ my
9         and [ < SO > ] she's } { \ [ HERE ] to VIdeo < _ TAPE > } { \ my [ < LECtui
10     s } { \ [ HERE ] to VIdeo < _ TAPE > } { \ my [ < LECture > ] } { \ [ < toDA
11     o < _ TAPE > } { \ my [ < LECture > ] } { \ [ < toDAY > ] } { = [ < SO > ] }
12     my [ < LECture > ] } { \ [ < toDAY > ] } { = [ < SO > ] } (.) { \ [ < ^ TOC
13     \ [ < toDAY > ] } { = [ < SO > ] } (.) { \ [ < ^ TOO > ] bad } { = [ < YOU
14     [ < SO > ] } (.) { \ [ < ^ TOO > ] bad } { = [ < YOU > ] } { = you'll [ NO1
15     < ^ TOO > ] bad } { = [ < YOU > ] } { = you'll [ NOT ] able to be < ON > }
```

Figure 4.22 The display for all prominences

The second and last item in this sub-menu is Word / Phrase Prominence, which displays only the instances of a particular word or phrase in which there is a prominence. Figure 4.23 shows the display for the word 'WELL' for the academic sub-corpus for all females, when Word / Phrase Prominence is selected. There are 109 concordances for 'WELL' with prominence.

```
Corpus_A_all_Females.txt                                                    _ □
Concordances for / WELL (PROMINENCE) /                                      _ □
1      s [ NOT ] a good < SENtence > } (.) { \ not a [ ^ WELL ] formed < SENtence > } (.) {
2      [ < SAY > ] } { \ just [ < THAT > ] } (.) { / [ < WELL > ] } (.) { = [ ^ Even ] from
3      > } { = and you've been [ < TAUGHT > ] } { / [ < WELL > ] } (.) { \ [ ENglish ] at
4      { \ [ < OH > ] } al:      ** { \ oh } a7:   { / [ < WELL > ] } al:  { / [ < WELL > ] }
5      ** { \ oh } a7:   { / [ < WELL > ] } al:  { / [ < WELL > ] } al:  { / [ < WELL > ] } { /
6      _ JUStiFIAble > } { ? [ < THAT > ] is } { \ [ < WELL > ] } { \ i can [ GIVE ] you
7      n be a < LINguist > } { \ [ < _ NOW > ] } { / [ < WELL > ] } { = [ < ER > ] } { \ it
8      THE > ] } { \ the word [ < BOOK > ] } (.) { / [ < WELL > ] } { = you [ UNderSTAND ]
9      = [ BUT ] DO you reMEMber < yesterDAY > } { = [ < WELL > ] } { = [ THERE ] was this
10     let's move [ < ON > ] } { = [ < ER > ] } { / [ < WELL > ] } { = [ SHALL ] we < SKIP
11     [ HOW ] about < beHIND > } ((laugh)) al:  { / [ < WELL > ] } { / [ < YES > ] } { = y
12     / [ < YES > ] } { = you can [ < SAY > ] } { \ [ < WELL > ] } { / [ < THESE > ]
13     poSItion > } al:  { = [ < beCAUSE > ] er } { / [ < WELL > ] } { \ [ < YEAH > ] } { =
14     occur < THIS > and } { / [ < SO > ] } (.) { \ [ < WELL > ] } { \ at [ < ^ LEAST > ]
15     HOST > ] } * { \ let's [ < SAY > ] } a3: { \ [ < WELL > ] } { \ okay [ ^ LET'S ] ta
```

Figure 4.23 The display for word/phrase prominence for 'WELL'

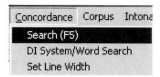

Figure 4.24 The Concordance Menu with the first item Search (F5) selected

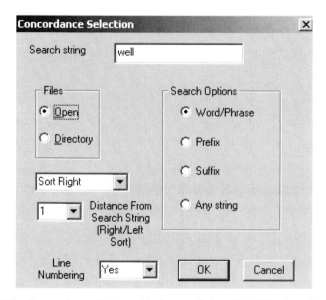

Figure 4.25 The Concordance Dialog with the search item 'WELL' selected

The concordance menu: search

The first item is for the basic concordance search (Figure 4.24). Selecting this initially presents the user with the Concordance Dialog which requires the user to input the search word or phrase as well as allowing various search preferences to be set. This is done by pressing the F5 key or clicking the left Concordance Search button ▢ ▢ for this dialog) (Figure 4.25).

Pressing 'OK' produces the following output (Figure 4.26). All instances of 'WELL' are shown; prominences are ignored as the searches are not case sensitive; and the total number of concordances listed for 'WELL' is 125. Referring back to

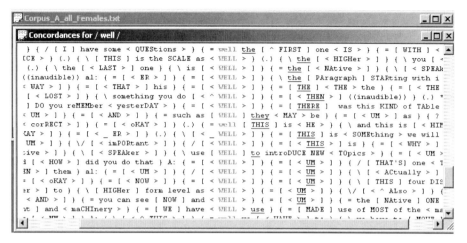

Figure 4.26 The concordance display for 'WELL' with both prominent and non-prominent examples

Figure 4.23 which shows 109 concordances for 'WELL' with prominence, by comparing the two figures, we can see that 'WELL' is normally spoken with prominence and only relatively rarely with no prominence.

The concordance menu: discourse intonation system/word search

The second menu item is the Discourse Intonation (DI) System/Word Search. This shows all the concordances showing all the positional and constituent variants of two or more DI system/words which occur within a given line width (set in characters). Selecting this second item (or clicking the right Search Button) brings up the DI System/Word Search Dialog, which requires the user to input the search items as well as allowing various search preferences to be set. A minimum of two search items must be specified (Figure 4.27).

In Figure 4.28, the display for ' _ / ^ ' shows all instances of co-occurrence of these discourse intonation systems. Altogether there are 457 concordances for ' _ / ^ ' listed. Figure 4.28 shows examples of low key/termination followed immediately by high key in consecutive tone units. Elsewhere, the concordance lines are able to display positional and/or constituent variation[1] where these are present for the search items.

---

1.   Positional variation refers to instances where the items can be in different positions relative to each other and constituent variation is when other items occur between the items searched.

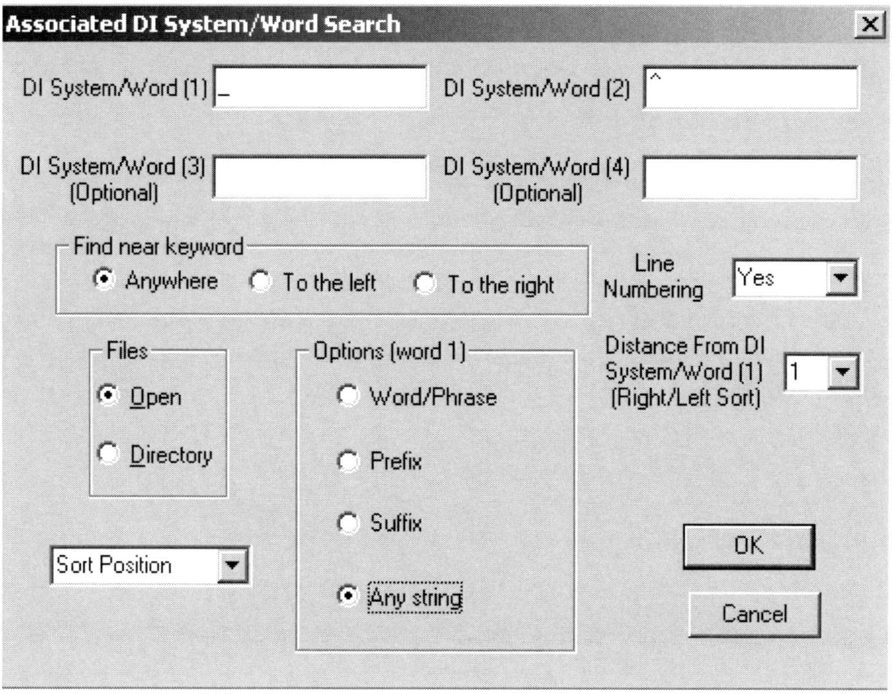

Figure 4.27 The DI System/Word Search Dialog with the search items '_ / ^ ' selected

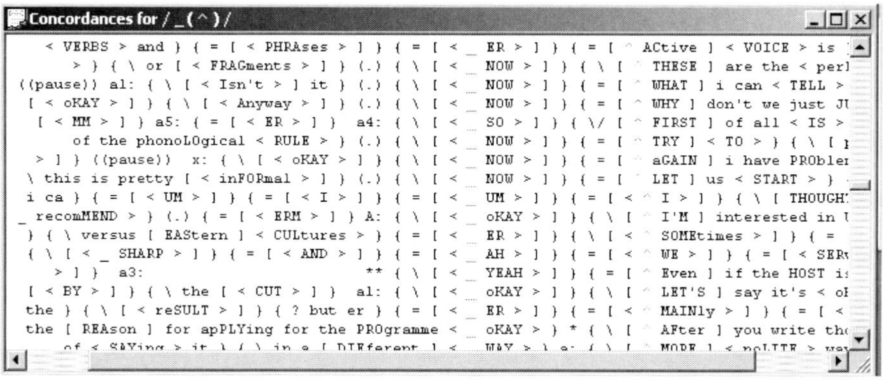

Figure 4.28 The display for ' _ / ^ ' showing low key/termination followed by high key

The statistics menu

The Statistics Menu has three functions:

1. Collocates View
2. Unique Words
3. Compare UW Lists

In Figure 4.29, the Statistics Menu is shown against a concordance search for 'WELL', here created with Right Sort selected from the Concordance Dialog.

The Collocates View requires a left or right sort option to be selected (not unsorted, which is the default setting), and the result lists the right hand collocates as shown in the Collocates View window in Figure 4.30.

Figure 4.29 The Statistics Menu with the concordance for 'WELL'

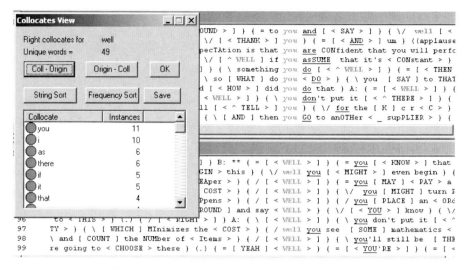

Figure 4.30 The Collocates View window for 'WELL' after the Frequency Sort button has been clicked

Figure 4.30 shows the concordance display resulting from selecting 'YOU' and pressing the Coll – Origin button. 'YOU' is listed as the most frequent right collocate of 'WELL', and selecting Coll – Origin centres 'YOU', showing 'WELL' as the co-occurring word with 'YOU'. The display is still right sorted, although the centred word is changed. The numbers for instances in the Collocates View refer to the number of instances of that word as a right collocate (the words which have been underlined, here sorted one word to the right of 'WELL'). Thus, for 'YOU' as a right collocate of 'WELL' there are 11 instances.

The display for 'YOU' is very different, and Figure 4.31 shows the result of a left sort with the collocate sorted one word to the left of 'YOU', with the Collocates View showing that 'IF' is the most frequently occurring left collocate of 'YOU'.

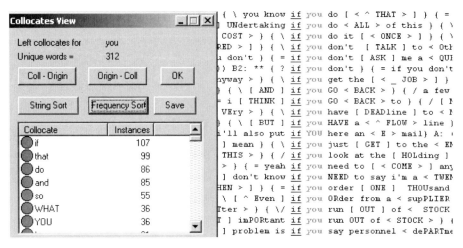

Figure 4.31 The Collocates View window for left collocates of 'YOU'

The statistics menu: unique words

The second function is the Unique Words List, as illustrated in Figure 4.32. This provides both a total word count and a count of the word types (unique words) together with the number of instances and frequency of occurrence (expressed as a percentage of the total) for each unique word. Figure 4.32 shows the Unique Words List for the merged Business sub-corpus after the Frequency Sort button has been clicked.

This shows that there are a total of 246,816 words in the merged business sub-corpus, of which 8,038 are unique words. The unique words function of the iConc program has been customized to ignore 'a:', 'b:' etc., which indicate speakers, as well as the symbols which are used to indicate the discourse intonation systems of the HKCSE (prosodic).

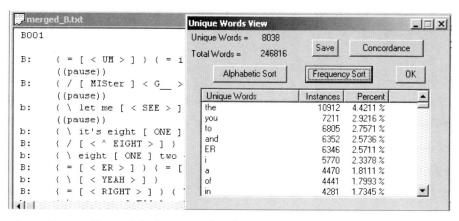

Figure 4.32 The Unique Words List window for the merged business sub-corpus after the Frequency Sort button has been clicked

The statistics menu: compare unique words lists

The third and final function on the Statistics Menu compares two unique word lists and lists the words which are in one of the lists but not the other. Before using this function, the user must first create and save unique word lists for the two files to be compared. Figure 4.33 shows the resulting figures comparing lists for the business and conversation sub-corpus files.

In Figure 4.33, the word 'YOU' is the second most frequent word in List 1 (the business sub-corpus), whereas for List 2 (the conversation sub-corpus) the second most frequent word is 'I'. Figure 4.33 also shows that 'TRANSCRIPTION' occurs 74 times in List 1 and is not used at all in List 2, whereas 'MAID' occurs 61 times in List 2 but not at all in List 1.

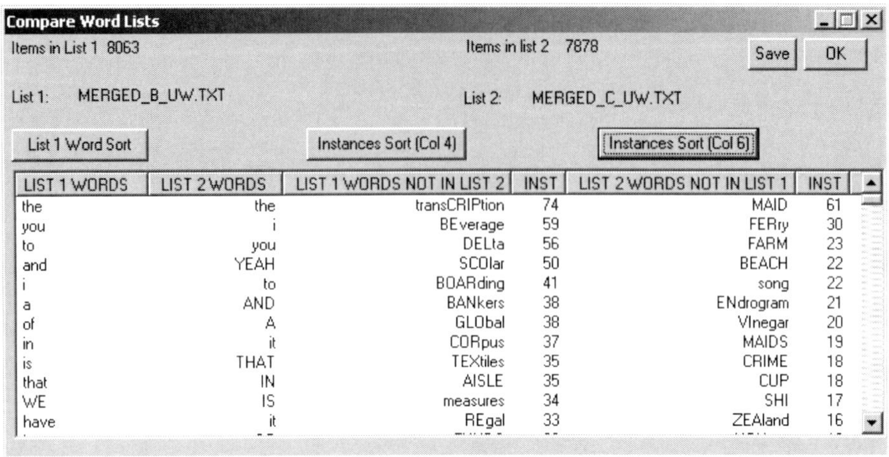

Compare Word Lists

Items in List 1 8063   Items in list 2 7878   Save   OK

List 1:   MERGED_B_UW.TXT   List 2:   MERGED_C_UW.TXT

List 1 Word Sort		Instances Sort (Col 4)		Instances Sort (Col 6)	

LIST 1 WORDS	LIST 2 WORDS	LIST 1 WORDS NOT IN LIST 2	INST	LIST 2 WORDS NOT IN LIST 1	INST
the	the	transCRIPtion	74	MAID	61
you	i	BEverage	59	FERry	30
to	you	DELta	56	FARM	23
and	YEAH	SCOlar	50	BEACH	22
i	to	BOARding	41	song	22
a	AND	BANkers	38	ENdrogram	21
of	A	GLObal	38	VInegar	20
in	it	CORpus	37	MAIDS	19
is	THAT	TEXtiles	35	CRIME	18
that	IN	AISLE	35	CUP	18
WE	IS	measures	34	SHI	17
have	it	REgal	33	ZEAland	16

Figure 4.33 The Compare Word Lists window for the merged business sub-corpus and the merged conversation sub-corpus

Conclusion

This chapter has described the software, iConc, designed specifically to interrogate the HKCSE (prosodic). The corpus and iConc are on the CD which accompanies this book, and it is hoped that it will prove to be a useful resource for researchers, as well as for teachers and students of the English language.

CHAPTER 5

Tone Units

Introduction

All speech is organised in tone units which are stretches of speech with one tonic segment comprising at least a tonic syllable. A tonic segment extends from an onset (first prominent syllable) to the tonic (final prominent syllable). In a tone unit with only one prominent syllable, the onset and tonic syllables are the same. In this chapter the tone units in the HKCSE (prosodic) are examined in terms of their distribution with regard to size; that is, the number of words found inside the tone units, in relation to text types and speakers in the sub-corpora. Some qualitative examples will be analysed with respect to how tone unit boundaries can function to disambiguate discourse meanings and delineate extended collocations, and how tone units relate generally to Linear Unit Grammar (Sinclair and Mauranen 2006).

There are no other corpora that have been transcribed based on the discourse intonation framework (Brazil 1997), and so direct comparisons with other spoken corpora cannot be made. However, Cauldwell (2003a, 2003b) has written an advanced listening and pronunciation textbook, which makes extensive use of naturally occurring spoken discourses. The data were transcribed using the same system as that used for the HKCSE (prosodic). While the data transcribed by Cauldwell only amount to 22 minutes in total, and were made up of extracts from eight different spoken discourses involving nine NES, the 1,205 tone units, the distribution of tones, and prominences are referred to in this study as points of reference, because both the data examined by Cauldwell and the HKCSE (prosodic) are spontaneous and identical in terms of the transcription of the discourse intonation systems.

Distribution of size of tone units

Tables 5.1 shows the distribution of tone units based on the number of words inside the tone units across the entire HKCSE (prosodic).

Table 5.1 Number of words in tone units in HKCSE (prosodic) and sub-corpora

Number of words in tone unit	HKCSE (prosodic)	Academic sub-corpus	Business sub-corpus	Conversation sub-corpus	Public sub-corpus
one	107,003 (33.05%)	26,748 (35.01%)	29,680 (33.88%)	31,642 (36.66%)	18,933 (25.78%)
two	70,651 (21.82%)	16,799 (22.00%)	18,146 (20.72%)	18,697 (21.66%)	17,009 (23.16%)
three	52,704 (16.28%)	11,965 (15.67%)	13,616 (15.55%)	12,748 (14.77%)	14,375 (19.57%)
four	35,954 (11.10%)	8,018 (10.50%)	9,692 (11.07%)	8,627 (10.00%)	9,617 (13.10%)
five	22,892 (7.07%)	5,210 (6.82%)	6,257 (7.14%)	5,607 (6.50%)	5,818 (7.92%)
six	14,079 (4.34%)	3,173 (4.15%)	4,021 (4.59%)	3,425 (3.97%)	3,460 (4.71%)
seven	8,275 (2.55%)	1,915 (2.51%)	2,417 (2.76%)	2,077 (2.41%)	1,866 (1.40%)
eight	4,541 (1.40%)	1,037 (1.36%)	1,305 (1.49%)	1,172 (1.36%)	1,027 (1.40%)
nine	2,420 (0.74%)	529 (0.69%)	728 (0.83%)	601 (0.70%)	562 (0.77%)
ten	1,298 (0.40%)	277 (0.36%)	408 (0.47%)	329 (0.38%)	284 (0.39%)
eleven	644 (0.20%)	127 (0.17%)	227 (0.26%)	164 (0.19%)	126 (0.17%)
twelve	304 (0.09%)	58 (0.08%)	106 (0.12%)	84 (0.10%)	56 (0.08%)
thirteen	156 (0.05%)	31 (0.04%)	56 (0.06%)	44 (0.05%)	25 (0.03%)
fourteen	70 (0.02%)	13 (0.02%)	26 (0.03%)	20 (0.02%)	12 (0.02%)
fifteen	27	1	10	9	7
sixteen	11	2	7	1	1
seventeen	8	1	3	4	0
eighteen	2	0	1	1	0
Total	323,703	76,380	87,582	86,304	73,437

The number of words in a tone unit clearly varies but in the majority of cases (89.86%) there are between one and five words in a tone unit. Tone units with up to ten words amount to 98.66% of all the tone units in the HKCSE (prosodic). The tiny minority (0.34%) that fall outside of this range extend all the way to 18 words

(2 instances), but are very rare. Cauldwell (2003b) has one instance of a 15-word tone unit among his 1,205 tone units, with almost all tone units falling within the one- to five-word range. These numbers fit well with the simple calculation of dividing the number of words in the HKCSE (prosodic) by the number of tone units which gives an average of 2.78 words per tone unit.

It is also interesting to note that the most frequently occurring tone unit is the one-word tone unit (33.05%). It needs to be pointed out that here, like Cauldwell (2003b), one-word tone units include interjections, such as 'oh', and the verbal fillers 'er', 'um' and 'erm' when they are on their own in a tone unit, although Cauldwell denotes all fillers as 'erm'. In Cauldwell's data one-word tone units are also the most common, although the proportion is lower at 20.16%. One-word tone units are discussed in more detail later in this chapter.

Table 5.1 shows an unbroken pattern. As the number of words in the tone unit increases, so the number of instances decreases. Two-word tone units are the next most frequent (21.82%), followed by 3-word (16.28%), 4-word (11.10%), 5-word (7.07%), 6-word (4.34%), 7-word (2.55%), 8-word (1.40%), 9-word (0.74%), and 10-word (0.40%). Remarkably, this pattern is unbroken all the way to the last table detailing the two instances of 18-word tone units. However, there are differences between the Public sub-corpus and the other three sub-corpora. It can be seen that the proportional usage of one-word tone units is less in the Public sub-corpus (25.78%), whereas across the other sub-corpora it ranges between 33.88%-36.66%. This pattern is reversed for the two-, three-, four-, and five-word tone units where the proportional usage is consistently higher in the Public-sub-corpus than in the other three sub-corpora. This is probably explained by the fact that there are more monologues in the Public sub-corpus reducing the incidence of single word tone units, and this is discussed in more detail below. Speakers, irrespective of first language, gender, or sub-corpus, conform to this pattern, but this is not to say that the various sets of speakers are the same in terms of the size of the tone units spoken proportionately by them.

While the general pattern outlined holds for all speakers, a closer look at the findings shows slight differences between the sets of speakers (Appendix 2). As described in Chapter 1, the number of words spoken by the different sets of speakers varies both in the HKCSE (prosodic) as a whole and from sub-corpus to sub-corpus. The distribution of words in the HKCSE (prosodic) between the HKC and the NES is 71.46% and 25.32% respectively, whereas the distribution of tone units between the two groups is 73.92% and 22.88% (Table 5.2).

Table 5.2 Number of words in tone units: HKC and NES

Number of words in tone unit	HKC	NES
one	80,856 (33.79%)	22,692 (30.64%)
two	53,850 (22.5%)	14,459 (19.52%)
three	40,081 (16.75%)	11,068 (14.94%)
four	26,388 (11.03%)	8,505 (11.48%)
five	16,101 (6.73%)	6,067 (8.19%)
six	9,454 (3.95%)	4,201 (5.67%)
seven	5,312 (2.22%)	2,701 (3.65%)
eight	2,794 (1.17%)	1,592 (2.15%)
nine	1,419 (0.59%)	889 (1.20%)
ten	743 (0.31%)	510 (0.69%)
eleven	361 (0.15%)	252 (0.34%)
twelve	148 (0.06%)	144 (0.19%)
thirteen	78 (0.03%)	69 (0.09%)
fourteen	31	33
fifteen	10	16
sixteen	3	7
seventeen	1	6
eighteen	1	1
Total	239,282 (73.92%)	74,058 (22.88%)

These proportions are not very different, but they do suggest that the HKC have a slight tendency to speak tone units containing fewer words than the NES and, of course, vice versa. It needs to be emphasised that this tendency is slight, given the differences in the proportional usage involved, but it is a tendency that is confirmed across all of the tables. The consistency of the pattern supports the claim, even though the tendency is slight.

When gender is factored, the same pattern is found (Table 5.3).

Table 5.3 Number of words in tone units: HKC males and females and NES males and females

Number of words in tone unit	HKC Males	NES Males	HKC Females	NES Females
one	38,028 (31.26%)	17,582 (29.78%)	42,828 (36.40%)	5,110 (33.98%)
two	27,632 (22.72%)	11,627 (19.70%)	26,218 (22.28%)	2,832 (19.84%)
three	21,176 (17.41%)	8,988 (15.23%)	18,904 (16.07%)	2,080 (13.83%)
four	14,131 (11.62%)	6,925 (11.73%)	12,257 (10.42%)	1,580 (10.51%)
five	8,735 (7.18%)	4,957 (8.40%)	7,366 (6.26%)	1,110 (7.38%)
six	5,102 (4.19%)	3,382 (5.73%)	4,351 (3.70%)	819 (5.45%)
seven	2,887 (2.37%)	2,177 (3.69%)	2,425 (2.06%)	524 (3.48%)
eight	1,509 (1.24%)	1,264 (2.14%)	1,285 (1.10%)	328 (2.18%)
nine	794 (0.65%)	723 (1.22%)	626 (0.53%)	166 (1.10%)
ten	411 (0.34%)	405 (0.69%)	332 (0.28%)	105 (0.70%)
eleven	194 (0.16%)	194 (0.33%)	167 (0.14%)	58 (0.39%)
twelve	82 (0.07%)	109 (0.18%)	66 (0.06%)	35 (0.23%)
thirteen	55 (0.05%)	58 (0.10%)	23 (0.02%)	11 (0.07%)
fourteen	22	27	9	6
fifteen	7	10	3	6
sixteen	2	5	1	2
seventeen	1	4	0	2
eighteen	1	1	0	0
Total	121,625	59,023	117,656	15,035

Table 5.3 shows that the differences are very small in the cases of the HKC and NES male and female speakers in the Business sub-corpus, and between the HKC and NES females in the Public sub-corpus. Beginning with the one-word tone units, the same pattern is found across the corpus, the sub-corpora and gender, although, again, the differences are very small in the Public sub-corpus. The pattern is repeated in the two-word tone units, and, again, the differences are very small in the Public sub-corpus. The same is the case for the three-word and four-word tone units with the Public sub-corpus following the same pattern, but to a lesser extent.

There is a shift in the pattern described for the tone units ranging in size from one to four words when the five-word tone units are studied. It is the NES who speak proportionately more of the five-word tone units, but as has been emphasised above, the differences are small. There are a few exceptions, possibly because it marks the borderline in terms of the patterns described. The Public sub-corpus has a proportional distribution which almost exactly matches the words spoken by the HKC and NES. The HKC females in the Business and Public sub-corpora use slightly more five-word tone units than the NES females. From the six-word through to the eighteen-word tone units, the NES, irrespective of sub-corpus or gender, steadily widen the gap in terms of their proportionate use of longer tone units, when compared to the HKC. Again, it needs to be stressed that tone units longer than five words represent only 10.14% of the tone units in the corpus. Nonetheless, the pattern is consistent. HKC speak proportionately more of the one- to four-word tone units, and the NES speak proportionately more of the tone units containing five words and up.

The fact that the Public sub-corpus shows a tendency, albeit quite weak, to contain longer tone units is probably due to the fact that some of the discourses are prepared speeches that might be read fully or partially from a script. Such discourses can be expected to contain longer tone units than those which have no pre-planning due to the real-time constraints of the latter.

Single word tone units

As described above, most of the tone units (33.05%) in the HKCSE (prosodic) contain only one word. In order to help to understand why one-word tone units are so common in naturally occurring data, the thirty words which are found most frequently in these tone units are listed below and discussed. Table 5.4 shows the thirty most frequent words[1] found amongst the 7,947 unique words found in the 107,003 one-word tone units.

---

1.   For the purposes of this table, contractions such as 'it's' and 'we'd' are excluded.

Table 5.4 Most frequent thirty words in one-word tone units

Most frequent thirty words in one-word tone units	Frequencies of occurrence	Most frequent thirty words in one-word tone units	Frequencies of occurrence
1. er	10,735 (10.03%)	16. no	1,290 (1.20%)
2. yeah	7,567 (7.07%)	17. to	1,005 (0.93%)
3. okay	4,117 (3.84%)	18. well	990 (0.92%)
4. and	3,973 (3.71%)	19. that	923 (0.86%)
5. mm	3,676 (3.43%)	20. in	888 (0.82%)
6. um	3,122 (2.91%)	21. now	884 (0.82%)
7. mhm	2,880 (2.69%)	22. because	851 (0.79%)
8. so	2,498 (2.33%)	23. it	847 (0.79%)
9. yes	2,398 (2.24%)	24. or	743 (0.69%)
10. the	1,892 (1.76%)	25. uhuh	676 (0.63%)
11. right	1,850 (1.72%)	26. you	672 (0.62%)
12. erm	1,680 (1.57%)	27. alright	656 (0.61%)
13. i	1,520 (1.42%)	28. is	652 (0.60%)
14. but	1,498 (1.40%)	29. we	639 (0.59%)
15. oh	1,430 (1.33%)	30. they	541 (0.50%)

It can be seen that the most frequent of these are 'affirmative' minimal responses, 'yeah' (7.07%), 'mm' (3.43%), 'mhm' (2.69%), 'yes' (2.24%), and 'uhuh' (0.63%), which are often spoken on their own as minimal responses, many of which are back-channels. It is interesting that 'no' (1.20%), while on the list, is much less frequent than the affirmative responses and confirms the notion of preference organisation (Schegloff et al. 1977). Another group of 'words' are fillers: 'er' (10.03%), 'um' (2.91%), and 'erm' (1.57%). These 'words' are associated with naturally-occurring spoken discourse in which speakers must communicate in real-time and, as a result, frequently fill what would otherwise be a pause because they need to plan what they will say next. The use of a filler signals that the utterance is not yet complete. Another large group in the list are words which often function as "discourse particles" (see, for example, Aijmer 2002; Lam 2007; Schiffrin 1987; Stenström 1994) in spoken discourse, 'okay' (3.84%), 'so' (2.33%,), 'right' (1.72%), 'well' (0.92%), 'now' (0.82%), and 'alright' (0.61%). This group of words is assumed to be predominantly used as discourse particles based on Lam's (2008) study of the HKCSE (prosodic) which finds that 97.6% of the instances of 'so' and 98.1% of the instances of 'well' are used as discourse particles. There are also a few conjunctions in the list, 'and' (3.71%), 'but' (1.40%), 'because' (0.79%), and 'or' (0.69%), which are quite often spoken in a separate tone unit apart from the segments that they connect. Another group are subject pronouns, 'i' (1.42%), 'you' (0.62%), 'we' (0.59%), and 'they' (0.50%), which seem to be another point at which speakers may employ a tone unit boundary before continuing with a verb phrase. There are also a number of one-word tone units containing 'the' (1.76%) which is also a product of real-time coding where the remainder of the noun phrase is delayed relative to the speaker uttering 'the'. All of these words can be seen to be indicative of the naturalness of the data and the high level of interactivity among the participants. Cauldwell (2003b) states that in his data, the use of fillers is the most common source of the one-word tone units. The fact that his data contain fewer one-word tone units (20.16%) than the HKCSE (prosodic) (33.05%) is probably a reflection of the type of discourse that he collected and the extracts that he chose to use. Cauldwell's book is concerned with providing models of NES speech and pronunciation for advanced learners of English, and so five of the eight extracts are monologic and the remaining three contain little interaction between the speakers and no back-channelling. The result is that there are fewer minimal responses and fewer discourse particles in Cauldwell's (2003b) data which then affects the number of one-word tone units.

Speaker choices and tone unit boundaries

As with all of the systems of discourse intonation, tone unit boundaries are not fully predictable because they are determined by the moment-by-moment real-time decisions of speakers as they construct their utterances. However, it is still possible to find patterns associated with the occurrence of tone units and their boundaries, and some of these are described below.

Tone unit boundaries and disambiguation

There are situations where a speaker's selection of tone unit boundaries can assist the hearer in interpreting the speaker's intended meaning. For example, Channel (1994: 136-40) discusses what she terms "intonation and tagging". She argues that in instances such as 'what about things like when you read sentences or something', the ambiguity as to what 'or something' might mean is reconciled in a real world context by the speaker's intonation. If 'read sentences or something' is said in one tone unit, the speaker effectively delimits the exemplar and the tag, and removes the ambiguity so that the hearer understands that it is the verb phrase 'read sentences' that is tagged (ibid.: 137).

In the HKCSE (prosodic), there are 126 instances of speakers saying 'or something' as a tag or as part of an elaborated form of the tag: 'or something' (76), 'or something like that' (40), and 'or something like' (4), 'or something like this' (3), 'or something else' (2), and 'or something of that nature' (1). The concordance lines are given below (Figure 5.1):

```
1    PHRASE > ] from } { \ [ CANtonese ] < ^ Opera > or something } { = i don't [ < _ reMEMber > ] } b: {
2    } { = i [ beLIEVE ] it's < ER > } (.) { \ [ C ] or something like < _ THAT > } { = [ < oKAY > ] }
3    like } { \ [ CANtonese ] is a GOOD < TOpic > * or something } y:
4    = [ < LIKE > ] er } { \/ in the [ < ^ SHOWER > ] or something } y: { \ [ < _ YEAH > ] } { = because [
5    > ] } } { / some [ KIND ] of houseHOLD apPLIANCE or something like < THAT > you know } a2: { / [ <
6    > ] seat } { = it's in [ SEventeen ] < H > } { = or something [ < LIKE > ] this } a: { = [ < ER > ]
7    ] is < aBOUT > um } { \ ((inaudible)) forty five or something to [ < CENtral > ] } a1:
8    { = er [ < DEEP > ] fried } * { \ [ < ^ CAKE > or something } a:
9    [ < _ FACT > ] } } { \ has [ COli ] < cysTItis > or something } { = and [ < THEY > ] } (.) * { = [ DO
10   [ KIND ] of < SEE > what we < TALK > about or something } ((pause)) { = [ < _ AND > ] er } { =
11   [ < LIKE > ] er } { = [ < proDUCtion > ] } } { = or something [ LIKE ] you < HAVE > to } { \ what you
12   { ? er a } { / a [ FAshion ] < deSIGner > } { / or something of [ THAT ] < NAture > } ((laugh)) a: {
13   ] well } b: { = [ < W__ > ] } } { / [ < ^ W__ > ] or something } { = or [ < DOCtor > ] } { = [ < W__ >
14   < WELL > } * { = just a [ BUNCH ] of < FLOWERS > or something } b:
15   < ONE > of those } { \ [ Asian ] < NIGHTS > * or something i don't } b:
16   > ] are like } { = [ TOWER ] of < ^ BAbel > or something } y: { ? he he } { \ [ < WELL > ] he }
17   as [ < opPOSED > ] to } { ? in the [ < BOdy > ] or something } ((pause)) B: { \ this [ < ^ eRAser >
18   ^ SING > } (.) { = [ LIKE ] an awful < PERson > or something } y: { \ [ < AWful > ] } ((laugh)) { \
19   > ] } * { \ [ PHARmacoloGY ] for a < MONTH > or something } { = [ < ERM > ] } (.){ = but in [
20   different < TIMES > or like } { = [ < TImer > ] or something } (.) { = is it a [ < TImer > ] } y: {
21   for < SORT > of } { = fifty [ < YEARS > ] } { = or something [ < _ LIKE > ] that } (.) { = [ < UM >
22   so [ THAT ] they can HAVE a new < MARket > } { \ or something like [ < THAT > ] } { = i think [ < ^
23            ** { \ he was a [ < CRIminal > ] or something } y: { \ [ < MM > ] } b: { \ [ < OH > ]
24   > ] b6: { \ [ < _ YEAH > ] } { \ [ enQUIry ] or something like < THAT > } a1: { = [ YEAH ] yeah <
25   i [ < ^ THINK > ] it } { = [ COME ] from a POEM or something < LIKE > this } { \ [ < _ YEAH > ] } {
26   < PLAY > ] um } { \ [ PLAY ] a < guiTAR > } { \/ or something [ LIKE ] in a BAR * or something < YOU
27   < THAT > } * { \/ and [ ^ JUST ] description OR something < LIKE > that } * { \ [ Overall ]
28   > ] your } { = [ RESpects ] to the < DEATHS > or something } { ? [ < THAT > ] } { = [ WHAT ] is it
29   > for } { \ [ < PIZza > ] } { \ [ LUNches ] or SOMEthing for the < ^ STUdents > but } b: { \ [ <
30   = [ < MAnagement > ] } { = [ < COURSE > ] } { \ or something like [ < THAT > ] } B: { \ [ < YEAH > ]
31   > ] around } { = with the [ < comPUter > ] } } { = or something [ < LIKE > ] that } b:
32   [ < WHEN > ] was it } { / [ < AUgust > ] } { \/ or something like [ < THAT > ] } { / [ < juLY > ] or
33   ] to FIND outwhere the mother's < GONE > } { \ or something like [ < THAT > ] } { \ [ < YEAH > ] }
34   ELSE > ] { \ he wants to go to [ < THAIland > ] or something } { \/ and he's [ LEFT ] it FAR too <
35   < YEAH > ] } { = [ < _ OR > ] } * ((Cantonese)) or something a:
36   > ] } } { \ [ _ I ] don't know < GERMAny > } { \ or something like [ < ^ THAT > ] } { \ and you [ GO
37   < ^ SURE > ] maybe } { \ some [ < EAR > ] rings or something } { \ i don't [ < KNOW > ] } { \ i'm
38   { ? [ < IN > ] } { \ in the ((inaudible)) } { ? or something like [ < THAT > ] i think * i'll } (.)
39   ] } { / or [ SWAM ] to the river < BANK > } { ? or something } a: { \ i do not [ KNOW ] the < DE *
40   } { = [ < TO > ] } { \ ((inaudible)) [ TO ] be or something like < THAT > } (.) { = we [ < MIGHT >
41   < DID > ] e } { / [ DIDN'T ] you have a < MEnu > or something like } { = [ < SO > ] you can } { = [ <
42   } { = [ < ERM > ] } } { / super [ < reLIgious > ] or something } * { = they [ DON'T ] want < TO > }
43   > ] A2: ** { \ [ MUST ] be a TEST on < MONday > or something } a: * { \/ a [ TEST ] on < ^ MONday >
```

44 { \ i don't know * [NINEty] < ^ EIGHT > } { ? or something like [< THAT >] and } B2:

45 < LINE > } * { / [GOing] to get < FOOD > } { \ or [SOMEthing] like THIS and < SAYing > } (.) { /

46 { = [< EAting >] } { \ [< SEAfood >] } * { \ or [SOMEthing] < LIKE > that } A:

47   >] } * { = [< POINT >] } { \ two [FIVE] or < SOMEthing > } (.) { \ [< _ YEAH >] } * { \

48 a3: { = says it's hi i_ } { = [< I_ >] } * { = or [SOMEthing] like that i < COULDN'T > } { \ hear

49 / or a [< JOURnalist >] } { / or an [Editor] or < SOMEthing > like that } a: { \ [< YEAH >] } *

50 [< supPOSE >] } { ? till [< HALF >] an hour or * something } b:

51   ** { = [< EIGHT >] times } { = [caPAcity] or < SOMEthing > } ** { \ [< YES >]

52 [< _ A >] } (.) { \ [< HAPpy >] place } { \/ or [SOMEthing] like < THAT >] * { = [< OR >] }

53 = [< CHANGEover >] } { \ [< ^ MUGS >] } { \ or [SOMEthing] like < THAT > } a: { \ not [< ^

54 UM >] } { = the [DRAINage] < PROblem > } { = or [SOMEthing] < UM > } { = [< UM >] } { = [

55   >] } { \ or the [< perFORmance >] } { \ or [SOMEthing] like < THAT > } u: ((inaudible))

56 > } { = [< _ ER >] } { = [< ^ FOOD >] } { = or [SOMEthing] like < THAT > } { = [< THEY >] }

57 < PUT >] er } { / [TEMporary] < SIGNS > } { = or [someTHING] < THAT > } { \ just to [< reMIND >

58 = [deDUCT] THAT < FROM > your } { ? [SAlary] or < SOMEthing > like that } a: { \ [< NO >] } { /

59 > er } { \ [JOURnal] of east Asian linGUIStics or < SOMEthing > } { = [< Isn't >] he } (.) { \ [

60 were [disCUSsing] < SOME > } { = [^ MAKE] up or < SOMEthing > } b1: { \ [< Uhuh >] } B: { = [

61 { \ [REAdy] for AFter their < ^ EXAM > } * { \ or [SOMEthing] like < THAT > } a1:

62 YOU >] } { / are you [CURrently] having a JOB or < SOMEthing > } { = [< LIKE >] } { / [

63 } (.) { / is [B] the known < VAlue > } (.) { \ or [SOMEthing] THAT we DON'T < _ KNOW > } (.) { /

64 [< oKAY >] } { \ [aCROSS] < ^ BANKS > } { \ or [SOMEthing] like < ^ THAT > } { = you know so [

65 { ? [MAYbe] you can < USE > the } { = [MEmo] or < SOMEthing > like that } (.) * { = [< COver >]

66] SOcial < STUdies > and } { / [communiCAtion] or < SOMEthing > } a: { \/ [< PRObably >] } { /

67 YOU'RE >] } { \ a [NAtive] < SPEAker > } { = or [SOMEthing] like < THAT > } { = [< OR >] } {

68 it [< CALLED >] } { \ [< mineRAlogy >] } { = or [SOMEthing] like < _ THAT > } b: { \ [< ^ YEAH

69 >] } { / you [GET] TWENty < TOASters > } { / or [< SOMEthing >] } { ? you know } a2: ((laugh))

70 < LIKE >] er } { \ [BATH] < _ TOWels > } { / or [< SOMEthing >] } a2: { \ [^ BATH] < TOWel >

71 } * { \ [ER] the END of the < ^ TERM > } { \ [OR] < SOMEthing > } a1:

72 \ you [GO] for a SWIM in the < ^ POOL > } { \ or [< SOMEthing >] } { ? [< OR >] } (.) { = [<

73 >] } { = [CANcer] or * < ^ maLIGnant > } { \/ or [< SOMEthing >] you know } B:

74   >] er } { \ [WALking] in the < RAIN > } { \ or [< SOMEthing >] } y: { \ [< YEAH >] }

75 < into >] } { \ [DREAM] or < whatEver > } { = or [< SOMEthing >] } { = [< AND >] } { \ make a

76 { = [< UM >] } { \ [< ((inaudible)) >] } { \ or [< SOMEthing >] } a: { \ yeah but [^ WE] are

77   ** ((laugh)) a2: { \ or [< SOMEthing >] } { \ [< oKAY >] } { = i [<

78   [< INternet >] } * { \ ((inaudible)) } { ? or [< SOMEthing >] } a3:

79 UM >] } { / is it [AFter] < proBAtion > } { = or [< SOMEthing >] } (.) { / [YEAH] you < CAN >

80 \ go [< ON >] } { \ to [< reSEARCH >] } { \ or [< SOMEthing >] } { and then } { = to give [< SOME

81 FLATS >] } { ? [< THEY >] } ((Cantonese)) { ? or [< SOMEthing >] } b: { \ i [< KNOW >] } y: {

82   } a2: { = [< NO >] } ((inaudible)) B: { = or [< SOMEthing >] } a2: { = [< NO >] } { = [<

83   >] } { / some [< VEgetables >] } { / or [< SOMEthing >] } a: { \ [< ^ YEAH >] } { / [

84 >] it's like } * { = [SEven] < FIFty > } { = or [< SOMEthing >] } a: ** { \ [SEven

85 } { ? [< TO >] } { = [< PHIlippines >] } { \ or [< SOMEthing >] } { / and one [TIME] i had an

86 eMAIL only in the AFternoon < aBOUT > one } { ? or [< SOMEthing >] } B: { \ [< _ YEAH >] } a: {

87   [< Evening >] } { \ [< _ PERhaps >] } { \ or * [SOMEthing] like < THAT > } { = and the [< ^

88   YEAH >] * yeah } b: ** { = [CANtonese] or < ^ SOMEthing > } y: { = [< YEAH >] yeah yeah }

89 know } { = we [WENT] out < toGEther > } * { = or [< SOMEthing >] you know } y:

90 they DON'T THREAten me with a < KNIFE > } * { \ or [< SOMEthing >] } { \ or [BEAT] me < UP > } {

```
91   ] } { ? hundred [ DOLlars ] a < ^ MONTH > } { \ or [ < SOMEthing > ] } } (.) * { \ that's all [ <
92   i think it was [ < unCHAINED > ] melody } * { = or [ < SOMEthing > ] } } { \ i can't [ < reMEMber > ]
93   ] er } { = the [ BANker ] to < PICK> it up } { = or [ < SOMEthing > ] like that } { \ [ THIS ] is <
94   about < DOing > } (.) { / a [ < COURSE > ] } } { = or [ < SOMEthing > ] } } { \ so there's [ THAT ] to <
95   } { ? [ < G > ] } } { / [ GOD ] of < FOOD > } { = or [ < SOMEthing > ] } y: { \ [ < OH > ] }
96   (.) { = [ < SOME > ] } } { / a [ < DISH > ] } } { / or [ < SOMEthing > ] } { / some [ < VEgetables > ] }
97   ] < THOUsand > ] } { \ five [ < HUNdred > ] } } { \ or [ < SOMEthing > ] } } { = but [ < I'M > ] } } { \ [
98       two hun } { = [ TWO ] hundred < MIL > ] } { \ or [ < SOMEthing > ] like that } { \ a [ < MONTH > ]
99   ] } } { = [ < Even > ] } } { \ [ < CAnada > ] } } { = or [ < SOMEthing > ] or } { \ [ < AUSTRAlia > ] } {
100  to trip < ER > } { = a [ < FIELD > ] trip } { \ or [ < SOMEthing > ] and then } { / he [ HAS ] to <
101 < WAS > ] er } { = some * [ < ^ conSTRUCtion > ] or } { ? something [ < LIKE > ] that } { = that was
103 > } { = you [ ALways ] need an < ARticle > } { = or [ < ^ SOMEthing > ] } } { \ [ < _ beFORE > ] that }
104 \ [ < _ YEAH > ] } } { \ [ < ^ REALly > ] } y: { \ or [ < _ SOMEthing > ] } } { = [ < BEcause > ] erm } {
105 } { = [ < FOR > ] } (.) { = for [ < MARriage > ] or } { = something [ < LIKE > ] } } { = er [ <
106 [ < YEAH > ] yeah yeah } { = ((inaudible)) } } { \ or [ < _ SOMEthing > ] } b: { \ [ < ALRIGHT > ] } y:
107   up } { / through the [ < CLASS > ] rep } * { \ or [ < _ SOMEthing > ] } * { = [ < ER > ] } a2:
108   / [ < BRIEfing > ] } } { = to the [ < STUdents > ] or } { = [ SOMEthing ] like < THAT > ] B: { \ [ <
109 TRAInee > } { = to [ < CROWN > ] counsel } * { \ or is it [ SOMEthing ] in < beTWEEN > } (.) * { \ or
110 > ] } { = to [ < FORM > ] } } { = [ < alLIANCE > ] or } { = [ SOMEthing ] we < NEED > to } { ? to [ <
111    > ] { = [ < FOR > ] my } { = [ < proMOtion > ] or } { \ [ SOMEthing ] like < THAT > } { = er [ <
112 aBOUT ] ONE point FIVE < ^ BILlion > } { = [ < _ OR > ] } { =something [ < LIKE > ] that } { = [ < _
113 { = [ < IT > ] will er } { = [ Over ] < BUDget > or } { \ [ < SOMEthing > ] } a14: { \ [ < YEAH > ] }
114 > the } { = [ linGUIStic ] < STRUCture > or some or } { = [ _ SOMEthing ] like < THAT > } { = [ < UM
115    > ] } { = [ < SOcial > ] } } { = [ < STRAta > ] or } { = [ < SOMEthing > ] } b: { = [ < FROM > ]
116 < _ WHAT > ] } (.) { = [ THREE ] million < NOW > or } { = [ < something > ] } { ? two million} b: {
117      > } { / [ inFLAtion ] was < EIGHT > } {? [ < oR > ] } { / [ SOMEthing ] was it * EIGHT and a <
118 ER > ] } { / a as a [ BAR ] < TENder > ] { = [ < OR  > ] } { / [ SOMEthing ] in the < BAR > } B: {
119 = [ < UM > ] } { / [ < PUnishment > ] } { = [ < OR  > ] } { \ [ someTHING ] like < THAT > } a1: { \/
120 { ? what [ DO ] you think of < THAT > } { = [ < OR  > ] } { \ [ SOMEthing ] like * < THAT > } a2:
121 { = [ < YEAH > ] } a3: { = [ LIKE ] using YAhoo or  like i c q < SOMEthing > like that } B: { \ [ <
122   [ DOing ] a < PROject > } { ? or so } { = [ < OR > ] } { / [ < SOMEthing > ] } a3: { = [ < IT'S >
123   } { = [ oKAY ] you can < USE > } { = [ BOOST ] or < SOME > } { \ [ SOMEthing ] < ELSE > } { \ [ <
124              ** { = [ < D__ > ] d__ } { = or [ T_ ] < D_ > } { = something [ LIKE ] < THAT > }
125 [ < MAYBE > ] } } { = [ manuFACturing ] TOlerance or < SOME > } { \/ [ < SOMEthing > ] } } { = now [ <
126 } { = [ < IN > ] } (.) { = [ < WORking > ] } } { = or [ < BUSIness > ] } { = something like [ < THAT >
```

Figure 5.1 Concordance lines for 'or something'

In the above concordance lines, it is possible to identify two general patterns associated with the tag 'or something'. The first pattern (41 instances) is when speakers utter the tag 'or something' in a tone unit that is separate from the exemplar, which has the communicative effect of not delimiting the possibilities that could be inferred by 'or something'. The second pattern (35 instances) is when 'or something' is said in the same tone unit as an exemplar, and so delimits what 'or something' could refer to.

Example 5.1 below illustrates the first pattern. Speaker B is talking about the perils of not coordinating the purchase of wedding gifts from family and friends in the UK. In line 1, the speaker says 'or something' in a separate tone unit, and so opens up the possibility of multiple gifts beyond the kitchenware variety.

Example 5.1

1   B: ... { / you [GET] TWENty < TOASters > } { / or [< SOMEthing >] } {?

2   you know }

Example 5.2 illustrates the second pattern when 'or something' is said in the same tone unit as an exemplar. Two friends are discussing possible gifts for speaker B's partner. In lines 2-3, speaker B says 'or something' in the same tone unit as 'ear rings', and so delimits the possibilities to items similar to the exemplar and, in so doing, concurs with his friend's suggestion of 'a piece of jewellery'.

Example 5.2

1   b: { \ you want to [BUY] her a piece of < JEWELLery > }

2   B: { \ well i'm not [< ^ SURE >] maybe } { \ some [< EAR >] rings or

3   something }...

Thus the discourse intonation selections made by the speakers in relation to 'or something' fit with the observations of Channell (1994), except that in the HKCSE (prosodic), delimiting is less common, and leaving the possibilities more open is preferred. Another pattern, which is not mentioned by Channell (1994), is that 'or something like', 'or something like this', 'or something like that', and 'or something of that nature' also typically occur in a separate tone unit to the item that they tag (41 out of 50 instances). The reason why this pattern is more predictable is probably because it lacks the same potential for ambiguity as 'or something', by having a component that specifically refers back to what is tagged (i.e. 'like', 'like that', 'like this' and 'of that nature').

Alternative 'or'

Tone unit boundaries can disambiguate meaning when 'or' is used in the presentation of alternatives (Crystal 1969: 263-73). Crystal provides the example 'would you like gin or whisky or tea?', and states that each alternative is normally uttered in a separate tone unit. He also states that the final item in the list is said with rise tone if the extent of the list is unspecified, and with fall tone if the alternatives represent the limit available. Crystal's observations about the speaker's selection of tone will be returned to in a later chapter.

Examples from the HKCSE (prosodic) are given below to illustrate the role of tone unit boundaries in the listing of alternatives. In the HKCSE (prosodic) there are 4,010 instances of 'or'; and in the majority of the instances (2,851, 71.09%), the alternatives are spoken in separate tone units. Of these, 2,449 (61.07%) have 'or' at the start of a new tone unit and 402 (10.02%) have 'or' at the end of the tone unit with the next alternative occurring on its own in the next tone unit. The remainder are made up of instances of 'or' occurring in the same tone unit as the alternatives (416, 10.37%), and instances of 'or' occurring in a separate tone unit (743, 18.52%).

Examples 5.3 and 5.4 are extracts from two academic lectures.

Example 5.3

1   B: ... { = [< ^ IF >] a } { = [< soCIEty >] } { = [OR] a < CULture > } { =
2   or a [NAtioNAlity] is a < ^ LOW > } { = [auTHOrity] soCIEty it <
3   MEANS > } { = [PEOple] do NOT < acCEPT > } { = [< DIFferences
4   >] } { = in [< POWer >] } { \ [< WILlingly >] }

Example 5.4

1   a: { \ it is er [< NOT >] } { \ about er the [< ^ DECibels >] } { \ or the
2   [< HERTZ >] } { \ or the [< FREquency >] } { = [< ER >] } { \ it's
3   [ACtually] about WHAT < ^ eXACTly > } { \ a [LIstener] can < HEAR
4   > } { \ [WHEther] it's GOOD or < BAD > }

In Example 5.3, the lecturer lists the alternatives 'society', 'culture' and 'nationality' in separate tone units. This has the communicative effect of making society, nationality, and culture distinct from each other. Similarly, in Example 5.4, the lecturer lists out three alternatives 'decibels', 'hertz' and 'frequency' and, by speaking each one in a separate tone units, he communicates that they are different.

In the following examples, 5.5 and 5.6, the speakers do not use tone unit boundaries to separate the alternatives, and the communicative effect changes as a result.

Example 5.5

1   B: ... { \/ [MOvies] i can TAKE or < _ LEAVE > }...

In Example 5.5, the alternatives, 'take or leave', are spoken in the same tone unit, and they are understood to be equivalent and not distinct in this context. In other words, in this context, the speaker is indifferent to movies, and watching them and not watching them are equivalent rather than alternatives.

In Example 5.6, speaker a says the alternatives, 'a boyfriend or girlfriend', in the same tone unit. In this local discourse context, they are equivalents not alternatives.

Example 5.6

1   a: ... { \ when you [WRITE] TO a BOYfriend or < GIRLFRIEND > } { =
2   you can [DO] this < WITH >...

Approximative versus specific use of numerals

Tone unit boundaries can also be employed to distinguish between approximative and specific uses of numerals. In the case of an utterance such as 'would you like one or two lumps of sugar', Channel (1994: 54-5) and Crystal (1969: 268) argue that if the meaning is approximative, rather than specific, 'one' or 'two' co-occur in the same tone unit. Conversely, when the numbers are uttered in separate tone units, they are interpreted as specific. In Example 5.7 speaker a is telling her friend about the buses she needs to take to get to work.

Example 5.7

1   a: ... < ER >] } { = [WAIting] for the two < FIVE > one } { \/ or two
2   [FIVE] < FIVE > now }

In lines 1 and 2, speaker a identifies two buses by their respective numbers, '251' and '255', and by saying the two numbers in separate tone units, she makes them specific.
    In Example 5.8, speaker B is reminiscing about his previous job.

Example 5.8

1   B: [THINK] i was there in ninety < ONE > } { \ or ninety [< TWO >] } { \
2   [THAT'S] when i < STARted > }

The two years, '91' and '92', are identified and understood to be distinct rather than equivalents because they are spoken in separate tone units.
    In Examples 5.9 and 5.10, the speakers say the numbers ('one or two months' and 'one million or two million') in the same tone unit, and the meaning becomes one of approximation rather than specific.

Example 5.9

1   a:] be } { \ i [< iMAgine >] } { \ a period of [ONE] or two months at <
2   ^ LEAST > }

Example 5.10

1   b:] company MAY < doNATE > } { \ [LET'S] say ONE million or

2   TWO million < TO > them }

Tone unit boundaries and Linear Unit grammar

Brazil's (1995) description of the grammar of speech and the new Linear Unit Grammar (LUG) developed by Sinclair and Mauranen (2005, 2006) are both based on the inherent linearity of language. Brazil's (1995: 14) grammar of speech is a "linear real-time description of syntax" which integrates phonological patterns, in particular tone unit boundaries and prominence, with the grammar. Sinclair and Mauranen's (2006) LUG is based on the way in which language is a strictly linear phenomenon produced in a succession of chunks. While these chunks are not defined (ibid.: 51), the boundaries of these chunks (provisional unit boundaries, PUBs) can be intuitively identified by people with considerable uniformity (ibid.: 58). Once identified, the chunks can be categorised as either message-oriented or organisation-oriented. Importantly, there is evidence that Brazil's tone unit boundaries tend to occur at the boundaries between the chunks identified in LUG, termed PUBs, (Sinclair and Mauranen, 2006: 51). LUG is not a grammar that is confined to spoken language, and its originators claim that all texts can be broken down into chunks based on whether a chunk is "incremental" in that it is message-oriented, or "non-incremental", that is contributing to the organisation of the text either interactively or textually (ibid.: 60). This division into message-elements and organisation-elements allows the analyst to eventually combine fragments of message elements, which come in a variety of forms (see detailed list of the forms below in Figure 5.2), into one finalised message-element which in turn is a "linear unit of meaning" (Sinclair and Mauranen 2006: 54). Using data from the HKCSE (prosodic), it is suggested that LUG may offer an explanation for the placement of tone unit boundaries.

Below is a discussion of how a speaker's selections in the form of tone unit boundaries may be explained with reference to LUG. The extract examined is taken from a conversation in the HKCSE (prosodic) between two friends in a restaurant (C113) as they study the menu and decide what to order for lunch. This extract was given to Sinclair and Mauranen (2005) without its prosodic transcription when they were refining their LUG. It has, therefore, been thoroughly analysed and described by Sinclair and Mauranen (2006), and by others at a workshop led by Sinclair and Mauranen at Michigan University in May, 2005 (the process of analysing this extract at the workshop is described in Sinclair and Mauranen 2006: 167-173).

Below are three sets of information. There is a key which summarises the different forms of elements in LUG (Figure 5.2). The extract from C113 is then analysed using the key (Figure 5.3). Lastly, the same extract is shown as it has been transcribed for the HKCSE (prosodic) with the discourse intonation plus the participants and their individual utterances are clearly shown (Figure 5.4). The latter observation is made because in Figure 5.3, prior to analysing the extract using LUG, all indications of speaker change are removed. This is an important principle in LUG, and, indeed, in Sinclair's very first spoken corpus compiled in the 1960s (Sinclair, Jones and Daley 1970), there is no indication of speaker change. This is no omission, according to Sinclair, because it is simply unnecessary if spoken discourse is seen as the joint construction of a coherent text in which collocations, for example, can occur across utterances (Sinclair, Jones and Daley 1970: 19).

Figure 5.2 presents a list of the analytical categories used in LUG, and examples of almost all of the categories are to be found in the analysis of the conversational extract shown in Figure 5.2.

At the very end of the analytical process of a spoken text in LUG (Sinclair and Mauranen 2006: 154-155), the elements that have been identified are organised into a string of linear units of meaning, each of which is comprised of a core M element and any dependent M-related elements. These units of meanings are connected by textual organiser (OT) elements. Other elements, termed "intermediate elements" (ibid.: 155) are excluded because they are either interactive-oriented organising (OI) elements or message fragment (MF) elements, and so contribute neither to the organisation of the units of meaning nor to their message content.

OI   = interactive-oriented organising element
OT   = text-oriented organising element
M   = completion of a message unit
M-   = anticipates a continuance
+M   = fulfils anticipation of a continuance
+M- = partial completion of message unit
MF   = message fragment
MA   = repeated message fragment
MS   = message supplement
MR   = replacement of all or part of a prior M

Figure 5.2 Key: designation of elements in LUG

1.	A:	yea	OI
2.	B:	deep-fried pork chop	M
3.	A:	yea	OI
4.	B:	and then	OT
5.		with the oil	M-
6.		butter	MR
7.		um	OI
8.		the	MF
9.		I	MF
10.		I'm not sure	OI
11.		it must be	M-
12.	A:	kind of mushroom	+M
13.	B:	it's a kind of mushroom	MR
14.	A:	the Japanese mushroom	MR
15.		okay okay	OI
16.		I know	OI
17.		I know	OI
18.		the	MF
19.		the long thin white one	M
20.		right	OI
21.	B:	yes	OI
22.		the long thin white one	MR
23.	A:	uhuh	OI
24.	B:	yea	OI
25.		and then	OT
26.		the other one is	MA
27.		um er	OI
28.		is the rice	+M
29.		um	OI
30.		like	OI
31.		the	MF
32.		I think	OI
33.		it's the	MA
34.		sort of	OI
35.		the roast beefs	+M

(Sinclair and Mauranen 2006: 115-116)

Figure 5.3 Conversational extract from C113 using LUG elements

Figure 5.4 below presents the prosodic transcription of the conversational extract. Speaker change is indicated, and this version makes the comparison that follows simpler to make.

```
 1    A:   { \ [ < YEAH > ] }
 2    a:   { \ deep-fried pork [ < CHOP > ] }
 3    A:   { / [ < YEAH > ] }
 4    a:   { / and [ < THEN > ] } { = with the ((inaudible)) < OIL > } { = [ < BUTter > ] }
 5         { = [ < UM > ] } (.) { = [ < THE > ] } (.) { = [ < I > ] } { \ i'm [ NOT ] < SURE > }
 6         (.) { = it must be }
 7    A:   { \ [ < KIND > ] of mushroom }
 8    a:   { \ it's a kind of mushroom } * { \ the [ < ^ JApanese > ] mushroom } { = [ <
 9    A:                                  ** ((laugh)) { = [ < oKAY > ] } { /\ [ ^ I ] know i
10    a:   oKAY > ] }
11    A:   know > } { { [ < THE > ] } } { \ the [ LONG ] thin < WHITE > ones } * { / [ <
12    a:                                             ** { \ [ < YES
13    A:   RIGHT > ] }
14    a:   > ] } { \ the [ LONG ] thin < _ WHITE > one }
15    A:   { / [ < Uhuh > ] }
16    a:   { \ [ < _ YEAH > ] } { \ [ < _ AND > ] then } { = the [ < Other > ] one is um } { =
17         < ER > } { \/ is the [ < RICE > ] } { = [ < UM > ] } { = [ < LIKE > ] the } { = i
18         think it's [ < THE > ] } { \ [ SORT ] of the ROAST < BEEFS > }
```

Figure 5.4 Prosodic transcription of the extract

A comparison of Figures 5.3 and 5.4 in terms of Sinclair and Mauranen's (2006: 51) LUG's boundaries (i.e. Provisional Unit Boundaries) and discourse intonation's tone unit boundaries provides more evidence of their similarities. First, interestingly, there are 35 elements in Figure 5.3 and 32 tone units in Figure 5.4, and the closeness of these totals suggests that there is one chunking process at work, rather than two. A closer examination reveals that 26 of the 32 tone units map precisely onto the elements identified. These are elements 1-15, 18-25, and 28-29, with element 15 counted as two OI elements based on the finalised transcription in the HKCSE (prosodic). In the instances where tone unit boundaries and Provisional Unit Boundaries do not match, they are all cases where an OI element is in the same tone unit as a form of M element. For example, the tone unit '{ \ [SORT] of the ROAST < BEEFS > }' has within it the OI element ' sort of' and +M element 'the roast beefs'. This is possibly the kind of division that is harder to determine in LUG when analysing naturally occurring spoken data, although there are other instances of OI elements fitting the boundaries of both LUG and discourse intonation. Nonetheless, the above analysis suggests that tone unit boundaries can be predicted with a fairly high success rate (i.e. 74%), employing the analytical framework of LUG.

Tone unit boundaries, Linear Unit Grammar and back-channels

In a preliminary study of back-channels in the HKCSE (prosodic) (Warren 2006), another link between discourse intonation and LUG is described with regard to back-channelling. Back-channels are listener attention signals that overlap with the talk of the current speaker. They have a variety of other names, for example, "accompaniment signals" (Kendon 1967), "continuers" (Schegloff 1982), and "reactive tokens" (Clancy *et al.* 1996). They are generally described as a means for the hearer to demonstrate a variety of ongoing feedback to the speaker such as interest, comprehension, agreement and involvement. Back-channelling typically occurs during extended turns when the discourse involves two or more participants, and its absence may be perceived as marked behaviour on the part of listeners in certain contexts. However, the threshold for the appropriate (i.e. unmarked) withholding of back-channels is unclear, but in certain genres, such as academic lectures, it tends to be withheld. Importantly, back-channelling cannot be done successfully in a random fashion. A current speaker is immediately aware of back-channelling that is not appropriately aligned with the ongoing talk. In his study, Warren (2006) argues that back-channels conform to systematic usage that should be possible to describe. He examines whether back-channelling is cued by the content of the current speaker's talk, or prosodically, i.e. by the current speaker's selection of discourse intonation within the system outlined by Brazil (1997), or by a combination of both content and prosody. The main conclusions are best illustrated with an example from the study. In Example 5.11, only the tone unit boundaries have been identified (indicated with double forward slash //), and the data have also been analysed in terms of LUG, which is indicated in brackets at the end of each element. The back-channels in the extract can be found in lines 2, 5, 7 and 11.

Example 5.11

1.   B: // well (OT) that's the average (M) // [// I think (OT) it depends what

2.   a: [// yeah (OI) //

3.   direction (MF) // // you're facing (M) // // if you've got a flat (MF) // //

4.   where you can watch (MF) // // the racing / (+M) // (.) [// then (OI) it's

5.   a: [// mm mm

6.   (MF) // // it costs (MR) a lot more (+M) // [// but (OT) my (MF) // // my

7.   a: mm mm (OI) //   [// mm mm mm mm mm

8.   (MF) my flat doesn't face the track (+M) // // er (OI) // // the (MF) the

9.   a: (OI) //

10.   race track (MR) // // it faces (MF) er (OI) // // they say that (OT) // // it has

11.   the mountain view (M) // [// which is a nice way of saying that (M) // //

12.   a: [// mhm (OI) //

13.   you look out across (MF) // // the factory estates (+M) // // of Fo Tan

14.   (+M) // ((laugh))

Example 5.11 provides evidence that there is a connection between the points at which hearers opt to back-channel, tone unit boundaries, and certain forms of M units in LUG. The back-channelling almost invariably takes place at the end of tone units. These tone unit boundaries typically correspond with the end of M and +M units. In other examples examined in the study, back-channelling also takes place at the end of MR units. Hearers do not seem to back-channel at the end of O units. The preliminary conclusions are that hearers appear to monitor the current speaker's talk for complete message unit boundaries, which also correspond with tone unit boundaries, in order to back-channel appropriately. It is probable, therefore, that a combination of discourse intonation and message increments is the determinant of appropriate back-channelling behaviour.

Tone unit boundaries and extended collocations

In a study of extended collocations (Cheng and Warren, 2008), the relationship between the phraseological characteristics of language and the communicative role of discourse intonation is explored. Contiguous lexically- and grammatically-rich word associations in the Public sub-corpus of the HKCSE (prosodic) were examined to see if the patterns of word association also reveal patterns of discourse intonation. The centrality of phraseology in language use expounded by Sinclair (1987, 1996, 1998, 2004) has led those working in the area of pattern grammar (e.g. Francis 1993, Hunston and Francis 2000, Hunston 1995, Partington 1998) to argue that corpus linguists will eventually be able to describe all lexical items in relation to their syntactic preferences, and all grammatical structures with regard to their lexis and phraseology (Francis 1993: 155). The study by Cheng and Warren examines the additional communicative value of discourse intonation (Brazil 1985, 1997) in the phraseology of spoken discourse.

Table 5.5 is a sample of the most frequent lexically-rich word associations studied. The sample is chosen to represent the spread of frequencies found. Two of the lexically-rich word associations examined are specific to Hong Kong and require a brief explanation. The year 'nineteen ninety-seven' is the year when Hong Kong returned to the People's Republic of China (PRC), and is often used as a synonym for that event. Another word association, 'asia's world city', was invented by Hong

Kong's political leaders to depict Hong Kong in a positive light. When first used around the year 2000, it was in the context of it being a long-term goal for Hong Kong to eventually become 'asia's world city'. However, very quickly, 'asia's world city' was adopted as a synonym of 'Hong Kong' by its political leadership.

Table 5.5 Lexically-rich word associations

Lexically-rich word associations	Frequency in a single tone unit	Overall frequency
nineteen ninety-seven	49 (89.1%)	55
hong kong people	54 (100%)	54
asia's world city	11 (44.0%)	25

Table 5.5 shows the frequencies with which the lexically-rich word associations are spoken within one tone unit. Two of the lexically-rich word associations are typically spoken in a single tone unit, and 'hong kong people' has a 100% occurrence. An exception to this pattern is 'asia's world city' (44%). All of the other instances of this word association are spoken in two, and sometimes three, tone units. In the instances where 'asia's world city' is spoken in a single tone unit, it seems that the speaker is saying that Hong Kong is 'Asia's world city' as a statement of fact, and 'asia's world city' is often preceded by 'as'. When 'asia's world city' is spoken across two or three tone units, which is the pattern for 56% of the instances, an interesting difference is found. Typically, this pattern occurs when the speaker is setting a future goal for Hong Kong to be classified as 'asia's world city' one day. These instances are typically preceded by 'will be', 'to be' or 'to become', for example '{ / [WE] will be Asia's < WORLD > } { \/ [< CIty >] }' and '{ = to be [< Asia's >] } { \ [WORLD] < _ CIty > }'.

Three of the most frequent grammatically-rich word associations (Table 5.6) are also examined by Cheng and Warren (2008), again, representing a spread of the frequencies found in the study.

Table 5.6 Grammatically-rich word associations

Grammatically-rich word associations	Frequency in a single tone unit	Overall frequency
a lot of	140 (98.6%)	142
we have to	76 (90%)	80
that we have	28 (44.4%)	63

These grammatically-rich word associations fall into the category of "lexical bundles" (Biber *et al.* 1999: 989-1025), belonging to three categories. The first one, 'a lot of', is a noun phrase fragment conveying a quantitative meaning (Biber *et al.* 1999: 1012). One is a declarative clause segment made up of a subject pronoun and a verb phrase (ibid.: 1002-1003), 'we have to'. The last is a *that*-clause fragment (ibid.: 1010), 'that we have'.

Table 5.6 shows that with the exception of 'that we have' (44.4%), the grammatically-rich word associations are spoken in a single tone unit. Again, this suggests that there may be a connection between the notion of chunking in LUG (Sinclair and Mauranen 2006) and tone unit boundaries. In other words, these word associations are co-selected as part of a chunk in the unfolding discourse and, as such, they are likely to be spoken within the same tone unit along with the rest of the chunk.

The grammatically-rich word association with the lowest proportion of instances spoken in a single tone unit – 'that we have' – is a *that*-clause fragment. According to LUG (Sinclair and Mauranen 2005, 2006), 'that we have' is made up of an organisational unit, 'that', and an incomplete message unit, 'we have'. The boundary between these non-incremental and incremental units is where the tone unit boundary occurs when this word association is spread across two tone units in most instances.

The main finding of Cheng and Warren's (2008) study is to confirm Brazil's (1997) suggestion that intonation is context-specific rather than word-specific. The occurrence of word associations in a single tone unit is found to be a strong tendency across both lexically-rich and grammatically-rich word associations, although it needs to pointed out that they may sometimes share the tone unit with other words. While patterns of discourse intonation have been identified and discussed, it is rare to find an intonation pattern that is 100% consistent for a particular word association. Only three of the ten lexically-rich word associations examined have 100% occurrence in a single tone unit. In addition, the principles underpinning LUG (Sinclair and Mauranen 2005, 2006) have also been found to be useful to explain word associations that are atypical with regard to discourse intonation, and also word associations which conform to the general patterns identified.

Conclusions

This chapter has examined the tone units in the HKCSE (prosodic). Most of the tone units (89.86%) contain between one and five words, with one-word tone units the most common (33.05%). There is a slight tendency for HKC to speak more of the shorter tone units. Conversely, the NES speak more of the tone units consisting of five words or more. The Public sub-corpus was found to have a slight tendency to contain longer tone units, probably due to the pre-planning of some of the discourses in this sub-corpus.

Other findings suggest that while discourse intonation selections in relation to tone unit boundaries are situation-specific, and are neither pre-determined nor guaranteed, it has been shown that patterns based on the occurrence of tone unit boundaries can be identified and described, and thus to some extent predicted. Tone unit boundaries can play a part in meaning-making in local contexts, for example, by helping to disambiguate what is said. They also play a role in determining back-channelling behaviour. A link exists between the increments outlined in LUG (Sinclair and Mauranen 2006), and that is, word associations that correspond to message or organisation-oriented units are typically spoken in one tone unit. However, while discourse intonation patterns are discernible, speakers, on occasion, deviate from them to align with discourse-specific communicative requirements.

CHAPTER 6

Prominence

Introduction

Prominence is used by speakers as a means of distinguishing those words which are situationally informative from those which are not (Brazil 1997: 23-25). Importantly, the assigning of prominence is not fixed on the basis of grammar or word-accent/stress, it is a choice made by the speaker in context. For Brazil (1997: 23), speakers have available to them two paradigms: existential and general. The existential paradigm is the set of possibilities that a speaker can select from in a given situation. The general paradigm is the set of possibilities that is inherent in the language system. The choice of prominence in naturally-occurring spoken discourse is made when the speaker selects from the existential paradigm that is available at that point in the discourse. It needs to be added that not every syllable in a word has to be made prominent for the word to have the status of prominence in a tone unit. Speaker decisions within the prominence system are made on the basis of the status of individual words (ibid.: 39). The other three systems in discourse intonation, tone, key and termination, are not attributes of individual words but of the tonic segment (i.e. that section of the tone unit that falls between the first and the last prominent syllable).

Brazil (1997: 18) states that there is a distinction between what is termed "word accent" and the choice available to speakers to superimpose upon an "accented" syllable the system of prominence. This is an important distinction and underlines the fact that it is the speaker who decides in what way his/her intonation choices "project a certain context of interaction" (ibid.: 27). Thus the choices with regard to prominent syllables are not reactive but rather proactive choices by speakers from perceived alternatives.

Distribution of prominences

Appendix 3 shows the distribution of prominences in tone units across the whole HKCSE (prosodic) and for each sub-corpus and each set of speakers. Table 6.1 below shows the distribution of prominences in tone units in the HKCSE (prosodic).

Table 6.1 Distribution of prominences in HKCSE (prosodic)

Number of prominences in a tone unit	Frequencies of occurrence in HKCSE (prosodic)
one	206,493 (63.79%)
two	81,958 (25.31%)
three	21,892 (6.76%)
four	4,907 (1.51%)
unclassified	8,453 (2.61%)
Total	323,703 (100%)

The number of prominences in a tone unit varies from one to four. In the HKCSE (prosodic) most tone units (63.79%) have one prominent word/syllable. There are less than half as many tone units with two prominent words/syllables (25.31%). Tone units with one or two prominences therefore make up 91.49% of all of the tone units, which is in line with Brazil (1997) who states that one or of two prominences per tone unit is the norm, while he recognises that more then two is possible. There are then a small number of tone units with three (6.76%) or four prominences (1.51%), plus those which are unclassified (8,453; 2.61%). This distribution can be compared with Cauldwell's (2003b: 101) findings, although it needs to be borne in mind that his data differ in significant ways from the HKCSE (prosodic) (see Chapter 5), which has an impact on the results. Cauldwell (2003b: 101) has a different distribution of prominences across the 1,205 tone units (Table 6.2).

Table 6.2 Comparison of prominence use: HKCSE (prosodic) and Cauldwell (2003b)

Number of prominences in a tone unit	HKCSE (prosodic)	Cauldwell (2003b)
one	206,493 (63.79%)	559 (46.39%)
two	81,958 (25.31%)	505 (41.90%)
three	21,892 (6.76%)	75 (6.22%)
four	4,907 (1.51%)	4 (0.33%)
unclassified	8,453 (2.61%)	62 (5.14%)
Total	323,703 (100%)	1,205 (100%)

In Cauldwell (2003b), single prominence tone units are the largest category (559; 46.39%), but not as large as in the HKCSE (prosodic) (63.79%). Next are tone units with double prominences (505; 41.90%). If these are combined with the single prominence tone units, the proportion (88.29%) is similar to that of the HKCSE (prosodic) (91.49%). The proportions of tone units with triple (6.22%) and quadruple (0.33%) prominences are close to those found in the HKCSE (prosodic), and there are 5.14% unclassified. The main difference is the distribution between the single and double prominences, when the two sets of findings are compared. This is probably linked to the higher incidence of one-word tone units (63.79%) in the HKCSE (prosodic) which is discussed in Chapter five.

In Tables 6.3 and 6.4, the frequencies of occurrence of the single, double, triple and quadruple prominence tone units are found to differ across sub-corpora and the sets of speakers. When comparing the sub-corpora and speakers in the use of prominence in tone units, both the number of tone units spoken and the proportions of words spoken have to be referred to (Appendices 1 and 2).

Table 6.3 Distribution of prominences in tone units: sub-corpora

Number of prominence in a tone unit	Academic sub-corpus	Business sub-corpus	Conversation sub-corpus	Public sub-corpus	Total
one	22.69%	27.3%	28.5%	21.34%	100%
two	24.71%	25.91%	23.05%	26.31%	100%
three	27.86%	26.17%	20.82%	25.13%	100%
four	31.2%	25.88%	19.21%	23.7%	100%

Table 6.4 Distribution of prominences in tone units: sets of speakers

	HKC	NES
Proportion of words spoken	71.46%	25.32%
Proportion of tone units spoken	73.92%	22.88%
Number of prominence in a tone unit		
one	74.5%	22.24%
two	74.34%	22.81%
three	71.78%	25.6%
four	69.86%	27.04%

In terms of sub-corpora, there is proportionately greater use of single prominence tone units in the Conversation sub-corpus (26.66% of all tone units, 28.5% of single prominence tone units) and less use of single prominence tone units in the Academic (23.59% of all tone units, 22.69% of single prominence tone units) and Public (22.6% of all tone units; 21.34% of single prominence tone units) sub-corpora. The proportions for the Business sub-corpus are almost unchanged (27.05% and 27.3%). This pattern reverses and strengthens when double prominence tone units are examined. Both the Conversation (26.66% of all tone units, 23.05% of double prominence tone units) and the Business sub-corpus have proportionately fewer of these tone units (27.05% of all tone units, 25.91% of double prominence tone units). The Academic and Public sub-corpora have proportionately more (23.59% of all tone units, 24.71% of double prominence tone units; 22.65% of all tone units, 26.31% of double prominence tone units, respectively). This pattern continues with the triple prominence tone units, and the differences grow wider between the Conversation and the Academic and Public sub-corpora. The Conversation and the Business sub-corpus have proportionately fewer of these tone units (26.66% of all tone units, 20.825% of triple prominence tone units; 27.05% of all tone units, 26.17% of triple prominence tone units, respectively). The Academic and Public sub-corpora have proportionately more (23.59% of all tone units, 27.86% of triple prominence tone units; 22.65% of all tone units, 25.13% of triple prominence tone units, respectively).

The same tendencies continue for the quadruple prominence tone units, although the Academic, Conversation, and Business sub-corpora have proportionately fewer of these tone units (26.66% of all tone units, 19.21% of quadruple prominence tone units; 27.05% of all tone units, 25.88% of quadruple prominence tone units, respectively). The Academic and Public sub-corpora have proportionately more, although the Academic sub-corpus has significantly more (23.59% of all tone units, 31.2% of quadruple prominence tone units; 22.65% of all tone units, 23.7% of quadruple prominence tone units, respectively).

These tendencies are also found between the sets of speakers. Table 6.4 summarises the comparative percentages of occurrence of the single, double, triple and quadruple prominence tone units across the sets of speakers, HKC and NES, in the context of the relative proportion of words and tone units spoken by the HKC and NES.

The distribution of words in the HKCSE (prosodic) between the HKC and the NES is 71.46% and 25.32% respectively, and the distribution of tone units is 73.92% and 22.88%, whereas there is a very slight tendency for the HKC to produce more single, as well as double, prominence tone units than the NES. For the triple and quadruple tone units, the trend reverses with the NES speaking proportionately more. These tendencies are linked to the slight tendency for the NES to speak longer tone units, as discussed in Chapter 5.

From Tables 6.3 and 6.4, it is shown that in terms of the sub-corpora and speaker sets, the same tendencies are found, except that the tendency for NES to speak more triple and quadruple prominence tone units is barely perceptible in the Public sub-corpus. The fact that more discourses in this sub-corpus are more likely to be pre-planned, and sometimes written to be spoken, explains why the findings for this sub-corpus differ from those of the other sub-corpora, especially conversations which are at the other end of the planned-unplanned continuum.

Table 6.5 Distribution of words with two and three prominences: HKCSE (prosodic) and sub-corpora

	HKCSE (prosodic)	Academic sub-corpus	Business sub-corpus	Conversation sub-corpus	Public sub-corpus
One word two prominences	1,026 (100%)	399 (38.88%)	193 (18.81%)	159 (15.49%)	275 (26.80%)
One word three prominences	3	1	1	1	0

Tables 6.5 shows the distribution of words which have double or triple prominences. These are rare occurrences with only 1,026 words with double prominences and merely 3 words with triple prominences.

Those words with double prominences are not evenly distributed if they are compared with the overall distribution of words in the HKCSE (prosodic) and the sub-corpora (see Table 1.1 in Chapter 1). There are proportionately fewer double prominence words in the Business (18.81% versus 27.41%) and Conversation (15.49% versus 25.50%) sub-corpora, and proportionately more of them in the Academic (38.88% versus 22.96%) and Public (26.80% versus 24.11%) sub-corpora, especially the Academic sub-corpus.

Brazil (1997: 142-143) discusses the phenomenon of double prominences in one word and states that it is typically associated with saying the equivalent of quotation marks in speech. The phenomenon also has the effect of holding up the word as an entity, perhaps in the case of the speaker introducing what he/she perceives to be a new word for the hearer. These two uses described by Brazil fit well with the fact that the instances in the HKCSE (prosodic) are more likely to be found in the Academic sub-corpus, where the use of quotes and the introduction of new words are probably more common than in other types of discourses. The uses described by Brazil also explain why this form of prominence selection happens very rarely in the whole HKCSE (prosodic). Examples are given later in this chapter.

In terms of speakers, with the exception of the Business sub-corpus, HKC produce more of the double prominence words than the NES, and HKC females tend to produce double prominence words proportionately slightly more than the HKC males (Table 6.6). The differences between the speakers are very small, however, relative to the proportion of words spoken and need to be handled cautiously given the relatively small number of instances involved.

Table 6.6 Distribution of words with two and three prominences: speakers and gender

	HKC	HKC Males	HKC Females	NES	NES Males	NES Females
One word two prominences	830	509	321	169	139	30
One word three prominences	3	2	1	0	0	0

Patterns in the selection of prominence

As has been mentioned before, discourse intonation is not fixed but is realised in its local discourse context based on moment-by-moment decisions by speakers. However, it is possible to find patterns relating to the selection of prominence, and to identify contexts in which prominence is likely to be used, or not used, to add communicative value. In the following sections, some of these patterns and contexts are described and discussed to illustrate this observation.

Prominence: the existential paradigm

What constitutes sense selection varies from one local discourse context to another. A speaker exploits the prominence system to project a particular perspective, but as Brazil (1997: 31) points out, "prominent syllables are not reflexes: we have to regard them as embodying speakers' choices from known alternatives". This overriding condition of prominence choice is fundamental in discourse intonation, but there are still patterns of prominence selection that can be discerned.

Opposites

One of these patterns is when a speaker sets up an antonymous relationship between elements in the information that is communicated in the local context. In Example 6.1, a Hang Seng Bank official presents the annual financial results at a press conference.

Example 6.1

  1 b: { = [^ HANG] seng < inCREASED > } { \ its [MARket] share of total <

  2   dePOsits > and loans } { \ for [USE] in HONG kong in two o o < TWO

  3   > }

In lines 2-3, speaker b says that the bank has increased its market share of deposits and loans in year 2002. The speaker selects prominence on 'deposits' which means that in the mind of the speaker, other sense selections are possible at this point in the discourse, i.e. other core bank activities. The speaker then says 'and loans' and does not select prominence on 'loans'. At this point in the discourse there is no sense selection. If the bank's market share of deposits has increased, then the opposite, loans, has also increased because the two are interconnected, and so in this local context of interaction 'loans' is projected as given.

In Example 6.2, speaker a1 is interviewing speaker a2 to determine her suitability for an internship in a 5-star hotel.

Example 6.2

1   a1: { = [< UM >] } (.) { \ [AS] a < ^ TRAInee > } { = i would [<

2   REcommend >] you to be } { \ [< ^ Open >] } { \/ [< MINded >] }

3   a2: { / [< Mhm >] }

4   a1: { = [< ER >] } { \ [TO] acCEPT a lot of < CHALlenges > } (.) { =

5   within [< THESE >] } (.) { \/ [MONTHS] that you'll < ^ BE > with us }

6   { \ [I'M] sure you will GO through } { \ a [^ LOT] of < HAPpy > times }

7   { \ but i will < ^ GUAranTEE > you } { \ you'll [< GO >] } { \ through a

8   [LOT] of miserable < _ TIMES > }

9   a2: { / [< Mhm >] }

Example 6.2 shows the effect of a speaker choosing from the existential paradigm when the interviewer says 'you will go through a lot of happy times' in line 6. The interviewer selects prominence on 'happy' as there are many possible adjectives that could be said at this point in the discourse, both positive and negative. The interviewer then says 'but I can guarantee you you'll go through a lot of miserable times' in lines 7-8. By using the adversative conjunction 'but', the interviewer has set up the probability that she is creating an antonymous relationship between 'happy times' and times which are not happy. Having established this as the most likely relationship, the interviewer does not select prominence on 'miserable' at this point in the discourse.

"Inevitability"

Other points in the local context when it is possible to identify patterns of prominence selection are when a speaker sets up a sequencing of elements that project a sense of "inevitability" in terms of what the speaker is going to say. In Example 6.3, the speaker is testing whether the recording equipment is working and says what speakers in similar contexts typically say.

Example 6.3

1   A: { = [< tesTING >] } { = [< tesTING >] } ((laugh)) (.) { \/ [< ONE >]

2   two three } { \ [< THREE >] two one }

Example 6.3 shows again the notion of speakers selecting from an existential paradigm at work in the selection of prominence. Twice the speaker says a series of numbers. On both occasions, it is only the first number in each of the series that is selected to be prominent because the next two numbers become an "inevitability" in this local context of interaction. The two series of numbers are each taken as sense units and only one prominence is necessary to make the whole sense unit selective.

Examples 6.4 and 6.5 are taken from a press conference as a bank official announces the annual results.

Example 6.4

1   b: { \ at the [END] of two o o < ONE > } } { = [< ^ FUNDS >] } } { = [<

2   conTINued >] } { \ to [< SHIFT >] } { = from [TIME] < dePOsits > }

3   { = to [< SAvings >] deposits }

Speaker b reports a shift of funds at the bank from time deposits to savings deposits (lines 2-3). When he says 'time deposits', he selects prominence on both 'time' and 'deposits' because he perceives that there are other possible selections at these points. However, when he says 'savings deposits', it is only 'savings' that is made prominent because 'deposits' have been perceived to be given in this context. In other words, it is "inevitable" given what has been said in line 2.

Example 6.5 shows speaker b's prominence selection when he details the average liquidity ratios in 2002 and 2001.

Example 6.5

1   b: { = we [< mainTAINED >] } { = [STRONG] < liQUIdity > } { \ and

2   [reMAINED] WELL < CApitalised > } { \/ the [Average] liQUIdity

3   RAtio in two o o < TWO > } { \ was [FORty] four POINT four <

4   perCENT > } { = [< comPARED >] with } { \ forty [FIVE] point SIX

5   perCENT in two o o < ONE > }

Speaker b's selections of prominence when he details the average liquidity ratios in 2002 and 2001 are reversed. In line 3, when he gives the percentage, it is 'forty' and 'point' which are prominent; whereas in line 4 it is not 'forty' but 'five' which is prominent. The word 'point' is non-prominent and 'six' is prominent. This selection reflects the fact that it is these two numbers, 'five' and 'six', which the speaker considers to be situationally informative in this local context where the two years are compared, because the items made prominent in line 2 are constant and so non-prominent.

Speakers' differing perspectives

Another usage associated with prominence selection is the way in which a speaker's selection of prominence can be used to convey differing perspectives in the local context. Example 6.6 is taken from an internship interview at a 5-star hotel and the interviewer has been questioning the interviewee about her choice of university programme (BA (Hons) in Hospitality and Tourism Management). The interviewer is asking the interviewee whether she had a choice of programme when she applied to university in terms of listing first and second choices.

Example 6.6

1 a2: { = i [< _ SEE >] } (.) { / [< DO >] you } { / have any other [<
2   CHOICE >] } { / apart from [< hoTEL >] } { = or [DO] you have
3   a FIRST < SEcond > } (.) { / [< CHOICE >] } { \/ [SOMEthing]
4   like < THIS > }
5 a1: { = [< UM >] } { \ [< ^ THIS >] course } { \ is the third [< ^
6   CHOICE >] } { \ [< ACtually >] }
7 a2: { \ [< ^ THIRD >] choice } { \ [< OH >] }

In lines 5-6, the interviewee replies that Hospitality and Tourism Management is *the third choice* and selects prominence on *choice*, which indicates that she projects *choice* to be situationally more informative at this point in the discourse. In this particular local context, it might be that the interviewee is seeking to exploit her choice of prominence to downplay her low ranking of her current programme of studies. For the interviewer, however, it can be seen that it is the fact that the interviewee placed Hospitality and Tourism Management *third* that is situationally informative because when she responds saying *third choice oh*, she selects prominence on *third* (line 7).

Examples 6.7 and 6.8 are both extracts from hotel service encounters when the guests are checking-out. In both examples, the hotel receptionist asks for the mini bar key which sometimes has the illocutionary force of asking the guest whether or not he/she has consumed anything from the mini bar in the hotel room.

Example 6.7

   1 b: { = [< ER >] } { / [HAVE] you got the mini bar < KEY > sir }

   2 A: { / [< NO >] } { \ i didn't [< HAVE >] one }

In Example 6.7 the hotel receptionist selects prominence on 'have' and 'key' (line 1), which for this speaker is where the existential paradigms occur. Interestingly, by not selecting prominence on 'mini bar', the speaker projects a shared understanding that there is only one key that he is concerned with in this discourse, and so the possibility of other keys, such as the room key, is excluded by selecting to make 'mini bar' non-prominent. By selecting prominence on 'have' in the question, the guest in turn makes prominent the words 'given' and 'have'. By doing so, the guest has interpreted the receptionist's question as a request for the return of the mini bar key in the context of this checking-out service encounter.

Example 6.8

   1 b: { / do you have the [KEY] of the MIni < BAR > }

   2 B: { \ [< NO >] } { \ [< _ NO >] nothing }

   3 b: { \ [< _ Okay >] }

A different choice of prominence by the receptionist in Example 6.8 results in a different response. Here the receptionist selects prominence on the words 'key' and 'mini bar' (line 1) and, by not selecting prominence on 'have' (line 1), presents an understanding that the guest has the key. The result of this is that the guest interprets the receptionist's question as if he has been asked whether or not he has used the mini bar during his stay at the hotel and responds 'no no nothing' (line 2).

    It could be argued that in terms of the choice of prominence, the receptionists' selections in Examples 6.7 and 6.8 are generally unmarked in terms of the expectations described by Brazil (1997), but, in the case of Example 6.8, the receptionist might have been seen to be asking a question devoid of an implicature if he had selected prominence on 'have' (line 1) in the context of guests checking out of the hotel.

Double-prominence on one word

Another discernible pattern is the distribution of words spoken with double prominence. Brazil (1997: 144) likens this use of double prominence as realising the difference between "this is the sense I select" and "this is the word that I use" by means of "word quotation" (ibid.: 143). He also states (ibid.: 163) that this usage is associated with lessons and lectures, which is the case in the HKCSE (prosodic).

Many of the instances of double prominences on one word are in the Academic sub-corpus, from which Examples 6.9-6.11 are taken.

In Example 6.9, speaker b1 is attending a university writing assistance programme. He is telling his English teacher about some upcoming tests and a presentation that he has to do as part of his undergraduate Business Studies programme.

Example 6.9

```
1   b1:  { = i will [ < HAVE > ] er } { \ [ TWO ] < TESTS > } { \ next [ < WEEK
2        > ] }
3   A:   { = oh [ < REALly > ] }
4   b1:  { = and also i will [ < HAVE > ] er } { = [ THIS ] one < presenTAtion > }
5        { \ next week [ < Also > ] }
6   A:   { \ on [ WHAT ] < ASpect > }
7   b1:  { = [ < MM > ] } { = [ < ON > ] the } { = [ < _ ER > ] } { \ [ <
8        dePREciAtion > ] }
```

In line 8, speaker b1 tells his English teacher the topic of his presentation and selects prominence on two of the syllables in 'depreciation'. Given that he is speaking to his English teacher about a Business Studies topic, this selection of double prominence can be explained as being a result of the students assuming that his teacher is unfamiliar with the topic, and so this particular term becomes a kind of "word quotation" (Brazil 1997: 143) by means of his selection of prominence. In other words, it represents a careful selection of words by the student.

In Example 6.10, a lecturer is outlining the contents of his upcoming lectures in his first lecture with the students.

Example 6.10

```
1   b:   ... { = [ < SO > ] } { = we'll [ SPEND ] a COUple of < CLASses
2        > } { \ on [ reSOURCE ] < alloCAtion > } { = [ LAter ] < ON > in the }
3        { / in the [ < SUBject > ] } { \/ [ AND ] < ^ LARGEly > } { = this will be
4        [ conCERNED ] < WITH > } { \ [ LInear ] < ^ PROgramming > } { =
5        [ WHICH ] is < ER > } { = a [ < MAtheMAtical > ] } { \ [ OPtiMIZAtion ]
6        < techniQUE > } { \/ that if [ NOthing ] < ELSE > } { \ at least you should
7        be [ < ^ aWARE > ] of } { / [ < THEN > ] } { = we will [ GO ] in for a
8        few WEEKS < inTO > } ...
```

In line 4, the lecturer says that later the course will be concerned with linear programming. He then elaborates a little on what this term entails 'which is er a mathematical optimization technique' (lines 5-6). The lecturer selects double prominence on both 'mathematical' and 'optimization', and so by means of word quotation projects them as a new and appropriate term for this concept. He thus signals that the students need to pay attention to these words.

Example 6.11 is taken from a lecture in the Academic sub-corpus.

Example 6.11

```
1  b:   and [ THEN ] i think FOR < THE > } { \ < ^ reMAINder > } { \ of

2       [ THAT ] < CLASS > } { ? [ ^ MOST ] of < WHAT > you } { / <

3       COvered > } { = [ WAS ] conCERNED < WITH > } { = [ proDUCtion ]

4       PLANning and < conTROL > } { \ [ IN ] the very BROAD < SENSE > }

5       { \/ [ beCAUSE ] it LOOKED at things LIKE < FORECASting > } { \/ or

6       it [ SHOULD ] have looked at THINGS LIKE < foreCASting > }
```

In Example 6.11, the lecturer is beginning a new topic and is relating it to another course taken by the students to do with 'production planning and control' (lines 3-4). In line 5 the lecturer states that the new topic is related to the previous class in a broad sense because that class has 'looked at things like forecasting'. He says 'forecasting' with double prominence because it is an exemplar which he highlights by means of "word quotation" which, again, indicates to the students something like "pay attention to this word".

Convergence

A less common pattern of prominence use that can be exploited by speakers is to indicate convergence or divergence with the other participants. The form of convergence described is from a study by Warren (2006). Chun (2002: 39-42) discusses other ways that speakers may select to use other forms of converging/diverging intonation behaviours to promote co-operation between themselves. For example, Yang (1995) describes speaker's pitch movements mirroring each other across utterances. Similarly, Brazil (1997) describes the prevalence of pitch concord, whereby the selection of pitch at the end of one speaker's utterance is echoed by the next speaker at the start of his/her utterance (see Chapter 8 for more on pitch concord). Also, Couper-Kuhlen and Selting (1996: 46) describe the exploitation by speakers of pitch, timing and rhythm between speakers to either converge or diverge to indicate their orientation to the other participants. In Warren's (2006) study convergence occurs when there is the possibility of choosing which syllable is made prominent. The speakers initially diverge in their choice, and they tend to converge and adopt the same syllable to be made prominent as the discourse unfolds.

Example 6.12 is a long extract, with 141 lines, taken from a job placement interview in a hotel, in which the speakers initially diverge in terms of which syllable is made prominent in 'front office' (in bold).

Example 6.12

B: interviewer   a: interviewee

1	B: { \ [< oKAY >] }] (.) { \ [R__] has TOLD me a < LITtle > bit } { / so [<
2	FAR >] } { ? [< THAT >] } { \ [< ^ I >] er } { = [< SORry >] } { \ i
3	should [< introDUCE >] myself } { = [I] work in the **front** < **OFfice** > }
4	* { \/ i'm the [**FRONT**] **office** < coORdinator > } * { / so you have the
5	a: ** { / [< Mhm >] } ** { / [< Mhm >] }
6	[FRONT] office < MAnager > } (.) * { = then you have the [< asSIStant
7	a: ** { / [< YES >] }
8	>] } { \ and [< THEN >] you have me } * { \/ [< AFterwards >] okay }
9	a: ** { / [< oKAY >] }
10	(.) { / [< R__ >] } { = has told me that you're [< INterested >] } { \ in
11	[WORking] in the **front** < **OFfice** > }
12	a: { \ [< YES >] }
13	B: { / is that [< ^ RIGHT >] }
14	a: { \ [< YES >] }
15	B: { = [WHY] would you be interested < IN > } (.) { \ [< COming >] to
16	**front office** }
17	a: { = [< MM >] } { \ [beCAUSE] i THINK er < **FRONT** > **office** } { ?
18	[< dePARTment >] } { = is a [< VEry >] } { = [< UM >] } { \/
19	[imPORtant] < ^ ROLE > } { = in [< THE >] } { = [hoTEL] < UM > }
20	{ \ [IN] a < hoTEL > } { = [< beCAUSE >] }
21	B: { / [< MM >] mm }
22	a: { = [< UM >] } { = the [^ MAIN] function of a < hoTEL > } { = is [<
23	TO >] } { / sell [< ROOMS >] } { \/ to [proVIDE] < ^

24   accommoDAtions > } { = [aPART] < FROM > } { \ food and [<

25   BEverage >] } { \ other [< SERvices >] } { = and [< UM >] } (.) { =

26   [AND] i THINK < ER > } { \ it's [ALso] < imPORtant > } { \ [<

27   beCAUSE >] } { = [< IT >] } { \ [proVIDES] < inforMAtion > } { \ to

28   [< _ GUESTS >] }

29   B: { / [< MM >] mm }

30   a: { \ and er [ANswer] < GUESTS' > } { \ [< enQUIries >] } { = [< MM

31   >] } { = [AND] < beCAUSE > } { = [< IT'S >] } (.) { \/ because of the

32   [CHALlenging] < ^ NAture > } { ? of the } (.) { / [< WORK >] } {? [<

33   AND >] } { \ [ALso] because of my < ^ persoNAlity > } { = [< I >] } (.)

34   { = [< beCAUSE >] } { = [< I'M >] } { \ [QUITE] er < SERvice > }

35   { \ [< oriENted >] } * { \ [< PERson >] } { = [< UM >] } (.){ \ [I]

36   B: ** { / [< Mhm >] }

37   a: LIKE to serve < ^ PEOple > } { \ and i [GAIN] < ^ satisFACtion > } { =

38   [WHEN] i } { ? [DEAL] with [< THEM >] and er } (.) { \ solve the [

       <

39   ^ PROblems >] } * { = [< MM >] }

40   B: ** { = [WHY] would you < CHOOSE > } { \ **front** [<

41   **OFfice** >] } { = [< Over >] } (.) { \ [FOOD] and < BEverage > } { \

42   what would [< BE >] } (.) { = [< WHY >] would you } { \ [preFER]

43   front < OFfice > } { \ more than food and [< _ BEverage >] }

44   a: { = [< UM >] } { = [< beCAUSE >] } (.) { = [< ER >] } (.) { = [I]

45   WANT to < LEARN > } { = more [aBOUT] < ER > } { \ [**FRONT**]

46   **office** < opeRAtion > }

47   B: { / [< Mhm >] }

48   a: { = [< ER >] } { \ [DAIly] < opeRAtion > and } { = [< UM >] } { / the

49   [< WAY >] } { = [< TO >] } { = [< UM >] } { = [< DEAL >] with }

50   { / [deMANding] < GUESTS > } { = [< AND >] } { = [< ALso >] }

51   { = [< ER >] } { = [beCAUSE] < I > } { = [^ INterest] < IN > the }

52   { = [CHECK] in CHECK out < proCEdures > } { = er [THAT] I <

53   LEARNED > } { / [FROM] the < SCHOOL > } * { / [< Mhm >] } (.)

54   B: ** { / [< oKAY >] }

55   { = [< UM >] } { = [I] don't < NE > } { / [DO] you know a LOT about

56   the < peNINsula > } (.) { ? about the } * { = the [HIStory] of the <

57 a: ** { = [< ER >] } { = [I] have

58   hoTEL > or }

59   < SOME > } { \ [BAsic] < KNOWledge > } { \ about [< THIS >] } { ?

60   [< beCAUSE >] } { = [< MM >] } { \/ [I'VE] READ some maTErials

61   < beFORE > } { = [< AND >] } { = [< aBOUT >] the } { = the

62   [PArent] COMpany is < THE > } { = [< HONG >] kong and } { \

63   [SHANGhai] hoTELS < LImited > }

64 B: { / [< Mhm >] }

65 a: { \/ and it was [< esTAblished >] } { / in ninety [TWENty] < EIGHT > }

66   (.) { = [AND] < ER > } { = the [hoTEL] has JUST < UM > } { = [< ER

67   >] } { \ [< ^ renoVAted >] } { = [AND] < UM > } { \ the [<

68   exTENsion >] } { = of [< THE >] } { = er [< FLOORS >] and } { =

69   [AND] the < ROOMS > } { = up to [< THREE >] hundred } { = er [<

70   ROOMS >] } (.) { = [< AND >] } { \ [< YEAH >] } { \ some [< KIND

71   >] of } { \ basic [< KNOWledge >] }

72 B: { \/ [< Okay >] } { = [< UM >] } (.) { = [< WHAT >] } (.) { \/ [< SAY

73   >] } { = [^ I] work in the **front** < **OFfice** > } * { = [< MAINly >] } { =

74 a: ** { / [< Mhm >] }

75   at the front [< DESK >] }

76 a: { / [< Mhm >] }

77 B: { \ [DEAling] with the < PRoblems > } { \ [< etCEtera >] } * { / as i

78 a: ** { / [< Mhm >] }

79   [COME] < aLONG > } { = [WE] have a < VEry > } (.) { \

80   [deMANding] < clienTELE > } { \ [_IN] this < _ hoTEL > } { ? [< _

81   SO >] } { ? [_ SAID] we < LIKE > } { = [< deMANding >] er } * { \

82 a: ** { / [< MM >] }

83   [deMANding] HELping deMANding < PEOple > } { = [< UM >] } (.)

84   { = [^ HOW] do you < FEEL > } (.) { = [< THAT >] } { = you can [<

85   HANdle >] } (.) { = [< SAY >] } { = a [< VEry >] } { / [AGgravated]

86   < GUEST > } { \ just [COME] off an eLEven hour < FLIGHT > } (.) { \/

87   [SEven] o'clock in the < MORning > } (.) * { \ [BUT] his < ROOM > }

88   a: ** { \ [< Mhm >] }

89   { \ is not [GOing] to be < REAdy > } (.) { \ [unTIL] ONE o' < CLOCK

90   > } (.) * { \ [WHAT] do you think you'll < DO > } (.) { \ for [< HIM >] }

91   a: ** { \ [< MM >] mm }

92   { \ when you [< MET >] him } { \ in the [< MORning >] } (.) { / he's

93   very [< TIRED >] } (.) { = he [WANted] to go to < BED > } { = [BUT]

94   there < JUST > was } { \ [NO] room for < HIM > }

95   a: { = [< MM >] } { / no [< ROOMS >] } * { / [< Mhm >] } { = i

96   B: ** { = no [< ROOMS >] }

97:     [THINK] i will < UM > } (.) { \ i will [< rePORT >] } { / to my

98   [suPErior] < FIRST > }

99   B: { / [< Mhm >] }

100 a: { \/ [aBOUT] the < situAtion > } { = [< AND >] um } { = to [SEE] if i

101   < CAN > } { = er [< FIND >] } { \ [ROOMS] for the < GUEST > } { =

102   in other [< hoTELS >] maybe } (.) { = [< ER >] } { \/ [< ^ nearBY >] }

103 B: { / [< Mhm >] }

104 a: { = [_ AND] < ER > } { = [MAYbe] i'll < CHECK > the } { \ er [<

105   VAcancies >] } (.) { \ in [OUR] < hoTEL > } { \ to [SEE] if any rooms

106   are < aVAILable > }

107 B: { \ [< Okay >] }

108 a: { / [< Mhm >] }

109 B: { = [< UM >] } { \ but [^ SAY] he's got a < BOOking > }

110 a: { / [< Mhm >] }

111 B: { = [< BUT >] } { \ the [ROOM] is not going to be < REAdy > for him }

112 a: { / [< Mhm >] }

113 B: { / until [TWO] o' < CLOCK > } { = [< AND >] } { \ your [<

114   superVIsor >] } (.) { \/ is not [< THERE >] }

115 a: { / [< Uhuh >] } { = [< UM >] } { = [I] THINK < I > will } { \/

116   [CHECK] with the < comPUter > } { = to [< SEE >] } { = [IF] < ER

117   > } { = any [ROOMS] can be < UM > } (.) { = [< CLEANED >] up }

118   { = [ER] < imMEdiately > } * { \/ by the [HOUSE] keeping <

119 B: ** { / [< Mhm >] }

119   dePARTment > } } { = [< UM >] } (.) { \ as [SOON] as < ^ POSsible > }

120   * { / [< Mhm >] }

121 B: ** { \/ [< Okay >] } { = and [WHAT] would you < DO > } { \ with the

122   [< GUEST >] } (.) { = [< _ WHILE >] }

123 a: { = [< UM >] } { = [I] THINK i < WILL > } { \ [< FIRST >] } { = [<

124   CALM >] } { / [CALM] him < DOWN > } { = [AND] < TO > } { =

125   [< aPOloGIZE >] } { \/ [aBOUT] the < ^ situAtion > }

126 B: { / [< Mhm >] }

127 a: { = [< AND >] } { = maybe [TO] < ER > } { \ [inVITE] him to GO to

128   the BAR or to < LOUNGE > } { = [< TO >] } { \ have a [< ^ DRINK

129   >] }

130 B: { ? quite good } { \ [< OKAY >] } ((inaudible))

131 a: { = [< Mhm >] }

132 B: { ? that's good } { \ i was i was [_ PUshing] < YOU > } * there } ((laugh))

133 a: ** ((laugh))

134 B: { \/ [< _ oKAY >] } (.) { = the [Other] THING < UM > } { = [< WITH

135   >] } { \ [WHEN] you're WORking in < **FRONT** > **office** } { ? [<

136   WHERE >] } { \ which [< dePARTment >] } { \ do you think you want

137   to [START] with < _ FIRST > }

138 a: { = [< MM >] }

139 B: { = [< WHICH >] } { \/ which way } { = do you [< SEE >] } { \ is the

140   [< BEST >] way } { \ to [< TRAIN >] } { \ [_ THROUGH] in <

141   **FRONT** > **office** }

In Example 6.12, the interviewee wishes to work in the front office of the hotel based at the front desk (i.e. reception area) and the interviewer is not keen to commit himself until he has 'tested' the interviewee. This divergence is realised in a number of ways but, interestingly, it is also realised through the selection of prominence chosen for 'front office' by the respective speakers. The interviewer selects prominence on 'office', up until lines 135 and 141, while the interviewee consistently selects to make 'front' prominent, except when he describes himself as the 'front office coordinator' (line 4). This serves to indicate what each speaker considers to be situationally informative in the discourse. The interviewer might be said to be exploiting his selection of prominence by downplaying the importance of where the interviewee may be placed to work in the hotel, while the interviewee does the opposite. In lines 72-132, the interviewer tests the interviewee's ability to handle difficult guests in the context of a front desk worker. Each time that the interviewee responds satisfactorily, the interviewer makes the scenario increasingly difficult by introducing an additional complication. Finally, in line 132, the interviewer appears to be satisfied that the interviewee is up to the task when he says 'that's good I was I was pushing you there ((laugh)) okay'. It is at this point that he converges with the candidate's selection of prominence and, for the first time in line 135, selects to make 'front' and not 'office' prominent when he says 'when you're working in front office where which department do you think you want to start with first'. The interviewer then continues with this selection of prominence for 'front office' (line 141). It is interesting to note that at the point in the discourse, when the interviewer's reticence with regards to the interviewee's suitability for the front office ends, his selection of prominence converges with that of the interviewee. This alignment in prominence selection may be heard as an additional indication that their views on the matter of where in the hotel the interviewee should be placed are now also aligned. The issue is resolved; the interviewee is to be placed in the front office in line with her preference, and it is now simply a matter of which department she wishes to start in.

Vague use of numbers

While the selection, or non-selection, of prominence is not fixed, it is still possible to observe patterns of recurrent discourse intonation choices because, while every context of interaction is unique, speaker behaviour is to some extent predictable in certain contexts though by no means guaranteed or pre-determined. An example of such an observable pattern in relation to the selection of prominence is illustrated and discussed below.

Speakers frequently use 'or' in combination with cardinal numbers to represent a vague approximation. In Figures 6.1 and 6.2 speakers can be seen using the vague approximatives 'two or three' and 'one or two'. These phrases are not to be interpreted as presenting alternatives, but are understood by the hearer to represent approximations within a range of the numbers stated. Thus 'two or three' has the sense of being in the range of these two numbers and equates to other vague terms such as 'few' and 'several'. Similarly, 'one or two', according to Quirk *et al.* (1985: 963), is to be understood as having the vague meaning of 'a small number'. Figures 6.1 and 6.2 contain the concordance lines for 'one or two' (27 instances in total) and 'two or three' (40 instances in total).

```
1      ] had to maNOEUvre our < WAY > } { = through [ < ONE > ] } { \ or [ < TWO > ] } { = [ < WITness > ] }
2           > ] } { = [ < I > ] think } { = er after [ < ONE > ] } { \/ or [ < TWO > ] months } { = [ < SHE >
3           > } { \ which [ ONE ] is < BETter > } * { \ [ ONE ] or < _ TWO > } b:
4      WIthin ] THESE few < YEARS > } { \ we'll [ DO ] ONE or < TWO > } { = [ EIther ] green < FIELD >   or
5           the < USE > of } { = [ < ONE > ] } { \ par- [ ONE ] or < TWO > } { = particular [ < KINDS > ] of }
6      < PRObLem > ] } { = er [ < IN > ] } { = er in [ ONE ] or < TWO > er } { \ [ < CORporates > ] but } {
7      [ < I > ] } * { = [ < I'VE > ] } { \ [ BEEN ] to one or < TWO > there } { = but i'm [ NOT ] sure if i
8      } { \ [ < COST > ] you } { = er [ < TAKE > ] you one } { = [ < _ OR > ] } { \ maybe two [ < HOUR > ] }
9           > ] } (.) { = there were [ < aBOUT > ] } { \/ [ ONE ] or two ((inaudible)) WARriors from where the <
10     be [ < LIStened > ] to } (.) * { \ [ < WHILE > ] one or two } al:                     ** { \
11     < ^ INteresting > stuff } { \ by [ FOcusing ] on ONE or two < ASpects > } { \ instead of focusing on
12     ] to } { = [ < ER > ] } { = [ < STAY > ] } { \ [ ONE ] or two < DAYS > to } { ? [ < TO > ] } { ? [ <
13     { \ [ occAsional ] < occURrence > of } { = the [ ONE ] or TWO < diSEASE > } (.) * { \ [ < _ YEAH > ] }
14     ^ aNOther > ] } { = or to [ < DROP > ] } { = [ ONE ] or two < Items > ] } { \ from your [ PROduct ] <
15     { = [ < ER > ] } (.) { / [ < SPEND > ] } { / [ ONE ] or two < MInutes > } { = [ < TO > ] } { \ [
16     [ YEAH ] it should < ^ NOT > be just } { \ er [ ONE ] or two < PROjects > } { = it should [ < BE > ]
17     at [ < LEAST > ] } { = at [ LEAST ] we prePARE ONE or two < SONGS > } { ? you know [ < ER > ] } { =
18     MIGHT ] be that WE would < HAVE > er } (.) { \ [ ONE ] or TWO < STUdents > } { \ [ WORking ] a few <
19     ] be } { \ i [ < iMAgine > ] } { \ a period of [ ONE ] or two months at < ^ LEAST > } { \ if the [ <
20     { = [ LINE ] < BAlancING > } { = and [ PERhaps ] one or two Other < _ TOpics > } { / [ < oKAY > ] }
21     [ ^ reCOvery ] may be < SLOWer > } { \ than [ ONE ] or two Others in the < REgion > } { = but we [
22     < probleMAtic > ] } *{ = and then [ ^ WE ] find ONE or TWO words < MOST > is the } { = [ < INspire >
23     [ < LANDscape > ] there } { = in the  [ NEXT ] one or two years but < WE > think } { = that there [
24     ] it's BEST TO < ER > } { = may be [ WORK ] in ONE outLET or < TWO > } * { \ for the [ < MOST > ] }
```

Figure 6.1 Concordance lines for 'one or two'

The selection of prominence by the speakers for these vague approximatives follows a fairly predictable pattern, which is that the first numeral is prominent (53 out of 64 instances), 'or' is almost always non-prominent (63 out of 64), and the second numeral is an even mixture of prominent and non-prominent (33 out of 64 instances). This general pattern fits with Brazil's (1997: 23) observation that when an item is predicted by a prior item, speakers are less likely to make the predicted item prominent. In commonplace vague approximatives such as these, once a speaker utters 'one or' and 'two or', he/she is more likely to perceive the next numeral to be non-selective in Brazil's sense of prominence selection, and it is therefore not perceived by the speaker to be situationally informative in approximately half (52.38%) of the instances, unlike the first numeral that is spoken which is prominent in 86.36% of instances. Given that discourse intonation selections are context-dependent, it is to be expected that the HKCSE (prosodic) also contains instances when this general pattern is not observed.

A second pattern is observed (25 instances) in which both numerals are prominent and 'or' is, again, non-prominent. In this pattern the speakers are effectively capping the range at 'two', or 'three', by the selection of prominence on the second numeral.

```
 1        ] then } { \ and we'll [ CALL ] you in the NEXT TWO or < THREE > days } a:   { \ [ < oKAY > ] } A:
 2                            ** { ? two or [ < THREE > ] weeks } B: { \ [ < ^ YEAH > ] }
 3        * { ? you will } { = you know [ I ] can say that TWO or three < REALly > } } { = [ TERrible ] < BOSses >
 4               > it } { \ you have to [ WAIT ] for some TWO or THREE < ^ ISsues > } { \ before it will
 5        } * { = [ < IN > ] } { ? in [ < SUCH > ] a } { \ two or three [ < ^ MONTHS > ] } (.) * { \ so [ HONG ]
 6        ] } B: { = for the next [ < TWO > ] } (.) * { = two or or three [ < ^ MONTHS > ] } a1:
 7        > ] he'll } { / he'll get [ WHAT ] promotion in two or < THREE > years a1: { = [ < UM > ] } { = [ <
 8        } { = [ < I > ] } { = [ I ] should < SAY > } { / two or [ < THREE > ] } { ? [ < BUT > ] } { / in [ <
 9        ] } { \/ in [ < FACT > ] } { = [ < ER > ] } { \ two or [ < ^ THREE > ] } { = [ < ER > ] } { \ is
10                  ** ((inaudible)) { \ MAYbe ] at least TWO or three < YEARS > } { = [ IN ] < THE > } A: { \
11        needs to [ < MAKE > ] er } { \/ for [ eXAMple ] TWO or THREE pina < coLAda > } { = [ < THAT > ] } { \
12        enTHUsiastic > } { \ for the last [ COUple ] of TWO or three < WEEKS > } { = [ AND ] < ER > } { \ [
13        > ] } { = [ multiLINgual ] < soCIEties > } { = [ TWO ] or three LANguages < CO > exist } { = [ < ER >
14          ] you to be the in < ^ CHARGE > } { \ in [ TWO ] or three year's < TIME > }  a2: { / [ beCAUSE ]
15        \ i what [ I ] will < SAY > } { ? he is } { \ [ TWO ] or < THREE > } { ? [ < beTWEEN > ] } { \ [ BAND
16          > } (.) * { = and [ < ^ NOT > ] } { = in [ TWO ] or three years < _ BUT > } { \ between [ FIVE ]
17        < ^ THERE > } { = they [ < SPEAK > ] er } { = [ TWO ] or three languages < ^ NOW > and } b: { = [ <
18            } { \ come to my [ < OFfice > ] } { = [ TWO ] or < THREE > times } * { = [ < TO > ] } (.) { \
19        > ] is } * { = for the [ < NEXT > ] } { \ [ TWO ] or three < WEEKS > } * { = [ < YOU > ] } { = [
20        > ] } a3: { = they [ < COST > ] me er } B: { = [ TWO ] or three < ^ HUNdred > } a1: * { \ [ < NO > ] }
21          > ] } { = you'll [ < HAVE > ] to wait } { \ [ TWO ] or three < MONTHS > } { \ but [ THAT ] *
22        } { \ from a very [ EARly ] < AGE > } { \ from [ TWO ] or < ^ THREE > } * { \ [ < YEAH > ] } { = [
23        ] } { / in the [ < NEXT > ] } { / i would say [ TWO ] or THREE < DAYS > } { / we'll get [ < BACK > ]
24        \ [ < SOUNDS > ] } { ? in [ < TWO > ] er } { \ [ TWO ] or three < TONES > in it } a: { = i think it's
25            [ TELL ] her to < ^ KEEP > er } (.) * { \ [ TWO ] or three < BOTtles > } b:
26        ] } { \ er this had [ THAT ] < _ Idea > } { \ [ TWO ] or THREE years < aGO > } { = [ < AND > ] } { =
27          DONE extremely < WELL > in the last } { \ [ TWO ] or three < YEARS > } A3: { = [ < AS > ] } { \
28        { ? [ < IN > ] } } { = [ < BEIjing > ] for } { = [ TWO ] or three < YEARS > } * { = [ < UM > ] } { = [ <
29        acCORding ] to them will < LAST > for er } { \ [ TWO ] or THREE < YEARS > } b2: { / [ DOES ] it <
30              > ] } { = take [ < CARE > ] of the } { = [ TWO ] or three < THOUsand > } { \/ [ PAtient ] but of
31        = i [ < WILL > ] } } { = [ < ^ Every > ] } { \/ [ TWO ] or three < HOUR > } { = [ < TO > ] } { \/ [
32        [ ^ IF ] the number should < GO > up to } { \ [ TWO ] or three < ^ THOUsand > } { = [ < _ THAT > ]
33        > ] } (.) { ? there's [ < ONly > ] } (.) { = [ < TWO > ] or three } (.) { \ [ < SOUNDS > ] } { ? in [
34        } { = [ < ER > ] } { = [ < LESS > ] than } { \ [ TWO ] weeks or THREE < WEEKS > } { = and [ < THEN > ]
35        / [ < WORK > ] } { = they [ SAY ] they only have TWO hundred or < THREE > hundred } { = [ < ER > ] } {
36        THEN ] i think it's < TWO > } { = [ < TAKES > ] two } * { ? or three } { ? takes [ TWO ] or takes
37        > } { \ [ < Usually > ] } { \ you only use [ < TWO > ] } { \ or [ < THREE > ] } { \ if you have [
38        PEriod > ] of time } { / are you really say [ < TWO > ] } { / or [ < THREE > ] } { = [ < OR > ] } a:
39        < SO > ] } (.) { = [ I ] would SAY there're < ^ TWO > } (.) { \ or [ THREE ] < PEOples > } { = if [ <
40        [ ^ DO ] not button < yourSELF > } { = with [ < TWO > ] sets } { \ or [ THREE ] < SETS > } { = and [
```

Figure 6.2 Concordance lines for 'two or three'

A third pattern, with seven instances, is when both the numerals are non-prominent. This seems to occur when the speaker is hesitant or if the numerals are preceded by an adverbial such as 'perhaps' which modifies the status of the approximative, indicating that 'perhaps' is perceived by the speaker to be more situationally informative context than the approximative itself.

Pre-modification of vague determiners

Another example of a recurrent prominence pattern is in the pre-modification of a vague determiner. Pre-modification of vague determiners refers to a determiner modified by an adverbial. Both the determiners and the adverbials are members of different sets of scalar implicature (Levinson 1983: 133-6) which are inherently vague in meaning and which require a shared understanding between the speaker and hearer in order to interpret their vague meanings in context. Figure 6.3 shows examples taken from the 37 instances of these particular commonly used vague expressions in the HKCSE (prosodic), which are comprised of a determiner, 'a lot (of)', 'a bit of' and '(a) few', which are modified by an adverbial, 'quite' and 'very'.

```
1    ] } { \ i [ underSTAND ] that there is er QUITE a lot of < PEOple > } * { \ will [ < GO > ] } B:

2              { = [ ONE ] of them you < DID > } { = [ QUITE ] a < LOT > of } { = [ < ER > ] } { \/ you [ COvered

3              { = [ < THERE'S > ] a } { = there's a [ QUITE ] a < LOT > of } { = [ < ERM > ] } { = that [ < KIND

4           think } (.) { = [ < QUITE > ] a } { = [ QUITE ] a < LOT > of you } { = know my [ < ^ NAME > ] } { /

5           THE > ] er } { = [ ER ] < VEry > } { = [ QUITE ] a < LOT > of } { = [ < ER > ] } { = [ C ] l < P > }

6           THE > ] er } { = [ ER ] < VEry > } { ? [ QUITE ] a < LOT > of } { = [ < ER > ] } { = [ C ]  l < P >

7           [ WE ] were < surPRISED > } { = that [ QUITE ] a < LOT > of people actually } { \ you know sort of

8        PHONE > ] } { = they [ < HAVE > ] } { = [ QUITE ] a < LOT > of } { = [ < _ ERM > ] } { \ [ <

9              > but } { ? [ < THEY > ] net } { = [ ^ QUITE ] a < LOT > of the } { \ [ < SINgaPOreans > ] } { \ [

10           < _ DONE > } { = [ < _ ER > ] } { = [ QUITE ] a < LOT > of er } { \ i [ THINK ] we are VEry

11           ] } { \ [ < PEriod > ] } { = there was [ QUITE ] a < LOT > of um } { \ [ < _ exhiBItion > ] } { \

12           [ < ER > ] } { = [ < WE > ] use } { = [ QUITE ] a < LOT > of } { = [ < ER > ] } { = [ < neuRO > ] }

13           ] < ^ SOUND > VEry much } { \ but it's [ QUITE ] a < LOT > of } (.) { \ quite a [ LOT ] of < WORDS >

14           ^ THAT ] is SOMEthing < THAT > } { = [ ^ QUITE ] a < LOT > of er } { = [ < ERM > ] } { = in [ < FACT

15        reMEMber when i was < ^ YOUNG > } { = [ QUITE ] a < LOT >of my } { = [ < ERM > ] } { \/ [ < ^

16              > ] } { = [ < THERE > ] was er } { \ [ QUITE ] a LOT of < ^ FOcus > } { \ on [ < Areas > ] } { =

17           [ PERsonal ] < SIDE > there are } { = [ QUITE ] a lot of < BANKruptcies > } { = and [ WHATnot ] and

18           are [ < conFRONted > ] with } { /\ [ QUITE ] a lot of < DIFficulties > } (.) { = [ < ONCE > ] }

19              = ((inaudible)) [ < _ TOOK > ] a } { / [ QUITE ] a lot of < MOney > } (.) { \ [ < YES > ] }

20              > } B: { \ [ < YEAH > ] } { \ that's [ QUITE ] a lot of < MOney > } a: ((laugh)) ((long pause)) B:

21              > ] one } ((pause)) B: { \ and that's [ QUITE ] a lot of < MOney > } { ? [ < THE > ] } { ? [ < THE

22           ] } { = you know you [ < AND > ] } { \ [QUITE] a LOT of < MEAsure > you know have } { = [ < ER > ]

23           ] < QUITE > a } { = [ < ERM > ] } { \ [ QUITE ] a LOT of < PRESsure > } { \ on the [ < ^ TEAcher >

24              > ] } { \ [ < _ YEAH > ] } { \ because [ QUITE ] a lot of < STUdent > } { = [ < ER > ] } { = [

25              > ] } { = [ < WE > ] have } { \ [ QUITE ] a lot of < TIME > } ((pause)) a3: { = [ HOW ] many
```

26   > } { = [< THERE >] is } { \ [QUITE] **a LOT of** < vaRIeties > } { \ in the [THREE]

27   [< AND >] er } { ? you've had } { \ [QUITE] **a lot of** exPEriences and CONtacts with our <

28   TWO > } { = [< _ THERE >] is } { = [^ QUITE] **a lot of** inforMAtion on < THAT > if } { = [< IF >

29   < THAT > you say } { \ usually occupy [QUITE] **a lot of** TIME < alREAdy > } { \ and [THAT]

30   it } { = [< YES >] } } { = cos i got [QUITE] **a lot of** WORK to do < BUT > * um } (.) { \ [< ^

31   [< DON'T >] feel it's } { = it's [< QUITE >] **a** } { \ a [**LOT**] **of** < _ MOney > } a1: { \ [<

32   >] } { ? [< THAT >] } (.) { ? [< ^ QUITE >] **a lot of** } { ? [< OF >] } { = of [< CHinese >]

33   know } { = [< I >] mean } { = [< ^ QUITE >] **a lot of** people } { \ you know [DO] things < THAT

34   ] er } { \ [< ^ NOW >] } { = er [< QUITE >] **a lot of** people } { = [< GO >] over to pearl } {

35   a < YEAR > } { \ which is really [< QUITE >] **a lot of** students } * { \ to [< MAnage >] } { \ [

36   < _ comMUnicating >] } { / and [< ^ QUITE >] **a lot of** them } { \ [< I >] } { \ [< WARNED >]

37   >] } { = you'll [< HAVE >] to do } { = [< quite **a** [< **LOT** >] **of** } { = [< ER >] } { = [<

38   ] } { = when [< HONG >] kong need } { ? quite **a** [< **LOT** >] **of** i } { = [< I >] t } { ? er er er

39   but it's [QUITE] **a** < **LOT** > **of** } (.) { \ quite **a** [LOT] **of** < WORDS > } a: { = [< MM >] } (.) {

40   [< QUITE >] er } { = [< _ ER >] } { \quite **a** [**LOT**] **of** other < inVESTments > } { \ into [<

41   ] through < THAT > } { = [^ reQUIring] QUITE **a lot of** < EFforts > } b: { = you mean the [< ONE

42   { = [< TO >] er } { \ to [acCOMmodate] quite **a lot of** < PEOple > } B: { / [< WHAT >] } { \ [

1   [< ^ taiWAN >] visitors } { \ spend [QUITE] **a bit of** < MOney > } * { = [< ON >] } { \ [<

2   >] } { = i [< deVOted >] } { ? [< QUITE >] **a** } { \ [**BIT**] **of** < SPACE > } { = [TALking] <

3   PROlong] SHEDding is because we give < QUITE > **a bit** } { \ [DOSE] **of** < STEroid > } { ? and of [

4   it here } { = [< SO >] } { \/ we [SEE] quite **a** < ^ **BIT** > **of** them } * { = we don't [< SEE >] }

5   ] < PROblem > } { \ [THAT] takes QUITE **a bit of** < TIME > } { ? and for [EACH] other to

6   [< DO >] } { \ we [STILL] need to do QUITE **a bit of** < WORK > on that } b1: { \ of [< COURSE >

7   **of** } { = [< ER >] } { \/ you [COvered] QUITE **a FAIR bit** of < maTErials > } { = [< ON >] } { \/

1   ] **a** < LOT > **of** } { = [< ^ ER >] } { \ er [< ^ **QUITE** >] **a few** } { \ [coLOnial] < BUILdings > } a:

2   > authority } (.) * { = he [< GOT >] **a** } { \ [**QUITE**] **a few** < OFfers > } { \ to come [< BACK >] }

3   where [< ^ I >] am } { \ that i've [GOT] quite **a FEW** english dePARTment < colLEAGUES > } { = in

4   = i [< beLIEVE >] } { = we [< HAVE >] } { = **quite a** [< **FEW** >] of those } { \ [< THESE >] days

5   } { = [YOU] have been to < HONG > kong } { \ [**QUITE**] **a few** < TIMES > } { = [BOTH] < beFORE > } { =

6   HOLD > them } { / [< WELL >] } { \ there's [**QUITE**] **a** < ^ **FEW** > } { = [REAsons] < WHY > } { \ [

7   ALL these < ER >] } { ? [< YOU >] have } { = [**QUITE**] **a** < **FEW** > } { = [QUEStions] < _ RAISED > } {

8   should [< SAY >] } { \/ [< toDAY >] } { \ [**QUITE**] **a few** < THOUGHTS > } { \ [WENT] through my <

1   BElieve] me in big < COMpanies > } { = [**VEry**] **very few** people < UNderstand > } { = [< AND >] } { \

2   { = of [< P >] r d } { = let me [JUST] say a < **VEry few** > WORDS > } { = [< aBOUT >] } { = [ONE]

3   ** { \ but you [HAVE] **very** < **FEW** > } { \ [< **VEry** >] few mistakes } { = [

4   < LANguage > one } b: { / [< ER >] } B: { = **VEry** < **FEW** > er } b: { = [NO] BUT if you } { = if

5   >] } { \ of [< dongGUAN >] } { \ there are [**VEry**] **few** GARment < COMpany > } { \ that can [emPLOY

6   { = [< ERM >] } { = [BUT] < NObody > } { \ [**VEry**] **few** people < WATCH > it } { = [< I >] mean in

7   in that < reSPECT > } { \ [I] would say that **very** < FEW > } { \ [< SCHOOLS >] } { \ that are [^

8   >] } (.) * { = [< BUT >] erm } (.) { = [^ **VEry**] **few** people < ACtually > } { = [VEry] few <

9   < HAVE >] } { \ er [< ^ PICtures >] } * { \ [**VEry**] **few** < WORDS > } { = [< BUT >] } { = [< MAYbe

10   < BUT >] erm } { = [< ERM >] } { \ you know [**VEry**] **few** people < ^ atTAIN > that } { \ [< YOU >]

11   NOT be GOOD for social < ^ staBIlity > } { \ [**VEry**] **few** GOvernment < ofFIcials > } { \ would be [

12   a HALF million < PEOple > } { ? in er } { \ [^ **VEry**] **few** < TIME > } { \ [THAT'S] < MEAN > } { \ [

13   [< ^ TIME >] } { = especially there were [^ **VEry**] **few** CHInese * there are < QUITE > } { \ quite a

14   have been < CANcelled > already } { \ because [**VEry**] **few** people < ^ REgister > } B: { \ [< OH >] }

15   [< SUFfering >] } * { \ [beCAUSE] of these < **VEry** > **few** } b:

16   IS >] that } { = i [< DON'T >] think } { = [**VEry**] **few** teachers who < comPLAINED > } { \ [aBOUT]

17   < THE >] k } { \ [N] d < Q > } { \ there are **VEry** < FEW > } { \ [D] < Q > s there } { = unless [

18   >] } { \ [< inSPECtion >] } { = there're [^ **VEry**] **few** who disPUted the < NEED > } { = to [<

19   >] } { \ [ARE] < inDEBted > } b: { \ [**VEry**] < FEW > } B: { \ [< _ YEAH >] } { \/ that

20   } { = [< AND >] } { = [< ER >] } { = [< **VEry** >] **few** of them } { = have oversea [< OFfice >

21   > } B: { = well i } { ? [< I >] } { \ i'm [^ **VEry**] < FEW > } { = i am one of [< THE >] } { \ [<

22   up } { ? only a [< COUple >] you know } { / [**VEry**] < FEW > } { \/ [VEry] low < reSPONSE > you

Figure 6.3 Pre-modification of vague determiners

A strong pattern of prominence selection can be seen in Figure 6.3. In 68 out of 79 instances (86.07%) of these forms of vague expression, the adverbial pre-modifying the determiner is said with prominence, and the determiner is said with a fairly even mixture of prominence and non-prominence (43 out of 79 instances, 54.43%). This suggests that speakers typically perceive the pre-modifier, and not necessarily the determiner, to be situationally informative in such contexts of interaction. When the overall instances of 'quite and 'very' in the HKCSE (prosodic) are examined, it is found that this high level of prominence selection is not typical. In the case of 'quite', of the 965 instances in the HKCSE (prosodic), 657 (68.08%) are said with prominence, and, of the 4,907 instances of 'very', 2,449 (49.9%) are made prominent.

Lexical cohesion

In spoken English, received wisdom is that it is generally lexical words that tend to be made prominent by speakers, while non-lexical, or grammatical, words tend not to be made prominent unless for a reason (see, for example, Chun 2002: 9; Clark and Yallop 1990: 296). Here the reasons for this observation are provided and the exploitation of prominence by speakers is investigated.

Speaker decisions within the prominence system are made on the basis of the speaker considering the status of individual words (Brazil 1997: 39). The selection between making lexical or non-lexical words prominent is linked to what speakers determine to be situationally informative at that point in the discourse (Brazil 1997). The other three systems in discourse intonation, tone, key and termination, are not attributes of individual words but of the tonic segment (i.e. that section of the tone unit that falls between the first and the last prominent syllable), and are not considered here.

A study by McCarthy (1988: 185) examines the lexical chains in the form of what he terms 'relexicalisations' across turns and across speakers in conversational data. These relexicalisations cover non-identical repetitions that have been re-formulated or re-structured. McCarthy's study is of particular interest because he also investigates the speakers' choice of discourse intonation. McCarthy (1988) makes the case that to fully understand reiteration (i.e. lexical chains), along with other forms of cohesion, the analyst working with spoken discourse needs to take into account the communicative role of intonation within the cohesive chain. McCarthy (1988: 183) argues that, in spoken discourse, intonation choices made by speakers also serve to signal "here-and-now lexical relationships projected by the speakers". One means by which speakers do this is through the selection of prominence.

A study by Warren (2006) builds on McCarthy's (1988) attempt to include an analysis of discourse intonation in the study of lexical cohesion, but differs in that it studies a wider range of words within a cohesive chain. By taking into account the interdependent relationship of lexical and non-lexical cohesion and speakers' intonation choices in the data, Warren's (2006) study examines the contribution of cohesion to the overall organisation of the discourse and the interactional management of cohesion over speaker turns. While some studies tend to distinguish between grammatical and lexical cohesion or repetition (see for example, Halliday and Hasan 1976, Hasan 1984), the notion of what may be considered to be part of the same cohesive chain in a discourse proposed by Winter (1974, 1979) is broader because he includes ellipsis, substitution, reference and lexical repetition. In Warren's study (2006), which examines cohesion in spoken discourse, Winter's (1974, 1979) approach to the ties between lexical and non-lexical cohesion is adopted as a more appropriate way of portraying the complexity of lexical cohesion, especially when the use of ellipsis and reference are generally far more prevalent in spoken discourse than in written discourse (see, for example, Cheng and Warren 1999a).

The communicative role played by prominence in cohesive chains is illustrated in the following example. The extract begins with the interviewer asking why the interviewee wishes to work at that particular hotel.

Example 6.13

B: interviewer   a: interviewee

1 B: { \ [VEry] < WELL > } } { = [< ER >] } { / [< ^ NOW >] } { = i'd

2   [LIKE] to < ASK > you er } { = my [SEcond] part of the < QUEStion >

3   which was } { / [< ^ WHAT >] } { \ you're interested in [< **HYATT** >] }

4   (.) { = [OR] is there < Any > } { \ special [< REAson >] } { / [OR]

5   you just dropped off in the m t < R > } { \ and you saw **HYATT** < OH > }

6   * { \ let me [WALK] in < **HERE** > } ((laugh))

7 a: ** ((laugh))

8 a: { = [< UM >] } (.) { \ [< ^ ACtually >] } { = [< UM >] } { \ [I'M]

9   BEing < asSIGNED > } { = to [< WORK >] in the } (.) { = [< HYATT

10   >] } (.) { \ [**HYATT**] < ^ REgency > }

11 B: { \ [OH] you've < BEEN > assigned } (.) * { \ it's [< ^ NOT >] your

12 a: ** { / [< YES >] }

13   * choice }

14 a: ** ((laugh))

15 a: { / [< YES >] } { = [< ER >] } { = [< BUT >] er } { = [< WHEN >]

16   i'm } { = [I] < KNOW > that } { \ i was [BEing] < asSIGNED > } { =

17   [< TO >] } { = [< ER >] } { = to [apPLY] for < ^ THE > } { \

18   [INternship] < trainEE > } { = to [WORK] in < THE > } { \ **hyatt** [<

19   **REgency** >] } { \ i'm [QUITE] < HAPpy > } { = [^ COS] < UM > }

20   ((laugh)) { \ its [< loCAtion >] } { = is [< VEry >] } { ? [< CON >] }

21   { \/ [< conVEnient >] } { ? [< **IT'S** >] } { = just [< NEAR >] the } { \/

22   m t r [< STAtion >] } { = [AND] < UM > } { = i [< JUST >] } { ? [<

23   ER >] } { \ come [< **HERE** >] } { = go [< **HERE** >] } { = [TO] <

24   UM > } { = [< BY >] } { / m t [< R >] }

25 B: { / [< Uhuh >] }

26 a: { = [< AND >] um } { \/ [< ^ ALso >] } { = [< UM >] } { \ i know [<

27   THAT >] } { \ er from the [< broCHURE >] } { \ of the **hyatt** [<

28   **REgency** >] } { = i [< KNOW >] the } { = i know [< _ THAT >] } { =

29   [< ER >] } { = [< **THIS** >] **hotel** } { = [< ALways >] } { \ [< ^

30   EMphasize >] } { \ [ON] the STAFF < ^ TRAIning > } } { = [AND]

31   **they** TREAT **their** < STAFF > } { = [NOT] < LIKE > their } (.) { \ [<

32   employEE >] } { \ just [LIKE] **their** < ^ GUEST > } (.) { = [< AND

33   >] } { = [**THEY**] have a < ^ GOOD > } { = [< AND >] } { = [< ER

34   >] } { ? [WELL] < ORganised > } { \/ training [< PROgrammes >] }

35   { \/ for the [< STAFF >] } { = [THEREfore] i'm quite HAPpy to be

36   asSIGNED < TO > } { \/ to [WORK] < **HERE** > }

In Example 6.13, there is a cohesive chain made up of both lexical and non-lexical words. The lexical words consist of 'Hyatt', 'Hyatt Regency' and 'hotel' in lines 3, 5, 9, 10, 18, 19, and 27-29. The speakers also consistently select to make these words prominent, perceiving them to be sense selections at those points in the discourse. The exception is 'this hotel' (line 29) uttered by the interviewee, where it is the demonstrative pronoun 'this' and not 'hotel' that is perceived to be more situation-ally informative. In this context of interaction, the speaker emphasises that this particular hotel has very good staff training, and so implies that other hotels do not. In the case of the non-lexical words in the cohesive chain (eleven in all) – 'here' (4 instances), 'it' (3 instances), 'they' (2 instances), 'their' (2 instances) – five are made prominent by the speaker, and in each case, 'here' (lines 6, 23 (twice) and 36) is perceived to be situationally informative. A possible explanation is that at this point in the interview, the focus is on why the interviewee wishes to work here in this particular hotel and not some other hotel. The other non-lexical words are typically non-prominent, and so are not perceived by the speaker to be sense selec-tions in their local contexts. The general pattern for selecting prominence in this extract provides evidence that, generally speaking, there is a connection between a speaker's choice of lexical or non-lexical words in a cohesive chain and what he/ she perceives to be situationally informative in the unfolding talk. However, it also shows that both lexical and non-lexical words can be made prominent or non-prominent by speakers.

Lexical words are more likely than non-lexical words to attract prominence in a cohesive chain, suggesting that speakers do not randomly select lexical or non-lexical words in a chain. Speakers may be guided in their choice between lexical and grammatical words, at least in part, by the decisions they make at the same time within the system of prominence in discourse intonation in terms of deter-mining what is situationally informative at that point in the discourse. In addition, in certain contexts of interaction this pattern may be reversed by speakers with lexical words made non-prominent and non-lexical words made prominent in a chain. This further supports the view that prominence is not an inherent property of words, but subject to context-specific speaker choices.

Word associations

Chapter 5 describes a study of word associations (Cheng and Warren 2008) in terms of tone unit boundaries, and here the same study is discussed in terms of prominence distribution across the word associations. In order to highlight some of the main findings, the same selection of lexically- and grammatically-rich word associations examined in Chapter 5 is analysed.

Table 6.7 shows the distribution of prominences across the three lexically rich word associations when they are spoken in one tone unit. The analysis is confined to one tone unit because the number of instances across more than one tone unit is too small to allow identification of any general patterns of prominence distribution.

Table 6.7 Distribution of prominence: lexically-rich word associations

1.	*nineteen*	*ninety-*	*seven*
	34 (69.4%)	0 (0%)	40 (100%)
2.	*hong*	*kong*	*people*
	37 (68.5%)	0 (0%)	35 (64.8%)
3.	*asia's*	*world*	*city*
	10 (90.9%)	3 (27.3%)	10 (90.9%)

First it should be noted that some of the words in Table 6.7 are predictable in terms of prominence or non-prominence. While it is quite rare for a word to be one hundred percent prominent or non-prominent in the HKCSE (prosodic), this pattern is found for some of the words in these word associations. Only 'seven' in 'nineteen ninety-seven' is always prominent, and both 'ninety' and 'kong' are always non-prominent. However, it is possible for these words to not conform to these patterns in other word combinations and in other communicative contexts.

Another finding is that there is a positional element in the typical distribution of prominence in one tone unit. In these three-word associations, it is the first and the final words that are typically chosen to be made prominent by the speakers. The selection and distribution of prominence within particular lexically-rich word associations can also be explained on the basis of Brazil's notion of the existential paradigm and sense selection. This can be illustrated by analysing one of the word associations: 'hong kong people'. When it occurs in a single tone unit, 'hong' (68.5%) and 'people' (64.8%) are typically made prominent, meaning that they are situationally informative. The selection to make the word 'hong' prominent sets up a situation in which 'kong' is non-selective, and then 'people' is selective because there are a range of possible words which could occupy this slot.

When a selection of grammatically-rich word associations are examined (Table 6.8 below), a number of the patterns can be accounted for with reference to Renouf and Sinclair's (1991) notion of a 'collocational framework'. Further, Brazil's (1997) notions of general versus existential paradigmatic speaker choices, which in the local context determine whether or not a syllable or a word is made prominent, are helpful here.

Table 6.8 Typical distribution of prominences: grammatically-rich word associations

1.	*a*	*lot*	*of*
	0	115 (81%)	0
2.	*we*	*have*	*to*
	9 (11.8%)	47 (61.8%)	0
3.	*that*	*we*	*have*
	10 (35.7%)	4 (14.3%)	0

An example of a collocational framework is 'a * of', in which 'lot' is occupying a slot. In each collocational framework, a large number of possible words (either single words or combinations of words) can occupy the empty slots in the framework, while the framework itself is invariant. Thus, the words in the framework, that is the grammatical core, are almost never spoken with prominence, and the word that is selected to complete the word association by occupying the framework is almost always spoken with prominence.

There is a similar pattern of prominence distribution in *we have to*, where the first word 'we' is usually not made prominent by speakers, and in the data studied there are no instances of the last word 'to' being made prominent at all. This is a case of subject pronoun plus semi-modal. It is 'have' in the semi-modal 'have to' that is most likely to be made prominent.

The last grammatically-rich word association has a relatively weaker tendency of prominence distribution. In the word association 'that we have', the first two words are sometimes prominent and the last word 'have' is non-prominent. 'That we have' is a mixture of organisation and message units in terms of Linear Unit Grammar (Sinclair and Mauranen 2006). The fact that this particular grammatically-rich word association cuts across the two types of chunks found in spoken discourse may account for the different patterns of prominence distribution, compared to the other two grammatically-rich word associations, 'a lot of' and 'we have to', both of which are parts of message elements.

Pronoun prominence

Two studies of Singapore English (Goh, 2000; Brown and Deterding 2005) suggest that different varieties of English might have different tendencies when it comes to the choice of prominence. Both provide evidence that speakers of Singapore English are more likely to select prominence on pronouns than speakers of British English, although they are careful not to claim that this is a general characteristic of Singapore English. Based on these studies, the HKCSE (prosodic) was examined to see whether the same pattern exists among the HKC when compared with the NES. The HKCSE (prosodic) was searched for personal pronouns, possessive pronouns and possessive determiners to examine the frequency with which the HKC and NES select prominence on these words (see Tables 6.9 and 6.10).

The findings in the tables below suggest that the tendency for speakers of Singapore English to select prominence on pronouns more frequently than speakers of British English is also to be found among HKC. Table 6.9 shows that across the personal pronouns, the HKC select prominence proportionately more often than the NES, although the differences vary from one personal pronoun to another between the two sets of speakers. For example, the differences for the personal pronouns *me* (24.2% versus 20.6%), *you* (17.9% versus 17.1%) and *we* (20.5% versus 16.4%) are quite small. In fact, HKC males have the smallest proportional usage of prominence for the personal pronoun *me*. For other personal pronouns, such as *she* (35.4% versus 6.7%) and *them* (24.6% versus 5.9%), the differences between the two sets of speakers are much greater.

A similar tendency can be found in Table 6.10 for the possessive pronouns and possessive determiners, except that it is not so uniform. In the case of *our* (26.8% versus 22.6%) and *ours* (100% versus 84.6%), it is the NES who select prominence proportionately more often. Again, for the remainder the differences between the HKC and the NES vary, but the extremes are not as great as those found for the personal pronouns. For example the smallest differences are found for *your* (17.1% versus 14.9%) and *their* (19.9% versus 18.6%) and the largest for *his* (20.7% versus 11.0%) and *its* (14% versus 6.2%).

It is also of interest to note that, across all of the personal pronouns examined, there is a very wide range when it comes to the speakers in general selecting prominence: from 12.7% and 11.7% for *its* and *it* to 86.7% and 100% for *ours* and theirs. The relationship between word frequency and the selection of prominence is probably part of the explanation for the wide spread that is found, and this will be examined in more detail later in this chapter.

Table 6.9 Personal pronouns

Pronoun	All speakers	HKC females	HKC males	All HKC	NES females	NES males	All NES
I	20,949	8,026	6,066	14,092	1,511	5,346	6,857
	(6,118)	(2,671)	(1,881)	(4,552)	(420)	(1,146)	(1,566)
	(29.2%)	(33.3%)	(31%)	(32.3%)	(27.8%)	(21.4%)	(22.8%)
me	1,627	598	558	1,156	110	361	471
	(378)	(178)	(103)	(281)	(24)	(73)	(97)
	(23.2%)	(29.8%)	(18.4%)	(24.2%)	(21.8%)	(20.2%)	(20.6%)
you	22,443	7,631	7,383	15,014	1,664	5,765	7,429
	(3,954)	(1306)	(1375)	(2681)	(342)	(931)	(1273)
	(17.6%)	(17.7%)	(18.6%)	(17.9%)	(20.6%)	(16.1%)	(17.1%)
one	24	7	10	17	1	7	8
	(15)	(5)	(7)	(12)	(1)	(2)	(3)
	(62.5%)	(71.4%)	(70.0%)	(70.6%)	(100.0%)	(28.6%)	(37.5%)
he	2,437	1054	440	1494	279	664	943
	(565)	(286)	(118)	(404)	(46)	(115)	(161)
	(20.6%)	(27.1%)	(26.8%)	(27.0%)	(16.5%)	(17.3%)	(17.1%)
him	367	155	57	212	46	109	155
	(97)	(54)	(16)	(70)	(5)	(22)	(27)
	(26.4%)	(34.8%)	(28.1%)	(33%)	(10.9%)	(20.2%)	(17.4%)
she	1,208	523	172	695	134	379	1723
	(361)	(180)	(66)	(246)	(41)	(74)	(115)
	(29.9%)	(34.4%)	(38.4%)	(35.4%)	(30.6%)	(19.5%)	(6.7%)
her	460	211	77	288	49	123	172
	(97)	(47)	(24)	(71)	(6)	(20)	(26)
	(21.1%)	(22.3%)	(31.2%)	(24.6%)	(12.2%)	(16.3%)	(15.1%)
it	14,963	4,954	4,222	9,176	1,091	4,696	5,787
	(1,755)	(781)	(540)	(1,321)	(75)	(359)	(434)
	(11.7%)	(15.8%)	(12.8%)	(14.4%)	(6.9%)	(7.6%)	(7.5%)
we	10,937	3610	4618	8228	526	2183	2,709
	(2,132)	(835)	(854)	(1,689)	(77)	(366)	(443)
	(19.5%)	(23.1%)	(18.5%)	(20.5%)	(14.6%)	(16.8%)	(16.4%)
us	994	365	404	769	44	181	225
	(284)	(122)	(117)	(239)	(7)	(38)	(45)
	(28.6%)	(33.4%)	(29%)	(31.1%)	(15.9%)	(21.0%)	(20%)
they	6,944	2,348	2,281	4,629	524	1,788	2,315
	(1,926)	(731)	(672)	(1,403)	(114)	(409)	(523)
	(27.7%)	(331.1%)	(29.5%)	(30.3%)	(21.8%)	(22.9%)	(22.6%)
them	1,471	544	417	961	114	396	510
	(26)	(135)	(101)	(236)	(6)	(24)	(30)
	(18.1%)	(24.8%)	(24.2%)	(24.6%)	(5.3%)	(6.1%)	(5.9%)

Table 6.10   Possessive pronouns and possessive determiners

Pronoun	All speakers	HKC females	HKC males	All HKC	NES females	NES males	All NES
my	2,164	1,014	607	1,621	176	367	543
	(662)	(324)	(200)	(524)	(37)	(101)	(138)
	(30.6%)	(32.0%)	(32.9%)	(32.3%)	(21%)	(27.5%)	(25.4%)
mine	55	14	20	34	4	17	21
	(46)	(13)	(19)	(32)	(2)	(12)	(14)
	(83.6%)	(92.9%)	(95%)	(94.1%)	(50%)	(70.6%)	(66.7%)
your	2,511	869	877	1,746	206	559	765
	(412)	(132)	(166)	(298)	(31)	(83)	(114)
	(16.4%)	(15.2%)	(18.9%)	(17.1%)	(15.0%)	(14.8%)	(14.9%)
yours	37	12	10	22	5	10	15
	(32)	(10)	(10)	(20)	(5)	(7)	(12)
	(86.5%)	(83.3%)	(100%)	(90.9%)	(100%)	(70%)	(80%)
his	449	188	106	294	47	108	155
	(78)	(36)	(25)	(61)	(2)	(15)	(17)
	(17.4%)	(19.1%)	(23.6%)	(20.7%)	(4.3%)	(13.9%)	(11%)
her	460	211	77	288	49	123	172
	(97)	(47)	(24)	(71)	(6)	(20)	(26)
	(21.1%)	(22.3%)	(31.2%)	(24.6%)	(12.2%)	(16.3%)	(15.1%)
hers	1	0	0	0	0	1	1
	(0)					(0)	(0)
	(0%)					(0%)	(0%)
its	393	140	189	329	13	51	64
	(50)	(28)	(18)	(46)	(0)	(4)	(4)
	(12.7%)	(20%)	(9.5%)	(14%)	(0%)	(7.8%)	(6.2%)
our	2,591	837	1,467	2,304	40	247	287
	(598)	(234)	(287)	(521)	(12)	(65)	(77)
	(23.1%)	(28%)	(19.6%)	(22.6%)	(30%)	(26.3%)	(26.8)
ours	15	7	6	13	0	2	2
	(13)	(7)	(4)	(11)		(2)	(2)
	(86.7%)	(100%)	(66.7%)	(84.6%)		(100%)	(100%)
their	1,343	500	553	1,053	80	210	290
	(264)	(102)	(108)	(210)	(13)	(41)	(54)
	(19.7%)	(20.4%)	(19.5%)	(19.9%)	(16.2%)	(19.5%)	(18.6%)
theirs	2	2	0	2	0	0	0
	(2)	(2)		(2)			
	(100%)	(100%)		(100%)			
one's	6	4	2	6	0	0	0
	(4)	(2)	(2)	(4)			
	(66.6%)	(50.0%)	(100%)	(66.6%)			

Word class and frequency

Brazil's (1997) underlying premise is that discourse intonation is context-specific and not pre-determined by, for example, word class. Nonetheless, it has been found that the distribution of prominence, while not fully predictable, appears to be related to both word class and word frequency. Figures 6.4-6.10 show four examples from each of the main word classes, i.e. conjunctions, prepositions, modal verbs, nouns, verbs, adjectives, and adverbs, drawn from the full HKCSE (prosodic). For each word class, the examples were selected to represent a spread in terms of frequency of occurrence. The examples also share the same number of syllables. Each Figure contains two graphs. The first graph details the raw frequencies of the words with the number of times the word is spoken with prominence in the shaded area. The second graph shows the words spoken with prominence as a percentage of the overall occurrence of the word in the HKCSE (prosodic).

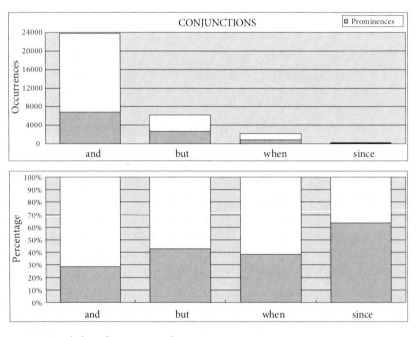

Figure 6.4 Word class, frequency and prominence: conjunctions

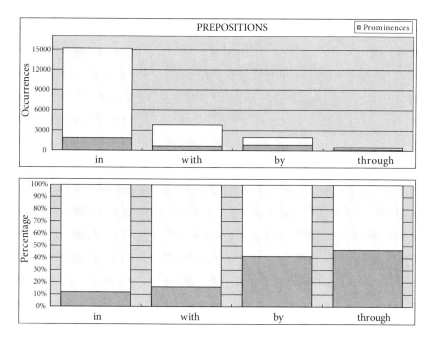

Figure 6.5 Word class, frequency and prominence: prepositions

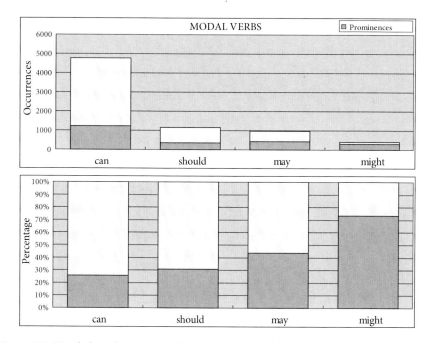

Figure 6.6 Word class, frequency and prominence: modal verbs

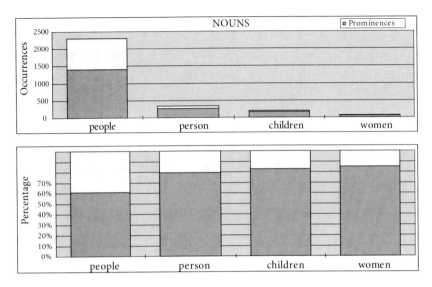

Figure 6.7 Word class, frequency and prominence: nouns

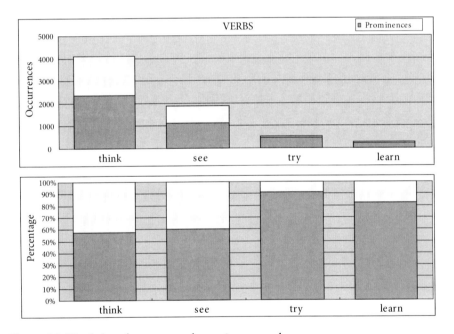

Figure 6.8 Word class, frequency and prominence: verbs

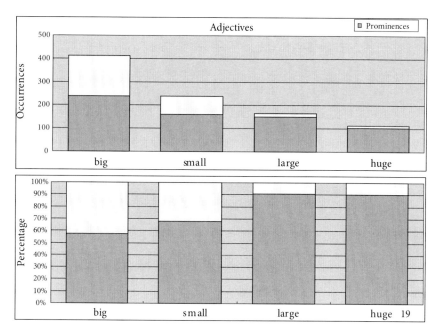

Figure 6.9 Word class, frequency and prominence: adjectives

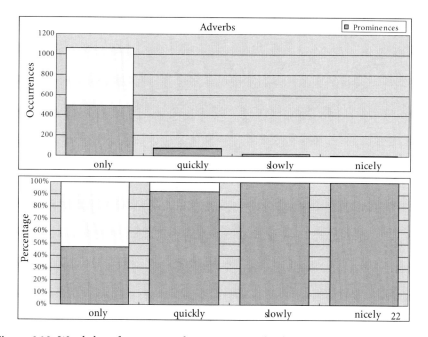

Figure 6.10 Word class, frequency and prominence: adverbs

What is most informative in the above figures is that none of the examples are ever always spoken without prominence, and only the least frequent are always spoken with prominence, e.g. 'slowly' (23 instances) and 'nicely' (7 instances). If we use the analogy of the tree line which can be seen on a tall mountain, above which no trees are found, further research into the distribution of prominence might uncover a 'prominence line' on word frequency lists, below which infrequent words can be predicted, with a very high degree of certainty, to be spoken with prominence.

Patterns are found with regard to both word class and word frequency. The 'grammatical' word classes have a smaller proportion spoken with prominence than the 'lexical' word classes. Within these two general categories, differences are found. For example, among the grammatical words, modal verbs are more likely to be spoken with prominence than prepositions, but such clear differences are not found among the lexical words. In terms of word frequency and speakers' selection of prominence, these examples, irrespective of word class, show an apparent connection between low relative frequency in the HKCSE (prosodic) and prominence. With the exceptions of the conjunctions 'but' and 'when', and the verbs 'try' and 'learn', all of the Figures 6.4-6.10 show that the more frequent a word is in the HKCSE (prosodic), the less likely it is to be spoken with prominence (and, of course, vice versa). This might seem to be logically the case (Sinclair, personal communication 2005), but these figures document this phenomenon for the first time. The notion of the "phraseological tendency" in language use (Sinclair 2004), i.e. language is typified by word associations representing units of meaning rather than by individual words, further supports the inverse relationship found here. The more frequent the word, the more functions it typically performs, and so the more likely it is that its contribution to meaning is in combination with other co-selections in lexical items (Sinclair 1996 and 1998). This is further evidence that meaning is determined from the association of words in the context of interaction rather than by individual words in isolation. Thus when, for example, nouns or adverbs are modified, they are less likely to be made prominent, and this is illustrated in Figures 6.11 and 6.12 below.

Nouns and adverbs such as *people* and *only* often collocate with other words such as *many, more* and *most,* and *just* and *not,* respectively. Figures 6.11 and 6.12 illustrate how the modification of words such as *people* and *only* reduces the likelihood that these words are said with prominence, and the pattern is more likely to be that prominence is selected for the preceding modifier. In the HKSCE (prosodic), *people* is spoken with prominence 60.92% of the time, but, when preceded by *most,* this drops to 31.37% of instances. Similarly, *only* is spoken with prominence in 46.83% of the instances in the whole HKCSE (prosodic), but, when preceded by *just,* this falls to 6.66% of instances.

```
 1  1       END ] up learning to be a bit more CAREful than most people HAVE to < BE > and } { = you [ LEARN ] to
 2     lot } { ? is [ < THAT > ] } { / is [ THAT ] what MOST people < TAKE > } { / [ < FIVE > ] } a: { \ [ < ^
 3        \ [ BEIjing ] < auTHOrities > } { \ i [ THINK ] MOST people would < acKNOWledge > } { \ that in the [
 4           > ] } { = [ < WELL > ] } { \ [ BAsically ] most people < aGREE > } { \ [ DOEsn't ] < eXIST > } {
 5           > } { \ which [ SOUNDS ] < HARSH > } { \ to most people [ outSIDE ] of new < YORK > } * { \ or [
 6        to the < PROperty > } { = it seems  [ LIKE ] MOST people have < ER > } { = [ GROSSly ] under
 7        } { \ [ < iNItiatives > ] } { \ [ ^ beCAUSE ] MOST  people < exPECted > } { \ the [ BUDget ] to be a
 8                     ** { \ [ ^ MOST ] people THINK syntax AS the < GRAMmar > } (.) *
 9     ] } { = [ < NOW > ] } { = [ GEORGE ] i think < ^ MOST > people when they } { = [ TALK ] about < ER > }
10         > ] } { = [ BUT ] i < ^ GUESS > like } { = [ MOST ] people would < HAVE > like } { \ [ DEEP ] <
11     to have } { \ for [ < WORK > ] } (.) { \ for [ ^ MOST ] people i < THINK > } { \ [ < THREE > ] } { \
12     ] d p  growth in CHIna has been EStimated by < ^ MOST > people to be } { = between  [ < SEven > ] } { \
13     { \ [ < MM > ] } a4: { \ [ < _ YEAH > ] } { \ [ MOST ] people < aGREE > } { = we [ < DON'T > ] have }
14      { \ [ OR ] you < WON'T > get it } { \ but [ ^ MOST ] people < GET > it } { = they [ < ^ ARE > ] no }
15     = at the [ END ] of the < DAY > } { = you know [ MOST ] people are NOT without < THAT > } { = [ < SORT
16     { \ [ < ^ sucCESS > ] } * { = but after all [ ^ MOST ] people < HERE > } { \ [ < ARE > ] } } { = i mean
17     SEE > er (.) { \ you [ < KNOW > ] } (.) { = [ MOST ] people have < GOT > } { ? [ < TEL > ] } { / [
18        > ] tax } { \ in [ HONG ] < ^ KONG > } { \ [ MOST ] people would iMAgine g s < T > } { = to be [
19        ] it on christmas < EVE > } { \ [ unLIKE ] < ^ MOST > people } { \ who [ < Open > ] } { \ on *
20     it's o } { = new [ VICE ] < CHANcellor > } { \ [ MOST ] people would have CRAWLED in at the < BACK > }
21     { = i [ < THINK > ] in } { = [ < IN > ] } { = [ MOST ] people's < MIND > } { \ [ parTIcularly ] in
22        > } { = [ OR ] is that < SOMEthing > } { \ that most [ PEOple ] who have DONE tertiary education < _
23        < MEAT > to cut } B1: { \ [ < HEY > ] } { = i ^ MOST ] people i < WORK > with } { = [ < WORK > ] till
24     ] < ^ HORses > } { \ and they're [ BETter ] than most < PEOple > } a: { \ you're [ < ^ JOking > ] } (.)
25     { \ [ BUT ] in their HEART of < ^ HEARTS > ] } { \ most [ PEOple ] < WANT > } (.) { \ they [ < WANT > ] }
26        only < REAson > } { = [ < I > ] mean } { ? [ ^ MOST ] people it seems to < GO > to } { \ [ < taiWAN >
27     minutes < LATE > ] } { = [ < AND > ] er } { \ [ ^ MOST ] people would have < THOUGHT > } { ? it's o } {
28     ] } } { \ [ ASK ] < QUEStions > } { = because [ < MOST > ] people wa } { \ [ LIKE ] to TALK about < _
29        < ^ HAVE > to take the risk } { = because [ MOST > ] people } { \ [ < _ WELL > ] } { \ everybody [
30     < BUT > ] erm er } { = and [ < AND > ] } { = and most [ < peoPLE > ] are } { = are [ VEry ] nervous
31                > } { \/ to [ < SAY > ] } } { = that  [ < MOST > ] people } { = are [ NOT ] < aWARE > } { = of [
32        > ] } { \ [ BUT ] THAT'S not < Usual > } { = as most [ < PEOple > ] } { = you know cos [ ^ THEY ] WORK
33     < BETter > } { = [ < beCAUSE > ] i think } { \ [ MOST ] < ^ PEOple > } { = if they [ LOST ] the < JOB >
34     BUT > ] i think this } { = [ < BRING > ] } { \ [ MOST ] of < PEOple > } { = [ < THEY > ] } { = [ < THEY
35     { \ [ GET ] mixed < UP > } { = [ < AND > ] } { = most [ M__ ] people that < I > } (.) { \ [ < HAD > ] }
36        [ < MUCH > ] } a3: { ? so because } { = [ ^ MOST ] other people < WERE > all } (.) { / [ < YOU > ]
37     < _ MM > ] } b: { \ [ < _ OH > ] } B: { = but [ MOST ] other people < HAVE > a VEry } { = [ < WIDE > ]
38     { = [ < THEY > ] } { = [ < SOME > ] } { = er [ MOST ] of the people i USED to < ^ WORK > with } { \
39     to } { \ take the [ < MAnagers > ] from } { \ [ MOST ] of the people in < Asia > } * { = and that's
40     deCIsion > } * { = [ < acCEPtable > ] to } { \ [ MOST ] of the PEOple in < HONG > kong }  b1:
41     [ < BUT > ] } { \ they're [ ^ NOT ] eXACTly the most straTEgic people in the < WORLD > } } { / [ < oKAY >
42        } { = then what [ < HAPpens > ] } a: { = [ < ^ MOST > ] } { = people i [ THINK ] would have < THOUGHT
43        > it yeah } { = like [ < MOST > ] of } { = [ < MOST > ] of the people that we } { = [ < HANG > ] } {
44     happy with WHAT they were < ^ DOing > } { = [ ^ MOST ] of the < PEOple > } { ? they [ < WENT > ] to }
45     { \ [ ^ FOURTH ] < COUNtry > } { = with the [ < MOST > ] } { \ [ PEOple ] with BILlion of < DOLlars >
46        > } { \ whatever it [ < COST > ] } (.) { \ but [ MOST ] of these < PEOple > } { \ were [ < ^ NOT > ] }
47        > ] } { \ [ THOSE ] in < NEW > town } { \ [ ^ MOST ] of these < PEOple > } { \ they [ DON'T ] have
```

48   } { \ [THIS] is < _ desPIcable > } * { = [**MOST**] hong kong < **PEOple** > } { \ [ˆ ARE] < exCLUded

49   from uniVERsity word list < THAT > um } { = [< **MOST** >] er } { \ [< **PEOple** >] } { = [< _ ER >] }

50   ˆ TOUrists >] } } (.) * { ? [< AND >] } { \ [ˆ **MOST**] of the local < **PEOple** > } { = in [THESE] <

51   { = i [< ˆ THINK >] } { ? i think } { = [< ˆ **MOST** >] of the } { \ [< **PEOple** >] } { = [< WHO] }

Figure 6.11 Concordance lines for 'most people'

1   ngs you [< ˆ CAN'T >] } a: * { \ she's <u>just</u> [< **ONly** >] } A: ** { = you [< KNOW >] she's just like }

2   * { / [< ˆ NO >] } A: ((laugh)) a: { \ [<u>JUST</u>] only < ˆ WORking > } A: ((laugh)) { \ [< OH >] } { \

3   of the [< CHILD >] } { \ if they have [<u>JUST</u>] only < ONE > } * { = so [ˆ ALL] the time i am enCOUra

4   ST >] } { = only for [< ME >] } { \ i [<u>JUST</u>] only < ONE > } ((pause)) B: { you don't [HAVE] < TI

5   [< WE >] } { ? [< JUST >] } b1: { = [<u>JUST</u>] only < ONE > night } x: { = [< YES >] } b1: { = [<

6   ? but [ˆ SOMEtimes] < WHEN > you } { = [<u>JUST</u>] only eat the < SANDwich > } { = [< WHEN >] } { = [<

7   mm } { = [< BUT >] } (.) { = [< <u>JUST</u> >] } { = only for [< ME >] } { \ i [JUST] only < ONE > } ((p

8   { \ [THIS] < SYStem > } { = is not [< <u>JUST</u> >] only for } { \ [toDAY'S] < USE > } { \ [< oKAY >]

9   { \ [THIS] < SYStem > } { = is not [< <u>JUST</u> >] only for } { \ [toDAY'S] < USE > } { \ [< oKAY >] }

10   ERman > feel } { = [< BUT >] } { = [< <u>JUST</u> >] only on the } { \ [acCEPt] the BRIGHT < LIGHting > }

11   < ˆ SOMEtimes >] } a: { = cos i'm [< <u>JUST</u> >] only s } { = [< SEE >] her only } * { \ [ORder] the

12   \ [< FACtors >] } (.) { = [THERE] is < <u>JUST</u> > only } { = [< _ ER >] } { \ [< PENnington >] } b2:

13   [< LIKE >] } { = we [ACtually] SAID it's JUST only a < beGINning > } { / it's a [< LONG >] } { = [

14   < LIKE >] } { = we [ACtually] SAID it's JUST only a < beGINning > } { / it's a [< LONG >] } { = [

15   ** { ? so [< WE >] } b: { \ [WE] have JUST only about < STUdents > } { = [Okay] * NOW it's < TUR

Figure 6.12 Concordance lines for 'just only'

Conclusions

This chapter finds that the most common distribution of prominence is in a single prominence tone unit. Single prominences are more common in the Conversation sub-corpus, whereas multiple prominences are more frequent in the Academic and Public sub-corpora. One possible explanation for this difference is that since conversations are impromptu, this absence of planning results in shorter tone units and thus more single prominences. There is a slight but consistent tendency for the HKC to speak more single prominence tone units, and for the NES to speak more multiple prominence tone units. Words with double and triple prominences are more frequent in the Academic sub-corpus which fits Brazil's (1997) description of this phenomenon, occurring when word quotation takes place.

While the selection of prominence is neither pre-determined nor guaranteed, a number of patterns are describable. No doubt many more can be found. For example, the establishment of antonymous relationships can produce patterns of prominence distribution as can other local contexts, which make the selection of certain words "inevitable". While lexical words are more likely to attract prominence than non-lexical words, this is not always the case when speakers select to use non-lexical words in a cohesive chain. Importantly, this suggests that speakers do not randomly select lexical or non-lexical words in a lexical chain. Speakers may be guided in their choice between lexical and grammatical words, at least in part, by the decisions they make at the same time within the system of prominence in discourse intonation, and so the selection of a lexical or grammatical word might be driven by what a speaker perceives to be situationally informative at that point in the discourse. A speaker's selection of prominence and the selection of a lexical or a grammatical word are not determined by the word class, i.e. lexical or grammatical words, but by the speaker's decision to project what is more important or relevant in a particular context of interaction.

Another pattern is when two speakers select prominence differently, in the sense of choosing prominence on different syllables in the same lexical word, or a different word in a fixed combination of words. Examples have been found of a tendency for speakers to converge and adopt the same practice, although such convergence might be delayed, or withheld, when the speakers disagree in terms of the subject under discussion.

A pattern of prominence selection found among speakers of Singapore English is also found among HKC. The HKC are more likely than the NES to select prominence on personal pronouns, possessive pronouns and possessive determiners. It would be interesting to see whether this pattern is found elsewhere in the usage of the HKC in future studies.

Patterns are also based on word class and word frequency. "Grammatical" word classes are less likely to be spoken with prominence than the "lexical" word classes. There are also differences within these two main categories, but the main pattern for all word classes is that there seems to be a link between low relative frequency in the corpus and prominence.

Finally, while prominence patterns are discernible, it needs to be emphasised that speakers may, and indeed do, deviate from them in order to alter their discourse-specific communicative role and negotiate the discourse-specific meaning in naturally occurring speech.

CHAPTER 7

Tones

Introduction

In discourse intonation, a particular communicative value is associated with each of the five possible tones. A tone is the *pitch* movement which begins at the tonic syllable, i.e. the last prominent syllable in a tone unit. Any spoken discourse unfolds on the basis of a considerable amount of shared knowledge between discourse participants, and it is for the speaker to decide moment-by-moment whether what he/she is saying is shared or not. Speaker-hearer convergence is not something which a speaker can be certain of, and so speakers make their choices on the basis of what they assume the common ground to be at any particular point in the discourse.

Speakers, according to Brazil (1997: 67-81), basically have a choice between fall-rise/rise tones and fall/rise-fall tones. Brazil calls the former "referring" tones and the latter "proclaiming" tones. When a speaker chooses referring tones, he/she effectively indicates that this part of the discourse will not enlarge the common ground assumed to exist between the participants. The choice of proclaiming tones, on the other hand, shows that the area of speaker-hearer convergence is about to be enlarged. The main distinctions between these tones are given below:

- Fall-rise tone is a referring tone which indicates that this part of the discourse will not enlarge the common ground assumed to exist between the participants.
- Rise tone is a referring tone which reactivates something which is part of the common ground between the participants.
- Fall tone is a proclaiming tone which shows that the area of speaker-hearer convergence is being enlarged.
- Rise-fall tone is a proclaiming tone which indicates addition to the common ground and to the speaker's own knowledge at one and the same time.

There is a fifth tone which falls outside of the binary distinction of referring and proclaiming tones: the level tone. This tone is neither a referring nor a proclaiming tone, and is associated with tone units which precede an encoding pause or otherwise "truncated" tone units. It is also associated with contexts in which speakers are saying something that is part of a pre-coded, well-rehearsed and routine performance. It may also be used when speakers employ self-quotation.

The choice of tone, as with other linguistic options, rests with the speaker, and the decision to present information as shared or new is based on a subjective assessment and is also open to exploitation should the speaker choose to do so.

Distribution of tones across speakers and sub-corpora

Table 7.1 below shows the overall distribution of tones across HKC and NES both separately and combined.

When the combined frequencies and distribution of tones for both HKC and NES are studied across the HKCSE (prosodic), the level tone is the tone most frequently selected (46.67%), followed by fall tone (38.75%), rise tone (5.81%), fall-rise tone (3.17%) and rise-fall tone (0.015%), with 5.56% of the tone units unclassifiable. This overall distribution differs when the frequencies for the HKC and the NES are examined separately. The ranking is the same for the HKC, but with proportionately more level tones (49.31%) and fewer fall, rise and fall-rise tones (37.13%, 5.66% and 2.95% respectively) than the NES. The opposite, of course, is the case for the NES who have a different ranking. For the NES, the most frequent tone is the fall tone (43.98%), followed by the level, rise and fall-rise tones (38.15%, 5.81% and 3.17%, respectively). The HKC use the rise-fall tone proportionately slightly more often (0.016% versus 0.012%), but this tone is used so infrequently in the HKCSE (prosodic) that this finding has to be viewed with caution. Possible explanations for these differences are examined later in the chapter.

Cauldwell (2003b: 107) describes a different distribution for the tones in his data. His speakers use the fall tone (35%) and the level tone (34%) almost equally, followed by the rise tone (12%), fall-rise tone (12%), and rise-fall tone (1%). While this ranking is the same as the NES in the HKSCE (prosodic), the higher proportion of level tones and subsequent smaller proportionate use of all of the other tones differentiate Cauldwell's data from the HKCSE (prosodic) for the NES and even

Table 7.1 Overall distribution of tones for HKC and NES

	level	fall	rise	fall-rise	rise-fall	unclassified	TOTAL
HKC	118,013	88,851	13,548	7,065	40	11,765	239,282
	(49.31%)	(37.13%)	(5.66%)	(2.95%)	(0.016%)	(4.91%)	(100%)
NES	28,254	32,571	4,664	2,888	9	5,672	74,058
	(38.15%)	(43.98%)	(6.29%)	(3.89%)	(0.012%)	(7.65%)	(100%)
HKC and NES	146,267	121,422	18,212	9,953	49	17,437	313,340
	(46.67%)	(38.75%)	(5.81%)	(3.17%)	(0.015%)	(5.56%)	(100%)

more so for the HKC. The use of fall-rise tone is lower in both the HKCSE (prosodic) and Cauldwell's data, but it is proportionately lower in the former. These findings seem to differ from the work of Brazil and might be linked to the greater use of the level tone in the HKCSE (prosodic), which is an important finding and suggests that this tone plays a central role in discourse intonation. Possible reasons for the frequent use of the level tone by all speakers are discussed later in this chapter.

Table 7.2 shows the distribution of the five tones across the HKCSE (prosodic) and the four sub-corpora.

Comparison across the sub-corpora needs to make reference to the overall distribution of tone units across the HKCSE (prosodic), the four sub-corpora, and the sets of speakers discussed in Chapter 5. In the following description of the main findings relating to the use of tones, the distribution of the five tones is compared with the distributions of tone units in general (see Tables 5.1-5.3, Chapter 5).

In the case of the level tone, the proportional use is lower in the Conversation sub-corpus (20.43%) than in the other sub-corpora (26.66%). The academic sub-corpus has the largest proportional usage of the level tone (26.52% versus 23.59%). A possible explanation for these differences is the way in which longer "telling increments" (Brazil 1995: 45) are constructed in certain discourse types in real-time, and this is returned to later in this chapter.

In terms of the fall tone, both the Conversation sub-corpus (28.96% versus 26.66%) and the Business sub-corpus (27.47% versus 27.05%) use slightly more fall tones, and the Academic (22.29% versus 23.59%) and Public (21.27% versus 22.6%) sub-corpora slightly less. Again, while these differences are small, the finding might be due to the existence of some longer and more complex telling increments in the Academic and Public sub-corpora, and this will be explored later in this chapter.

Table 7.2 Distribution of tones across sub-corpora

Sub-corpora	level	fall	rise	fall-rise	rise-fall
Academic sub-corpus	39,933 (26.52%)	28,037 (22.29%)	3,732 (19.91%)	2,705 (26.72%)	7 (13.20%)
Business sub-corpus	42,307 (28.10%)	34,554 (27.47%)	5,060 (26.99%)	2,282 (22.54%)	3 (5.66%)
Conversation Sub-corpus	30,760 (20.43%)	36,423 (28.96%)	6,487 (34.61%)	2,770 (27.36%)	41 (77.35%)
Public sub-corpus	37,556 (24.94%)	26755 (21.27%)	3,463 (18.47%)	2,366 (23.37%)	2 (3.77%)
Total	150,556 (100%)	125,769 (100%)	18,742 (100%)	10,123 (100%)	53 (100%)

The Conversation sub-corpus (34.61% versus 26.66%) makes proportionately more use of the rise tone than the other three sub-corpora, although the Business sub-corpus (26.99% versus 27.05%) is only very slightly lower, whereas the Academic sub-corpus (19.91% versus 23.59%) and the Public sub-corpus (18.49% versus 22.6%) are down more. This higher use of the rise tone in the Conversation sub-corpus could be a result of the use of the rise tone to exert speaker dominance and control which is available to all speakers in conversation due to their relative equality in terms of speaker rights, compared to discourses in the sub-corpora where there is a designated dominant speaker, or more. Also, the Academic and Public sub-corpora have a higher incidence of monologic discourses where this function is less relevant. These differences are returned to later in this chapter.

The fall-rise tone is used proportionately more often in the Academic (26.72% versus 23.59%), Conversation (27.36% versus 26.66%) and Public (23.37% versus 22.6%) sub-corpora, but less often in the Business sub-corpus (22.54% versus 27.05%). As mentioned earlier, the occurrence of the fall-rise tone is less frequent than one might expect from the work of Brazil (1985 and 1997), and this might be due to the higher proportional occurrence of the level tone across all speakers and sub-corpora. This in turn might be the result of studying naturally-occurring data which have a higher number of instances of encoding presenting some form of difficulty for the speakers.

The number of instances of the rise-fall tone is very small (53), and so this needs to be borne in mind when looking at the spread of this tone across the sub-corpora. There is a much higher proportional usage of this tone in the Conversation sub-corpus (77.3% versus 26.66%) than in the other three sub-corpora: Academic (13.20% versus 23.59%), Business (5.66% versus 27.05%) and Public (3.77% versus 22.6%). This difference may be related to the more interactive nature of conversations in which speakers of perceived equal status are more likely to speak out if something unexpected happens or if they suddenly think of something to say.

When the proportional usage of the tones is examined across the two main sets of speakers, HKC and NES, and across genders, there are some interesting findings. The level tone is used proportionately more often by the HKC (78.38% versus 73.92%) than the NES (18.77% versus 22.88%) across the HKCSE (prosodic). This is also the case for each of the sub-corpora, although the difference is very small for the Public sub-corpus. This pattern is also found across the males and females across all of the sub-corpora. The pattern of distribution for the level tone is reversed for the fall tone with the HKC (70.65% versus 73.92%) using this tone proportionately less than the NES (25.90% versus 22.88%). Again, the difference is very small in the case of the Public sub-corpus. No gender differences are found for these patterns of usage. The rise tone is used proportionately more often by the NES (24.89% versus 22.88%) than the HKC (72.29% versus 73.92%) across the HKCSE (prosodic). However, this pattern is only found in the Academic sub-corpus where the difference is large. In the other three sub-corpora the pattern is reversed. Again, these patterns are found irrespective of gender. The use of the fall-rise tone across the HKCSE (prosodic) is also higher for the NES (28.53% versus 22.88%) than the HKC (69.79% versus 73.92%). However, this pattern is not uniform across the sub-corpora. The pattern is found in the Academic and Conversation sub-corpora where the differences are quite large, but it is reversed in the Business and Public sub-corpora. The number of instances of the last tone, rise-fall, is so small that the findings need to be read with caution. The HKC (75.47% versus 73.92%) use the level tone proportionately more often than the NES (16.98% versus 22.88%) across the whole HKCSE (prosodic). This pattern holds for the Conversation and Public sub-corpora, but the opposite is the case for the other sub-corpora. These patterns hold across the gender divide except in the Business sub-corpus, where the HKC females use the rise-fall tone more than any other speaker set. However, again, the number of instances makes generalisations difficult for this tone.

Patterns of tone use

In the following sections, some of the patterns of tone choice present in the HKCSE (prosodic) are identified and discussed.

Proclaiming and referring tones

One central pattern of tone usage described by Brazil (1997: 67-81) is the speaker's choice between rising and falling tones. This choice is based on the speaker's perception as to whether or not the common ground assumed to exist between the participants is enlarged by what is said. This usage is well-known and central to discourse intonation and can be found across all of the data.

Example 7.1 is extracted from a conversation between two friends. Speaker a is describing a recent open day at the hospital where she works and the role of a particular doctor in the preparations for this event.

Example 7.1

1   a: ... { = [< AND >] } { = [< DOCtor >] } { / [< C__ >] }
2   { \ want to [< SHOWS >] } { = all [< OUR >] } { \
3   [EXcellence] to the < PEOple > } * { / so [SHE] <

4 A: ** { \ [< YEAH >] }

5 a: prePARE > eVErything } { = [< SET >] the } {= [< THEatre

6 A: { \ [< YEAH >] }

7   >] in the } (.) { \ [MOST] Elegant < LOOK > }

8 A: { \ [< YES >] }

9 a: { / and she [WANT] to show < OFF > } { \ the [< comPUter

10   >] }

11 A: { \ [< RIGHT >] }

Example 7.1 shows a speaker making moment-by-moment decisions in terms of
what she perceives as shared information between herself and the hearer and
what she perceives to be new. The speakers have been discussing Doctor C__.
After two truncated tone units with level tone (line 1), speaker a selects rise tone
when she says the doctor's name (line 1), which signals the reactivation of shared
knowledge. She then chooses fall tone (line 3) when she says that Doctor C__
wanted to show people how excellent the unit is, because she perceives this to be
new information for the hearer. In the next tone unit (lines 3 and 5), she employs
a rise tone when she says 'so she prepare everything', as she perceives this to be
the reactivation of shared information. In other words, it is a known requirement to prepare everything ahead of showcasing it. After two tone units with
level tone (lines 5 and 7), she then uses fall tone on 'most elegant look' (line 7),
as this is perceived as new information that this was the method used to arrange
the theatre. She then continues by saying 'and she wanted to show off' (line 9),
using a rise tone as this is now the reactivation of shared information that was
said with a fall tone earlier, but the last part of her utterance, concerning what
was to be shown off, 'the computer' (lines 9-10) is perceived as new information
and is said with fall tone.

In Example 7.2, speaker A is telling her friend about being busy the previous week.

Example 7.2

1 A: { \ well i had a [< ^ VEry >] busy week } { / [< LAST >] week }

2   * { = [< beCAUSE >] } { \/ i was doing [^ LOTS] of < TEAching > }

Speaker A begins with fall tone on 'well I had a very busy week' (line 1), and so she
perceives this to be new information to the hearer. She then selects rise tone when
she says 'last week' (line 1), as she considers this to be the reactivation of shared
knowledge. In other words, when someone says 'I had a very busy week', the hearer
will infer that the speaker means 'last week'. After employing level tone for a part
of the utterance, 'because' (line 2), she chooses fall-rise tone which signals that the

fact she teaches is shared knowledge between the two friends. But 'lots' (line 2), said with contrastive high key, is not the norm, and hence the reason for high key on 'very' (line 1).

These examples demonstrate the patterning to be found as speakers make real-time decisions with regard to their perceptions of shared knowledge. However, the relatively low occurrence of the two rise tones (rise and fall-rise) in the HKCSE (prosodic) suggests that the choice between referring (rising tones) and proclaiming (falling tones) is not always as strongly represented in the data as these two examples suggest. The two tones that dominate the HKCSE (prosodic) are the level and fall tones for all speakers, although the ranking shifts as to which is the more prevalent of the two tones between the HKC and NES. Therefore, it is the choice between the level tone and the fall tone which predominates in the HKCSE (prosodic) in terms of frequency of occurrence. The ways in which this interplay is manifested are examined in the next section.

Level tone

The use of the level tone merits particular attention because it is the most prevalent of the five tones in the HKCSE (prosodic). This frequency pattern holds for the HKC, while for the NES, it is the second most commonly selected tone after the fall tone. Given its prevalence, the main usages of the level tone are analysed to better understand why the level tone is so frequently selected by speakers in the HKCSE (prosodic). Brazil himself provides one possible reason for the frequent use of level tone when he predicts that the occurrence of level tone due to encoding problems would be much higher in naturally-occurring data because "the more a speaker is 'thinking on his/her feet' the more common they are" (ibid: 140).

Functions of the level tone

The other four tones in discourse intonation are oriented towards the "interactive" nature of the speech (Brazil 1995: 244), meaning that "speakers have in mind the impact of what they say upon particular hearers at particular times in particular verbal communicative events" (ibid: 244). The level tone is used when the speaker is not being sensitive, in a moment-by-moment way, to "the details of a hearer's perspective" (ibid: 244). Rather the speaker is sensitive to the "non-interactive business of assembling the linguistic resources" (ibid.: 244) to plan the next part of the discourse.

Brazil (1997) provides a detailed description of two main contexts that favour a set towards the linguistic organization of the utterance, rather than towards the hearer. It is under these contexts that the level tone is used. The first context is met when a speaker chooses an "oblique presentation" (ibid: 133), or when a speaker is saying something, on paper or in the speaker's memory, that is either pre-coded or partially coded information (ibid: 136-139). The second context is when encoding has not yet been achieved or when encoding presents some form of difficulty for the speaker (ibid: 139). These two contexts are described and exemplified below.

Context 1

A speakers' choice of the level tone denotes the tone unit "as part of oblique orientation" (Brazil 1997: 134). By "oblique orientation", Brazil means that the speaker is effectively "reading out" (ibid.: 134) the words that he/she is speaking and does not commit himself/herself to interpreting them, as he/she would normally do by selecting either referring or proclaiming tones. As a result, the speaker treats the words as an entity rather than as being of communicative significance (ibid.: 133). Brazil distinguishes between "reading out" and "reading aloud". In the case of reading aloud, the speaker makes contextual projections in the same way as in most other spoken discourse contexts. In other words, the speaker still makes a distinction between referring tones (the rise and the fall-rise) and proclaiming tones (the fall and the rise-fall). In this study, examples similar to those termed "reading out" by Brazil are also found when speakers draw the hearer's attention to a particular word or phrase in, for example, educational settings. For this reason, both are grouped together and termed "oblique presentation".

Apart from situations where a speaker is doing an oblique orientation, such as "reading out", there are also times when speakers impart to hearers pre-coded or partially coded information, and this is often done by means of the level tone. Examples include such rituals as parade-ground command; public recitation of prayers and other liturgical material; classroom interaction as semi-ritualised practice, with a string of directives being a recurrent feature of a large number of lessons; classroom teaching when the teacher presents information as "immutable knowledge" (ibid.: 138); and last, classroom teaching when the teacher uses a kind of "template' technique" (ibid: 138) for eliciting contributions from students, particularly used in language lessons when most of the material is introduced as samples of the context-free target language.

An example of oblique orientation is given below (Example 7.3) taken from a university seminar in which the lecturer highlights new terminology for the benefit of the students.

Example 7.3

  1 b: { \ [< _ YES >] } { = so [< CALLED >] } { = [FORward] <

  2   DIFference > } { = [BACKward] < DIFference > }

A student has been describing a technical process in the field of building services engineering and uses terminology that the lecturer perceives as being unknown to other students in the class, and so the lecturer repeats the terms 'forward difference' and 'backward difference'. The lecturer highlights the language as an entity with the expression 'so called'. The three tone units in which he highlights the terminology are all said with the level tone. Also, all the words being highlighted are all said with prominence when one might have expected the second 'difference" in line 2 to not have prominence. It might be that this additional prominence is also a feature of oblique orientation.

In Example 7.4, three friends are engaged in a conversation and the topic turns to a well-known furniture store in Hong Kong, but they struggle to recall its name.

Example 7.4

  1 a1: { = [< ER >] } { = [< ^ WHAT'S >] that called } (.) { = [< BAMboo

  2   >] } (.) { = [< TREE >] or } (.) * { ? [baNAna] < TREE > or }

  3 B: ** { \ [< SOMEthing >] } * { =

  4 a2:   ** { ? [< WHE

  5 B: [BANyang] < TREE > }

  6   >] }

  6 a1: { = [< BANyang >] tree yeah } * { = [< BANyang >] tree } { \ [<

  7 a2:   ** { ? where ((inaudible)) }

  8   WHERE'S >] it } { \ [< OH >] } { \ where's it [< _ NOW >] }

In Example 7.4, the topic digresses briefly and the focus shifts to the name of the shop as a linguistic entity. As the speakers offer suggestions for the name, the level tone is used and, when speaker B remembers the name, 'Banyang Tree' (line 5), speaker a then repeats the name twice in line 6, again with level tone. The repetitions in line 6 might be instances of the speaker perceiving the name of the shop as a linguistic entity rather than as shared or unshared common ground when she confirms that her friend has been able to recall the correct name of the shop.

Examples 7.5-7.8 are all the closing sequences of service encounters and serve to illustrate the selection of level tone when saying routine and partly or fully pre-coded utterances. The advantage of using extracts of service encounters is that these kinds of discourse can be widely recognised and accepted as routine, and hence pre-coded at certain points, because we have all experienced such discourses many times. In all of these examples of service encounter closing sequences, both the HKC service providers and the NES customers use level tones throughout.

Example 7.5

   1 b: { = [< BYE >] bye }

   2 B: { = [< BYE >] bye }

Example 7.6

   1 b: { \ would you [MIND] coming over this < WAY > } { ? [< SIR >] }

   2 B: { = [< oKAY >] } { = thank [< YOU >]

   3 B: { = [< oKAY >] } { = [< BYE >] bye }

   4 a: { = [< BYE >] bye }

Example 7.7

   1 b: { = have a [< ^ NICE >] trip }

   2 B: { = [< THANKS >] }

   3 b: { = [< BYE >] }

Example 7.8

   1 A: { \ thank you very [< MUCH >] }

   2 a1: { = my [< PLEAsure >] }

   3 A: { = [< THANK >] you }

   4 a1: { = [< Okay >] }

In the following set of examples, Examples 7.9-7.11, again service encounters are the site for more instances of routine pre-coded utterances.

Example 7.9

   1 b: { = [< MAY >] i have } { = [^ ONE] hundred for the airport < TAX >

   2   please }

   3   ((pause))

Example 7.10

   1 b2: { = [GOOD] afternoon < ^ SIR > }

   2 B2: { \ just one [< QUEStion >] } { = where [CAN] i buy < ^ STAMPS > }

   3 b2: { ? oh [< HERE >] }

Example 7.11

  1 b1: { = you [preFER] the room with no < ^ SMOking > }
  2 B1: { \ [< YEAH >] } { \ [NO] < SMOking > }

In each of the above examples, it is the HKC service provider who says the routine pre-coded utterance. In Example 7.9, an airline employee manning the check-in asks for the airport tax using level tone, and this is something that is asked of every passenger checking-in. In Example 7.10 a receptionist at a five-star hotel says the obligatory salutation to the guest with level tone. It is interesting to note that, as is quite often the case in such service encounters, the guest does not return this greeting which would be marked behaviour in other contexts. The guest then asks the receptionist a non-routine question also with level tone, 'where can I buy stamps', but, having prefaced the question with 'just one question', the need for a hearer-sensitive tone choice would seem to be redundant. In Example 7.11, a hotel receptionist asks with level tone another very routine question with regard to the guest's preferred room type.

Context 2

The second context for oblique orientation also has two forms: when encoding has not yet been achieved and when encoding presents some form of difficulty for the speaker. In order to understand the first form of oblique orientation, it is necessary to understand the basic principle underlying Brazil's (1995) description of the grammar of speech. According to Brazil, spoken language serves real world communicative needs and is basically made up of "telling and asking exchanges" (ibid.: 41-46). When engaged in either of these exchanges, the speaker has in mind a target state which requires one or more "telling or asking increments" (ibid.: 38-39) to be realised, with the latter requiring a response to achieve its target state. Brazil reminds us of Halliday's (1989) key point that discourse is both a process and a product, and he notes that speakers may have to speak a sequence of "elements" (Brazil 1997: 40) before completing an increment on their way to reaching the target state. A target state is a point of possible completion in terms of information, although Brazil acknowledges that it not possible to state an exact point at which "a speaker's purpose of telling will be achieved" (ibid.: 42) in the real-time construction of utterances. When a speaker has not yet arrived at the target state by means of either a telling increment, or the initiation of an asking increment, or the response in an asking increment, the speaker may elect to temporarily disengage from hearer-sensitive "direct" discourse to "oblique" discourse (Brazil 1995: 244). This disengagement then enables the speaker to change focus to "the non-interactive business of assembling the linguistic resources that the next step will need" (ibid.: 244). An analogy might be that of someone using stepping stones to cross a river where the river bank on the far side is the end of a telling increment, and the stones represent the elements that have to be said on the way to achieving the telling increment of crossing the river.

The same phenomenon is described in linear unit grammar (Sinclair and Mauranen 2006), which is based on Brazil's notion of the incremental co-construction of spoken language. Indeed, as discussed in Chapter 5, Sinclair and Mauranen (2006) ignore speaker boundaries in their analyses, and this is in line with Brazil's description of the achievement of the target state in "asking", in which the response is needed to achieve the target state. This also applies to other phenomena, such as utterance completion, commonly found in many spoken discourse types in which speaker boundaries are crossed in the achievement of a target state. In their description, Sinclair and Mauranen (2006) have a number of different elements that might occupy this role for what Brazil terms "elements" in a sequence leading to an increment. Certain organising elements such as 'and then' (OT) or 'I think' (OI), and "message element fragments" which prospect continuance (i.e. M- and MA), might be found occupying the middle ground leading to the target state.

In the HKCSE (prosodic), the use of the level tone outlined above has been found to be the most commonplace in the data. Examples of this use of the level tone are described below. They are grouped together irrespective of whether or not they are organising elements or message fragment elements, and are termed "incremental elements". In example 7.12, the speaker is a well-known former Hong Kong Government official giving a speech at a formal luncheon. She reflects on the options available to her when making a speech of this kind. All of the tone units with level tone are underlined in the transcript.

Example 7.12

1   a: { = [< BUT >] } { = [^ HOW] to enCOMpass all < THIS > } { \/ in the

2   [SHORT] time we < HAVE > } { = [< AFter >] this } { \ [SPLENdid]

3   < LUNCH > } { = a [< SPEECH >] } { = [PACKED] with <

4   REminiscences > } { = a [SHOPping] < LIST > } { = [< PACkaging >] }

5   { = our [< PROgress >] } { = over the [< LAST >] } { = [< FORty

6   >] years } { = a [< ^ KISS >] } { \ and [< TELL >] speech } { = [<

7   reVEAling >] } { = some [< REAL >] } { = or [iMAgined] secrets or <

8   SCANdals > } { \ from the [< PAST >] } { = [< WELL >] } { \ i'm

9   [VEry] < SORry > } { = that's [< NOT >] } { \ my [< _ STYLE >] }

10   { = so [I] have < deCIded > to do } { \ what i [Usually] < DO > } { =

11   and [< THAT >] is } { \ to [SPEAK] < FRANKly > } { = on a [< ^

12   NUMber >] of issues } { = [< aBOUT >] which } { \ i feel [< _

13   STRONGly >] }

In Example 7.12, the use of level tone for tone units which are incremental elements is consistent with the real-time construction of each of her telling increments. These incremental elements may only be one incremental element, for example, 'after this' (line 2), but they can also be quite numerous. For example, there
are nine incremental elements in lines 3-6, and all are spoken with level tone, except for the one in lines 1-2 which is said with fall-rise tone.

In Example 7.13, the speaker is announcing the annual results for one of the
utility companies in Hong Kong.

Example 7.13

1   b: { = let's [NOW] TURN to the < HONG > kong } { \ [elecTRIcity] < _

2   BUSIness > } { = the [TOtal] units < SALES > } { = for the < FIRST >

3   six months } { = of < THIS > year } { = < inCREASED > } { = < BY > }

4   { = three point < SIX > percent } { \ [comPARE] to the SAME period <

5   LAST > year } { = [THIS] was < enCOUraging > } { = given the

6   [STATE] of < eCOnomy > } { \ we are < IN > } { = the < TOtal > units }

7   { = < SALES > } { = < exCLUding > } { = [manuFACturing] < SECtor

8   > } { = were < UP > } { \ [FIVE] point one < perCENT > }

The speaker selects the level tone when he says the incremental elements that are
needed to complete each of his telling increments. Each telling increment can be
seen to represent the speaker's perception of a discrete chunk of information which
contributes to the realization of the target state.

Example 7.14 is an extract from a televised panel discussion in which the host,
speaker b1, questions a government official about the procedures for presenting
legislation for discussion.

Example 7.14

1   b1:   ... { = are you [TALking] about a < WHITE > bill }

2   B: { = i'm [TALking] about DRAFT legislation < WHICH > is } { = [<

3   DRAFted >] in the form } { \ that we're [< USED > to] }

4   b1:   { = [< ER >] } { \ [THAT] will be preSENted to < LEGco > }

5   B: { = i [THINK] the CURrent < THINking > is } { = the [< BILL >] } { \

6   will be [preSENted] to < LEGco > } { \ that's [< _ corRECT >] }

In Example 7.14, there are two asking increments: in lines 1-3 and lines 4-6. Brazil (1995: 41) states that an asking increment is only complete when the speaker doing the asking gets a response from the hearer (the speaker may or may not then acknowledge the response). As with telling increments, an asking increment typically contains one proclaiming tone. In lines 1-3, speaker b1 asks a question choosing the level tone, and speaker B's response consists of three tone units. The first two are incremental elements with the level tone, and this asking increment is completed with a fall tone in the last tone unit (line 3). In the second asking increment beginning in line 4, speaker b1 begins with a verbal filler said in a tone unit with level tone, followed by a question with fall tone. Speaker B's response comprises four tone units. The first two are incremental elements and have level tones and the third is said with the fall tone. At this point the speaker might have completed this particular asking increment, but he adds an emphatic 'that's correct' also spoken with the fall tone. They also illustrate Brazil's key point that all increments contain the "telling" ingredient (Brazil 1997: 41).

The next example, Example 7.15, is from the Q&A session at the end of a formal public speech.

Example 7.15

1   B: ... { \/ [WHAT] i WANted to < ^ ASK > you though } { = < WAS > }

2   { = < HOW > } { \ [HONG] < ^ KONG > could help } { = < ER > } { =

3   in the < DRIVE > for } { = < susTAInaBIlity > } { = < WITH > the } { =

4   [BUILding] < conTRACtors > } { = < AND > } { \ < ^ deVElopers > }

5   { = < ERM > with } { = [Everything] that is < HAPpening > } { \ in

6   hong < ^ KONG > } { = can < THAT > then } { = < BE > } { = < SET >

7   into } { \ < CHIna > } { \ and can [HONG] kong HELP < LEverage > }

8   { \ [sustainaBIlity] through < THAT > route }

9   a: { \ i [^ CERtainly] THINK that < HONG > kong } { \ has a [VEry]

10   imPORtant ROLE to PLAY < _ HERE > }...

In line 1, speaker B begins the introduction to his question with fall-rise on 'what I wanted to ask you though' which acknowledges that he has said quite a lot in the build-up to his question, and so he has not yet fulfilled his role in the discourse; that is, to ask a question. He then needs a number of incremental elements as he pieces together two questions, and most of the tone units are said with the level tone (see underlined tone units).

Across all of the above examples, it is typical in the telling increments that the speaker ends with a fall tone when the increment is completed. Indeed, Brazil (1995: 250) states that both telling and asking increments require a proclaiming tone (i.e. fall or rise-fall) to be complete. This is certainly the pattern that is found to be predominant in the HKCSE (prosodic). However, in routinised contexts (see examples 7.5-7.8) in which pre-coded language is frequently employed, it is possible to find increments which only contain tone units said with the level tone, suggesting that a proclaiming tone is not an absolute requirement.

The second context for oblique orientation, resulting in the occurrence of the level tone, also includes instances when the speaker encounters what Brazil (1997: 139-140) terms "momentary problems in coding". These problems have an impact on verbal planning and message organization, and are the inevitable product of spontaneous speech when the speaker is thinking on his or her feet. When encoding has not yet been achieved and is presenting some difficulty for the speaker, the speaker may shift to focusing on the linguistic properties of the utterance itself, usually a tendency for hesitation markers, pauses and pause fillers to follow instances of level tone (ibid.: 139). In this context, there are usually "single tone units interpolated into direct discourse" (ibid.: 140).

The first example of encoding problems, Example 7.16, is taken from a point in a conversation between two friends where one of the speakers has difficulty articulating her feelings towards a group of her work colleagues.

Example 7.16

```
1   a:    ... { = < I > } { = i < HAVE > er } { = < ER > } { = < I > } { = < I >
2         mean you know } { = < I > } { = < I > } { = < I > } { = i REALly [ LIKE ]
3         you know the < MEdical > } { \ < PEOple > } * { = < AND > er } { = <
4   B1:                                          ** { \ < _ YEAH > }
5         THEY > } { = < THEY > } { = < THEY > } { = < REALly > do } { \ their
6         < WORK > }
```

In Example 7.16, speaker a employs both the filler 'er' (lines 1 and 3) and repetition (lines 1-2 and 4) of subject pronouns to handle her encoding problems and hold onto her turn.

Example 7.17 is an extract of a postgraduate research student's presentation of his research in a departmental seminar at a point where he experiences difficulties expressing his ideas.

Example 7.17

1 b1: ...{ = in [< MAny >] difference } { = [< WAYS >] } { = and [< SUCH
2   >] er } { = for [<INstance >] } { = [< I >] } { = [< IF >] the } { = [<
3   IF >] the } { = [< IF >] } { = [< IF >] the } { = [< ER >] } { = [< IF
4   >] the } { = if [< THE >] } { = [< ER >] } { = chilled [WAter]
5   distribution SYStem < OF > the } { = [< OF >] the } { = [< ER >] } { =
6   hong kong [< C >] c ex } { = [exTENsion] is too < LARGE > } { = [I]
7   can break it < DOWN > } { = and [< RUN >] the indi } { = [<
8   indiVIdual >] } { = [< ERM >] } { = [BRANches] < FIRST > } { =
9   [AND] then < comBINE > it } { = [< toGEther >] } { = [< TO >] } { \
10   [FIND] out the Operational < PROblems > } ...

The speaker uses the fillers 'er' (lines 2-5), 'erm' (line 8) and repetition (lines 2-4 and 5). The pattern for repetition is to repeat the first part of the noun phrase, 'if the' (lines 2-4) and 'of the' (lines 4-5), which, like a filler, serves to signal that more is on the way. After 27 tone units said with the level tone, some of which are incremental elements, some of which represent purely encoding problems, and yet others a mixture of the two, he gets to the end of this telling increment and chooses a fall tone in the last tone unit in lines 9-10.

   Examples of the use of the level tone for Context 2 have presented the two forms of (i.e. incremental elements and encoding problems) as if a speaker is simply engaged in one of the two forms. In reality, of course, speakers typically use the level tone to handle what is very often a mixture of both incremental elements and encoding problems. In Example 7.18, a senior Hong Kong Government official is at a public forum and is being pressured by a group of journalists to respond to their questions.

Example 7.18

1 b: { = [I'LL] be < ANswering > } { = [< _ UM >] } { = [<
2   QUEStions >] } { = [< IN >] } { = [< WHEN >] we we } { =
3   when [< ^ I >] } { = and [Other] government < ofFIcials > } { =
4   and [< PRINcipal >] officials } { \ [MEET] the < MEdia > }

Example 7.18 contains nine tone units, the first eight of which are said with the level tone. These eight level tones are a mixture of tone units. Some of them are incremental elements while others are the products of encoding problems. The five incremental elements are underlined in the transcript, and the three tone units containing instances of encoding problems are in bold font. When the flustered government official finally ends this telling increment, he does so with a fall tone (line 4).

Frequencies of use of the level tone for Contexts 1 and 2

A random sample of 1,000 tone units (i.e. 500 instances for each group, HKC and NES), in which the speakers have chosen the level tone, was examined to determine the spread of the use of the level tone across the two contexts described above. Determining the functions of the level tones was not an unproblematic process, and it was finalised by means of an "inter-rater" comparison within the research team. Table 7.3 below contains the results of this analysis.

Table 7.3 Distribution of level tones for Contexts 1 and 2

Contexts	HKC	NES	Total
Context 1a: Oblique presentation (reading out)	9 (1.8%)	14 (2.8%)	23 (2.3%)
Context 1b: Pre-coded/partially coded information	46 (9.2%)	73 (14.6%)	119 (11.9%)
Context 2a: Incremental element	309 (61.8%)	299 (59.8%)	608 (60.8%)
Context 2b: Encoding difficulty	136 (27.2%)	114 (22.8%)	250 (25.0%)
Total	500 (100%)	500 (100%)	1,000 (100%)

Table 7.3 shows that in this sample of 1,000 level tones, when all speakers are considered, incremental elements (Context 2a) account for 60.8% of the level tones used. The next most common usage is when speakers encounter problems encoding (25.0%) followed by the use of the level tone when giving pre-coded or partially encoded information (11.9%). The use of the level tone for the purposes of oblique presentation accounts for only 2.3% of all instances.

When the two sets of speakers are compared, they both use the level tone most frequently when speaking incremental elements with similar levels of proportional usage (HKC 61.8% and NES 59.8%), and the rankings for the other uses of the level tone are the same, but the proportional usage differs. The HKC use the level tone more for encoding problems (27.2% versus 22.8%) and the NES make more use of Context 1b (14.6% versus 9.2%) and Context 1a (2.8% versus 1.8%), but this difference should not be over-emphasised, given the small proportion of occurrences for both sets of speakers. It should be remembered that when there are encoding problems, the use of the level tone is not a deliberate choice by the speaker but rather a consequence of the encoding problem.

To summarise, the HKC are more likely to encounter momentary encoding problems than the NES, and we can also see that the HKC are less likely to perceive "chunks" of information as pre-coded or partially coded, and so they make proportionately less use of the level tone in such local contexts, compared to the NES. Both of these findings possibly reflect the consequences of the HKC operating in a second language, even though the HKC do so very effectively and experience no difficulty in communicating with the other participants. It is important to restate that both sets of speakers make quite frequent use of the level tone due to local encoding problems.

Disambiguation and tones

Chapter 5 examines how a speaker's choice of tone unit boundaries could help to disambiguate meaning, and shows that a speaker's choice of tone could also play a role. Here this claim is examined. According to Crystal (1969), there are patterns of tone choice associated with points of potential ambiguity. The term "potential ambiguity" is used here because in the local context of interaction, speakers and hearers have a number of strategies to avoid ambiguity, one of which is tone choice, and ambiguity is rarely found in reality. In Crystal's (1969: 263-73) example, 'would you like gin or whisky or tea?', he states that each alternative is normally uttered in a separate tone unit and that the final item in the list is said with rise tone if the extent of the list is unspecified, and with fall tone if the alternatives represent the limit available. Two examples from the HKCSE (prosodic) are given below to illustrate the role of intonation in such potentially ambiguous contexts, and which confirm Crystal's claim.

In Example 7.19, the speaker offers to buy lunch and lists the alternatives.

Example 7.19

```
1   b:   { \ it's [ RAIning ] < outSIDE > } { \ i'll [ BUY ] you < LUNCH > } { \
2        [ WHAT ] would you < LIKE > } { = [ < HOTdog > ] } { \ or [ <
3        HAMBURger > ] }
```

The speaker limits the list of options for lunch to just 'hotdog' and 'hamburger', by choosing fall tone on 'hamburger', and so the use of alternative 'or' in this context is to offer the hearer only these two alternatives.

In the second example, 7.20, two friends are discussing whether speaker a had held other career ambitions when she was younger. Speaker B lists some alternative career options.

Example 7.20

1 B: ... { \ [< ^ OH >] } { = [< LIKE >] } { = [< LIKE >] } { \/ like a [<

2   SCRIPT >] writer } * { = [OR] < OR > }

3 a: ** { \ [< YEAH >] }

4 B: { = [< OR >] } { \ [< YEAH >] } { / or a [< JOURnalist >] } { / or an

5   [Editor] or < SOMEthing > like that }

6 a: { \ [< YEAH >] } * { \ [< YEAH >] } { \ [< YEAH >] }

7 B: ** { \ [< YEAH >] } { \ [< YEAH >] }

The full enumeration of the list provided by speaker B in lines 1-2 and 4-5 is unspecified by the speaker choosing the rise tone in the last tone unit. The unspecified nature of the list is further confirmed by the speaker ending with 'or something like that' (line 5).

In the HKCSE (prosodic), there is an additional pattern of tone choice in such
contexts that are not described by Crystal (1969). A number of the alternative
questions in the data are from service encounters and job interviews, in which the
service providers and interviewers sometimes ask routine, pre-coded and highly
practised alternative questions. As Brazil (1997: 36 and 136) predicts, the speakers
frequently choose the level tone when asking these questions. Some typical examples of these kinds of questions are given below.

Example 7.21 i-iv

i) a: { = [YOU] like to pay by < CREdit > card } { = or by [< CASH >] }

ii) b: { = you pay [< CASH >] or } { = [< CREdit >] card }

iii) a: { = [SO] you preFER a < WINdow > seat } { = or [< ^ AISLE >] seat }

iv) B: { = do you have [< ^ Any >] } (.) { \/ [< PROblem >] } { = or [<
        QUEStion >] }

The speakers in Examples 7.21 i-iv all choose level tone rather than rise or fall tone
when saying the final item in their lists in these oft-repeated questions involving
the use of alternative 'or'. It can be assumed that this choice presents no problems
for the hearer, assuming that the hearer is equally familiar with the context of interaction. The hearers will understand these to be clearly delimited in the context
and not exemplars from a longer list of alternatives. This pattern of use for the level
tone is another means of communicating to the hearer that the enumerated items
are specified rather than unspecified.

Question intonation

A use of intonation that even those not trained in matters of intonation often refer to is that there is a highly predictable intonation for questions when it comes to tone choice. This received wisdom of the existence of "question intonation", especially the use of rise tone on declarative mood questions and yes/no questions, is challenged in discourse intonation. Brazil (1995: 193) asks whether there is such a thing as question intonation, which he acknowledges is a widely held belief. Many textbooks, for example, still contain the mantra that the rise tone is used for yes/no questions, a category which includes declarative mood questions, and fall tone is used for *wh*-questions. Brazil (1995: 193-197) argues that there is no fixed question intonation and states that it is the local context of interaction that determines a speaker's choice of tone, and not the form of the question, which in turn is based on the broad distinction between two basic questioning functions: "finding out" and "making sure" (ibid.: 193).

Declarative-mood questions

The case that the choice of tone is not a fixed property in questions is examined by looking more closely at speakers' tone choice in declarative mood questions. This question form is highlighted because it is often argued that this question type, which is in effect an indirect speech act, is only identified as such by the hearer thanks to the speaker's choice of intonation, often portrayed as rise tone in textbooks and the literature (e.g. Quirk et al. 1985, Givón 1993, Halliday and Matthiessen 2004). In this study, declarative mood questions are identified with reference to the unfolding discourse. In other words, a question is classified in relation to the presence of a response by the hearer, or other evidence that the speaker is asking a question.

According to Brazil (1997: 100-101), the significance of tone choice for declarative-mood questions needs to be examined against a background of non-intonational facts, namely the state of understanding existing between speaker and hearer. Generally speaking, if the fall tone is used, the speaker is more likely to be asking the hearer to respond to the tentative assertion that he/she makes, and hence the "declarative-mood" question has an interrogative function of "I don't know whether you do or not – please tell me" (ibid.: 106). If the rise tone is used, the speaker is "projecting a context of interaction in which the context of the referring tone unit is common ground" (ibid.: 160), and if the fall-rise tone is used, the speaker is heard as offering "a tentative assessment of common ground and asking the hearer to concur with, or adjudicate with respect to, its validity" (ibid.: 160).

The usage described above can be illustrated by looking at an example from the HKCSE (prosodic). In Example 7.22 below, two friends are comparing the availability, quality, and price of local and imported lettuce. Speaker B has said that he likes to buy local lettuce, with the extract beginning with speaker b asking his colleague if he purchased the lettuce from a specific food retailer, 'Seibu', which is a Japanese-owned department store based in Hong Kong.

Example 7.22

1 b: { \ [< ^ OH >] } { = you [< BOUGHT >] from } (.) { \

2   you bought from [< SEIbu >] }

3 B: { / [< Mhm >] }

4 b: { / you [FIND] it very < GOOD > }

5 B: { / [< YEAH >] }

6 b: { = [< YEAH >] }

In lines 1 and 2, speaker b asks his friend a declarative-mood question with the fall tone whether he bought the lettuce from Seibu. The communicative value of his choice of tone is that he does not know whether it was Seibu or not. In line 4, speaker b employs another declarative-mood question to ask about the quality, but this time with the rise tone with the meaning "am I right in thinking". These two questions conform to the broad distinction made by Brazil (1995: 193) between "finding out" and "making sure", respectively.

In addition to asking declarative-mood questions with the fall and rise tones, speakers can also be found asking them with the level tone. In Example 7.23, the speakers are discussing the repairs carried out by speaker B as a result of a leaking ceiling.

Example 7.23

1 B: { \ see it's [< ALL >] } { / [< MOULdy >] } { / and [< WET >] }

2 a1: { \ [< YES >] }

3   ((pause))

4 a1: { \ [< OH >] } { ? [< SO >] you } { = you [PURposely] < Opened > it }

5   { / and [LET] < THEM > } { = have a [LOOK] < OR > }

6 B: { \ oh [< YEAH >] } { \/ i [Opened] it up < ^ FOR > them }

7 a1: { = ah [< _ HA >] ha }

8   ((pause))

In line 4, speaker a uses a declarative-mood question to ask her friend about the logistics of showing the relevant authorities the problem. It can be seen that her utterance is truncated and spoken with the level tone. However, speaker B has no problem in responding to the question.

Example 7.24 is from a conversation between two friends in a Chinese dim sum restaurant as they collectively decide which dim sum dishes they will have for lunch.

Example 7.24

1   a: { / you like [GLUtinous] < RICE > }

2   B: { \ [< ^ YEAH >] } { \ [< YEAH >] } { \ [STICky] rice < YEAH > }

3   a: { / [STICky] < RICE > } (.) { = [< AND >] } { = [THEN] < THE > }

4   B: { \ and [DO] you want to < GET > a } (.) { = [< SOME >] } { / a [<

5   DISH >] } { / or [< SOMEthing >] } { / some [< VEgetables >] } { / or

6   [< SOMEthing >] }

7   a: { \ [< ^ YEAH >] } { / [< VEgetable >] } { = you [< LIKE >] }

8   B: { \ [YEAH] < VEgetable > }

9   a: { \/ [< BEEF >] ball } { = you [< LIKE >] }

10 B: { \ [< ^ YEAH >] } { \ get [_ SOME] of those < TOO > }

11 a: { = [< _ MM >] } { = [OR] MAYbe SOME < TURnip > } { \ [RICE]

12   < CAKE > }

13 B: { \ [< SURE >] }

In lines 1, 7, 9 and 11-12, speaker a employs a series of declarative-mood questions to ask her friend what he would like to eat. The first of these is spoken with the rise tone as she is reactivating common ground, as speaker B has just been trying to recall the name of glutinous rice in Cantonese, and so she makes the assumption that he likes that form of rice. The next two declarative-mood questions in lines 7 and 9 have the same pattern. Speaker a first names the food in question with referring tones, and 'vegetable' (line 7) is said with the rise tone because speaker b has just mentioned vegetables as a possible dish to order, and 'beef ball' (line 9) is said with the fall-rise tone as speaker a assumes this dish is common ground (beef balls are a dim sum staple). Interestingly, 'you like' (line 7 and line 9) in both of these declarative mood questions is spoken with the level tone. A possible explanation as to why the level tone is used on both occasions is that these are examples of a speaker adopting an "oblique orientation" (Brazil 1997: 134) to what is said because 'you like' is a routine and formulaic "add on" to the naming of this dish, which in itself could have served as the declarative mood question. In other words, in this context, once the dish has been named, the 'you like' is pre-coded information, which is associated with the selection of the level tone.

The last declarative mood question is in lines 11-12 when speaker a asks her friend if he would also like to order turnip rice cake. This time the fall tone is selected, reflecting the fact that unlike the glutinous or 'sticky' rice and vegetables which attract referring tones because of the prior mention of these items by speaker B, speaker a is finding out, rather than making sure, whether her friend wants to order this dim sum.

A study by Cheng and Warren (2002) examines thirteen hours of data in the Conversation sub-corpus of the HKCSE (prosodic) and analyzes all of the instances of declarative-mood questions in terms of the distribution of tone choices between HKC and NES. The number of words spoken by each set of speakers is almost the same, allowing for direct comparisons to be made. Table 7.4 details the main findings.

Table 7.4 Declarative-mood questions in Conversation sub-corpus: distribution of tones for HKC and NES

	Total	fall-rise	rise	fall	rise-fall	level
HKC	138	5	39	71	2	21
	(100%)	(3.62%)	(28.26%)	(51.45%)	(1.45%)	(15.2%)
NES	96	4	30	59	2	1
	(100%)	(4.17%)	(31.25%)	(61.46%)	(2.08%)	(1.04%)

The findings show that HKC and NES are different in two main ways. First, the HKC have a stronger tendency to perform interrogative functions by means of declarative-mood questions. The HKC use declarative-mood questions for expressing interrogative functions 44% more frequently than NSE. Second, the tone choices used to express declarative-mood questions by HKC and NSE are different in certain aspects. Proportionately, NES use more fall tones (61.46%) than the HKC (51.45%) and marginally more rise tones (31.25%) than HKC (28.26%). However, when actual instances are compared, HKC use four of the five tones, except for the rise-fall tone, more frequently than NES. Among the five tones, rise and fall tones are more frequently used by both HKC and NES; fall-rise and rise-fall tones are very rarely used by both HKC and NES; and the level tone is almost exclusively used by HKC. For HKC, the frequencies of use of tones in descending order are fall, rise, level, fall-rise, and rise-fall; for NES, the frequencies are fall, rise, fall-rise, rise-fall, and level. Possible reasons for the higher use of level tone are explored elsewhere in this chapter.

The pattern of tone choices can perhaps be explained in two ways. First of all, in Cantonese, questions are formed "not by changes in word order as in English, but by a number of interrogative constructions and by sentence-final particles" (Matthews and Yip 1994: 310). The syntactic structure of the Cantonese question which is a declarative sentence may therefore explain the high frequency of "declarative-mood" questions used by the HKC. The second explanation is the difference in cultural backgrounds between HKC and NES. The prevalence for use of "declarative-mood" questions by HKC could be accounted for in terms of the purported cultural attributes. In communication, the Chinese, in comparison with westerners, are said to emphasise more the maintenance of group harmony, or integration (Bond 1986, 1996), cooperation, modesty and humility (Markus and Kitayama 1991 and 1994). These may explain the higher tendency for the HKC in this study to use a rise tone which offers the hearer a tentative assessment of common ground and invites the hearer to indicate agreement or otherwise to its validity, and also a fall tone which communicates only a tentative assertion and invites the hearer to respond to it. Both of these tones, fall and rise, may indicate the HKC's concern with consensual opinions.

Question types and tone choice

A study by Lin (2008), based on the Business sub-corpus of the HKCSE (prosodic), examines the forms and functions of questions and responses. Lin (ibid.) identifies six question types, *wh-*, yes/no, declarative, tag, alternative, and insert. Insert questions are named by Lin after a term used by Biber *et al.* (1999: 1082) to describe a set of invariable items that are characterized in general by their inability to enter into syntactic relations with other structures. For Lin, "insert questions" include 'pardon me', 'sorry' and 'excuse me'. Lin's study is the largest of its kind to date to examine the discourse intonation of all questions types in the HKCSE (prosodic). Altogether, 1,827 questions are found in the Business sub-corpus, and are analysed in terms of their form, function and discourse intonation. The tone choices for these questions are shown in Table 7.5 below.

   Table 7.5 confirms, again, that tone choice is not a fixed property of question types. In Lin's (2008) study, all of the question types have instances of speakers selecting across the full range of tones, with the exception of the rise-fall tone, which is not surprising given its extremely low occurrence in the HKCSE (prosodic) as a whole. The three most common question types are yes/no, *wh-*, and declarative-mood questions. None of them have fixed tones. In the case of yes/no questions, contrary to received wisdom, the level tone is the most common tone selected, followed by the rise tones (rise and fall-rise tones combined) and then the fall tone. For *wh*-questions, most are said with the fall tone, which better fits received wisdom, but 21.53% are spoken with the level tone and 12.11% with the rise tone. In the case of declarative-mood questions, almost half are spoken with the fall tone, 28.48% with the rise tone, and the level tone accounts for 21.53% of instances. Tag questions are mostly spoken

Table 7.5 Distribution of tone choices across question types in Business sub-corpus

	yes/no	wh-	declarative	tag	alternative	insert	Total
fall	173	335	227	25	35	3	798
	(29.93%)	(64.42%)	(47.19%)	(16.33%)	(44.87%)	(17.64%)	(43.67%)
rise-fall	0	0	0	0	0	0	0
rise	161	52	110	49	11	2	394
	(27.85%)	(10.00%)	(22.86%)	(32.02%)	(14.10%)	(11.76%)	(21.56%)
fall-rise	20	11	27	54	4	1	117
	(3.4%)	(2.11%)	(5.62%)	(35.29%)	(5.12%)	(5.88%)	(6.40%)
level	212	112	109	19	24	2	478
	(36.67%)	(21.53%)	(22.66%)	(12.41%)	(30.76%)	(11.76%)	(26.16%)
unclassified	12	10	8	6	4	0	40
	(2.07%)	(1.92%)	(1.66%)	(3.79%)	(5.12%)		(2.18%)
Total	578	520	481	153	78	17	1,827
	(100%)	(100%)	(100%)	(100%)	(100%)	(100%)	(100%)

(Lin, 2008)

with rise tones (67.31%), especially the fall-rise tone (35.29%). Alternative questions also have a tendency to be spoken with the fall tone (44.87%), followed by the level tone (30.76%), and then rise tones (19.22%). Thus, while no question form is associated with one particular tone choice, there are, nonetheless, patterns of tone choice associated with question forms and these differ across the various forms.

Lin (2008) has yet to study the differences, if any, between HKC and NES in the Business sub-corpus, but she argues that the role of the speaker in the discourse (e.g. interviewer or interviewee, meeting chair or meeting member) influences the choice of the forms and functions of questions.

Speaker dominance and control

Another pattern to be found in the HKCSE (prosodic) relates to the observation by Brazil (1997: 82-98) that there are tone choices which may be characterised as being participant-specific in specialised discourse types (e.g. supervisions, interviews, meetings), but not in conversations in which the speakers have the perception of equal speaker rights (Warren 2006). Brazil (1997) states that the decision to choose whether to use the rise or rise-fall tone is dependent, in part, on the role relationships of the participants in the discourse. In discourse types where one speaker is dominant, in the sense of having greater responsibility for the discourse and greater freedom in making linguistic choices, that speaker monopolises the rise/rise-fall choice, as for example, in the case of the teacher in classroom talk, the interviewer in an interview, the doctor in a doctor/patient consultation, and so on. Similarly, although the rise-fall tone is by far the least prevalent of the tones, again Brazil (1997) claims that it tends to be the dominant speaker(s) in a discourse, in which the participants are of unequal status, who alone makes this selection. The types of discourse in which one participant is dominant, and thus is designated "all-knowing" by the institutionalised relationships in force, would limit the selection of the rise-fall tone to that participant. In other words, in the same kinds of discourse in which one finds the use of the rise tone the preserve of a particular participant, the selection of the rise-fall tone is similarly restricted.

In conversations, however, the selection of the rise and the rise-fall tones is not restricted by the existence of institutionalised inequalities between the participants, and if a speaker, for whatever reason, wishes to assert dominance and control through the selection of these tones he/she has the option to do so. Consequently, in conversation these tones are selected by all, some or none of the participants, depending on the moment-by-moment decisions of those involved and not on the basis of restrictive conventions. Brazil (1985: 131) argues that in conversation there is "an ongoing, albeit incipient, competition for dominance". However, he adds that this does not necessarily imply aggressiveness or rudeness on the part of speakers, rather it can be characterised as "to remind, underline, emphasize, insist or convey forcefulness" (Brazil 1997: 98), when a speaker selects a rise or rise-fall tone, and so overtly assumes the status of the dominant speaker. The important point is that dominant speaker status is neither predetermined nor fixed in conversation, and is typically interchangeable among the participants as the discourse unfolds.

It needs to be made clear that while the words "dominance and control" have a generally negative "semantic environment" or "semantic prosody" (e.g. Sinclair 1991: 112, Louw 1993: 158-159), the fact that speakers choose to use the rise and the rise-fall tones to exert dominance and control locally in a discourse is not an inherently negative behaviour. While it is possible that the overuse of these tones by a participant not deemed to be in an institutionalised dominant role might be heard to be usurping the designated dominant speaker, this would require repeated rather than isolated use of these tones by the speaker. The primary function of the rise and the rise-fall tones is to facilitate the smooth exchange of control of the discourse between the discourse participants (Brazil 1997: 86). In any discourse, there is the need at times for speakers to exert dominance and control of the discourse. What is of interest here is whether this, to an extent, is predetermined by the roles assigned to speakers in particular discourse types, and hence whether it therefore constitutes a predictable pattern of tone choice.

Functions of the rise and rise-fall tones

A number of controlling or dominating uses are given (Brazil 1997: 89) for the rise and the rise-fall tones. These are illustrated with examples below from the HKCSE.

Continuative use of the rise tone

The continuative use of rise tone underlines the expectation that the speaker will be allowed to continue to speak (Brazil 1997: 88-93). Examples 7.25 and 7.26 are extracts from a televised discussion in which a speaker lists the issues Hong Kong faced in the 1960s and then lists some of the government policies initiated in the 1970s.

Example 7.25

1   b2: { = [^ FIRST] we < HAVE > the } { / [< REfugees >] } { = [< THE >]
2   er } (.) { / the [< RIOTS >] } { = [< THE >] } { / the [WAter] <
3   shorTAGE > } { \ the [< BANK >] runs }

Example 7.26

1   b2: … { / at [THAT] time they have the TEN year housing < PROject > }
2   { = [< THEIR >] } { / ten [YEAR] < eduCAtion > } { / [TEN] year
3   social < WELfare > } { \ all [< THESE >] }

In Examples 7.25 and 7.26, the speaker uses rise tone when he says his lists. By means of his choice of tone, he asserts control of the discourse at these points in order to hold on to his turn and so complete his list. The completion of the list is indicated in both examples with fall tone.

In Example 7.27, the speaker is giving an academic lecture, and lists the characteristics of Hong Kong's workforce.

Example 7.27

1   b: kong's } { \ [DRIving] < ^ FORCE > } { \ they're from < Everywhere > }
2   { = < BEcause > } { \ they are < Agile > } { / [LIKE] < ^ yourSELF > }
3   { = [THEY] are < CREative > } { / [LIKE] < yourSELF > } { ? and
4   they [ALso] have a < CAN > do } { \ < ^ menTAlity > } { \ [LIKE] < ^
5   yourSELF > }

As the lecturer lists the characteristics of Hong Kong's workforce, he also ascribes these characteristics to the students attending his lecture. He does this by repeating 'like yourself' after each characteristic and, interestingly, it is on 'like yourself' that he selects the continuative use of rise tone (lines 2 and 3), until he gets to the end of his list and then 'like yourself' (lines 4-5) is said with fall tone.

In Example 7.28, the interviewer in an internship interview at a hotel asks if the interviewee has a preference within the field of food and beverage.

Example 7.28

```
1  B:   ... { \ [ < oKAY > ] } } { = i [ < DO > ] } { \ i [ THINK ] we will < LOOK >
2        on that } { \/ [ DO ] you have any speCIfic < ^ Area > } (.) { = you would
3        [ < LIKE > ] to concentrate on } { \ within your [ < TRAIning > ] in } { \
4        [ FOOD ] and < BEverage > } (.) { \ [ IS ] there a speCIfic < _ Area > }
5        { / like [ COFfee ] < SHOP > } (.) { / [ < BANquets > ] } { = room [ <
6        SERvice > ] } { / is there a [ speCIfic ] area you're < MORE > interested
7        in }
```

In this example, the speaker again uses rise tone (line 5) as he lists the possibilities available, and then ends the list on level tone (lines 5-6) rather than the usual fall tone. This further confirms that not all lists have the pattern of rise/rise/rise/fall.

Use of the rise tone to exert pressure on hearer to speak

Speakers choose the rise tone in certain contexts to put pressure on the hearer to respond to what they have said (Brazil 1997: 93). For example, in Example 7.28, the speaker repeats his question three times. Twice with fall tone in lines 2-4 and line 4, and then with rise tone in lines 6-7 which exerts pressure on the interviewee to respond.

Examples 7.29 and 7.30 show the openings of service encounters recorded at an information counter at Hong Kong airport involving two different female service providers.

Example 7.29

```
1  a1:  { = good [ < EVEning> ] sir } { / [ CAN ] i < HELP > you }
2  B:   { = [ < ER > ] } { \ i'm a [ TRANsit ] < PASsenger > } { = and i
3        [ WONder ] if < THERE > is a } { = any [ < SPEcial > ] } { / [ < RATES
4        > ] } { ? for the } { / [ < hoTEL > ] }
```

Example 7.30

1 a: { = good [< EVEning >] } { / [< CAN >] i help you sir }
2 B: { \ [YEAH] i have JUST a < QUEStion > }
3 a: { / [< YES >] }

In Examples 7.29 and 7.30, the same tone choices can be seen. After greeting with a choice of level tone, and, as in earlier examples, this greeting is not returned, the service providers then select rise tone with 'can I help you' and 'can I help you sir'. Brazil (1997: 95) also gives an example of a service provider's use of the rise tone with 'can I help you', arguing that the question is probably perceived as warmer when the rise tone is used than if it was uttered with the fall-rise tone. The speaker's choice of rise tone to control the response would be understood as a more "wholehearted" (Brazil 1997: 95) attempt to ensure that the offer of help is taken up. These examples confirm that the choice to assert dominance and control should not be associated with either positive or negative behaviour. The service provider in Example 7.30 selects rise tone on 'yes' (line 3) to convey that she is keen to hear and respond to the query. Brazil (1997: 95) states that such questions are asked 'for the benefit of the hearer" and the choice of rise tone "would probably be heard as a warmer offer" than fall-rise tone.

Use of the rise tone to openly remind the hearer(s) of common ground

The dominant speaker in a discourse can choose to assert dominance through the use of the rise tone to openly assert that the hearer needs to be reminded of something that is common ground between the participants (Brazil 1997: 96). Example 7.31 is taken from an internship placement interview at a 5-star Hong Kong hotel. The purpose of the interview is to determine whether the student is suitable to be placed in the hotel and, if so, which department of the hotel he will be placed in.

Example 7.31

1 b: { = [< UM >] } { = [< I >] } { \ i [WANT] to < ASK > } { = if i [<
2   HAVE >] } { / any [CHANCE] to < WORK > } { = [< ER >] } { / a as
3   a [BAR] < TENder > } { = [< OR >] } { / [SOMEthing] in the < BAR
4   > }
5 B: { \/ [< oKAY >] } { = if [< YOU >] } { \ [< ^ ACtually >] } { \ [^
6   WANT] to < WORK > } { = [< ER >] } {? [< A >] } { \/ as a [< ^
7   BAR >] tender } * { = [< ER >] } { \/ we can [< reFER >] you } { = [<

8   TO >] er } { / [^ BACK] to the < personNEL > } } { = and they will

9   [GET] in conTACT with < THE > } } { / the [BEverage] < dePARTment

10   > } ...

Earlier in the interview, speaker b told the interviewer that he would like to work in the bar. The interview is nearing its conclusion, when the interviewer asks speaker b whether he has any questions, and above is his first question. The interviewee repeatedly chooses the rise tone in lines 2-3 to reactivate common ground; and in so doing, reminds the interviewer that he is very keen to work as a bartender or in any other capacity in the hotel's bar. This choice by the interviewee might also be due to the relative tentativeness of a rise tone, compared to a fall, in this context, when the interviewee has to repeat the question but does not want to be seen to be too demanding.

In Example 7.32, a lecturer interrupts a presentation by one of his students to remind him of the need to adhere to the time limit.

Example 7.32

1   B: ** { \ [< R__ >] } } { = [< UM >] } { = [< WE'RE >] } } { = we are [<

2   RUNning >] } { \ a [LONG] way over < TIME > } { = [< SO >] } } { =

3   [< COULD >] you } { \ you [MAY] NOT be able to include <

4   EVerything > } { = [< BUT >] er } { / could you sort of [WRAP] it up

5   within the NEXT FIVE minutes or < SO > } } { / [< PLEASE >] }

In lines 4-5, the speaker selects rise tone as he reminds the student to come to a close. By doing so, speaker B openly asserts that the hearer needs to be reminded of something that is common ground between the participants.

Change in the speaker's world view

The rise-fall tone is used by speakers to indicate how "the world view of speaker and hearer are to be regarded as relating" (Brazil 1997: 97). In other words, the use of the rise-fall tone allows the speaker to overtly (i.e. in a dominant or controlling fashion) modify her/his own world view as events both internal and external to the discourse unfold, and hence the extent of convergence between the speaker and the hearer. In addition, according to Brazil (1997: 97), the rise-fall tone indicates to the hearer that no feedback is expected or that the speaker intends to continue to speak and so asserts control of the progress of the discourse. The use of the rise-fall tone is very rare (there are only 53 instances in the HKCSE (prosodic) because it is employed when what is being said is news to both the speaker and the hearer at that point in the discourse. It usually happens when something suddenly springs into the mind of the speaker, as he/ she is speaking, or if something unexpected happens during the discourse and the speaker comments on it.

Example 7.33 is taken from a conversation between two female friends recorded in a restaurant.

Example 7.33

1   a: { / and < THEN > } { = with the ((inaudible)) < OIL > } { = < BUTter > }

2   { = < UM > } (.) { = < THE > } (.) { = < I > } { \ i'm [NOT] < SURE > }

3   (.) { = it must be }

4   A: { \ < KIND > of mushroom }

5   a: { \ it's a kind of mushroom } * { \ the < ^ JApanese > mushroom } { = <

6   A: ** ((laugh)) { = < oKAY > } { /\ [^ I]

7   a: oKAY > }

8   A: know i know < THE > } { \ the [LONG] thin < WHITE > ones } * { / <

9   a: ** { \ <

10 A: RIGHT > }

11 a: YES > } { \ the [LONG] thin < _ WHITE > one }

In lines 1-3, speaker a is describing a dish on the menu, and is not able to be very specific about the exact kind of mushroom in the dish. Speaker A acknowledges her friend's description with a laugh and 'okay' (line 6). It then suddenly dawns on speaker A exactly what the mushroom is, and she chooses the rise-fall tone when she says 'I know' (line 6 and line 8). Her choice of the rise-fall tone marks the modification of her world view at the very moment that she succeeds in remembering. Locally, it might be heard as equivalent to 'Eureka!'. Brazil states that it is heard as this precisely because the use of the rise-fall tone isolates that part of the discourse from the rest of the discourse through the speaker choosing to use the dominant and controlling form of proclaiming tone. Speaker A's actual description of the mushrooms as 'the long thin white ones' (line 8) is said with a fall tone as the moment of the modification of the speaker's world view has passed.

The last example, Example 7.34, is from a conversation recorded between two friends, and the extract occurs when one of the women notices something strange about the recording device.

Example 7.34

    1   a: …{ /\ [JUST] a SEcond < STOP > } } { \ we're [< reCORding >] } } { =

    2   [< BUT >] } * { = er it [< SOUNDS >] }

    3   A: ** { \/ i [< ^ HOPE >] so } ((laugh))

    4   a: { = it [< SEEMS >] }

    5   A: { = shall [< WE >] } } { \ er [< reWIND >] it } { \ and [< LIsten >] }

    6   a: { = [< oKAY >] }

In line 1, speaker a immediately says 'just a second stop' when she notices what she thinks is a problem with the recording device. This is proclaimed with the rise-fall tone as new information to both the hearer and the speaker in this particular context.

Distribution of the rise and the rise-fall tones across discourse types

A study by Cheng and Warren (2005) examines a cross-section of text types in the four sub-corpora of the HKCSE (prosodic) to determine the use of the rise and the rise-fall tones by speakers to exert dominance and control. Six discourse types were selected: conversations (31,255 words), service encounters (4,642 words), informal office talk (19,715 words), placement interviews (23,653 words), business meetings (14,632 words) and academic supervisions (25,837 words). These text types were chosen on the basis that, in theory, some of them do not have an institutionalised designated dominant speaker (i.e. conversations and informal office talk) while the remainder do. The discourses were also chosen on the basis that in each discourse the talk is spread evenly across the participants in terms of the number of words spoken by each participant, in order to make it possible to make direct comparisons when analysing the data.

For each discourse type, a search was conducted to determine the frequency with which each participant used the rise and the rise-fall tones when speaking. The findings are presented with regard to the use of the rise tone from across the six different discourse types on a continuum in Figure 7.1 below. At one end of the continuum, the use of the rise tone is evenly spread between the discourse participants (i.e. 50:50 in a two-party discourse) and at the other extreme end of the continuum, the use of the rise tone is entirely monopolised by a designated dominant speaker (i.e. 100:0).

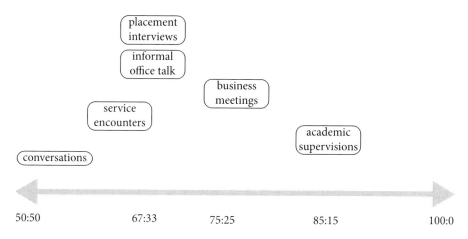

Figure 7.1 Distribution of rise tone across discourse types

Conversations are at one extreme end where the use of the rise tone is evenly distributed (i.e.50:50) across the participants enjoying equal staus. Moving towards the other end of the continuum shows that the degree to which designated dominant speakers use the rise tone more frequently than the other discourse participants steadlily increases. The first discourse type on the continuum is the service encounter, followed by placement interview and informal office talk. Next is the business meeting and, finally, academic supervision which is the furthest removed from conversation in this respect.

It is also clear from the findings that there are degrees of dominance and control from one discourse to another. It would appear, for example, that the role of the academic supervisor might be one of greater dominance and control than that of, for example, the placement interviewer with regard to choosing to use these tones. This suggests that the extent of dominance and control vested in the designated dominant speaker is not fixed but rather seems to vary across discourse types. In other words, there is a continuum with conversations at one end in which the power relationship is equal, and then other discourse types which have a designated dominant speaker can be plotted on the continuum, depending on the extent of the power difference that is manifested in the speakers' roles. In addition, while no discourse type reveals a designated dominant speaker with a complete monopoly on the use of these tones, there does seem to be a connection between the use of the rise and the rise-fall tones and the participant role of being the designated dominant speaker. Interestingly, Cheng and Warren (2005) find no evidence that either gender or first language plays a role in this pattern of intonation behaviour.

It is only possible to plot the use of the rise tone. With regard to speakers' use of the rise-fall tone, it is more problematic to make similarly bold claims simply because its occurrence is extremely infrequent. Cheng and Warren (2005) note that the very infrequent occurrence of the rise-fall tone means that, in effect, the assertion of dominance and control through the speaker's tone choice is essentially achieved by choosing the rise tone. They also caution that while Brazil (1997) argues that the use of the rise and the rise-fall tones is made by speakers asserting dominance and control at certain points in the discourse, there are, of course, many other ways in which speakers can exert dominance and control in spoken discourse. The use of the rise and the rise-fall tones is only one contributing element to such behaviour at a local level, and it should not be viewed as either the major or the determining factor.

Conclusions

This chapter has examined the distribution of tone choice in the HKCSE (prosodic), and described and discussed patterns of tone usage in the corpus. In terms of the distribution of tones, the main finding is the prevalence of level tones across all sub-corpora and all speakers. In the case of the HKC, the level tone is the most used of all of the five tones available to speakers, while for NES it is ranked second after fall tone. The two rise tones are used relatively infrequently, especially the fall-rise tone, by all speakers. Cauldwell (2003b: 107) makes the point that in other systems for describing tones, the level tone is regarded as "a type of rising tone", and he argues strongly that level tones deserve "a category to themselves". The prevalence of level tone use in the HKCSE (prosodic) is an important finding, suggesting that the level tone use in naturally-occurring data merits further study.

Patterns of tone use have been discussed. One of these has been related to the well-known referring and proclaiming use of tones, but additional emphasis has been placed on examining the use of level tone due to its high frequency. The main use of the level tones occurs when speakers are constructing longer telling and asking increments and need incremental elements, typically said with level tone, to achieve the target state. This usage of the level tone is further supported by a number of the message and organisation elements described in Linear Unit Grammar (Sinclair and Mauranen 2006). Another major source of level tones is when speakers encounter encoding problems and divert their focus from direct discourse, i.e. hearer-sensitive, to oblique discourse. Again, this finding is attributable to the spontaneous naturally occurring data in the HKCSE (prosodic), which results in a higher incidence of this usage compared to planned speech. Tone choice patterns also play a role in disambiguation in certain contexts with regard to setting limit, or not, when alternative 'or' is used.

The notion of question intonation is examined. It is found that while no question type comes with a fixed tone choice, a study by Lin (2008) shows that the distribution of tones across question types does differ. Finally, rise and rise-fall tones can be used to assert dominance and control in a discourse, and a study by Cheng and Warren (2005) shows that this usage varies across genres. In genres with a designated dominant speaker, the use of the rise tone is higher for this participant relative to the other participants. Conversely, in discourses with greater equality between the participants, the use of rise tone is spread more evenly.

CHAPTER 8

Key and termination

Introduction

The last two systems concern pitch level selections available to speakers and are best looked at in combination. Brazil (1997: 40-66) suggests that speakers can select from a three tier system, high, mid and low, in terms of the relative "key" at the onset of a tone unit which is the first prominent syllable in a tone unit. The selection of key is made on the first prominent syllable, and whether the speaker selects high, mid or low key will affect the meaning of what is said. High key selection has contrastive value; mid key selection has additive value; and low key selection has equative value, i.e. with the meaning "as to be expected" (Brazil 1985: 75-84).

Brazil (1997) states the speaker also selects pitch level again at the end of the tonic segment on the tonic syllable (i.e. the last prominent syllable in the tone unit), and he terms this system "termination" (ibid.: 11). Again, this is a three tier system of high, mid and low. By means of this selection, the speaker can seek to constrain the next speaker to respond if he/she selects high or mid termination. Due to the seeming preference for "pitch concord" (Brazil 1985: 86) found in spoken discourse across turn boundaries, the next speaker frequently "echoes" the election of termination of the previous speaker in her/his selection of key. If the speaker selects low termination, this means the speaker makes no attempt to constrain the next turn, and thus leaves the next speaker to initiate a new topic or for the discourse to come to a close.

The local meaning of selecting high or mid termination at the end of a declarative or a question varies according to the functional value of what is being said, and can be briefly summarized based on three broad scenarios. In yes/no questions, the speaker's selection of high termination carries the meaning that adjudication is invited from the hearer while mid termination seeks concurrence (Brazil 1997: 54-55). In *wh*-questions, high termination carries the meaning that "an improbable answer is expected" and mid termination is a "straightforward request for information" (ibid.: 56). In declaratives, the selection of high termination denotes the meaning "this will surprise you" and mid-termination the meaning "this will not surprise you" (ibid.: 58).

As described in Chapter 5, many tone units in the HKCSE (prosodic) have only one prominence. In fact, of the 323,703 tone units, 206,493 (63.79%) have one prominence, and such tone units are said to have "minimal tonic segments" (ibid.: 61). When one syllable is made prominent in a tone unit, the speaker in effect selects both key and termination simultaneously (ibid.: 61). If there is only one prominence in a tone unit, this is designated "key + termination" (ibid.: 61-66), and the hearer needs to determine in the local context whether the selection of high, mid or low level is to be interpreted within the key or termination systems.

Distribution of key and termination across the HKCSE (prosodic)

The following Tables (8.1-8.9) show the distribution of key, termination, and key + termination across the HKCSE (prosodic), the sub-corpora, and the sets of speakers. Reference is made to the overall distribution of words (see Tables 1.5 to 1.7 in Chapter 1) to enable comparisons to be made.

Table 8.1 Distribution of key: HKC and NES

Speakers	High key	Mid key	Low key	Total
HKC	7,528 (9.52%)	71,311 (90.25%)	173 (0.21%)	79,012 (100%)
NES	2,214 (8.73%)	23,009 (90.77%)	125 (0.49%)	25,348 (100%)
HKC and NES	9,724 (9.33%)	94,320 (90.37%)	298 (0.28%)	104,360 (100%)

Table 8.2 Distribution of termination: HKC and NES

Speakers	High termination	Mid termination	Low termination	Total
HKC	7,767 (9.79%)	69,037 (87.06%)	2,487 (3.13%)	79,291 (100%)
NES	3,611 (14.11%)	20,965 (81.95%)	1,006 (3.93%)	25,582 (100%)
HKC and NES	11,378 (10.84%)	90,002 (85.81%)	3,493 (3.33%)	104,873 (100%)

Table 8.3 Distribution of key + termination: HKC and NES

Speakers	High key + termination	Mid key + termination	Low key + termination	Total
HKC	15,670 (10.05%)	131,986 (84.69%)	8,181 (5.24%)	155,837 (100%)
NES	5,339 (11.45%)	38,145 (81.87%)	3,106 (6.66%)	46,590 (100%)
HKC and NES	21,009 (10.37%)	170,131 (84.04%)	11,287 (5.57%)	202,427 (100%)

Tables 8.1-8.3 show that key is selected proportionately more often by the NES, given that HKC speak 71.46% and NES speak only 25.32% of the words in the whole corpus. The same distribution is found for the selection of termination. The HKC also make proportionately greater use of "key + termination" (Brazil 1997: 61-66). The finding that HKC use more "key + termination" is the result of the HKC speaking more one word tone units, which then has an impact on the availability of separate key and termination selections.

Among all instances of key selection, mid key is chosen most frequently by both sets of speakers and the distribution of high and low key selections is very even across the two sets of speakers (Table 8.1), although the HKC do make slightly more use of high key and the NES slightly more use of low key, which is the least common of the selections available to speakers in these two discourse intonation systems. In Table 8.2, while both sets of speakers mainly select mid termination, the HKC make proportionately greater use of this selection than the NES (87.06% versus 81.95%). The NES select high termination more than the HKC (14.11% versus 9.79%) and the same is the case for low termination, although the proportional difference is less (3.93 versus 3.33%). Table 8.3 shows that mid key and termination is the most frequently selected by both HKC and NES (84.69% versus 81.87%), and the slightly higher proportional use by the HKC results in them selecting high and low termination proportionately less compared with the NES.

Table 8.4 shows the distribution of key across the four sub-corpora and Table 8.5 across HKC and NES males and females.

Table 8.4 Distribution of key: HKCSE (prosodic) and sub-corpora

Sub-corpora	High key	Mid key	Low key	Total
Academic sub-corpus	2,182 (7.96%)	25,198 (91.89%)	43 (0.16%)	27,423 (100%)
Business sub-corpus	2,828 (10.06%)	25,164 (89.59%)	95 (0.34%)	28,087 (100%)
Conversation sub-corpus	1,845 (7.67%)	22,115 (91.87%)	113 (0.47%)	24,073 (100%)
Public sub-corpus	3,138 (11.29%)	24,610 (88.50%)	57 (0.2%)	27,805 (100%)
HKCSE (prosodic)	9,993	97,087	308	107,388

Table 8.5 Distribution of key: gender

Gender	High key	Mid key	Low key	Total
HKC Males	4,134	37,802	101	42,037
	(9.83%)	(89.92%)	(0.24%)	(100%)
HKC Females	3,394	33,509	72	36,975
	(9.18%)	(90.63%)	(0.19%)	(100%)
NES Males	1,832	18,730	100	37,662
	(4.86%)	(94.73%)	(0.27%)	(100%)
NES Females	382	4,279	25	4,686
	(8.15%)	(91.30%)	(0.53%)	(100%)
Total	9,742	94,320	298	121,360

Table 8.4 shows that across the sub-corpora, the use of high key is not evenly spread, with it being used proportionately more frequently in the Business and Public sub-corpora, especially the latter, and it is used proportionately less in the other two sub-corpora, especially the Conversation sub-corpus. The same distribution patterns are to be found across the gender divide (Table 8.5). The use of mid key across the sub-corpora is also uneven, with proportionately higher use in the Academic and Public sub-corpora and lower in the other two sub-corpora (Table 8.4). These patterns are found across both male and female speakers (Table 8.5). The selection of low key has the most uneven distribution across the sub-corpora (Table 8.4), but it is also rarely used with only 298 instances for HKC and NES combined (Table 8.5). Low key is used proportionately much more in the Conversation and Business sub-corpora, with relatively low frequencies of occurrence in the Academic and Public sub-corpora (Table 8.4). This finding might be related to the relatively lower numbers of NES in the latter corpora as the NES tend to make more use of low key overall.

Table 8.6 Distribution of termination: sub-corpora

Sub-corpora	High termination	Mid termination	Low termination	Total
Academic sub-corpus	2,319	24,409	727	27,455
	(8.45%)	(88.90%)	(2.65%)	(100%)
Business sub-corpus	2,828	24,337	1,104	28,269
	(10.00%)	(86.09%)	(3.91%)	(100%)
Conversation sub-corpus	2,731	21,005	633	24,369
	(11.20%)	(86.20%)	(2.60%)	(100%)
Public sub-corpus	3,809	22,791	1,236	27,836
	(13.68%)	(81.88%)	(4.44%)	(100%)
HKCSE (prosodic)	11,687	92,542	3,700	107,929

Table 8.7 Distribution of termination: gender

Gender	High termination	Mid termination	Low termination	Total
HKC Males	4,585	36,025	1,536	42,146
	(10.88%)	(85.48%)	(3.64%)	(100%)
HKC Females	3,182	33,012	951	37,145
	(8.57%)	(88.87%)	(2.56%)	(100%)
NES Males	3,135	16,899	820	20,854
	(15.03%)	(81.03%)	(3.93%)	(100%)
NES Females	476	4,066	186	4,728
	(10.06%)	(86.00%)	(3.93%)	(100%)
Total	11,378	90,002	3,493	104,873

Table 8.6 shows the distribution of termination across the four sub-corpora, and Table 8.7 across HKC and NES males and females.

In terms of the selection of termination across the sub-corpora (Table 8.6), there are some interesting similarities and differences. For high termination, the distribution follows a similar pattern to that of high key. High termination is used proportionately more in the Business and Public sub-corpora and less in the other two, especially in the Academic sub-corpus. This pattern is found for both male and female speakers. In terms of mid termination, it again follows the pattern observed for mid key with proportionately higher use in the Academic and Public sub-corpora and lower for the other two sub-corpora, although the differences are slight they are found across both males and females. The patterns for the distribution of low termination are not the same as that found for low key. Low termination is used more in the Business and Public sub-corpora, especially the Public, and used quite a lot less in the Academic and Conversation sub-corpora. Again, this pattern holds for males and females (Table 8.7).

Table 8.8 shows the distribution of key + termination across the four sub-corpora, and Table 8.9 across HKC and NES males and females.

The spread of key + termination selections across the sub-corpora differs (Table 8.8). In the case of high key + termination, proportionately greater use is found in the Conversation sub-corpus and less for the other three sub-corpora. This pattern is found for the male and female speakers (Table 8.9). The use of mid key + termination is proportionately higher in the Academic and Conversation sub-corpora, in line with expectations for the Business sub-corpus and proportionately less in the Public sub-corpus. Low key + termination is used proportionately more in the Business and Conversation sub-corpora and less in the other two (Table 8.8). Again, male and female speakers follow these patterns of distribution (Table 8.9). This finding might be related to a higher use of metalanguage in the

Table 8.8 Distribution of key + termination: sub-corpora

Sub-corpora	High key + termination	Mid key + termination	Low key + termination	Total
Academic sub-corpus	3,992 (8.37%)	41,375 (86.73%)	2,339 (4.90%)	47,706 (100%)
Business sub-corpus	5,518 (9.65%)	48,269 (84.39%)	3,408 (5.96%)	57,195 (100%)
Conversation sub-corpus	6,275 (10.49%)	49,873 (83.41%)	3,643 (6.09%)	59,791 (100%)
Public sub-corpus	5,881 (13.16%)	36,484 (81.63%)	2,328 (5.21%)	44,693 (100%)
HKCSE (prosodic)	21,666	176,001	11,718	209,385

Table 8.9 Distribution of key + termination: gender

Gender	High key + termination	Mid key + termination	Low key + termination	Total
HKC Males	8,454 (10.92%)	64,480 (83.32%)	4,459 (5.76%)	77,393 (100%)
HKC Females	7,216 (9.20%)	67,506 (86.06%)	3,722 (4.74%)	78,444 (100%)
NES Males	4,271 (11.64%)	29,935 (81.60%)	2,479 (6.76%)	36,685 (100%)
NES Females	1,068 (10.78%)	8,210 (82.89%)	627 (6.33%)	9,905 (100%)
Total	21,009	170,131	11,287	202,427

Academic and Public sub-corpora, which can be used to explicitly signal the organisation of the discourse and which is one of the functions of low key + termination, and could be investigated further.

Patterns of usage

In the following sections, some of the patterns of usage of key and termination selections in the HKCSE (prosodic) are described.

Contrastive use

One pattern of usage found in the HKCSE (prosodic) is for speakers to use the selection of high key, or high key + termination, on its own to denote contrast or that what is being said is perceived to be in some way unexpected. On occasion, the selection of high key, or high key + termination, is selected following low key, or low key + termination, in order to contrast or juxtapose different propositions in the local context. Examples of these patterns of usage are described and discussed below.

Example 8.1 is from a university writing assistance programme supervision in which the teacher gives advice to a student on what to include in his job application letter.

Example 8.1

```
1   A:   ... { = [ < I > ] } } { = [ < I > ] } { = [ < I > ] know } { \ i will just put a [ <
2        DASH > ] there } { \ [ MAKES ] it a little BIT easier to < READ > } (.)
3        { = [ < ERM > ] } (.) { \/ you may [ _ NOT ] HAVE an < Email > } { =
4        [ < BUT > ] } { \ he [ ^ PRObably ] < DOES > }
```

In Example 8.1, the speaker employs a combination of both low and high key in lines 3-4. When she says 'you may not have an e-mail but he probably does', she selects low key on 'not' (line 3), and then high key on 'probably' (line 4). The selection of low key has an equative meaning (i.e. as expected) and the selection of high key has a contrastive meaning which, in this example, contrasts with the first part of what the speaker says. It needs to be added that this discourse was collected in the late 1990s, when students typically did not have e-mail addresses whereas individuals working in most business and professional organisations had e-mail addresses, hence the assumptions made here by the speaker.

In Example 8.2, speaker A is describing the extent of gender equality in Ireland in a conversation with her friend.

Example 8.2

```
1   A:   { \ it's quite [ < INteresting > ] actually } { \ to [ SEE ] how < ^ QUICKly
2        > } { \ in [ JUST ] in ONE < geneRAtion > } { ? [ < HOW > ] it's }
3        * { \ just [ <     CHANGED > ] } { = [ < ALmost > ] } { = [ < WHERE > ]
4   a:   ** { \ [ < ^ YEAH > ] } { \ [ < YEAH > ] }
5        it's } { \ [ TOtally ] < ^ Equal > }
```

In line 1, speaker A selects high termination on 'quickly' and again on 'equal' in line 5 when she says that in a generation, it has quickly moved to a situation of almost complete gender equality. The selection of high termination has the communicative value of "this will surprise you" (Brazil 1997: 58), and so this rapid change in Irish society is perceived by the speaker to be unexpected information for the hearer.

Example 8.3 is from a televised panel discussion and the host asks one of the panel members about his prediction for Hong Kong after the SARS[1] crisis.

Example 8.3

1   b1: ... (.) { = do [^ YOU] think < THAT > er } { = [< WHEN >] } { \ when

2   [ALL] of this is < Over > } { \ [HONG] kong may < eMERGE > } { =

3   as a [< ^ BETter >] place } { \ than it was [< _ beFORE >] }

4   b2: { = [< WE >] } { = [< DO >] need to have } { \ [LONG] term < PLAN

5   > }...

In line 3, speaker b1 asks if Hong Kong will be 'a better place', and selects high key + termination on 'better' which seeks adjudication. He then adds 'than it was before' with low key + termination on 'before' (line 3). This last part of his utterance, in this local context, is self-evident and, given what he has said earlier, it is already implied. It is therefore argued that it is probably something of an afterthought, and, in this local context, does not have the effect of removing the constraint on speaker b2 to respond.

In Example 8.4, the speakers are from another televised panel discussion discussing the health and safety standards in post-SARS Hong Kong.

Example 8.4

1   b3: ... (.) { \ [< WE >] must } { \ [PLAY] < SAFE > }

2   b1: { \ [< _ RIGHT >] } { = [< BUT >] } { \ is the [HIGHest] standard

3   being aDOPted < ^ toDAY > } { \ the [HIGHest] < STANdard > }

4   b3: { = [< NO >] }

5   b1: { = [< NOT >] } { \ [NOT] even < _ toDAY > }

In line 3, the host of the panel discussion, speaker b1, asks if the highest standards are 'being adopted today' and selects high termination on 'today' which would seek adjudication from speaker b3, but he then continues and ends his question

---

1.   In 2003 Hong Kong, and other countries in South East Asia, suffered from the Severe Acute Respiratory Syndrome (SARS) epidemic which had a devastating impact on the local population and economy.

with mid termination on 'standard' (line 3). The selection of mid termination invites speaker b3 to concur with his implication that the highest standard is not being adopted today. Speaker b1, the panel discussion host, seems to test speaker b3's claim that 'we must play safe'. Speaker b3 responds to his question with a simple 'no' (line 4) which does concur with speaker b1's implied meaning. In line 5, speaker b1 selects low termination on 'today', and this time it has the communicative value of 'as expected' and does not prospect a response. This serves to further underline that speaker b3's response in line 4 concurs with the assumption behind speaker b1's question. In other words, it is not unexpected given the context of Hong Kong in the immediate post-SARS period.

Disagreements

Disagreements between speakers are a particular kind of behaviour that is considered separately here in terms of patterns of discourse intonation associated with their occurrence. Pomerantz (1984) has shown that disagreements between participants in spoken discourse are dispreferred and thus marked in various ways, and agreements are preferred and so unmarked. However, a disagreement can be either a preferred or dispreferred response, depending on the local context in which it occurs in a discourse. For example, disagreement is considered a preferred response following self-deprecation, and may be a dispreferred response following assessment, or following a question, as in the case of a negative answer.

Studies of disagreements encompass a range of genres. For example, in a study of focus group discussions, Myers (1998: 99) found that participants manage disagreements by means of "markers of dispreferred turns, hedges, concessions, and attributions". Myers also observes that even for a direct disagreement between participants, the disagreement is often presented within a shared view, namely by agreeing with one aspect of the previous turn, using repetition, concessions, or repair. Similarly, in Gardner's (2000) study of conversation in a family setting, he finds that disagreements are delayed in the turn sequence and typically hedged or mitigated. As Mey (2001: 166-167) states, "the phenomenon of '(dis)preferred' response sequences is probably universal, the way (dis)preference is realized is not", and individual manifestations of this probably universal phenomenon of conversational organization in different languages may vary a great deal. Cheng (2003) finds in her study of intercultural conversational that HKC are more likely than their NES interlocutors to use disagreements, which are heavily redressed to mitigate the imposition of the disagreement on the NES interlocutor, to disclaim an all-knowing and authoritative status, and to coerce and involve the interlocutor in

the reasoning and in claiming common ground. HKC's disagreements are therefore more likely than NES's to be realized in the form of a dispreferred response.

In a study by Cheng and Warren (2005), the additional communicative role
played by discourse intonation when speakers perform the speech act of disagreement is examined. This is an aspect that is typically absent from other studies examining disagreement in spoken discourse. Specifically, the analysis focuses on
the use of various strategies by the speakers to perform disagreement. The most
commonly used strategy typically involves the use of high key or high key + termination, to indicate that what the current speaker is saying is in contrast to what the
previous speaker has said, or that it goes against expectations given what the previous speaker has said.

The study (Cheng and Warren 2005) identifies instances of disagreement in the
Business sub-corpus of the HKCSE (prosodic), excluding speakers other than HKC
and NES, and examines the disagreement strategies employed by the speakers.
Altogether, they identify 151 disagreements and the most common strategy for both
sets of speakers (72%) tends to have a particular pattern of high key, high key + termination or high termination selection, by the speakers. The strategy is described
(ibid.: 253) as "positive acknowledgement (mitigating device), disagree, inductive or
deductive rhetorical strategy". This involves the speaker who is performing the disagreement beginning with a positive acknowledgment/ evaluation of what the previous speaker has said, with the option to then use some form of mitigating device,
before proceeding to disagree by means of either an inductive or deductive rhetorical
strategy. The examples below illustrate this strategy, with a focus on a discussion of
the discourse intonation pattern typically associated with its use.

Example 8.5 is taken from a business meeting, and two colleagues are discussing the best time to advertise for new staff.

Example 8.5

1   a1: { = maybe the [< END >] } { = maybe the [END] of April or < Even > }
2   { = [SOME] some time in < ^ MAY > }
3   B: { \ [< _ Okay >] }
4   a1: { \ [< YEAH >] }
5   B: { \ [< YEAH >] } { / [< alRIGHT >] } { \ so you will [^ HAVE] to <
6   apPLY > } { \/ the [Other] thing that I was MENtioning the other < DAY
7   > } { \ which [MEANS] advertising < EARlier > }
8   a1: { = [< WE >] } { \ [< WE >] } { \ we can [< disCUSS >] that }

In lines 1-2, speaker a1 suggests advertising at 'the end of April or even some time in May' and selects high termination on 'May' which seeks to constrain the hearer to adjudicate. In line 3, speaker B selects low key + termination on 'okay', and this seems to denote that speaker a's suggestion is a foregone conclusion. In other words, it does not require adjudication (this is an example of 'pitch discord' which is discussed later in this chapter). However, in lines 5-7, speaker B disagrees with his colleague. He begins with a positive acknowledgement 'yeah alright' and then refers to something that he mentioned a few days ago 'so you will have to apply' with high key on 'have'. Speaker B selects high key on 'have' (line 5) which has a contrastive value. This key selection carries the local meaning of 'against expectations', and serves to underline the fact that the speaker believes that what he was 'mentioning the other day' is applicable despite the previous speaker's contrary position. The consequence is that the advertisement will have to be placed earlier than the dates proposed by speaker a. The use of 'so' (line 5) is also interesting because it gives the impression that his upcoming disagreement follows on from what has just been said.

Example 8.6 has been examined (see Example 8.2), but here the extract is extended to include speaker a's response.

Example 8.6

```
1   A:   { \ it's quite [ < INteresting > ] actually } { \ to [ SEE ] how < ^ QUICKly
2        > } { \ in [ JUST ] in ONE < geneRAtion > } { { ? [ < HOW > ] it's }
3        * { \ just [ < CHANGED > ] } } { = [ < ALmost > ] } } { = [ < WHERE > ]
4   a:   ** { \ [ < ^ YEAH > ] } { \ [ < YEAH > ] }
5        it's } { \ [ TOtally ] < ^ Equal > } (.) * { \ [ < YEAH > ] }
6   a:                        ** { \ [ < YEAH > ] } { = [ < ER > ] }
7        { \/ not [ < ^ TOtally > ] } { \ but [ < NEARly > ] }
8        ((laugh))
```

Speaker A asserts that women in Ireland now enjoy total gender equality (lines 1-3 and 5). In lines 6-7, speaker a disagrees with her friend's assessment of the extent of the equality. Speaker a begins her turn with a positive acknowledgement 'yeah' (line 6), hesitates momentarily, 'er', and then in line 7 says 'not totally but nearly' with high key + termination on 'totally'. This selection is contrastive and serves to underline the point of disagreement, after which she offers her an alternative assessment of the current extent of gender equality with the word 'nearly'.

Example 8.7 is from a radio interview. Speaker A is the interviewer, and speaker a is a well-known Hong Kong politician who is a champion for greater democracy in Hong Kong. They are discussing a new law, which, as argued by speaker a, is aimed at limiting the pro-democracy organizations and their rights to mount street protests.

Example 8.7

```
1   a:   ... { \ so they [ HAVE ] already taken VEry significant < ^ STEPS > } { \
2        in [ < eROding > ] } { \ our [ CIvil ] < LIberties > } { \ the [ QUEStion ] <
3        IS > } { \ [ WHEN ] will be the COMmissioner of < poLICE > } { \
4        [ Exercise ] those < POWers > } { \ to [ CRACK ] down on < US > }
5   A:   { \ so [ SO ] far there HAven't been < _ CAses > } { \ where [ SAY ] a
6        group either WANTS to register AS an < organiZAtion > } { = or
7        [ WANTS ] to have a < PROtest > } { \/ [ AND ] it's < BEEN > refused }
8   a:   { \/ [ < THAT'S > ] true } { \/ you can [ < SAY > ] that } { = [ < BUT > ] }
9        { = [ < THE > ] } { \ you must [ ASK ] the < QUEStion > } { \ of [ WHY ]
10       did they change the LAW a few < ^ MONTHS > ago } ...
```

In lines 1-4, speaker a asserts that the new law gives power to the police to curtail civil liberties. In lines 5-7, speaker A says that there has been no change in the status quo. In line 8-10, speaker a disagrees with speaker A, and she does so by beginning with a positive acknowledgement, 'that's true you can say that' and then says 'but', which is an adversative conjunction. She then goes on to argue that if the government intends to maintain the status quo 'why did they change the law a few months ago' with high termination on 'months' (line 10). This selection of termination seeks adjudication by way of rhetorical effect to emphasise that if the government wanted to maintain the status quo, they would not have changed the law.

Example 8.8 is from a TV panel discussion, and the panel guests are discussing their different views on tackling corruption in China mainland.

Example 8.8

```
1   a:   { = [ < ERM > ] } { \ i [ < ^ aGREE > ] } { \ i [ < THINK > ] } { \
2        [ THAT ] < IS > a challenge } { = [ < ER > ] } { = the [ ^ STARting ] <
3        POINT > of course } { \ is to [ < reMEMber > ] } { = [ < THAT > ] er }...
```

In Example 8.8, the speaker selects high key + termination on 'agree' (line 1) which has contrastive communicative value. In this context the panel guests have very different views on how to tackle a problem due to their differing views on its underlying causes, and so this initial expression of agreement with the other panel guest is contrary to expectations given their very different political standpoints. In line 2, speaker a selects high key on 'starting' which has contrastive value in keeping with the different views between the speaker and the other panel guest with regard to the underlying causes of the problem which the speaker then proceeds to outline.

Example 8.9 is from a job interview. Speaker a1 and B are interviewers and speaker a3 is the interviewee. The interviewee has been asked about her experience as a journalist, and whether it is relevant to the post for which she is now being interviewed.

Example 8.9

1 a3: { \ [SO] it's VEry < DIFferent > }

2 a1: { \ [< YEAH >] yeah }

3 B: { \ [< ^ DIFferent >] } * { = but [< I >] think } { = [< I >] think } { =

4 a3:   ** { = [< IT >] s depend on } { ? on on }

5 B: [< I >] think } { ? if you } { ? if you >

6 a3: { = [< THE >] } { ? [< obJECtive >] * er } (.) { = [< WHAT >] } (.)

7 a1:   ** { = [< SURE >] } { \ [< _ YEAH >] }

8 a3: * { \ what do you [< WANT >] }

9 B: ** { \ [< _ YEAH >] } { \ [< YEAH >] }

10 a1: * { = [< _ Mhm >] }

11 B: ** { \ [< YEAH >] } { \ but i [< THINK >] } { \ i think [< STILL >] }

12   { = if you've [HAD] < exPErience > } { = [< OF >] } { \ [colLECting]

13   DAta as a < JOURnalist > } { = and [< THEN >] } * { \ trying to make

14 a3:   ** { / [< Mhm >] }

15   sense of it [< AFterwards >] } { ? i think that } { \ [^ exPErience] is <

16   USEful > } { = [alTHOUGH] it is a < DIFferent > } { \/ [< _ exPErience

17   >] } * { = and your [< deMANDS >] } { \ are [< ^ LESS >] } { ? in in }

18 a3;   ** { = [< MM >] }

19   { \ [< ONE >] sense } { = [< IT'S >] } { \ it's [< ^ USEful >] }

In line 1, speaker a3 says that her experience as a journalist is very different. In lines 3 and 5, speaker B seems to try to voice his disagreement with high key + termination on 'different' (line 3), followed by 'but I think' (line 3). He is then interrupted by speaker a3, and he gives the floor to her after a brief period of simultaneous talk. In lines 11-12, 15-17 and 19, speaker B manages to make the case that the experience of the job applicant, although different, is nonetheless useful. In line 11, he begins with a positive acknowledgement, 'yeah', and then the adversative conjunction 'but', followed twice by the hedge 'I think', which leads him into his disagreement. His view differs from that of speaker a1 and, to add communicative value to his contrasting position, he selects high key on 'experience' (line 15) and high key + termination on 'less' and 'useful' (lines 17 and 19). These discourse intonation selections serve to underline his contrary position with regard to the usefulness of the interviewee's experience which is that while her experience was less demanding than that of the post she is being interviewed for this does not diminish its usefulness in speaker B's opinion.

In Example 8.10, two colleagues are having a business meeting. They digress momentarily to talk about the merits of various kinds of equipment for keeping Hong Kong's humidity at bay.

Example 8.10

```
1  B:   ... { = i've [ GOT ] THREE < BIG > } { \ [ < WARdrobes > ] } { \ each
2       [ ONE'S ] GOT ONE of those < HEAters > in }
3  a1:  { \ i [ DON'T ] < USE > them } { = i [ DON'T ] like < Using > them }
4  B:   { / [ < NO > ] }
5  a1:  { = [ < NO > ] } { = i [ DON'T ] want to < FEEL > } { \ [ ^ FEEL ] the <
6       HEAT > } { = [ < WHEN > ] } { = [ whenEver ] i o < Open > } { = [ <
7       Open > ] it }
8  B:   { \ [ < YEAH > ] } { \ [ < WELL > ] } { \ you [ < ^ DON'T > ] } { \ you
9       [ < DON'T > ] } { \/ it's [ ^ NOT ] that < HOT > } ...
```

Speaker a1 says that she is not in favour of using wardrobe heaters because she fears that it would result in a blast of hot air whenever she opens her wardrobes. In line 8, speaker B begins with a positive acknowledgement, 'yeah', followed by 'well', and then selects high key + termination on 'don't' which has contrastive communicative value followed by high key on 'not' in line 9. These selections of contrastive high key underline the speaker's point that one does not feel the heat from the heater because it is not hot enough to create that effect and further imply "I think you're wrong" in this local context.

The above examples illustrate that speakers employ high key, high key + termination or high termination to indicate that what they are saying is either in contrast to or has the sense of "this will surprise you" (Brazil 1997: 58). In other words, the speakers' selections from these two systems of discourse intonation add additional local meaning and help the speaker to convey, and the hearer to understand, that a disagreement is taking place. The consistent use of these discourse intonation selections may be accounted for in part by the fact that, having begun by positively acknowledging the contribution of the previous speaker, it is of importance to convey the sense of contrast, or going against expectations, in relation to the ensuing disagreement.

Particularising use of high key

Another pattern of use associated with the selection of high key is what Brazil (1997: 45-46 and 163) terms the "particularising" use. It is not used to contrast propositions but rather to "reject all of the existentially possible alternatives" (ibid.: 45). This pattern of usage is exemplified below. Example 8.11 is from a speech by a senior Hong Kong politician.

Example 8.11

1 b: { \/ [FOLlowing] the < SEries > } { = of [^ eduCAtion] < reFORMS

2   > } { \ that [beGAN] < LAST > year }

In line 1, speaker b talks about 'education reforms' and selects high key on 'education'. The speech was delivered at a time when a number of reforms across a range of public services was underway, and so the speaker highlights by means of this selection of particularizing high key that it is 'education' rather than 'social service reforms', or any other kind of reforms, that he is addressing.

Example 8.12 is taken from a conversation between two friends in a restaurant. The speaker is explaining that whenever HKC have a dim sum lunch (i.e. a typical Cantonese lunch), they always order a particular dish.

Example 8.12

1 b: … { = for [CHInese] < PEOple > } (.) { = [< WE >] } (.) { \ we [<

2   ALways >] have ((Cantonese)) } { \ for [< _ LUNCH >] } { / when we

3   go to [DIM] sum < LUNCH > } { = it is [< ACtually >] } { = it is [<

4   ACtually >] } { \ [^ SHRIMP] < DUMpling > } { \ [SHRIMP] <

5   DUMpling > } …

In line 4, speaker b names the favourite dim sum dish, 'shrimp dumpling', for the Chinese and selects high key on 'shrimp' which has the particularising function of emphasising the specific type of dumpling in this local context of interaction.

Example 8.13 is from a public speech by a senior government official.

Example 8.13

1   b: ... { \ [FInally] we have < CONfidence > } { \ [beCAUSE] we can <

2   LEverage > } { / on the [^ supPORT] of the central < GOvernment > }...

In the above example of the speaker choosing high key, the speaker is talking about 'the support of the central government' (line 2), and selects high key on 'support'. Again, this use of high key carries with it the situation-specific sense that of all the things that can be leveraged by Hong Kong to help it become a major economic centre in the region, it is 'support' from the government in Beijing in this context.

Topic development

If the speaker selects low termination, he/she makes no attempt to exert control over the next turn, and this can lead to the next speaker initiating a new topic or for the discourse to come to a close (Brazil 1997). One of the functions of low termination is to close a pitch sequence which constitutes a stretch of speech comprising one or more tone units and, importantly, represents some "discrete part of the discourse" (Brazil 1995: 246). A pattern of use that may be selected by speakers, and which is related to this function, is to employ low termination to signal the close of a topic in a discourse. This may be used in combination with high key which a speaker may select to indicate the start of the next topic, which has the communicative value of contrasting the commencement of a new topic with the close of a prior topic.

The process of moving from one topic to another can be realised in a number of ways. Stenström (1994: 150-162), for example, identifies six topical strategies used by speakers to manage this process. Five of the strategies described by Stenström involve the use of prefaces (e.g. 'now I want to talk about ...', 'first I'd like to examine ...') and discourse markers (e.g. 'well', 'okay', 'so') by speakers to signal to the hearer that topic movement is underway. Extra-linguistic phenomena, such as pauses and laughter, may also be employed. On occasion, especially in conversation, speakers do not linguistically signal topic development, and the topic develops imperceptibly (Stenström, 1994: 151 and 157-8).

Brown and Yule (1983) describe the role that can be played by intonation in topic development. They describe "paratones" as intonational behaviour that is equivalent to a writer using paragraphing to separate one topic from another (ibid.: 100-106). Where a writer uses indentation to signal "a division in the discourse structure" or "topic shifts", a speaker creates "speech paragraphs" or "paratones" (ibid.: 100), by means of intonational selections and other linguistic and paralinguistic strategies. Brown and Yule (1983: 101) describe the boundary markers for these paratones. At the start the speaker may use a preface or discourse marker and, in terms of intonation, the first clause or sentence may be said with raised pitch. The end of the paratone may be marked by low pitch "even on lexical items" (ibid.: 101), a summarising phrase, or repetition, and a pause of more than one second (ibid.: 101), or the use of fillers. Examples of this discourse intonation pattern are discussed below.

Example 8.14 is from the start of a televised interview of a well-known former senior government official in Hong Kong.

Example 8.14

1 B: { \ [BAroness] < _ DUNN > } { = [HONG] kong is < SEEN > as } { =

2   having [< ^ LOST >] } } { = [< SOME >] of its } { \ [< comPEtitiveness

3   >] } } { \ in [< REcent >] years } { = is [THAT] a < FAIR > assessment }

In line 1, the speaker selects low termination in the first tone unit when he says 'Baroness Dunn'. This occurs right at the start of a televised interview between the interviewer, speaker B, and Baroness Dunn. This represents the end of a discrete part of the discourse which is the use of a vocative by the interviewer, before asking the guest the first question in the interview. The question is the start of a new topic, and the speaker selects high key on 'lost' (line 2).

In Example 8.15, the speaker is a senior government official giving a speech to a group of financiers.

Example 8.15

1 b: ... { = [fiNANcial] < SERvices > } { = is [REALly] a < SECtor > } { =

2   i'm [< PLEASED >] to see } { \ is [< ^ BROAdening >] } } { = its [<

3   BASE >] } { = with [< NEW >] products } { = and [NEW] <

4   LEgislation > } { = to [< enHANCE >] } { \ the [< QUAlity >] } { \ of

5   the [< _ MARket >] } (.) { [< ^ toDAY >] } { = as you [QUITE]

6   rightly say i am < ^ NOT > } { = going to [< TALK >] about } { = [<

7   MARkets >] } { \ or [MAking] < MOney > }...

At the start of Example 8.15, speaker b talks about the improving market for the financial services industry in Hong Kong (lines 1-5). He ends this topic by stating that the Hong Kong Government has recently introduced 'new legislation to enhance the quality of the market', and he finishes this topic with low termination on 'market'. This intonation selection indicates to the hearers the end of the current topic. He then pauses briefly before using a preface, 'today as you quite rightly say

I'm not going to talk...', with high key on 'today' (line 5) when he introduces the new topic.

Example 8.16 is from a press conference at which a senior official of a Hong Kong bank announces the bank's annual results.

Example 8.16

1   b: ... { = [^ speCIfic] < proVIsions > } { \ [PLUS] < colLAteral > } { =
2   [THAT] is conSERvatively < estiMAted > } { = [aMOUNted] to
3   ALmost a < HUNdred > percent } { = of our non [< perFORming >] }
4   { \ [< _ adVANces >] } (.) { = [^ HANG] seng < inCREASED > } { \ its
5   [MARket] share of total < dePOsits > and loans } { \ for [USE] in
6   HONG kong in two o o < TWO > } { = [CUStomer] < dePOsits > } { \
7   were [< ^ mainTAINED >] } { = at [< FOUR >] hundred } { \ and
8   [THIRteen] point SEven < BILlion > }...

In lines 1-4, speaker b describes the constituents of the bank's 'non performing advances' with low termination on 'advances' which signals the close of the topic. Speaker b then pauses in line 4 before beginning a new topic with high key on 'Hang' in which he moves on to talk about deposits and loans.

Endings

The above examples have illustrated how the selection of low or high voice pitch is an option available to speakers to signal points of topic development in the local context. In the case of low termination, it is sometimes selected at the end of the discourse, or to signal the end of the speaker's contribution to the discourse. Example 8.17 (i-iv), provides four examples of this pattern of use.

Example 8.17 i-iv

i)

1   b: ... { \ we have the [FORmula] for < ^ sucCESS > } { = we [SHALL] <
2   JOIN > hands to achieve it } { \ [THANK] you very < _ MUCH > }

ii)

1   b: ... { \ it [< ^ canNOT >] } { \ [< superCEDE >] } { = [< OR >] }
2   { = [< OR >] } { \ [< ^ overRIDE >] } { = [< THE >] }
3   { \ [S] f < C > } { \ [< _ THAT'S >] all }

iii)

1   b2:   ...{ = there'll be more [DEtails] < LAter > } } { = i'm going to

2   [< HAND >] over that } { = to [< PEter >] } { = to [< GO >] through

3   the } { \ the [Operations] of the < _ GROUP > }

4   ((pause))

iv)

1   b: { = [< JUST >] } } { \ [TAking] an < INterest > } { \ in the [afFAIRS]

2   of hong < ^ KONG > } } { = we should [< ALL >] } } { \ [TAKE] < PART

3   > } } { ? [< BE >] it } { { ? a [< VEry >] } } { \ [< SMALL >] part } { = in

4   [< SHAping >] } } { = [OUR] < DEStiny > } { \ and our [< _ FUture >] } }

In the above examples, the speakers select low key + termination or low termination in the last tone unit to signal the end of the discourse or a discrete segment of the discourse. Instances of the latter category include a speaker ending his answer to a question in Q&A session (8.17 ii) and a speaker passing the floor to another speaker (8.17 iii).

Equative

A pattern of use for low key is to signal an "equative" value to what is said in the sense of "as expected" in that what is said is self evident and so a foregone conclusion (Brazil 1997: 49-53). The following examples illustrate this selection in a variety of local contexts. In the examples which feature single prominence tone units, where the speaker has to select key + termination simultaneously, it is the selection of low key that is the focus of the analyses.

Example 8.18 is from a public speech delivered by a senior official of the Hong Kong government to a conference attended by venture capitalists.

Example 8.18

1   b: ... { = i [^ THINK] you will < aGREE > } } { = that we are the [<

2   WORLD'S >] } } { = [< MOST >] } } { = [BUSIness] < FRIENDly > } { \

3   [< CIty >] } } { = an [^ ENtrepreneurial] < CIty > } } { = [< MADE >] } }

4   { \ for venture [< _ CApitalists >] } } { = but [^ DON'T] take my <

5   WORD > for it } } { = you [< ARE >] } } { \ the [< _ EXperts >] } } { =

6   when it [^ COMES] to < eVAluating > } } { = the [< viaBIlity >] } } { = of

7   a [< BUSIness >] } }...

In Example 8.18, the speaker twice selects low key when he refers to his audience of venture capitalists: 'capitalists' (line 4) and 'experts' (line 5). These both have the meaning of "self evident" in this context.

Example 8.19 is from an internship interview at a five-star hotel. The interviewer, speaker B, describes the anti-social working hours that are inherent to the industry.

Example 8.19

1 B: { \ [AND] < ^ LONG > hours } { ? in our industry } { \/ [IS] very < ^

2   EAsy > } { \/ for [^ ONE] simple < REAson > } { \ is that the [hoTEL]

3   never < _ CLOses >}

4 a: { \ [< MM >] }

5 B: { = [< SO >] } { \ [YOU] can BAsically < ^ BE > here } { \ [_

6   TWENty] four hours a < DAY > }

Speaker B, in line 3, states what he perceives to be the end of a discrete section of the discourse, 'that the hotel never closes' with low termination on 'closes'. He then selects low key in lines 5-6 when he summarises the point he has made earlier, stating that 'you can basically be here twenty four hours a day' with low key on 'twenty' (line 6), which has the sense of "self-evident" given that he has said that the hotel never closes.

Example 8.20 is from an academic lecture in the field of accounting in which the lecturer is explaining a formula for arriving at the simplified version of the total cost.

Example 8.20

1 b: ... { = and we [< PUT >] this } { / [< exPRESsion >] } { / [INto] the

2   FORmula < HERE > } { = [< AND >] we } { \/ [REarRANGE] the < ^

3   ALgebra > } { / because [THIS] equals < THIS > } { = [< THEN >] }

4   { = you [COME] up with < THIS > } { ? [< S >] } { \/ [SIMplified] <

5   VERsion > } { \ of the [TOtal] < COST > } { = the [^ FIRST] < PART

6   > } { / shown [< THERE >] } { = [< IS >] } { \/ the [< ^ GROUping

7   >] } { \/ of the [< ORder >] } { / [AND] the HOLding < ^ COST > }

8   { = and the [LAST] < PART > } { \ is the [Unit] < _ COST > } { \ so

9   [_ THAT'S] where it < COMES > from }...

In lines 1-5, the speaker is describing a formula for calculating the simplified version of the total cost. He then mentions two components of the total cost, the 'holding cost' (line 7) and the 'unit cost' (line 8). He then concludes by saying 'so that's where it comes from' (lines 8-9), referring back to the simplified total cost, and says 'that's' with low key to signal self-evidence in the sense of having gone full circle in terms of explaining the concept.

Example 8.21 is from a conversation between two friends in which they discuss the size of speaker B's house in Australia.

Example 8.21

```
 1  b:   { \ it's fifteen [ < THOUsand > ] }
 2  B:   { \ square [ < FEET > ] }
 3  b:   { \ fifteen [ < ^ THOUsand > ] } { \ square [ < FEET > ] }
 4  B:   { ? it [ CAN'T ] be < RIGHT > }
 5  b:   { ? [ < SUCH > ] a } { \/ such a [ < BIG > ] one }
 6  B:   { / [ < NO > ] } { / [ < WELL > ] } { = if you've [ < GOT > ] }
 7  b:   { \ [ < NO > ] } { \ you are [ TALking ] about INside or < OUTside > }
 8       * { \ or [ < BOTH > ] }
 9       ** { \/ [ < Inside > ] } { \ [ < _ INside > ] }
10  b:   { /\ [ ^ INside ] it is fifteen < THOUsand > } { \ it must be a [ _ VEry ]
11       BIG < HOUSE > }
12  B:   ((laugh)) { = [ < HANG > ] on } { \ we've [ ^ GOT ] something <
13       WRONG > here }
14  b:   ((laugh))
```

Speaker B seems to be muddled when converting the size of his house into square feet. In line 4, he expresses doubt as to whether the size he has stated is correct. Speaker b in line 5 seems to think his friend has 'such a big one' if it's fifteen thousand square feet. The confusion persists and speaker B sticks with this figure for the inside dimensions when asked by his friend, which causes him to respond 'inside it is fifteen thousand it must be a very big house' in lines 10-11. The self evidence of his comment is reinforced by his selection of low key on 'very'. Speaker B finally admits his error (lines 12-13), and the friends share a laugh together.

Pitch concord and discord

A pattern related to a speaker's selection of intonation at the start of a turn is described by Brazil (1997: 54-61). Brazil states that there is a tendency for speakers to select "pitch concord" at these points in the discourse. Pitch concord is realised in two ways. The first situation is when the first speaker ends his/her utterance with high termination, or high key and termination, and then the second speaker begins his/her utterance with high key, or high key and termination. The second situation is when the first speaker ends his/her utterance with mid termination, or mid key and termination, and then the second speaker begins his/her utterance with mid key, or mid key and termination. Also, pitch concord is a phenomenon which applies whether the prior speaker has uttered an interrogative or a declarative (ibid.: 165).

Pitch concord is therefore another way in which speakers may use forms of converging and diverging intonation behaviours to add communicative value to what they are saying. Other forms are discussed in Chapter 6 (see also Chun 2002: 39-42). The phenomenon of pitch concord is not a rule, however, and a speaker may select to begin a turn without matching the termination, or key + termination, selection of the previous speaker. Brazil (1997: 55-56) terms such instances "concord-breaking", but the term "pitch discord" is used here for these instances because concord-breaking suggests that a rule has been broken, and hence a mistake of some kind made. This is potentially misleading because pitch discord also carries important communicative value in the local context, and is certainly not some kind of mistake It is simply that "there is a discrepancy between the ways the two parties assess the context of interaction" (Brazil 1997: 54).

Below examples of pitch concord are discussed. The form that the pitch concord takes is given at the start of each example, high termination ('ht') followed by high key ('hk'), for instance, is shown as 'ht → hk'. In the first example, Example 8.22, the two speakers have been discussing the achievements of speaker a's daughter in piano playing. Speaker a has been very modestly telling her friend that her daughter has been recommended to sit for a prestigious scholarship exam. Throughout, speaker a downplays the achievements of her daughter and projects a very muted reaction to all that her daughter has accomplished.

Example 8.22

(ht → hk)

1. B: { \ you must be very [< ^ PROUD >] }
2. a: { / i [< ^ HOPE >] } { = she [< CAN >] } { = she [< CAN >] } { \ [<
3.   GAIN >] it } { = [BUT] er NEver < MIND > } { ? if she } { \ [<
4.   canNOT >] }

In line 1, speaker B says that speaker a 'must be very proud' of her daughter; in other words, contrary to the very humble way in which speaker a has been talking about her daughter's impressive piano-playing achievements. Speaker B selects high termination on 'proud', which has the communicative meaning that this is an unexpected comment and, in this local context in which parental pride is not being overtly displayed, it is unexpected and speaker B expects the hearer to adjudicate. In line 2, speaker a responds 'I hope she can she can gain it...'. She can be seen to select pitch concord by her selection of high key on 'hope' at the start of her utterance. This selection has a contrastive meaning and, in the local context of this discourse, it functions to contrast her indirect response to the direct assertion in line 1 by speaker B. Speaker a does not openly admit to being proud of her daughter, and selects instead to do it indirectly by talking about her hope that her daughter will do well.

In the next example, Example 8.23, two friends are having a conversation and the topic is the increasing affluence among Chinese in China mainland.

Example 8.23
(ht → hk)

> 1. a: { \ [< OH >] } { \ [SOME] are much much < ^ RIcher > }
> 2. B: { \ [< ^ SURE >] } { = [< WATches >] } { = and [< SO >] on }

In line 1, speaker a makes the point that although all Chinese living in the PRC are more affluent these days, 'some are much much richer'. She selects high termination on 'richer', which invites speaker B to adjudicate in the sense of "don't you agree". In line 2, speaker B responds by saying 'sure watches and so on' and selects high key on 'sure', and this pitch concord signals agreement with his friend's claim and he goes on to give an example.

In Example 8.24, two friends have been discussing a project that speaker a has been working on.

Example 8.24
(ht → hk)

> 1. B: { = so the [< JOB'S >] } { \ [< ^ FInished >] }
> 2. a: { \ [< ^ FInished >] }

In line 1, speaker B asks a declarative mood question as to whether 'the job's finished', and selects high termination on 'finished'. This selection has the communicative meaning of seeking adjudication from the hearer. In other words, speaker B does not know whether the project that speaker a has been working on has finished or not, and so he is not seeking confirmation of what he has said. When speaker a responds, she says 'finished' (line 2) with high key and this pitch concord serves to underline the fact that there is no question that the job is finished.

In Example 8.25, the two speakers are colleagues in a business meeting and they are discussing the date by which a report has to be submitted.

Example 8.25
(mt → mk)

1. b: { / on the [< THIRD >] }
2. a: { \ [< FOURTH >] }
3. b: { \ on the [< FOURTH >] } { \ that's a [< THURSday >] }

In line 1, speaker b asks a declarative mood question and selects mid termination on 'third' which has the communicative function of seeking concurrence from the hearer. In other words, speaker b thinks that the deadline date is the third, and is seeking confirmation from speaker a that this is indeed the case. What is interesting here is that speaker a responds with mid key when she says 'fourth' (line 2), despite the fact that this answer contrasts with speaker b's belief that it is the third. We might have expected speaker a to not select pitch concord and to select high key with its contrastive value in this context. Brazil (1997) notes that discourse intonation is open to exploitation by speakers, and here speaker a is effectively correcting her colleague, but in a less face threatening way, by exploiting discourse intonation. This makes what she says appear to concur with the previous speaker. This sense of the fourth being the known, or expected, date continues in line 3, when speaker b takes the correction is his stride with mid-key selection on 'fourth'.

In the last example of pitch concord, Example 8.26, two friends are discussing the location of a restaurant that speaker B has recently visited.

Example 8.26
(mt → mk)

1. B: { / it's called the [MANdarin] < HOUSE > } { / do you [< KNOW >]
2.   that } { / on [LOCKhart] < ROAD > }
3. a: { / [LOCKhart] < ROAD > } { \ [< MM >] } (.) { ? [< I >] } { \ i
4.   [SELdom] < GO > there }

In lines 1-2, speaker B asks his friend if she knows the 'Mandarin House... on Lockhart Road' and, by choosing mid termination on 'road', he is expecting his friend to concur by saying that she does know it because it is quite well-known, and also the road that it is on is very well-known. By responding with mid-key selection on 'Lockhart', speaker a concurs that she knows the road, but then goes on to indirectly say that she doesn't know the restaurant itself, by saying that she rarely goes to that particular road 'I seldom go there' (lines 3-4).

Pitch discord

As explained above, in this study the term pitch discord has been coined to describe situations when the first speaker selects high termination or mid termination at the end of her utterance, and the next speaker selects a different level key at the start of her utterance. It needs to be made clear that pitch concord is not correct discourse intonation behaviour and, similarly, that pitch discord is not incorrect usage in terms of discourse intonation selections. Brazil (1997: 54) makes it clear that while the first speaker's selection of termination sets up constraints on the next speaker's selection of utterance initial key selection, these constraints can be overridden by the next speaker. Instances of pitch discord, termed "concord-breaking" by Brazil (1997: 54), occur when there is "a discrepancy between ways the two parties assess the context of interaction", and such discrepancies are not related to notions of correct and incorrect discourse intonation usage. Examples of pitch discord are discussed below.

Example 8.27 is taken from a job interview, with the interviewer asking the interviewee about her current teaching post in a secondary school.

Example 8.27
(ht → mk)

1. a1: { \ what [SUBjects] are you < ^ TEAching > }
2. a3: { \ [< ENglish >] }

In line 1, speaker a1 selects high termination on 'teaching', and this has the communicative value of seeking adjudication from the hearer as the answer is not anticipated by speaker a1. In the context of a wh-question, this key selection indicates that an improbable answer is anticipated (Brazil, 1997: 57). Speaker a3 responds with 'English' (line 2), said with mid key which has the communicative function of stating something additive. In other words, she perceives her answer to not be improbable and hence possible to anticipate given the context of the interview. The job interview is for a research assistant in a university English department, and this might explain speaker a3's selection of pitch discord.

In Example 8.28, pitch discord takes place when the two participants are talking about some mutual acquaintances who are submitting a work-related project proposal which they need to submit that day.

Example 8.28
(mt → hk)

1. B: { / did they [SAY] they would GET it in < toDAY > }
2. b: { \ oh [^ F__] asked < THEM > before } { \ they [SAID] they <

3.   WOULD > }

In line 1, speaker B is in effect asking the hearer to double-check with regard to what has been said, and ends his question with mid termination in line 1 which seeks concurrence from the hearer. In other words, speaker B expects a positive response from speaker b beginning with mid key. However, speaker b selects contrastive high key on the name of 'F__' when he responds by saying 'oh F__ asked them before...' (line 2). This selection of pitch discord by speaker b has the communicative meaning of undermining speaker B's assumption that double-checking is required because a third party, F__, has already double-checked and they will submit the proposal that day.

The following example, Example 8.29 is taken from a conversation between friends discussing food, which is a popular topic in Hong Kong.

Example 8.29
(ht → lk)

  1. b: { \ [SO] it's < ^ FRIED > }
  2. a: { \ [< _ NO >] } { \ cos it's [< CHEAP >] } { \ it's [< CHEAP >] }

Speaker b asserts that the food being discussed is fried, and selects high termination on 'fried' (line 1) which has the meaning that this information is perceived by him to be unexpected or surprising to the hearers. In line 2, the speaker selects low key on 'no', which has the meaning of self-evident given what she goes on to explain. She says that speaker b's assertion is incorrect, i.e. 'cos it's cheap', which implies that it is a forgone conclusion that the food being discussed could not be both fried and cheap. Her selection of pitch discord adds further communicative value to her different opinion.

The last example, Example 8.30, shows both pitch concord and pitch discord. The extract is taken from a conversation between two friends, who are discussing the fact that one of them has a tough job. His friend then asks if he is too tired.

Example 8.30
(ht → hk) and (mt → hk)

  1 b1: { / [WERE] you too < ^ TIRED > }
  2 b2: { = [< UM >] } { \/ i was a [< ^ LITtle >] bit tired } { = but [< I >] er }
  3   { = [< I >] er } { = [< I >] } { \ i [< beLIEVE >] } { = i [< COULD >]
  4   er } { = i [< COULD >] * er }
  5 b1:   ** { = did you [TELL] anyone that you were
  6   < TIRED > }

7   b2: { \ [< ^ NO >] } { \ [NOT] at < ALL > } { \ [NOT] at < ALL > }...

At the start of the Example 8.30, speaker b1 asks his friend 'were you too tired' and selects high termination on 'tired'. Speaker b2 begins with a filler, 'um', in line 2 and then admits that he was 'a little bit tired' and selects high key on 'little' which puts distance between the assumption in speaker b1's question and his answer. Speaker b1 then asks whether or not his friend has told anyone where he works that he gets tired in (line 5). He selects mid termination on 'tired', which expects concurrence from the hearer. In other words, he expects his friend to say that he has told someone. In line 2, speaker b2 responds by saying 'no', selecting contrastive high key which is appropriate given that his response is not what speaker b1 anticipates.

Frequency distribution of pitch concord and discord

In this section the relative frequencies of occurrence of pitch concord and pitch discord across the two sets of speakers are examined to see whether or not a preference exists for pitch concord, as opposed to pitch discord as stated by Brazil (1997). Table 8.10 below shows the results of a sample of 1,000 instances of studying the concord or discord that exists between the first speaker's selection of termination at the end of his/her utterance and the second speaker's utterance initial selection of key. These 1,000 instances are comprised of 500 instances spoken by HKC and 500 instances spoken by NES. The percentages refer to the proportional distributions of concord and the two possible forms of discord when the prior speaker ends with mid termination, and then the same again for when the prior speaker ends with high termination.

Table 8.10 shows that in the data examined, pitch concord is more prevalent than pitch discord, which confirms the claims of Brazil (1997). When the prior speaker selects mid termination, the next speaker selects mid key in 83.57% of all the instances and, for high termination, pitch concord accounts for 70.87% of

Table 8.10 Frequency and distribution of pitch concord and discord

	mt → mk concord	mt → hk discord	mt → lk discord	ht → hk concord	ht → mk discord	ht → lk discord	Total
HKC	390	25	38	33	8	6	500
	(86.09%)	(5.51%)	(8.38%)	(70.21%)	(17.02%)	(12.76%)	(100%)
NES	368	44	42	40	11	5	500
	(81.05%)	(9.69%)	(9.25%)	(71.42%)	(19.64%)	(8.92%)	(100%)
Total	758	69	80	73	19	11	1,000
	(83.57%)	(7.60%)	(8.82%)	(70.87%)	(18.44%)	(10.67%)	(100%)

instances. Table 8.10 also shows that pitch discord is more commonplace (29.01% across both sets of speakers) at points in the discourse, where the second speaker is being constrained to adjudicate by the first speaker's selection of high termination. Pitch discord is therefore less likely (13.89% of instances for HKC and 18.94% of instances for NES) in situations, where the first speaker is constraining the hearer to concur through the selection of mid termination. This difference is possibly linked to the inherent difference between seeking adjudication and seeking concurrence, in which the latter is more likely to be in line with the first speaker's assessment of the context of interaction. While levels of pitch discord are similar in the case of first speakers selecting high termination, there is a slightly higher level of pitch discord in the cases of NES responding to mid termination utterances (i.e. 18.94% versus 13.89%). However, this difference is not very great, and so it might be overstating the case to suggest that HKC are more likely to concur with their interlocutors than NES. As to what form the pitch discord takes, there seems to be an even spread for both sets of speakers in terms of what level of key is chosen when the termination selection of the prior speaker is mid. However, when it is high termination, there is higher proportional use of mid key, compared with low key, for both sets of speakers.

Most frequent word classes in single word tone units

The high number of single word tone units, as well as the most frequent words found in this kind of tone unit, are described and discussed in Chapter 5. Table 8.11 returns to these words to examine whether there are discernible patterns in speakers' selection of key + termination for these single word tone units. The fact that many tone units are single word tone units, or tone units with a single prominence, means that there are many instances of speakers simultaneously selecting key and termination. This is because in "minimal tonic segments there is no possibility of making the two selections independently" (Brazil 1997: 61). The selection of key + termination on the same syllable does not impede the hearer's interpretation of its communicative value in the local context of interaction (ibid.: 162-167).

Before individual words, and groups of similar word classes, are discussed, it is of interest to note that in Table 8.11, no word has a one hundred percent occurrence of a particular key + termination selection, and there are no zero instances of a key + termination selection. Again, this underlines the fact that discourse intonation selections are not fixed properties. Across all of the words, the selection of mid key + termination by speakers is the most frequent selection, but there is a wide range from 98.83% on 'it' down to 53.34% on 'now'. Low key + termination is the second most selected option by speakers across all these words, but, again, the

Table 8.11 Patterns of key + termination in thirty most frequent one-word tone units[2]

Word	Low key + termination	Mid key + termination	High key + termination	Total
er	2,233 (21.23%)	8,220 (78.16%)	63 (0.59%)	10,516 (100%)
yeah	1,761 (23.83%)	4,987 (67.50%)	640 (8.60%)	7,388 (100%)
okay	529 (13.89%)	3,055 (80.24%)	223 (5.80%)	3,807 (100%)
and	79 (2.04%)	3,748 (97.17%)	30 (0.77%)	3,857 (100%)
mm	408 (11.26%)	3,008 (83.07%)	205 (5.66%)	3,621 (100%)
um	227 (7.34%)	2,835 (91.68%)	30 (0.97%)	3,092 (100%)
mhm	79 (2.79%)	2,719 (96.31%)	25 (0.88%)	2,823 (100%)
so	191 (8.40%)	2,154 (94.76%)	100 (4.39%)	2,273 (100%)
yes	298 (12.62%)	1,838 (77.84%)	225 (9.52%)	2,361 (100%)
the	26 (1.41%)	1,805 (98.52%)	1 (0.054%)	1,832 (100%)
right	382 (21.34%)	1,350 (75.41%)	58 (3.24%)	1,790 (100%)
erm	261 (15.83%)	1,376 (83.49%)	11 (0.66%)	1,648 (100%)
i	3 (0.23%)	1,233 (98.16%)	20 (1.59%)	1,256 (100%)
but	9 (0.61%)	1,419 (96.33%)	45 (3.05%)	1,473 (100%)
oh	116 (8.23%)	856 (60.75%)	437 (31.01%)	1,409 (100%)
no	227 (17.98%)	881 (69.80%)	154 (12.20%)	1,262 (100%)
to	9 (0.91%)	972 (98.78%)	3 (0.30%)	984 (100%)
well	176 (18.29%)	704 (73.18%)	82 (8.52%)	962 (100%)
that	6 (0.82%)	694 (95.98%)	23 (3.18%)	723 (100%)
in	7 (0.80%)	856 (98.39%)	7 (0.80%)	870 (100%)
now	346 (39.95%)	462 (53.34%)	58 (6.69%)	866 (100%)
because	8 (0.98%)	747 (91.76%)	59 (7.24%)	814 (100%)
it	1 (0.29%)	338 (98.83%)	3 (0.87%)	342 (100%)
or	27 (3.76%)	680 (94.70%)	11 (1.53%)	718 (100%)
uhuh	20 (3.03%)	631 (95.89%)	7 (1.06%)	658 (100%)
you	2 (0.35%)	541 (95.24%)	25 (4.40%)	568 (100%)
alright	47 (7.87%)	511 (85.59%)	39 (6.53%)	597 (100%)
is	12 (1.86%)	628 (97.51%)	4 (0.62%)	644 (100%)
we	1 (0.18%)	518 (96.46%)	18 (3.35%)	537 (100%)
they	1 (0.20%)	470 (97.91%)	9 (1.87%)	480 (100%)

---

2.   The rank order in Table 8.11 follows the raw frequencies of the words occurring in single word tone units, the differences in totals in this table is a result of some tone units being unclassifiable

proportional use of this selection has a wide range from 39.95% on 'now' to 0.18% on 'we'. There is also a wide range of usage for high key + termination with 31.01% on 'oh' and a mere 0.054% on 'the'.

When groups of similar words are examined, different tendencies can be observed. If the 'affirmative' minimal responses, 'yeah', 'mm', mhm', 'yes', and 'uhuh' are grouped together, three of them have quite a relatively high usage of low key + termination (ranging from 23.83% for 'yeah' to 11.26% for 'mm') and also quite a high usage of high key + termination (ranging from 9.52% for 'yes' to 5.66% for 'mm'). Two members of this group, 'mhm' and 'uhuh', are much more likely to be spoken with mid key + termination, 96.31% and 95.89% respectively, than the other members of this group. Another minimal response is 'no', which also has a high incidence of low key + termination (17.98%) and high key + termination (12.20%). The minimal response 'oh' has quite a high usage of low key + termination (8.23%), and the highest usage of high key + termination (31.01%).

The three fillers in the list, 'er', 'um' and 'erm', also have a distinct pattern of usage, with all of them having a relatively high proportional usage of low key + termination, ranging from 21.23% for 'er' to 7.34% for 'um', but a very low usage of high key + termination, ranging from 0.97% for 'um' to 0.59% for 'er'. The group of discourse particles[3] on the list, 'okay', 'so', 'right', 'well', 'now', and 'alright', also make proportionately greater use of low and high key + termination selections than other kinds of single word tone units, and with a higher proportional usage of low, as opposed to high, key + termination.

The conjunctions, 'and', 'but', because' and 'or', have a lower proportionate usage of low and high key + termination, especially low key + termination, although 'because' has quite a high usage of high key + termination (7.24%). The pronouns, 'i', 'it', 'you', 'we', and 'they', are also comparatively rarely spoken with low or high key + termination, especially low key + termination. Similarly, the group of 'fragments', 'the', 'to', 'that', 'in' and 'is', has the lowest usage of low and high key + termination out of all of the groupings.

Conclusions

This chapter has examined the distribution of key, termination, and key + termination in the HKCSE (prosodic). As expected, mid key, mid termination, and mid key + termination are by far the most frequent selections across all speakers and

---

3.   Here all instances are labeled discourse particles, but some may be used propositionally. In her study of discourse particles in the HKCSE (prosodic), Lam (2008) finds that 97.60% of the instances of 'well' and 98.10% of 'so' are discourse particles.

sub-corpora, followed by high and then low. There are differences, however, in the proportional usages of the various options across the HKC and the NES and across the sub-corpora.

A number of patterns of use relating to key and termination selections have been described and discussed. The contrastive use of high selections, sometimes in combination with low selections, has been found to be related to this basic contrastive use is the use of high key and high termination when speakers perform disagreement in certain local contexts. High key is also used to particularise, and some of the forms that this can take have been examined. The use of intonation to signal topic development is another use that may combine both low and high selections, and the ending of a discourse with low termination is another quite common phenomenon. Low key and low termination are also used to convey propositions which are perceived as self evident. Pitch concord is a pattern of use which seems to be the typical selection of both sets of speakers, but there is also evidence of pitch discord when the participants' perceptions differ. Lastly, frequently occurring single word tone units are analysed. While the selection of key + termination is not fixed, there are patterns associated with both specific words and word classes.

CHAPTER 9

Conclusions and implications

Concluding comments

The corpus-driven study described in this book has examined, both quantitatively and qualitatively, the Hong Kong Corpus of Spoken English (prosodic) in terms of the four systems and thirteen choices of discourse intonation (Brazil 1985, 1997). The study contributes to our knowledge in the field of discourse intonation in a number of ways.

First of all, while the study does not claim to be fully comprehensive, it is the first large-scale study that has trialled and tested the discourse intonation framework in its entirety on authentic discourses. Brazil (1997) at times describes and exemplifies his framework with "constructed – and perhaps fanciful – situations" (ibid.: x). The spoken corpus investigated here has almost one million words, covering the major domains of spoken communication: academic, business, social (conversation) and public, each of which is made up of a range of contexts of interaction located in Hong Kong, and collected over seven years (1997-2003). The scope of corpus analysis covers all of the thirteen choices of the four systems across the entire HKCSE (prosodic), in each of the sub-corpora, used by all participants and different participant groups. The depth of corpus analysis ranges from frequency counts of individual intonational choices and comparison of the frequencies of instances of these choices across sub-corpora and participant groups, to detailed qualitative analysis of selected sequences of interaction in support of the quantitative discussions.

The second strength and contribution of this study is that the discourse intonation framework has been consistently and meticulously applied throughout the study. The framework is characterized by a finite set of meaningful intonational oppositions, each of which is regarded as "an occasion for setting up *ad hoc* categories in the light of the speaker's apprehensions of how things presently stand between them and a putative hearer" (Brazil, 1997: xii). The application began from the stage of conception and design of the study and formulation of research questions; the reiterative process of data transcription, checking, double-checking, mark-up and annotation of the transcriptions; the design and implementation of the software programme (iConc) to read and search the transcribed data; and up to the analysis, interpretation and explanation of the quantitative and qualitative findings. The study confirms that the conceptual framework of discourse intonation (Brazil 1985, 1997) is most useful in accounting for the moment-by-moment intonational choices made by discourse participants to project, negotiate and mediate meanings as the spoken discourse unfolds.

Third, the study contributes to a highly unique area of language study in intercultural contexts, namely the communicative role and value of discourse intonation in intercultural communication primarily between Hong Kong Chinese and native speakers of English, particularly the different resources and options that are available for discourse participants to make meanings and the way in which these resources are actually employed in real-life discourses. This study adds to the existing huge body of research literature in language study in intercultural communication which has employed an array of methodologies, primarily textual analysis, ethnography, and survey research; adopted different approaches to language study, including linguistics, sociolinguistics, pragmatics, conversation analysis, discourse analysis, and critical language study (see, for example, Austin 1962, Brown and Levinson 1987, van Dijk 1993, Fairclough 2001, Scollon and Scollon 2001); and drawn upon different concepts, theories, taxonomies, and frameworks that account for the relation between culture and communication (see, for example, Chinese Culture Connection 1987, Hall 1976, Hofstede 1980, Bond 1996).

The fourth contribution is that, being a corpus-driven study, the study has unified observations, based on "corpus evidence of the repeated patterns" (Tognini-Bonelli, 2001: 14-18), in theoretical statements about the systems of discourse intonation. Patterns have been identified and described for each of the four systems of discourse intonation, and also for the delineation of tone units. In terms of discourse intonation in general, it has proved to be a robust framework to work within, and the analyses described confirm the systems described by Brazil. The results suggest that two phenomena in particular deserve further investigation, and perhaps need to be highlighted more in descriptions of the systems. The first is the prevalence of the level tone in the HKCSE (prosodic). It is the tone most commonly used by the HKC, and it is the second most common tone used by the NES after the fall tone. These high levels of usage merit further study to better understand the functions of the level tone, and, arguably, the level tone should be more foregrounded in accounts of discourse intonation. The second significant result that has implications for descriptions of the discourse intonation systems is the high incidence of single prominence tone units, the largest group of which is single word tone units, and hence the potential for the prevalence of key and termination being selected simultaneously, dependent on the local context of interaction. Again, this reality needs to be more foregrounded in descriptions of discourse intonation, and more research is needed on how hearers interpret the communicative value of the occurrence of this selection in the local context.

Implications for future research

Still another contribution of the study is the implications for future research. Regarding future research, the findings and conclusions of the present study could be of value to various types of research. The first type is research into the communicative value of discourse intonation specific to other groups of speakers in other contexts of communication. Another type is studies which make use of other models of intonation, which would also find the findings and conclusions of the present study useful for comparison purposes. Language studies of spoken discourse with an additional focus on discourse intonation in order to make a fuller investigation are another research pathway. As shown in Appendix 1, the HKCSE (prosodic) has already yielded a number of studies in the areas of discourse analysis, intercultural pragmatics, and intercultural communication, all with an additional focus on the communicative role of discourse intonation. For instance, in Warren's (2007) study of vague language, discourse intonation plays an additional role in adding situation-specific meaning to the use of vague language by discourse participants. Warren's study shows that a speaker's selection of intonation can serve to disambiguate vague language use or add additional layers of meaning to vague items, based on the speaker's perceptions of the context, including the perceived shared knowledge between the participants. While discourse intonation selections are situation specific, and are neither pre-determined nor guaranteed, such studies show that patterns of discourse intonation can be described, and thus to some extent predicted in local contexts. Another area that merits further research is the contribution that LUG can make to discourse intonation, and vice versa. For example, it has been shown that LUG helps to explain speakers' selection of tone unit boundaries, the contents of tone units and the selection of prominence with respect to extended word associations, and the use of the level tone in tone units that constitute incremental elements. Further research is recommended to explore links between LUG and discourse intonation.

Another interesting finding is that when comparing the two groups of speakers in terms of the quantitative distribution of use of the discourse intonation systems, the differences are relatively few and, where there exist, they tend to be slight. For instance, in Chapter 6, it is found that there is a slight but consistent tendency for the HKC to speak more single prominence tone units, and for the NES to speak more multiple prominence tone units. In addition, the HKC are more likely than the NES to select prominence on personal pronouns, possessive pronouns and possessive determiners. In Chapter 7, the HKC is found to use the level tone, among all of the five tones, most frequently, whereas for the NES the level tone is ranked second after fall tone. Therefore the overwhelming pattern is the similarity of discourse intonation usage of the HKC and NES, as reflected in the relative proportion of usages. This suggests, as others have before (see, for example, Koester 1990, Mansfield 1990, Wulffson 1990), that the systems of discourse intonation may extend beyond the English language. A study by Cheng and Warren (2006) further supports this view. The study analyses the discourse intonation selections of the Cantonese-speaking host and contestants in a television game show and finds that all of the systems of discourse intonation operate in Cantonese, even though Cantonese is one of the most complex tonal languages in the world. Again, the extent of the universality of discourse intonation requires further study. Similarly, while a number of patterns of discourse intonation usage have been identified and discussed in this study, the likelihood is that there are more to be uncovered. It is to be hoped that other studies will be conducted on the HKCSE (prosodic) in the future, particularly studies that qualitatively examine the use of discourse intonation systems.

Implications for learning and teaching

The last, but not least, contribution is pedagogical. The use of English language corpora such as the HKCSE (prosodic) as a potential resource for learning and teaching has yet to be fully tapped, but language corpora can clearly make important and useful pedagogical contributions to the learning and teaching of English language and English language studies. With respect to pedagogy, the learning and teaching of discourse intonation has yet to find its way into mainstream English language learning and teaching materials (Chun 2002: 199). In the upper secondary schools in Hong Kong, for instance, discourse intonation has yet to be given attention in the teaching materials, despite studies that have advocated or investigated this area, including Brazil, Coulthard, and Johns (1980), Hewings (1986), McCarthy (1988), Cauldwell (2003a, 2003b), Cheng (2004a, 2004b, 2004c), Cheng and Warren (2003), Warren (2004), Cheng, Greaves and Warren (2005). However, where discourse intonation has been introduced (see, for example, Cauldwell 2003a, 2003b), examples drawn from real instances of language use can serve as models for learners to discuss and replicate. Through analysing the intonation of the speakers in the corpus, learners will better understand discourse intonation and how it works across a variety of speakers and discourse types.

The main advantage of describing discourse intonation with Brazil's systems, as pointed out by McCarthy (1991: 114), lies in the possibility to deal with the four different parts of the system individually, "while not losing sight of either the sense of the importance of speaker choice and adjustment to the constantly changing state of play between participants in the talk". Arguably, McCarthy's assessment has been borne out by the increasing number of listening and pronunciation publications for English language learners in recent years that are based on Brazil's systems (see, for example, Bradford 1988, Brazil 1994, Cauldwell 2003a, 2003b, Chun 2002, Hewings and Goldstein 1999).

The combination of an intercultural corpus which is also prosodically transcribed means that the HKCSE (prosodic) is a potentially rich resource. Having access to a very large number of naturally-occurring examples for learners and teachers to draw upon would also help to avoid the dangers of learning and practising discourse intonation devoid of context which Brazil (1997: 142) strongly warns against. The HKCSE (prosodic) could, therefore, serve as the basis for learning and teaching materials, and offer learners the opportunity for both the quantitative and qualitative study of discourse intonation in real world contexts. Advanced learners of English language or applied linguistic studies should be able to use the HKCSE (prosodic) in "data-driven learning" activities (Johns, 1991), and research students in their research projects and theses.

This research study has clearly shown that intonation is a set of meaningful choices, and that discourse intonation serves as an additional important level of the linguistic dimension of culture in English language teaching. Instructional materials and activities that illustrate the intonation choices available to speakers and the effects those choices have on local meaning are an obvious way to proceed. For example, Bradford (1988) encourages learners to experiment with different intonation choices and to discuss their effect on the meaning potential of utterances. Such activities, supported with a corpus of examples, would be a useful addition for the language learner. The fundamental idea that discourse intonation represents a set of speaker choices, rather than a fixed system that is tied to words, attitudes, or the grammar, is underlined throughout this study, and should serve to empower both learners and teachers alike.

References

Aijmer, K. 2002. *English Discourse Particles: Evidence from a Corpus.* Amsterdam: John Benjamins.

Austin, J.L. 1962. *How to Do Things with Words.* Oxford: OUP.

Bargiela-Chiappini, F. & S. Harris. 1997. *Managing Language. The Discourse of Corporate Meetings.* Amsterdam: John Benjamins.

Biber, D., S. Conrad, F. Edward, S. Johansson & G. Leech. 1999. *Longman Grammar of Spoken and Written English.* Harlow: Longman.

Bolt, P. & K. Bolton 1996. The International Corpus of English in Hong Kong. In *Comparing English Worldwide: The International Corpus of English,* S. Greenbaum (ed.),197–214. Oxford: Clarendon Press.

Bolton, K. 2002. Introduction. In *Hong Kong English Autonomy and Creativity*, K. Bolton (ed.), Hong Kong: Hong Kong University Press.

Bolton, K. (ed.). 2002. *Hong Kong English: Autonomy and Creativity.* Hong Kong: Hong Kong University Press.

Bond, M.H. (ed.). 1986. *The Psychology of the Chinese People.* Hong Kong: OUP.

Bond, M.H. (ed.) 1996. *The Handbook of Chinese Psychology.* Hong Kong: OUP.

Boxer, D. 2002. Discourse issues in cross-cultural pragmatics. *Annual Review of Applied Linguistics* 22: 150–67.

Bradford, B. 1988. *Intonation in Context.* Cambridge: CUP.

Brazil, D. 1975. *Discourse Intonation* [Discourse Analysis Monograph 1]. Birmingham: University of Birmingham, English Language Research.

Brazil, D. 1985. *The Communicative Value of Intonation.* Birmingham: University of Birmingham, English Language Research.

Brazil, D. 1994. *Pronunciation for Advanced Learners of English.* Cambridge: CUP.

Brazil, D. 1995. *A Grammar of Speech.* Oxford: OUP.

Brazil, D. 1997. *The Communicative Role of Intonation in English.* Cambridge: CUP.

Brazil, D., M. Coulthard & C. Johns. 1980. *Discourse Intonation and Language Teaching.* Harlow: Longman.

Brown, A. & D. Deterding. 2005. A checklist of Singapore English pronunciation features. In *English in Singapore: Phonetic Research on a Corpus,* D. Deterding, A. Brown & Low Ee Ling (eds.), 7–13. Singapore: McGraw-Hill.

Brown, G., K. Currie & J. Kenworthy. 1980. *Questions of Intonation.* Baltimore MD: University Park Press.

Brown, G. & G. Yule. 1983. *Discourse Analysis.* Cambridge: CUP.

Brown, P. & S.C. Levinson. 1987. *Politeness: Some Universals in Language Usage.* Cambridge: CUP.

Cauldwell, R.T. 1997. Tones, attitudinal meanings, and context. *Speak Out! Newsletter of the* IATEFL Pronunciation Special Interest Group 21: 30–35.

Cauldwell, R.T. 2002. The functional irrhythmicality of spontaneous speech: A discourse view of speech rhythms. *Apples* 2(1): 1–24.

Cauldwell, R.T. 2003a. *Streaming Speech: Listening and Pronunciation for Advanced Learners of English.* (Windows CD-ROM). Birmingham: speechinaction.

Cauldwell, R.T. 2003b. *Streaming Speech: Listening and Pronunciation for Advanced Learners of English.* (Student's book). Birmingham: speechinaction.

Cauldwell, R.T. 2007. SpeechinAction Research Centre (SPARC). (http://www.speechinaction.com/, accessed 16 June 2007).

Cauldwell, R.T. & M. Hewings. 1996. Discourse intonation and listening. In *Speak Out! Changes in Pronunciation,* M. Vaughan-Rees (ed.), 49–57. Cambridge: CUP.

Channell, J. 1994. *Vague Language.* Oxford: OUP.

Cheng, W. 2002. Indirectness in intercultural communication. Conference on the Pragmatics of Interlanguage English. Münster University, Germany, 22–25 September 2002.

Cheng, W. 2003. *Intercultural Conversation.* Amsterdam: John Benjamins.

Cheng, W. 2004a. // → did you TOOK // ↗ from the miniBAR //: What is the practical relevance of a corpus-driven language study to practitioners in Hong Kong's hotel industry? In *Discourse in the Professions: Perspectives from Corpus Linguistics,* U. Connor & T. Upton (eds.), 141–166. Amsterdam: John Benjamins.

Cheng, W. 2004b. // → FRIENDS // ↘↗ LAdies and GENtlemen //: Some preliminary findings from a corpus of spoken public discourses in Hong Kong. In *Applied Corpus Linguistics: A Multidimensional Perspective,* U. Connor & T. Upton (eds.), 35–50. Amsterdam: Rodopi.

Cheng, W. 2004c. // → well THANK you DAvid for // → THAT question //: The intonation, pragmatics and structure of Q&A sessions in public discourses. *The Journal of Asia TEFL* 1(2): 109–133.

Cheng, W. 2007. The use of vague language across spoken genres in an intercultural corpus. In *Vague Language Explored,* J. Cutting (ed.), 161–181. London: Palgrave Macmillan.

Cheng, W., C. Greaves & M. Warren. 2005. The creation of a prosodically transcribed intercultural corpus: The Hong Kong Corpus of Spoken English (prosodic). *International Computer Archive of Modern English (ICAME) Journal* 29: 5–26.

Cheng, W. & M. Warren. 1999a. Inexplicitness: What is it and should we be teaching it? *Applied Linguistics* 20(3): 293–315.

Cheng, W. & M. Warren. 1999b. Facilitating a description of intercultural conversations: The Hong Kong Corpus of Conversational English. *International Computer Archive of Modern English (ICAME) Journal* 20: 5–20.

Cheng, W. & M. Warren. 2001a. The functions of *actually* in a corpus of intercultural conversations. *International Journal of Corpus Linguistics* 6(2): 257–280.

Cheng, W. & M. Warren. 2001b. "She knows more about Hong Kong than you do isn't it": Tags in Hong Kong conversational English. *Journal of Pragmatics* 33(9): 1419–1439.

Cheng, W. & M. Warren. 2001c. The use of vague language in intercultural conversations in Hong Kong. English World-Wide 22(1): 81–104.

Cheng, W. & M. Warren. 2002. The intonation of declarative-mood questions in a corpus of Hong Kong English: // ↘↗ beef ball // → you like //. *Teanga: Journal of the Irish Association of Applied Linguistics. Special Issue of Corpora, Varieties and the Language Classroom* 21: 151–165.

Cheng, W. & M. Warren. 2005. // → well I have a DIFferent // ↘ THINking you know //: A corpus-driven study of disagreement in Hong Kong business discourse. In *Asian Business Discourse(s),* F. Bargiela-Chiappini & M. Gotti (eds.), 241–270. Frankfurt: Peter Lang.

Cheng, W. & M. Warren. 2006. // ↗ you need to be <u>RUTH</u>less //: Entertaining cross-cultural differences. *Language and Intercultural Communication* 6(1): 35–56.

Cheng, W. & M. Warren 2008. // → ONE country two <u>SYS</u>tems //: The discourse intonation patterns of word associations. In *Corpora and Discourse: The Challenges of Different Settings,* A. Ädel & R. Reppen (eds.), 135–153. Amsterdam: John Benjamins.

Chinese Culture Connection, T. 1987. Chinese values and the search for culture-free dimensions of culture. *Journal of Cross-Cultural Psychology* 18: 143–164.

Chomsky, N. & M. Halle. 1968. *The Sound Pattern of English.* New York: Harper.

Chu, S.Y.S. 2002. Using Brazil's system to transcribe a corpus of Hong Kong English: A report on some preliminary findings and difficulties encountered. AAAL 2002 Annual Convention: (Re)Interpreting Applied Linguistics, 6–9 April 2002, Salt Lake City UT, USA.

Chun, D.M. 2002. *Discourse Intonation in L2: From Theory and Research to Practice.* Amsterdam: John Benjamins.

Clancy, P., S. Thompson, R. Suzuki & H. Tao. 1996. The conversational use of reactive tokens in English, Japanese, and Mandarin. *Journal of Pragmatics* 26: 355–387.

Clark, J. & C. Yallop. 1990. *An Introduction to Phonetics and Phonology.* Oxford: Basil Blackwell.

COLT website: http://torvald.aksis.uib.no/colt/cd/CDINTRO.PDF, 12.07.07.

Coulthard, M. & D. Brazil. 1981. The place of intonation in the description of interaction. In *Analyzing Discourse: Text and Talk,* D. Tannen (ed.), 94–112. Washington DC: Georgetown University Press.

Coulthard, M. & M. Montgomery (eds.). 1981. *Studies in Discourse Analysis.* London: Longman.

Couper-Kuhlen, E. & M. Selting. 1996. Towards an interactional perspective on prosody and a prosodic perspective on interaction. In *Prosody in Conversation,* E. Couper-Kuhlen & M. Selting (eds.), 11–56. Cambridge: CUP.

Cresti, E. & M. Moneglia (eds.). 2005. *C-ORAL-ROM: Integrated Reference Corpora for Spoken Romance Languages.* Amsterdam: John Benjamins.

Cruttenden, A. 1986[1997]. *Intonation.* Cambridge: CUP.

Crystal, D. 1969. *Prosodic Systems and Intonation and in English.* Cambridge: CUP.

Crystal, D. 1975. *The English Tone of Voice.* London: Edward Arnold.

Crystal, D. 1995. *The Cambridge Encyclopaedia of the English Language.* Cambridge: CUP. Fairclough, N. 2001. *Language and Power,* 2nd edn. London: Longman.

Fishman, J. 1972. Domains and the relationship between micro and macrosociolinguistics. In *Directions in Sociolinguistics: The Ethnography of Communication,* J. Gumperz & D. Hymes (eds.), 435–454. New York NY: Holt, Rinehard and Winston.

Francis, G. 1993. A corpus-driven approach to grammar: Principles, methods and examples. In *Text and Technology: In Honour of John Sinclair,* M. Baker, G. Francis, & E. Tognini-Bonelli (eds.), 137–156. Amsterdam: John Benjamins.

Gardner, R. 2000. Resources for delicate manoeuvres: Learning to disagree. *Australian Review of Applied Linguistics Supplement* 16: 31–47.

Givón, T. 1993. *English Grammar: A Functional-based Introduction* II. Amsterdam: John Benjamins.

Grabe, E. & B. Post. 2002. The transcribed IViE corpus. University of Oxford, Phonetics Laboratory.

Goh, C. 1998. The level tone in Singapore English. *English Today* 14(1): 50–53.

Goh, C. 2000. A discourse approach to the description of intonation in Singapore English. In *The English Language in Singapore: Research on Pronunciation*, A. Brown, D. Deterding & E. L. Low (eds.), 35–45. Singapore: Singapore Association for Applied Linguistics.

Hall, E.T. 1976. *Beyond Culture*. Garden City NY: Anchor Press.

Halliday, M.A.K. 1963. Class in relation to the axes of chain and choice in language. *Linguistics* 2.

Halliday, M.A.K. 1967. *Intonation and Grammar in British English*. The Hague: Mouton.

Halliday, M.A.K. 1970. *A Course in Spoken English: Intonation*. London: OUP.

Halliday, M.A.K. 1989. *Spoken and Written Language*. Oxford: OUP.

Halliday, M.A.K. 1994. *An Introduction to Functional Grammar*. London: Arnold.

Halliday, M.A.K. & W. Greaves. 2008. *Intonation in the Grammar of English*. London: Equinox.

Halliday, M.A.K. & R. Hasan. 1976. *Cohesion in English*. London: Longman.

Halliday, M.A.K. & C. Matthiessen. 2004. *An Introduction to Functional Grammar*, 3rd edn. Oxford: OUP.

Harris Z. 1988. *Language and Information*. New York NY: Columbia University Press.

Hasan, R. 1984. Coherence and cohesive harmony. In *Understanding Reading Comprehension*, J. Flood (ed.), 181–219. Newark, Delaware: International Reading Association.

Hewings, M. 1986. Problems of intonation in classroom interaction. *Guidelines* 2(1): 45–51.

Hewings, M. (ed.). 1990. *Papers in Discourse Intonation*. Birmingham: English Language Research.

Hewings, M. & R. Cauldwell. 1997. Foreward. In *The Communicative Role of Intonation in English*, D. Brazil (ed.), i–vii. Cambridge: CUP.

Hewings, M. & S. Goldstein. 1999. *Pronunciation Plus: Practice through Interaction: North American English*. Cambridge: CUP.

Hofstede, G.H. 1980. *Culture's Consequences, International Differences in Work-related Values*. Beverly Hills CA: Sage.

Hunston, S. 1995. A corpus study of some English verbs of attribution. *Functions of Language* 2(2): 133–158.

Hunston, S. & G. Francis. 2000. *Pattern Grammar. A Corpus-driven Approach to the Lexical Grammar of English*. Amsterdam: John Benjamins.

Johns, T. 1991. Should you be persuaded: Two samples of data-driven learning materials. In *Classroom Concordancing* [English Language Research Journal 4], T. Johns & P. King (eds.), 1–16. Birmingham: English Language Research.

Kendon, A. 1967. Some functions of gaze-direction in social interaction. *Acta Psychologica* 26: 22–63.

Knowles, G. 1991. Prosodic labelling: The problem of tone group boundaries. In *English Computer Corpora*, S. Johannson & A.-B. Stenström. (eds.), 149–163. Berlin: de Gruyter.

Knowles, G., A. Wichmann, & P. Alderson (eds.). 1996. *Working with Speech*. London: Longman.

Koester, A. 1990. Intonation in agreeing and disagreeing in English and German. In *Papers in Discourse Intonation* [Discourse Analysis Monograph 16], M. Hewings (ed.), 83–102. Birmingham: English Language Research.

Lam, P. 2007. What a difference the prosody makes: The role of prosody in the use of discourse particles. The 10th International Pragmatics Conference, Gothenburg, Sweden, 8–13 July 2007.

Lam, P. 2008. *Discourse Particles in an Intercultural Corpus of Spoken English*. PhD dissertation,The Hong Kong Polytechnic University, Hong Kong.

Leech, G. 1996. Foreword: The spoken English corpus in its context. In *Working with Speech: Perspectives on Research into the Lancaster/IBM Spoken English Corpus,* G. Knowles, A. Wichmann & P. Alderson (eds.), ix–xii. London: Longman.

Lee, L.S. May, 2005. Message from the commissioner for official languages [Electronic version]. *Word Power* 1, 2.

Levinson, S.C. 1983. *Pragmatics.* Cambridge: CUP.

Liberman, M. & A. Prince. 1977. On stress and linguistic rhythm. *Linguistic Inquiry* 8: 249–336.

Lin, I. 2008. Questions and Responses in Business Communication in Hong Kong. PhD dissertation, The Hong Kong Polytechnic University, Hong Kong.

Louw, B. 1993. Irony in the Text or Insincerity in the Writer? The Diagnostic Potential of Semantic Prosodies. In *Text and Technology: In Honour of John Sinclair,* F. Baker & E. Tognini-Bonelli (eds.), 157–176. Amsterdam: John Benjamins.

Lustig, M.W. & J. Koester. 2006. *Intercultural Competence: Interpersonal Communication Across Cultures,* 5th edn. London: Longman.

Mansfield, G. 1990. Discourse intonation in English and Italian news broadcasts. In *Papers in Discourse Intonation* [Discourse Analysis Monograph 16], M. Hewings (ed.), 71–82. Birmingham: English Language Research.

McCarthy, M. 1988. Some vocabulary patterns in conversation. In *Vocabulary and Language Teaching,* R. Carter & M. McCarthy (eds.), 181–200. London: Longman.

Markus, H. & S. Kitayama. 1991. Culture and the self: Implications for cognition, emotion, and motivation. *Psychological Review* 98: 224–253.

Markus, H. & S. Kitayama. 1994. The cultural construction of self and emotion: Implications for social behaviour. In *Emotion and Culture: Empirical Studies of Mutual Influence,* S. Kitayama & H. Markus (eds.), 89–130. WashingtonDC: American Psychological Association.

Matthews, S. & V. Yip. 1994. *Cantonese: A Comprehensive Grammar.* London: Routledge.

Mey, J. 2001. *Pragmatics: An Introduction.* Boston MA: Blackwell.

Myers, G. 1998. Displaying opinions: Topics and disagreement in focus groups. *Language in Society* 27: 85–111.

McCarthy, M. 1988. Some vocabulary patterns in conversation. In *Vocabulary and Language Teaching* R. Carter & M. McCarthy (eds.), 181–200. London: Longman.

McCarthy, M. 1991. *Discourse Analysis for Language Teachers.* Cambridge: CUP.

O'Connor, J. & G. Arnold. 1973. *Intonation of Colloquial English,* 2nd edn. London: Longman.

Partington, A. 1998. *Patterns and Meanings: Using Corpora for English Language Research and Teaching.* Amsterdam: John Benjamins.

Pickering, L. 2001. The role of tone choice in improving ITA communication in the classroom. *TESOL Quarterly* 35: 233–255.

Pickering, L. 2004. Establishing priorities in teaching intonation to adult English language learners. In *IATEFL 2003 Brighton Conference Selections*: IATEFL, A. Pulverness (ed.), 138–140.

Pierrehumbert, J. 1980. The Phonology and Phonetics of English Intonation. PhD dissertation, MIT.

Pierrehumbert, J. & J. Hirschberg. 1990. The meaning of intonational contours in the interpretation of discourse. In *Intentions in Communication* P. Cohen, J. Morgan, & M. Pollock (eds.), 271–312. Cambridge MA: The MIT Press.

Pomerantz, A. 1984. Agreeing and disagreeing with assessments: Some features of preferred/dispreferred turn shapes. In *Structures of Social Action: Studies in Conversation Analysis,* J. M. Atkinson & J. Heritage (eds.), 57–101. Cambridge: CUP.

Quirk, R., S. Greenbaum, G. Leech, & J. Svartvik. 1985. *A Comprehensive Grammar of the English Language*. London: Longman.

Schegloff, E. A. 1982. Discourse as an interactional achievement: Some uses of 'uh huh' and other things that come between sentences. In *Analyzing Discourse: Text and Talk,* D. Tannen (ed.), 71–93. Washington DC: Georgetown University Press.

Schegloff, E. A., G. Jefferson, & H. Sacks. 1977. The preference for self-correction in the organization of repair in conversation. *Language* 53(2): 361–382.

Schiffrin, D. 1987. *Discourse Markers*. Cambridge: CUP.

Scollon, R. & S. Scollon. 2001. *Intercultural Communication: A Discourse Approach,* 2nd edn. Oxford: Blackwell.

SCOLAR. 2005. *Corporate Interview*. Retrieved 11 May 2006 from http://www.english.gov.hk/eng/html/wec_news_interview_in01.htm/.

Sinclair, J. McH. 1987. *Looking Up: An Account of the COBUILD Project in Lexical Computing*. London: Collins.

Sinclair, J. McH. 1991. *Corpus, Concordance, Collocation*. Oxford: OUP.

Sinclair, J. McH. 1996. The search for units of meaning. *TEXTUS* IX(1): 75–106.

Sinclair, J. McH. 1998. The lexical item. In *Contrastive LexicalSemantics,* W. Weigand (ed.), 1–24. Amsterdam: John Benjamins.

Sinclair, J. McH. 2004. *Trust the Text*. London: Routledge.

Sinclair, J. McH. 2005. Dial-a-corpus. Tuscan Word Centre International Workshop, Certosa di Pontignano, Italy, June 29– July 2, 2005.

Sinclair, J. McH. & D. Brazil. 1982. *Teacher Talk*. Oxford: OUP.

Sinclair, J. McH., S. Jones, & R. Daley. 1970. *English Lexical Studies. Report to OSTI on Project C/LP/08*. Department of English, University of Birmingham.

Sinclair, J. McH. & A. Mauranen. 2005. Workshop on Linear Unit Grammar. AAACL 6 and ICAME 26, University of Michigan, 12–15 May 2005.

Sinclair, J. McH. & A. Mauranen. 2006. *Linear Unit Grammar*. Amsterdam: John Benjamins.

Sinclair, J.McH. & A. Renouf. 1991. Collocational frameworks in English. Reprinted in J. A. Foley (Ed.), 1996). *J. M. Sinclair on Lexis and Lexicography,* 55–71. Singapore: Unipress.

Spencer-Oatey, H. 2000. Introduction: language, culture and rapport management. In *Culturally Speaking: Managing Rapport through Talk across Cultures* H. Spencer-Oatey (ed.), 1–8. New York NY: Continuum.

Stenström, A.-B. 1994. *An Introduction to Spoken Interaction*. New York NY: Longman.

Svartvik, J. (ed.). 1990. *The London-Lund Corpus of Spoken English: Description and Research*. Lund: Lund University Press.

Taylor, L. 1996. The compilation of the Spoken English Corpus. In *Working with Speech* G. Knowles, A. Wichmann, & P. Alderson (Eds.), (pp. 20–37). London: Longman.

Tognini-Bonelli, E. 2001. *Corpus Linguistics at Work*. Amsterdam: John Benjamins. The University of Ljubljana. 1998). The Attitudinal Approach of O'Connor and Arnold, and Brazil's Communicative Approach. MA paper, Faculty of Arts, University of Ljubljana, October 1998. Retrieved on 6 August 2007, http://www2.arnes.si/~nhirci/articles/intonat.htm.

van Dijk, T.A. 1993. Principles of critical discourse analysis. *Discourse & Society* 4(2): 249–83.

Warren, M. 2004. // ⌵ so what have YOU been WORking on REcently //: Compiling a Specialized Corpus of Spoken Business English. In *Discourse in the Professions: Perspectives from Corpus Linguistics,* U. Connor & T. Upton (eds.), 115–140. Amsterdam: John Benjamins.

Warren, M. 2006. A corpus-driven analysis of back-channels. Third Inter-Varietal Applied Corpus Studies (IVACS) International Conference: Language at the Interface. University of Nottingham, UK, 23–24 June 2006.

Warren, M. 2007. { / [OH] not a < ^ LOT > }: Discourse intonation and vague lagnauge. In *Vague Language Explored,* J. Cutting (ed.), 182– 197. London: Palgrave Macmillan.

Wichmann, A. 2000. *Intonation in Text and Discourse.* London: Longman.

Winter, E. O. 1974. Replacement as a Function of Repetition: A Study of Some of its Principal Features in the Clause Relations of Contemporary English. Unpublished PhD dissertation, University of London.

Winter, E. O. 1979. Replacement as a fundamental function of the sentence in context. *Forum Linguisticum* 4(2): 95–133.

Wulffson, M. 1990. Gnomes in context: A look at discourse intonation in Swedish. In *Papers in Discourse Intonation* [Discourse Analysis Monograph 16], M. Hewings (ed.), 47–70. Birmingham: English Language Research.

Yang, L. 1995. Intonational Structures of Mandarin Discourse. PhD dissertation, Georgetown University, Washington DC.

Yau, F.M. 1997. Code switching and language choice in the Hong Kong legislative council [Electronic version]. *Journal of Multilingual and Multicultural Development* 18 (1): 40–53.

HKCSE-Related scholarly output to date

1.   Cheng, W. and Warren, M. 1999. Facilitating a description of intercultural conversations: the Hong Kong Corpus of Conversational English. *ICAME Journal* Vol. 23, 5-20.

2.   Cheng, W. and Warren, M. 1999. Inexplicitness: what is it and should we be teaching it? *Applied Linguistics* Vol. 20/3, 293-315.

3.   Cheng, W. and Warren, M. 2000. The Hong Kong Corpus of Spoken English: language learning through language description. In L. Burnard and T. McEnery (eds.) *Rethinking Language Pedagogy from a Corpus Perspective.* Frankfurt main: Peter Lang. 133-144.

4.   Cheng, W. and Warren M. 2001. The use of vague language in cross-cultural conversations. *English World-Wide*, 22(1): 81-104.

5.   Cheng, W. and Warren, M. 2001. "She knows more about Hong Kong than you do isn't it": Tags in Hong Kong conversational English. *Journal of Pragmatics*, 33/9, 1419-1439.

6.   Cheng, W. and Warren, M. 2001. The functions of *actually* in a corpus of intercultural conversations. *International Journal of Corpus Linguistics*. 6(2): 257-280.

7.   Cheng, W. and Warren, M. 2002. The intonation of declarative-mood questions in a corpus of Hong Kong English: // ↘↗ beef ball // → you like //. Special Issue: Corpora, varieties and the language classroom. *Teanga, Journal of the Irish Association of Applied Linguistics* 21, 151-165.

8.   Cheng, W., Warren, M. and Xu, X. 2003. The Language Learner as Language Researcher: Corpus Linguistics on the Timetable. *System* 31/2: 173-186.

9.   Cheng, W. 2003. Humour in intercultural conversation. *Semiotica* 146 (1/4): 287-306.

10.   Cheng, W. and Warren, M. 2003. Indirectness, inexplicitness and vagueness made clearer. *Pragmatics* 13 (3/4): 381-400.

                                TOOK

11.   Cheng, W. 2004 // → did you   // ↗ from the miniBAR //: what is the practical relevance of a corpus-driven language study to practitioners in Hong Kong's hotel industry? In U. Connor and T. Upton (eds.) *Discourse in the Professions: Perspectives from Corpus Linguistics.* Amsterdam: John Benjamins, 141-166.

12. Warren, M. 2004. // ↘ so what have YOU been WORking on REcently //: Compiling a Specialized Corpus of Spoken Business English. In U. Connor and T. Upton (eds.) *Discourse in the Professions: Perspectives from Corpus Linguistics*. Amsterdam: John Benjamins, 115-140.

13. Cheng, W. 2004 // → FRIENDS // ↘↗ LAdies and GENtlemen //: some preliminary findings from a corpus of spoken public discourses in Hong Kong. In U. Connor and T. Upton (eds.) *Applied Corpus Linguistics: A Multidimensional Perspective*. Rodopi, 35-50.

14. Warren, M. 2004. A corpus-driven analysis of the use of intonation to assert dominance and control. In U. Connor and T. Upton (eds.) *Applied Corpus Linguistics: A Multidimensional Perspective*. Rodopi, 21-33.

15. Cheng, W. 2004. // → well   THANK   you DAvid for // → THAT question //: the intonation, pragmatics and structure of Q&A sessions in public discourses. *The Journal of Asia TEFL* Vol. 1, No. 2, 109-133.

16. Cheng, W. and Warren, M. 2005 // ↗ CAN i help you //: The use of *rise* and *rise-fall* tones in the Hong Kong Corpus of Spoken English. *International Journal of Corpus Linguistics* 10/1: 85-107.

17. Cheng, W., Greaves, C. and Warren, M. 2005. The creation of a prosodically transcribed intercultural corpus: The Hong Kong Corpus of Spoken English (prosodic). *ICAME Journal 29*: 47-68.

18.[1] Cheng, W., Warren, M., and Xu Xun-feng. (2005). Towards a description of spoken English in Hong Kong: Some findings and applications.. In School of Foreign Studies Editorial Committee, South China Normal University, (Eds.), *Yuliaoku Yuyanxue de Yanjiu Yu Yingyong*. (pp. 57-63). China: Northeast Normal University Press.

19. Cheng, W. and Warren, M. 2005 // → well   I   have a DIFferent // ↘ THINking you know //: Disagreement in Hong Kong business discourse: A corpus-driven approach. In F. Bargiela-Chiappini and M. Gotti (eds.) *Asian Business Discourse(s)*. Frankfurt main: Peter Lang, 241-270.

20. Cheng, W. and Warren, M. 2006. // ↗ you need to be RUTHless //: Entertaining Cross-cultural Differences. *Language and Intercultural Communication* 6/1: 35-56.

21. Cheng, W. and Warren, M. 2006. *I would say be very careful of....*: Opine markers in an intercultural business corpus of spoken English. In J. Bamford and M. Bondi (eds.) *Managing interaction in professional discourse. Intercultural and interdiscoursal perspectives*. Officina Edizioni: Roma, 46-57.

---

1. One third of this paper is authored by Xu Xunfeng and is unrelated to the HKCSE.

22.   Cheng, W. 2006. Interpreting the meaning of lexical cohesion in a corpus of SARS-related discourses. Special edition: Corpus Studies of Lexical Cohesion. J. Flowerdew and M. Mahlberg (eds.). *International Journal of Corpus Linguistics* 11/3: 325-344.

23.   Warren, M. 2006. *because of the role of er front office um in hotel*: lexical cohesion and discourse intonation. Special edition: Corpus Studies of Lexical Cohesion. J. Flowerdew and M. Mahlberg (eds.). *International Journal of Corpus Linguistics* 11/3: 305-324.

24.   Cheng, W., Greaves, C. and Warren, M. 2006. From n-gram to skipgram to concgram. *International Journal of Corpus Linguistics* 11/4: 411-433.

25.   Lam, P. 2006. *Well but that's the effect of it*: The use of *well* as a discourse particle in talk shows. *Sprache und Datenverarbeitung. International Journal for Language Data Processing* 30/1: 99-108.

26.   Cheng, W. 2007. The use of vague language across spoken genres. In J. Cutting (ed.) *Vague Language Explored*. Basingstoke and New York: Palgrave Macmillan, 161-181.

27.   Warren, M. 2007. { / [OH] not a < ^ LOT > }: Discourse intonation and vague language. In J. Cutting (ed.) *Vague Language Explored*. Basingstoke and New York: Palgrave Macmillan, 182-197.

28.   Cheng, W. and Warren, M. 2007. Checking understanding in an intercultural corpus of spoken English. Special edition: Corpus-based Studies of Language Awareness: A. O'Keefe and S. Walsh (eds.) *Language Awareness* 16/3: 190-207.

29.   Fung, L. 2007. The Communicative Role of Self-Repetition in a Specialized Corpus of Business Discourse. Special edition: Corpus-based Studies of Language Awareness: A. O'Keefe and S. Walsh (eds.) *Language Awareness* 16/3: 224-238.

30.   Cheng, W. 2007. Co-constructing prejudiced talk: ethnic stereotyping in intercultural communication between Hong Kong Chinese and English-speaking westerners. In A. Lin, (Ed.), *Gender, ethnicity, and identity: symbolic struggles of everyday worlds*. Lawrence Erlbaum.

31.   Greaves, C. and Warren M. 2007. Concgramming: A corpus-driven approach to learning the phraseology of English. *ReCALL Journal* 17/3: 287-306.

32.   Lam, P. 2008. Discourse Particles in an Intercultural Corpus of Spoken English. Unpublished PhD dissertation, Department of English. The Hong Kong Polytechnic University.

33.   Cheng, W. and Warren, M. 2008. // → ONE country two SYStems //: The discourse intonation patterns of extended collocations. In A. Ädel and R. Reppen (eds.), *Corpora and Discourse: The Challenges of Different Settings*. Amsterdam: John Benjamins, 135-153.

34.   Lin, I. (2008). Questions and Responses in Business Communication in Hong Kong. Unpublished PhD dissertation, Department of English. The Hong Kong Polytechnic University.

Quantitative data

Distribution of words

Table 1 Total Words - L1

Total Words	HKC	NES	Other Speakers	Unidentified Speakers	All Speakers
HKCSE (Prosodic)	643286 (71.46%)	227894 (25.32%)	28682 (3.19%)	382 (0.04%)	900214 (100%)
A- corpus	168784 (81.64%)	30526 (14.76%)	7421 (3.59%)	31 (0.01%)	206750 (100%)
B- corpus	174135 (70.55%)	68807 (27.88%)	3849 (1.56%)	45 (0.02%)	246816 (100%)
C- corpus	107825 (46.97%)	107851 (46.98%)	13584 (5.92%)	306 (0.13%)	229568 (100%)
P- corpus	192542 (88.7%)	20710 (9.54%)	3828 (1.76%)	0 (0%)	217080 (100%)

Table 2 Total words – gender

Total Words	HKC Males	NES Males	Other speakers Males	All Males (M)	HKC Females	NES Females	Other Speakers Females	All Females (F)
HKCSE (Prosodic)	337927 (63.11%)	183150 (34.2%)	14406 (2.69%)	535463 (100%)	305371 (83.8%)	44756 (12.28%)	14288 (3.92%)	364391 (100%)
A- corpus	88708 (79.23%)	23265 (20.78%)	0 (0%)	111969 (100%)	80080 (84.51%)	7265 (7.67%)	7421 (7.83%)	94758 (100%)
B- corpus	59060 (48.18%)	59875 (48.85%)	3660 (2.99%)	122581 (100%)	115083 (92.66%)	8940 (7.12%)	197 (0.16%)	124204 (100%)
C- corpus	46682 (33.83%)	82104 (59.49%)	9216 (6.68%)	138004 (100%)	61143 (67%)	25747 (28.21%)	4368 (4.79%)	91258 (100%)
P- corpus	143477 (88.07%)	17906 (10.99%)	1526 (0.94%)	162909 (100%)	49065 (90.57%)	2804 (5.18%)	2302 (4.25%)	54171 (100%)

Table 3 Unique Words – L1

Unique Words	HKC	NES	Other Speakers	Unidentified Speakers	All Speakers
HKCSE (Prosodic)	14899 (87.73%)	8697 (51.21%)	2730 (16.07%)	144 (0.85%)	16983
A- corpus	6620 (92.24%)	2390 (33.3%)	961 (13.39%)	18 (0.25%)	7177
B- corpus	7034 (87.51%)	4122 (51.28%)	790 (9.83%)	25 (0.31%)	8038
C- corpus	5504 (68.26%)	5849 (72.54%)	1705 (21.15%)	116 (1.44%)	8063
P- corpus	9252 (94.95%)	2837 (29.12%)	841 (8.63%)	0 (0%)	9744

Table 4 Unique Words – gender

Unique Words	HKC Males	NES Males	Other speakers Males	All Males (M)	HKC Females	NES Females	Other Speakers Females	All Females (F)
HKCSE (Prosodic)	11313 (82.26%)	7873 (57.25%)	1839 (13.37%)	13752	10369 (92.87%)	3525 (31.57%)	1720 (15.4%)	11165
A- corpus	4800 (90.06%)	2052 (38.5%)	0 (0%)	5330	4622 (93.56%)	943 (19.09%)	961 (19.45%)	4940
B- corpus	4401 (72.74%)	3877 (64.08%)	765 (12.64%)	6050	5393 (97.22%)	1294 (23.36%)	90 (1.62%)	5547
C- corpus	3567 (55%)	5143 (79.31%)	1273 (19.63%)	6485	4009 (80.5%)	2481 (49.82%)	888 (17.83%)	4980
P- corpus	7763 (94.13%)	2577 (31.25%)	500 (6.06%)	8247	5072 (95.45%)	804 (15.13%)	511 (9.62%)	5314

Quantitative data

Tone units

Table 1 All tone units – L1

All tone units	HKC	NES	Other Speakers	Unidentified Speakers	All Speakers
HKCSE (Prosodic)	239282 (73.92%)	74058 (22.88%)	10237 (3.16%)	134 (0.04%)	323703 (100%)
A- corpus	65777 (86.12%)	8339 (10.92%)	2256 (2.95%)	10 (0.01%)	76380 (100%)
B- corpus	64124 (73.22%)	22310 (25.47%)	1133 (1.29%)	16 (0.02%)	87582 (100%)
C- corpus	43840 (50.8%)	37097 (42.98%)	5263 (6.1%)	108 (0.13%)	86304 (100%)
P- corpus	65541 (89.25%)	6312 (8.6%)	1585 (2.16%)	0 (0%)	73437 (100%)

Table 2 All tone units – gender

All tone units	HKC Males	NES Males	Other speakers Males	All Males (M)	HKC Females	NES Females	Other Speakers Females	All Females (F)
HKCSE (Prosodic)	121625 (65.38%)	59023 (31.73%)	5389 (2.9%)	186034 (100%)	117656 (85.54%)	15035 (10.93%)	4848 (3.52%)	137537 (100%)
A- corpus	34934 (85.05%)	6140 (14.95%)	0 (0%)	41074 (100%)	30841 (87.38%)	2199 (6.23%)	2256 (6.39%)	35296 (100%)
B- corpus	19399 (48.88%)	19230 (48.45%)	1058 (2.67%)	39687 (100%)	44726 (93.41%)	3080 (6.43%)	75 (0.16%)	47881 (100%)
C- corpus	18565 (36.73%)	28143 (55.69%)	3834 (7.59%)	50539 (100%)	25275 (70.88%)	8954 (25.11%)	1429 (4.01%)	35657 (100%)
P- corpus	48727 (89.03%)	5510 (10.07%)	497 (0.91%)	54734 (100%)	16814 (89.9%)	802 (4.29%)	1088 (5.82%)	18703 (100%)

Table 3 One-word tone units (ALL) – L1

1-word tone units (ALL)	HKC	NES	Other Speakers	Unidentified Speakers	All Speakers
HKCSE (Prosodic)	80856 (75.56%)	22692 (21.21%)	3390 (3.17%)	65 (0.06%)	107003 (100%)
A- corpus	24219 (90.55%)	1831 (6.85%)	694 (2.59%)	4 (0.01%)	26748 (100%)
B- corpus	22370 (75.37%)	6994 (23.56%)	308 (1.04%)	8 (0.03%)	29680 (100%)
C- corpus	17371 (54.9%)	12392 (39.16%)	1826 (5.77%)	53 (0.17%)	31642 (100%)
P- corpus	16896 (89.24%)	1475 (7.79%)	562 (2.97%)	0 (0%)	18933 (100%)

Table 4 One-word tone units (ALL) – gender

1-word tone units (ALL)	HKC Males	NES Males	Other speakers Males	All Males (M)	HKC Females	NES Females	Other Speakers Females	All Females (F)
HKCSE (Prosodic)	38028 (66.28%)	17582 (30.64%)	1766 (3.08%)	57376 (100%)	42828 (86.41%)	5110 (10.31%)	1624 (3.28%)	49562 (100%)
A- corpus	12774 (92.22%)	1078 (7.78%)	0 (0%)	13852 (100%)	11445 (88.78%)	753 (5.84%)	694 (5.38%)	12892 (100%)
B- corpus	5360 (46.63%)	5858 (50.96%)	277 (2.41%)	11495 (100%)	17010 (93.58%)	1136 (6.25%)	31 (0.17%)	18177 (100%)
C- corpus	6988 (39.45%)	9348 (52.78%)	1376 (7.77%)	17712 (100%)	10383 (74.82%)	3044 (21.94%)	450 (3.24%)	13877 (100%)
P- corpus	12906 (90.14%)	1298 (9.07%)	113 (0.79%)	14317 (100%)	3990 (86.44%)	177 (3.83%)	449 (9.73%)	4616 (100%)

Table 5 One-word tone units (with prominence only) – L1

1-word tone units (with prominence only)	HKC	NES	Other Speakers	Unidentified Speakers	All Speakers
HKCSE (Prosodic)	79813 (75.5%)	22476 (21.26%)	3356 (3.17%)	63 (0.06%)	105708 (100%)
A- corpus	23760 (90.53%)	1796 (6.84%)	688 (2.62%)	2 (0.01%)	26246 (100%)
B- corpus	22177 (75.4%)	6920 (23.53%)	307 (1.04%)	8 (0.03%)	29412 (100%)
C- corpus	17249 (54.9%)	12313 (39.19%)	1805 (5.74%)	53 (0.17%)	31420 (100%)
P- corpus	16627 (89.25%)	1447 (7.77%)	556 (2.98%)	0 (0%)	18630 (100%)

Table 6 One-word tone units (with prominence only) – gender

1-word tone units (with prominence only)	HKC Males	NES Males	Other speakers Males	All Males (M)	HKC Females	NES Females	Other Speakers Females	All Females (F)
HKCSE (Prosodic)	37410 (66.14%)	17408 (30.78%)	1745 (3.09%)	56563 (100%)	42403 (86.39%)	5068 (10.33%)	1611 (3.28%)	49082 (100%)
A- corpus	12482 (92.23%)	1051 (7.77%)	0 (0%)	13533 (100%)	11278 (88.73%)	745 (5.86%)	688 (5.41%)	12711 (100%)
B- corpus	5302 (46.64%)	5790 (50.93%)	276 (2.43%)	11368 (100%)	16875 (93.56%)	1130 (6.27%)	31 (0.17%)	18036 (100%)
C- corpus	6929 (39.41%)	9295 (52.86%)	1359 (7.73%)	17583 (100%)	10320 (74.87%)	3018 (21.89%)	446 (3.24%)	13784 (100%)
P- corpus	12697 (90.18%)	1272 (9.03%)	110 (0.78%)	14079 (100%)	3930 (86.35%)	175 (3.85%)	446 (9.8%)	4551 (100%)

Table 7 Two-word tone units – L1

2-word tone units	HKC	NES	Other Speakers	Unidentified Speakers	All Speakers
HKCSE (Prosodic)	53850 (76.22%)	14459 (20.47%)	2313 (3.27%)	29 (0.04%)	70651 (100%)
A- corpus	15050 (89.59%)	1375 (8.19%)	372 (2.21%)	2 (0.01%)	16799 (100%)
B- corpus	13662 (75.29%)	4283 (23.6%)	197 (1.09%)	4 (0.02%)	18146 (100%)
C- corpus	9889 (52.89%)	7467 (39.94%)	1318 (7.05%)	23 (0.12%)	18697 (100%)
P- corpus	15249 (89.65%)	1334 (7.84%)	426 (2.5%)	0 (0%)	17009 (100%)

Table 8 Two-word tone units – gender

2-word tone units	HKC Males	NES Males	Other speakers Males	All Males (M)	HKC Females	NES Females	Other Speakers Females	All Females (F)
HKCSE (Prosodic)	27632 (68.03%)	11627 (28.63%)	1359 (3.35%)	40618 (100%)	26218 (87.38%)	2832 (9.44%)	954 (3.18%)	30004 (100%)
A- corpus	8179 (88.71%)	1041 (11.29%)	0 (0%)	9220 (100%)	6871 (90.68%)	334 (4.41%)	372 (4.91%)	7577 (100%)
B- corpus	4093 (51.19%)	3721 (46.54%)	182 (2.28%)	7996 (100%)	9569 (94.31%)	562 (5.54%)	15 (0.15%)	10146 (100%)
C- corpus	4306 (38.94%)	5691 (51.46%)	1062 (9.6%)	11059 (100%)	5583 (73.32%)	1776 (23.32%)	256 (3.36%)	7615 (100%)
P- corpus	11054 (89.56%)	1174 (9.51%)	115 (0.93%)	12343 (100%)	4195 (89.91%)	160 (3.43%)	311 (6.67%)	4666 (100%)

Table 9 Three-word tone units – L1

3-word tone units	HKC	NES	Other Speakers	Unidentified Speakers	All Speakers
HKCSE (Prosodic)	40081 (76.05%)	11068 (21%)	1547 (2.94%)	12 (0.02%)	52704 (100%)
A- corpus	10340 (86.42%)	1284 (10.73%)	341 (2.85%)	1 (0.01%)	11965 (100%)
B- corpus	10141 (74.48%)	3318 (24.37%)	156 (1.15%)	3 (0.02%)	13616 (100%)
C- corpus	6584 (51.65%)	5375 (42.16%)	781 (6.13%)	8 (0.06%)	12748 (100%)
P- corpus	13016 (90.55%)	1091 (7.59%)	269 (1.87%)	0 (0%)	14375 (100%)

Table 10 Three-word tone units – gender

3-word tone units	HKC Males	NES Males	Other speakers Males	All Males (M)	HKC Females	NES Females	Other Speakers Females	All Females (F)
HKCSE (Prosodic)	21176 (68.39%)	8988 (29.03%)	801 (2.59%)	30965 (100%)	18904 (86.99%)	2080 (9.57%)	746 (3.43%)	21730 (100%)
A- corpus	5576 (84.51%)	1022 (15.49%)	0 (0%)	6598 (100%)	4763 (88.76%)	262 (4.88%)	341 (6.35%)	5366 (100%)
B- corpus	3295 (51.95%)	2903 (45.77%)	145 (2.29%)	6343 (100%)	6846 (94.14%)	415 (5.71%)	11 (0.15%)	7272 (100%)
C- corpus	2832 (37.8%)	4098 (54.7%)	562 (7.5%)	7492 (100%)	3752 (71.49%)	1277 (24.33%)	219 (4.17%)	5248 (100%)
P- corpus	9473 (89.94%)	965 (9.16%)	94 (0.89%)	10532 (100%)	3543 (92.17%)	126 (3.28%)	175 (4.55%)	3844 (100%)

Table 11 Four-word tone units – L1

4-word tone units	HKC	NES	Other Speakers	Unidentified Speakers	All Speakers
HKCSE (Prosodic)	26388 (73.39%)	8505 (23.66%)	1048 (2.91%)	12 (0.03%)	35954 (100%)
A- corpus	6601 (82.33%)	1181 (14.73%)	235 (2.93%)	1 (0.01%)	8018 (100%)
B- corpus	7063 (72.87%)	2490 (25.69%)	138 (1.42%)	1 (0.01%)	9692 (100%)
C- corpus	4155 (48.16%)	3951 (45.8%)	511 (5.92%)	10 (0.12%)	8627 (100%)
P- corpus	8569 (89.1%)	883 (9.18%)	164 (1.71%)	0 (0%)	9617 (100%)

Table 12 Four-word tone units – gender

4-word tone units	HKC Males	NES Males	Other speakers Males	All Males (M)	HKC Females	NES Females	Other Speakers Females	All Females (F)
HKCSE (Prosodic)	14131 (65.38%)	6925 (32.04%)	558 (2.58%)	21614 (100%)	12257 (85.55%)	1580 (11.03%)	490 (3.42%)	14327 (100%)
A- corpus	3585 (79.05%)	950 (20.95%)	0 (0%)	4535 (100%)	3016 (86.62%)	231 (6.63%)	235 (6.75%)	3482 (100%)
B- corpus	2439 (51.26%)	2188 (45.99%)	131 (2.75%)	4758 (100%)	4624 (93.74%)	302 (6.12%)	7 (0.14%)	4933 (100%)
C- corpus	1812 (35.01%)	3007 (58.11%)	356 (6.88%)	5175 (100%)	2343 (68.07%)	944 (27.43%)	155 (4.5%)	3442 (100%)
P- corpus	6295 (88.09%)	780 (10.92%)	71 (0.99%)	7146 (100%)	2274 (92.06%)	103 (4.17%)	93 (3.77%)	2470 (100%)

Table 13 Five-word tone units – L1

5-word tone units	HKC	NES	Other Speakers	Unidentified Speakers	All Speakers
HKCSE (Prosodic)	16101 (70.33%)	6067 (26.5%)	723 (3.16%)	3 (0.01%)	22892 (100%)
A- corpus	4093 (78.56%)	926 (17.77%)	192 (3.69%)	0 (0%)	5210 (100%)
B- corpus	4365 (69.76%)	1797 (28.72%)	95 (1.52%)	0 (0%)	6257 (100%)
C- corpus	2470 (44.05%)	2782 (49.62%)	353 (6.3%)	3 (0.05%)	5607 (100%)
P- corpus	5173 (88.91%)	562 (9.66%)	83 (1.43%)	0 (0%)	5818 (100%)

Table 14 Five-word tone units – gender

5-word tone units	HKC Males	NES Males	Other speakers Males	All Males (M)	HKC Females	NES Females	Other Speakers Females	All Females (F)
HKCSE (Prosodic)	8735 (62.16%)	4957 (35.28%)	360 (2.56%)	14052 (100%)	7366 (83.34%)	1110 (12.56%)	363 (4.11%)	8838 (100%)
A- corpus	2157 (74.66%)	732 (25.34%)	0 (0%)	2889 (100%)	1936 (83.38%)	194 (8.35%)	192 (8.27%)	2322 (100%)
B- corpus	1594 (48.44%)	1608 (48.86%)	89 (2.7%)	3291 (100%)	2771 (93.43%)	189 (6.37%)	6 (0.2%)	2966 (100%)
C- corpus	1151 (32.8%)	2134 (60.82%)	224 (6.38%)	3509 (100%)	1319 (62.96%)	648 (30.93%)	129 (6.16%)	2095 (100%)
P- corpus	3833 (87.85%)	483 (11.07%)	47 (1.08%)	4363 (100%)	1340 (92.1%)	79 (5.43%)	36 (2.47%)	1455 (100%)

Table 15 Six-word tone units – L1

6-word tone units	HKC	NES	Other Speakers	Unidentified Speakers	All Speakers
HKCSE (Prosodic)	9454 (67.15%)	4201 (29.84%)	426 (3.03%)	0 (0%)	14079 (100%)
A- corpus	2378 (74.94%)	652 (20.55%)	143 (4.51%)	0 (0%)	3173 (100%)
B- corpus	2661 (66.18%)	1283 (31.91%)	77 (1.91%)	0 (0%)	4021 (100%)
C- corpus	1376 (40.18%)	1886 (55.07%)	165 (4.82%)	0 (0%)	3425 (100%)
P- corpus	3039 (87.83%)	380 (10.98%)	41 (1.18%)	0 (0%)	3460 (100%)

Table 16 Six-word tone units – gender

6-word tone units	HKC Males	NES Males	Other speakers Males	All Males (M)	HKC Females	NES Females	Other Speakers Females	All Females (F)
HKCSE (Prosodic)	5102 (58.83%)	3382 (38.99%)	191 (2.2%)	8673 (100%)	4351 (80.5%)	819 (15.15%)	235 (4.35%)	5405 (100%)
A- corpus	1187 (69.78%)	514 (30.22%)	0 (0%)	1701 (100%)	1190 (80.9%)	138 (9.38%)	143 (9.72%)	1471 (100%)
B- corpus	1019 (45.86%)	1128 (50.77%)	75 (3.38%)	2222 (100%)	1642 (91.27%)	155 (8.62%)	2 (0.11%)	1799 (100%)
C- corpus	579 (27.72%)	1423 (68.12%)	89 (4.26%)	2089 (100%)	797 (91.27%)	463 (34.66%)	76 (5.69%)	1336 (100%)
P- corpus	2317 (87.07%)	317 (11.91%)	27 (1.01%)	2661 (100%)	722 (90.36%)	63 (7.88%)	14 (1.75%)	799 (100%)

Table 17 Seven-word tone units – L1

7-word tone units	HKC	NES	Other Speakers	Unidentified Speakers	All Speakers
HKCSE (Prosodic)	5312 (64.19%)	2701 (32.64%)	260 (3.14%)	1 (0.01%)	8275 (100%)
A- corpus	1377 (71.91%)	444 (23.19%)	94 (4.91%)	0 (0%)	1915 (100%)
B- corpus	1555 (64.34%)	810 (33.51%)	52 (2.15%)	0 (0%)	2417 (100%)
C- corpus	766 (36.88%)	1210 (58.26%)	99 (4.77%)	1 (0.05%)	2077 (100%)
P- corpus	1614 (86.5%)	237 (12.7%)	15 (0.8%)	0 (0%)	1866 (100%)

Table 18 Seven-word tone units – gender

7-word tone units	HKC Males	NES Males	Other speakers Males	All Males (M)	HKC Females	NES Females	Other Speakers Females	All Females (F)
HKCSE (Prosodic)	2887 (55.74%)	2177 (42.04%)	115 (2.22%)	5179 (100%)	2425 (78.35%)	524 (16.93%)	145 (4.68%)	3095 (100%)
A- corpus	654 (65.01%)	352 (34.99%)	0 (0%)	1006 (100%)	723 (79.54%)	92 (10.12%)	94 (10.34%)	909 (100%)
B- corpus	621 (44.97%)	709 (51.34%)	51 (3.69%)	1381 (100%)	934 (90.15%)	101 (9.75%)	1 (0.1%)	1036 (100%)
C- corpus	338 (25.92%)	913 (70.02%)	53 (4.06%)	1304 (100%)	428 (55.44%)	297 (38.47%)	46 (5.96%)	772 (100%)
P- corpus	1274 (85.62%)	203 (13.64%)	11 (0.74%)	1488 (100%)	340 (89.95%)	34 (8.99%)	4 (1.06%)	378 (100%)

Table 19 Eight-word tone units – L1

8-word tone units	HKC	NES	Other Speakers	Unidentified Speakers	All Speakers
HKCSE (Prosodic)	2794 (61.53%)	1592 (35.06%)	151 (3.33%)	3 (0.07%)	4541 (100%)
A-corpus	698 (67.31%)	287 (27.68%)	52 (5.01%)	0 (0%)	1037 (100%)
B-corpus	811 (62.15%)	463 (35.48%)	31 (2.38%)	0 (0%)	1305 (100%)
C-corpus	422 (36.01%)	689 (58.79%)	57 (4.86%)	3 (0.26%)	1172 (100%)
P-corpus	863 (84.03%)	153 (14.9%)	11 (1.07%)	0 (0%)	1027 (100%)

Table 20 Eight-word tone units – gender

8-word tone units	HKC Males	NES Males	Other speakers Males	All Males (M)	HKC Females	NES Females	Other Speakers Females	All Females (F)
HKCSE (Prosodic)	1509 (53.15%)	1264 (44.52%)	66 (2.32%)	2839 (100%)	1285 (75.68%)	328 (19.32%)	85 (5.01%)	1698 (100%)
A-corpus	317 (58.92%)	221 (41.08%)	0 (0%)	538 (100%)	381 (76.35%)	66 (13.23%)	52 (10.42%)	499 (100%)
B-corpus	316 (42.65%)	394 (53.17%)	31 (4.18%)	741 (100%)	495 (87.77%)	69 (12.23%)	0 (0%)	564 (100%)
C-corpus	195 (26.42%)	520 (70.08%)	27 (3.64%)	742 (100.13%)	227 (53.29%)	169 (39.67%)	30 (7.04%)	426 (100%)
P-corpus	681 (83.25%)	129 (15.77%)	8 (0.98%)	818 (100%)	182 (87.08%)	24 (11.48%)	3 (1.44%)	209 (100%)

Table 21 Nine-word tone units – L1

9-word tone units	HKC	NES	Other Speakers	Unidentified Speakers	All Speakers
HKCSE (Prosodic)	1419 (58.64%)	889 (36.74%)	112 (4.63%)	0 (0%)	2420 (100%)
A- corpus	314 (59.36%)	161 (30.43%)	54 (10.21%)	0 (0%)	529 (100%)
B- corpus	429 (58.93%)	279 (38.32%)	19 (2.61%)	0 (0%)	728 (100%)
C- corpus	204 (33.94%)	362 (60.23%)	35 (5.82%)	0 (0%)	601 (100%)
P- corpus	472 (83.99%)	87 (15.48%)	4 (0.71%)	0 (0%)	562 (100%)

Table 22 Nine-word tone units – gender

9-word tone units	HKC Males	NES Males	Other speakers Males	All Males (M)	HKC Females	NES Females	Other Speakers Females	All Females (F)
HKCSE (Prosodic)	794 (51.09%)	723 (46.53%)	37 (2.38%)	1554 (100%)	626 (72.29%)	166 (19.17%)	75 (8.66%)	866 (100%)
A- corpus	151 (56.34%)	117 (43.66%)	0 (0%)	268 (100%)	163 (62.45%)	44 (16.86%)	54 (20.69%)	261 (100%)
B- corpus	196 (42.33%)	249 (53.78%)	18 (3.89%)	463 (100%)	234 (88.3%)	30 (11.32%)	1 (0.38%)	265 (100%)
C- corpus	93 (23.85%)	282 (72.31%)	15 (3.85%)	390 (100%)	111 (52.61%)	80 (37.91%)	20 (9.48%)	211 (100%)
P- corpus	354 (81.76%)	75 (17.32%)	4 (0.92%)	433 (100%)	118 (91.47%)	12 (9.3%)	0 (0%)	129 (100%)

Table 23 Ten-word tone units – L1

10-word tone units	HKC	NES	Other Speakers	Unidentified Speakers	All Speakers
HKCSE (Prosodic)	743 (57.24%)	510 (39.29%)	46 (3.54%)	0 (0%)	1298 (100%)
A-corpus	166 (59.93%)	86 (31.05%)	25 (9.03%)	0 (0%)	277 (100%)
B-corpus	226 (55.39%)	174 (42.65%)	9 (2.21%)	0 (0%)	408 (100%)
C-corpus	108 (32.83%)	209 (63.53%)	12 (3.65%)	0 (0%)	329 (100%)
P-corpus	243 (85.56%)	41 (14.44%)	0 (0%)	0 (0%)	284 (100%)

Table 24 Ten-word tone units – gender

10-word tone units	HKC Males	NES Males	Other speakers Males	All Males (M)	HKC Females	NES Females	Other Speakers Females	All Females (F)
HKCSE (Prosodic)	411 (49.64%)	405 (48.91%)	12 (1.45%)	828 (100%)	332 (70.49%)	105 (22.29%)	34 (7.22%)	471 (100%)
A-corpus	71 (58.2%)	51 (41.8%)	0 (0%)	122 (100%)	95 (61.29%)	35 (22.58%)	25 (16.13%)	155 (100%)
B-corpus	105 (38.32%)	160 (58.39%)	9 (3.28%)	274 (100%)	121 (89.63%)	14 (10.37%)	0 (0%)	135 (100%)
C-corpus	44 (21.26%)	160 (77.29%)	3 (1.45%)	207 (100%)	64 (52.46%)	49 (40.16%)	9 (7.38%)	122 (100%)
P-corpus	191 (84.89%)	34 (15.11%)	0 (0%)	225 (100%)	52 (88.14%)	7 (11.86%)	0 (0%)	59 (100%)

Table 25 Eleven-word tone units – L1

11-word tone units	HKC	NES	Other Speakers	Unidentified Speakers	All Speakers
HKCSE (Prosodic)	361 (56.06%)	252 (39.13%)	31 (4.81%)	0 (0%)	644 (100%)
A- corpus	79 (62.2%)	37 (29.13%)	11 (8.66%)	0 (0%)	127 (100%)
B- corpus	125 (55.07%)	95 (41.85%)	7 (3.08%)	0 (0%)	227 (100%)
C- corpus	55 (33.54%)	97 (59.15%)	12 (7.32%)	0 (0%)	164 (100%)
P- corpus	102 (80.95%)	23 (18.25%)	1 (0.79%)	0 (0%)	126 (100%)

Table 26 Eleven-word tone units – gender

11-word tone units	HKC Males	NES Males	Other speakers Males	All Males (M)	HKC Females	NES Females	Other Speakers Females	All Females (F)
HKCSE (Prosodic)	194 (48.38%)	194 (48.38%)	13 (3.24%)	401 (100%)	167 (68.72%)	58 (23.87%)	18 (7.41%)	243 (100%)
A- corpus	38 (61.29%)	24 (38.71%)	0 (0%)	62 (100%)	41 (63.08%)	13 (20%)	11 (16.92%)	65 (100%)
B- corpus	54 (38.57%)	79 (56.43%)	7 (5%)	140 (100%)	71 (81.61%)	16 (18.39%)	0 (0%)	87 (100%)
C- corpus	22 (21.36%)	75 (72.82%)	6 (5.83%)	103 (100%)	33 (54.1%)	22 (36.07%)	6 (9.84%)	61 (100%)
P- corpus	80 (83.33%)	16 (16.67%)	0 (0%)	96 (100%)	22 (73.33%)	7 (23.33%)	1 (3.33%)	30 (100%)

Table 27 Twelve-word tone units – L1

12-word tone units	HKC	NES	Other Speakers	Unidentified Speakers	All Speakers
HKCSE (Prosodic)	148 (48.68%)	144 (47.37%)	12 (3.95%)	0 (0%)	304 (100%)
A- corpus	35 (60.34%)	21 (36.21%)	2 (3.45%)	0 (0%)	58 (100%)
B- corpus	51 (48.11%)	51 (48.11%)	4 (3.77%)	0 (0%)	106 (100%)
C- corpus	17 (20.24%)	64 (76.19%)	3 (3.57%)	0 (0%)	84 (100%)
P- corpus	45 (80.36%)	8 (14.29%)	3 (5.36%)	0 (0%)	56 (100%)

Table 28 Twelve-word tone units – gender

12-word tone units	HKC Males	NES Males	Other speakers Males	All Males (M)	HKC Females	NES Females	Other Speakers Females	All Females (F)
HKCSE (Prosodic)	82 (41.21%)	109 (54.77%)	8 (4.02%)	199 (100%)	66 (62.86%)	35 (33.33%)	4 (3.81%)	105 (100%)
A- corpus	16 (53.33%)	14 (46.67%)	0 (0%)	30 (100%)	19 (67.86%)	7 (25%)	2 (7.14%)	28 (100%)
B- corpus	23 (33.82%)	41 (60.29%)	4 (5.88%)	68 (100%)	28 (73.68%)	10 (26.32%)	0 (0%)	38 (100%)
C- corpus	6 (11.11%)	47 (87.04%)	1 (1.85%)	54 (100%)	11 (36.67%)	17 (56.67%)	2 (6.67%)	30 (100%)
P- corpus	37 (78.72%)	7 (14.89%)	3 (6.38%)	47 (100%)	8 (88.89%)	1 (11.11%)	0 (0%)	9 (100%)

Table 29 Thirteen-word tone units – L1

13-word tone units	HKC	NES	Other Speakers	Unidentified Speakers	All Speakers
HKCSE (Prosodic)	78 (50%)	69 (44.23%)	8 (5.13%)	0 (0%)	156 (100%)
A- corpus	12 (38.71%)	16 (51.61%)	3 (9.68%)	0 (0%)	31 (100%)
B- corpus	29 (51.79%)	23 (41.07%)	3 (5.36%)	0 (0%)	56 (100%)
C- corpus	15 (34.09%)	27 (61.36%)	2 (4.55%)	0 (0%)	44 (100%)
P- corpus	22 (88%)	3 (12%)	0 (0%)	0 (0%)	25 (100%)

Table 30 Thirteen-word tone units – gender

13-word tone units	HKC Males	NES Males	Other speakers Males	All Males (M)	HKC Females	NES Females	Other Speakers Females	All Females (F)
HKCSE (Prosodic)	55 (47.41%)	58 (50%)	3 (2.59%)	116 (100%)	23 (58.97%)	11 (28.21%)	5 (12.82%)	39 (100%)
A- corpus	7 (38.89%)	11 (61.11%)	0 (0%)	18 (100%)	5 (38.46%)	5 (38.46%)	3 (23.08%)	13 (100%)
B- corpus	20 (46.51%)	20 (46.51%)	3 (6.98%)	43 (100%)	9 (75%)	3 (25%)	0 (0%)	12 (100%)
C- corpus	9 (27.27%)	24 (72.73%)	0 (0%)	33 (100%)	6 (54.55%)	3 (27.27%)	2 (18.18%)	11 (100%)
P- corpus	19 (89.36%)	3 (13.64%)	0 (0%)	22 (100%)	3 (100%)	0 (0%)	0 (0%)	3 (100%)

Table 31 Fourteen-word tone units – L1

14-word tone units	HKC	NES	Other Speakers	Unidentified Speakers	All Speakers
HKCSE (Prosodic)	31 (44.29%)	33 (47.14%)	6 (8.57%)	0 (0%)	70 (100%)
A- corpus	2 (16.67%)	6 (50%)	4 (33.34%)	0 (0%)	12 (100%)
B- corpus	14 (53.85%)	10 (38.46%)	2 (7.69%)	0 (0%)	26 (100%)
C- corpus	6 (30%)	14 (70%)	0 (0%)	0 (0%)	20 (100%)
P- corpus	9 (75%)	3 (25%)	0 (0%)	0 (0%)	12 (100%)

Table 32 Fourteen-word tone units – gender

14-word tone units	HKC Males	NES Males	Other speakers Males	All Males (M)	HKC Females	NES Females	Other Speakers Females	All Females (F)
HKCSE (Prosodic)	22 (43.14%)	27 (52.94%)	2 (3.92%)	51 (100%)	9 (47.37%)	6 (31.58%)	4 (21.05%)	19 (100%)
A- corpus	1 (16.67%)	5 (83.33%)	0 (0%)	6 (100%)	1 (16.67%)	1 (16.67%)	4 (66.67%)	6 (100%)
B- corpus	9 (47.37%)	8 (42.11%)	2 (10.53%)	19 (100%)	5 (71.43%)	2 (28.57%)	0 (0%)	7 (100%)
C- corpus	4 (23.53%)	13 (76.47%)	0 (0%)	17 (100%)	2 (66.67%)	1 (33.33%)	0 (0%)	3 (100%)
P- corpus	8 (88.89%)	1 (11.11%)	0 (0%)	9 (100%)	1 (33.33%)	2 (66.67%)	0 (0%)	3 (100%)

Table 33 Fifteen-word tone units – L1

15-word tone units	HKC	NES	Other Speakers	Unidentified Speakers	All Speakers
HKCSE (Prosodic)	10 (37.04%)	16 (59.26%)	1 (3.7%)	0 (0%)	27 (100%)
A- corpus	0 (0%)	1 (100%)	0 (0%)	0 (0%)	1 (100%)
B- corpus	4 (40%)	5 (50%)	1 (10%)	0 (0%)	10 (100%)
C- corpus	0 (0%)	9 (100%)	0 (0%)	0 (0%)	9 (100%)
P- corpus	6 (85.71%)	1 (14.29%)	0 (0%)	0 (0%)	7 (100%)

Table 34 Fifteen-word tone units – gender

15-word tone units	HKC Males	NES Males	Other speakers Males	All Males (M)	HKC Females	NES Females	Other Speakers Females	All Females (F)
HKCSE (Prosodic)	7 (38.89%)	10 (55.56%)	1 (5.56%)	18 (100%)	3 (33.33%)	6 (66.67%)	0 (0%)	9 (100%)
A- corpus	0 (0%)	0 (0%)	0 (0%)	0 (0%)	0 (0%)	1 (100%)	0 (0%)	1 (100%)
B- corpus	2 (33.33%)	3 (50%)	1 (16.67%)	6 (100%)	2 (50%)	2 (50%)	0 (0%)	4 (100%)
C- corpus	0 (0%)	6 (100%)	0 (0%)	6 (100%)	0 (0%)	3 (100%)	0 (0%)	3 (100%)
P- corpus	5 (83.33%)	1 (16.67%)	0 (0%)	6 (100%)	1 (100%)	0 (0%)	0 (0%)	1 (100%)

Table 35 Sixteen-word tone units – L1

16-word tone units	HKC	NES	Other Speakers	Unidentified Speakers	All Speakers
HKCSE (Prosodic)	3 (27.27%)	7 (63.64%)	1 (9.09%)	0 (0%)	11 (100%)
A- corpus	0 (0%)	2 (100%)	0 (0%)	0 (0%)	2 (100%)
B- corpus	2 (28.57%)	5 (71.43%)	0 (0%)	0 (0%)	7 (100%)
C- corpus	0 (0%)	0 (0%)	1 (100%)	0 (0%)	1 (100%)
P- corpus	1 (100%)	0 (0%)	0 (0%)	0 (0%)	1 (100%)

Table 36 Sixteen-word tone units – gender

16-word tone units	HKC Males	NES Males	Other speakers Males	All Males (M)	HKC Females	NES Females	Other Speakers Females	All Females (F)
HKCSE (Prosodic)	2 (28.57%)	5 (71.43%)	0 (0%)	7 (100%)	1 (25%)	2 (50%)	1 (25%)	4 (100%)
A- corpus	0 (0%)	1 (100%)	0 (0%)	1 (100%)	0 (0%)	1 (100%)	0 (0%)	1 (100%)
B- corpus	2 (33.33%)	4 (66.67%)	0 (0%)	6 (100%)	0 (0%)	1 (100%)	0 (0%)	1 (100%)
C- corpus	0 (0%)	0 (0%)	0 (0%)	0 (0%)	0 (0%)	0 (0%)	1 (100%)	1 (100%)
P- corpus	0 (0%)	0 (0%)	0 (0%)	0 (0%)	1 (100%)	0 (0%)	0 (0%)	1 (100%)

Table 37 Seventeen-word tone units – L1

17-word tone units	HKC	NES	Other Speakers	Unidentified Speakers	All Speakers
HKCSE (Prosodic)	1 (12.5%)	6 (75%)	1 (12.5%)	0 (0%)	8 (100%)
A- corpus	0 (0%)	0 (0%)	1 (100%)	0 (0%)	1 (100%)
B- corpus	1 (33.33%)	2 (66.67%)	0 (0%)	0 (0%)	3 (100%)
C- corpus	0 (0%)	4 (100%)	0 (0%)	0 (0%)	4 (100%)
P- corpus	0 (0%)	0 (0%)	0 (0%)	0 (0%)	0 (0%)

Table 38 Seventeen-word tone units – gender

17-word tone units	HKC Males	NES Males	Other speakers Males	All Males (M)	HKC Females	NES Females	Other Speakers Females	All Females (F)
HKCSE (Prosodic)	1 (20%)	4 (80%)	0 (0%)	5 (100%)	0 (0%)	2 (66.67%)	1 (33.33%)	3 (100%)
A- corpus	0 (0%)	0 (0%)	0 (0%)	0 (0%)	0 (0%)	0 (0%)	1 (100%)	1 (100%)
B- corpus	1 (50%)	1 (50%)	0 (0%)	2 (100%)	0 (0%)	1 (100%)	0 (0%)	1 (100%)
C- corpus	0 (0%)	3 (100%)	0 (0%)	3 (100%)	0 (0%)	1 (100%)	0 (0%)	1 (100%)
P- corpus	0 (0%)	0 (0%)	0 (0%)	0 (0%)	0 (0%)	0 (0%)	0 (0%)	0 (0%)

Table 39 Eighteen-word tone units – L1

18-word tone units	HKC	NES	Other Speakers	Unidentified Speakers	All Speakers
HKCSE (Prosodic)	1 (50%)	1 (50%)	0 (0%)	0 (0%)	2 (100%)
A- corpus	0 (0%)	0 (0%)	0 (0%)	0 (0%)	0 (0%)
B- corpus	1 (100%)	0 (0%)	0 (0%)	0 (0%)	1 (100%)
C- corpus	0 (0%)	1 (100%)	0 (0%)	0 (0%)	1 (100%)
P- corpus	0 (0%)	0 (0%)	0 (0%)	0 (0%)	0 (0%)

Table 40 Eighteen-word tone units – gender

18-word tone units	HKC Males	NES Males	Other speakers Males	All Males (M)	HKC Females	NES Females	Other Speakers Females	All Females (F)
HKCSE (Prosodic)	1 (50%)	1 (50%)	0 (0%)	2 (100%)	0 (0%)	0 (0%)	0 (0%)	0 (0%)
A- corpus	0 (0%)	0 (0%)	0 (0%)	0 (0%)	0 (0%)	0 (0%)	0 (0%)	0 (0%)
B- corpus	1 (100%)	0 (0%)	0 (0%)	1 (100%)	0 (0%)	0 (0%)	0 (0%)	0 (0%)
C- corpus	0 (0%)	1 (100%)	0 (0%)	1 (100%)	0 (0%)	0 (0%)	0 (0%)	0 (0%)
P- corpus	0 (0%)	0 (0%)	0 (0%)	0 (0%)	0 (0%)	0 (0%)	0 (0%)	0 (0%)

Table 41 Tone Units – HKCSE (prosodic) – L1

Tone Unit { }	HKC	NES	Other Speakers	Unidentified Speakers	All Speakers
All tone units	239282	74058	10237	134	323703
	(73.92%)	(22.88%)	(3.16%)	(0.04%)	(100%)
1-word tone units (ALL)	80856	22692	3390	65	107003
	(75.56%)	(21.21%)	(3.17%)	(0.06%)	(100%)
1-word tone units (with prominence only)	79813	22476	3356	63	105708
	(75.5%)	(21.26%)	(3.17%)	(0.06%)	(100%)
2-word tone units	53850	14459	2313	29	70651
	(76.22%)	(20.47%)	(3.27%)	(0.04%)	(100%)
3-word tone units	40081	11068	1547	12	52704
	(76.05%)	(21%)	(2.94%)	(0.02%)	(100%)
4-word tone units	26388	8505	1048	12	35954
	(73.39%)	(23.66%)	(2.91%)	(0.03%)	(100%)
5-word tone units	16101	6067	723	3	22892
	(70.33%)	(26.5%)	(3.16%)	(0.01%)	(100%)
6-word tone units	9454	4201	426	0	14079
	(67.15%)	(29.84%)	(3.03%)	(0%)	(100%)
7-word tone units	5312	2701	260	1	8275
	(64.19%)	(32.64%)	(3.14%)	(0.01%)	(100%)
8-word tone units	2794	1592	151	3	4541
	(61.53%)	(35.06%)	(3.33%)	(0.07%)	(100%)
9-word tone units	1419	889	112	0	2420
	(58.64%)	(36.74%)	(4.63%)	(0%)	(100%)
10-word tone units	743	510	46	0	1298
	(57.24%)	(39.29%)	(3.54%)	(0%)	(100%)

Tone Unit { }	HKC	NES	Other Speakers	Unidentified Speakers	All Speakers
11-word tone units	361	252	31	0	644
	(56.06%)	(39.13%)	(4.81%)	(0%)	(100%)
12-word tone units	148	144	12	0	304
	(48.68%)	(47.37%)	(3.95%)	(0%)	(100%)
13-word tone units	78	69	8	0	156
	(50%)	(44.23%)	(5.13%)	(0%)	(100%)
14-word tone units	31	33	6	0	70
	(44.29%)	(47.14%)	(8.57%)	(0%)	(100%)
15-word tone units	10	16	1	0	27
	(37.04%)	(59.26%)	(3.7%)	(0%)	(100%)
16-word tone units	3	7	1	0	11
	(27.27%)	(63.64%)	(9.09%)	(0%)	(100%)
17-word tone units	1	6	1	0	8
	(12.5%)	(75%)	(12.5%)	(0%)	(100%)
18-word tone units	1	1	0	0	2
	(50%)	(50%)	(0%)	(0%)	(100%)

Table 42 Tone Units – Academic sub-corpus – L1

Tone Unit { }	HKC	NES	Other Speakers	Unidentified Speakers	All Speakers
All tone units	65777 (86.12%)	8349 (10.93%)	2256 (2.95%)	10 (0.01%)	76380 (100%)
1-word tone units (ALL)	24219 (90.55%)	1831 (6.85%)	694 (2.59%)	4 (0.01%)	26748 (100%)
1-word tone units (with prominence only)	23760 (90.53%)	1796 (6.84%)	688 (2.62%)	2 (0.01%)	26246 (100%)
2-word tone units	15050 (89.59%)	1375 (8.19%)	372 (2.21%)	2 (0.01%)	16799 (100%)
3-word tone units	10340 (86.42%)	1284 (10.73%)	341 (2.85%)	1 (0.01%)	11965 (100%)
4-word tone units	6601 (82.33%)	1181 (14.73%)	235 (2.93%)	1 (0.01%)	8018 (100%)
5-word tone units	4093 (78.56%)	926 (17.77%)	192 (3.69%)	0 (0%)	5210 (100%)
6-word tone units	2378 (74.94%)	652 (20.55%)	143 (4.51%)	0 (0%)	3173 (100%)
7-word tone units	1377 (71.91%)	444 (23.19%)	94 (4.91%)	0 (0%)	1915 (100%)
8-word tone units	698 (67.31%)	287 (27.68%)	52 (5.01%)	0 (0%)	1037 (100%)
9-word tone units	314 (59.36%)	161 (30.43%)	54 (10.21%)	0 (0%)	529 (100%)
10-word tone units	166 (59.93%)	86 (31.05%)	25 (9.03%)	0 (0%)	277 (100%)

Tone Unit { }	HKC	NES	Other Speakers	Unidentified Speakers	All Speakers
11-word tone units	79 (62.2%)	37 (29.13%)	11 (8.66%)	0 (0%)	127 (%)
12-word tone units	35 (60.34%)	21 (36.21%)	2 (3.45%)	0 (0%)	58 (100%)
13-word tone units	12 (38.71%)	16 (51.61%)	3 (9.68%)	0 (0%)	31 (100%)
14-word tone units	2 (16.67%)	6 (50%)	4 (33.34%)	0 (0%)	12 (100%)
15-word tone units	0 (0%)	1 (100%)	0 (0%)	0 (0%)	1 (100%)
16-word tone units	0 (0%)	2 (100%)	0 (0%)	0 (0%)	2 (100%)
17-word tone units	0 (0%)	0 (0%)	1 (100%)	0 (0%)	1 (100%)
18-word tone units	0 (0%)	0 (0%)	0 (0%)	0 (0%)	0 (0%)

Table 43 Tone Units – Business sub-corpus – L1

Tone Unit { }	HKC	NES	Other Speakers	Unidentified Speakers	All Speakers
All tone units	64124 (73.22%)	22310 (25.47%)	1133 (1.29%)	16 (0.02%)	87582 (100%)
1-word tone units (ALL)	22370 (75.37%)	6994 (23.56%)	308 (1.04%)	8 (0.03%)	29680 (100%)
1-word tone units (with prominence only)	22177 (75.4%)	6920 (23.53%)	307 (1.04%)	8 (0.03%)	29412 (100%)
2-word tone units	13662 (75.29%)	4283 (23.6%)	197 (1.09%)	4 (0.02%)	18146 (100%)
3-word tone units	10141 (74.48%)	3318 (24.37%)	156 (1.15%)	3 (0.02%)	13616 (100%)
4-word tone units	7063 (72.87%)	2490 (25.69%)	138 (1.42%)	1 (0.01%)	9692 (100%)
5-word tone units	4365 (69.76%)	1797 (28.72%)	95 (1.52%)	0 (0%)	6257 (100%)
6-word tone units	2661 (66.18%)	1283 (31.91%)	77 (1.91%)	0 (0%)	4021 (100%)
7-word tone units	1555 (64.34%)	810 (33.51%)	52 (2.15%)	0 (0%)	2417 (100%)
8-word tone units	811 (62.15%)	463 (35.48%)	31 (2.38%)	0 (0%)	1305 (100%)
9-word tone units	429 (58.93%)	279 (38.32%)	19 (2.61%)	0 (0%)	728 (100%)
10-word tone units	226 (55.39%)	174 (42.65%)	9 (2.21%)	0 (0%)	408 (100%)

Tone Unit { }	HKC	NES	Other Speakers	Unidentified Speakers	All Speakers
11-word tone units	125	95	7	0	227
	(55.07%)	(41.85%)	(3.08%)	(0%)	(100%)
12-word tone units	51	51	4	0	106
	(48.11%)	(48.11%)	(3.77%)	(0%)	(100%)
13-word tone units	29	23	3	0	56
	(51.79%)	(41.07%)	(5.36%)	(0%)	(100%)
14-word tone units	14	10	2	0	26
	(53.85%)	(38.46%)	(7.69%)	(0%)	(100%)
15-word tone units	4	5	1	0	10
	(40%)	(50%)	(10%)	(0%)	(100%)
16-word tone units	2	5	0	0	7
	(28.57%)	(71.43%)	(0%)	(0%)	(100%)
17-word tone units	1	2	0	0	3
	(33.33%)	(66.67%)	(0%)	(0%)	(100%)
18-word tone units	1	0	0	0	1
	(100%)	(0%)	(0%)	(0%)	(100%)

Table 44 Tone Units – Conversation sub-corpus – L1

Tone Unit { }	HKC	NES	Other Speakers	Unidentified Speakers	All Speakers
All tone units	43840 (50.8%)	37097 (42.98%)	5263 (6.1%)	108 (0.13%)	86304 (100%)
1-word tone units (ALL)	17371 (54.9%)	12392 (39.16%)	1826 (5.77%)	53 (0.17%)	31642 (100%)
1-word tone units (with prominence only)	17249 (54.9%)	12313 (39.19%)	1805 (5.74%)	53 (0.17%)	31420 (100%)
2-word tone units	9889 (52.89%)	7467 (39.94%)	1318 (7.05%)	23 (0.12%)	18697 (100%)
3-word tone units	6584 (51.65%)	5375 (42.16%)	781 (6.13%)	8 (0.06%)	12748 (100%)
4-word tone units	4155 (48.16%)	3951 (45.8%)	511 (5.92%)	10 (0.12%)	8627 (100%)
5-word tone units	2470 (44.05%)	2782 (49.62%)	353 (6.3%)	3 (0.05%)	5607 (100%)
6-word tone units	1376 (40.18%)	1886 (55.07%)	165 (4.82%)	0 (0%)	3425 (100%)
7-word tone units	766 (36.88%)	1210 (58.26%)	99 (4.77%)	1 (0.05%)	2077 (100%)
8-word tone units	422 (36.01%)	689 (58.79%)	57 (4.86%)	3 (0.26%)	1172 (100%)
9-word tone units	204 (33.94%)	362 (60.23%)	35 (5.82%)	0 (0%)	601 (100%)
10-word tone units	108 (32.83%)	209 (63.53%)	12 (3.65%)	0 (0%)	329 (100%)

Tone Unit { }	HKC	NES	Other Speakers	Unidentified Speakers	All Speakers
11-word tone units	55	97	12	0	164
	(33.54%)	(59.15%)	(7.32%)	(0%)	(100%)
12-word tone units	17	64	3	0	84
	(20.24%)	(76.19%)	(3.57%)	(0%)	(100%)
13-word tone units	15	27	2	0	44
	(34.09%)	(61.36%)	(4.55%)	(0%)	(100%)
14-word tone units	6	14	0	0	20
	(30%)	(70%)	(0%)	(0%)	(100%)
15-word tone units	0	9	0	0	9
	(0%)	(100%)	(0%)	(0%)	(100%)
16-word tone units	0	0	1	0	1
	(0%)	(0%)	(100%)	(0%)	(100%)
17-word tone units	0	4	0	0	4
	(0%)	(100%)	(0%)	(0%)	(100%)
18-word tone units	0	1	0	0	1
	(0%)	(100%)	(0%)	(0%)	(100%)

Table 45 Tone Units – Public sub-corpus – L1

Tone Unit { }	HKC	NES	Other Speakers	Unidentified Speakers	All Speakers
All tone units	65541 (89.25%)	6312 (8.6%)	1585 (2.16%)	0 (0%)	73437 (100%)
1-word tone units (ALL)	16896 (89.24%)	1475 (7.79%)	562 (2.97%)	0 (0%)	18933 (100%)
1-word tone units (with prominence only)	16627 (89.25%)	1447 (7.77%)	556 (2.98%)	0 (0%)	18630 (100%)
2-word tone units	15249 (89.65%)	1334 (7.84%)	426 (2.5%)	0 (0%)	17009 (100%)
3-word tone units	13016 (90.55%)	1091 (7.59%)	269 (1.87%)	0 (0%)	14375 (100%)
4-word tone units	8569 (89.1%)	883 (9.18%)	164 (1.71%)	0 (0%)	9617 (100%)
5-word tone units	5173 (88.91%)	562 (9.66%)	83 (1.43%)	0 (0%)	5818 (100%)
6-word tone units	3039 (87.83%)	380 (10.98%)	41 (1.18%)	0 (0%)	3460 (100%)
7-word tone units	1614 (86.5%)	237 (12.7%)	15 (0.8%)	0 (0%)	1866 (100%)
8-word tone units	863 (84.03%)	153 (14.9%)	11 (1.07%)	0 (0%)	1027 (100%)
9-word tone units	472 (83.99%)	87 (15.48%)	4 (0.71%)	0 (0%)	562 (100%)
10-word tone units	243 (85.56%)	41 (14.44%)	0 (0%)	0 (0%)	284 (100%)

Tone Unit { }	HKC	NES	Other Speakers	Unidentified Speakers	All Speakers
11-word tone units	102 (80.95%)	23 (18.25%)	1 (0.79%)	0 (0%)	126 (100%)
12-word tone units	45 (80.36%)	8 (14.29%)	3 (5.36%)	0 (0%)	56 (100%)
13-word tone units	22 (88%)	3 (12%)	0 (0%)	0 (0%)	25 (100%)
14-word tone units	9 (75%)	3 (25%)	0 (0%)	0 (0%)	12 (100%)
15-word tone units	6 (85.71%)	1 (14.29%)	0 (0%)	0 (0%)	7 (100%)
16-word tone units	1 (100%)	0 (0%)	0 (0%)	0 (0%)	1 (100%)
17-word tone units	0 (0%)	0 (0%)	0 (0%)	0 (0%)	0 (0%)
18-word tone units	0 (0%)	0 (0%)	0 (0%)	0 (0%)	0 (0%)

Table 46 Tone Units – HKCSE (prosodic) – gender

Tone Unit { }	HKC Males	NES Males	Other Speakers Males	All Males	HKC Females	NES Females	Other Speakers Females	All Females
All tone units	121625 (65.38%)	59023 (31.73%)	5389 (2.9%)	186034 (100%)	117656 (85.54%)	15035 (10.93%)	4848 (3.52%)	137537 (100%)
1-word tone units (ALL)	38028 (66.28%)	17582 (30.64%)	1766 (3.08%)	57376 (100%)	42828 (86.41%)	5110 (10.31%)	1624 (3.28%)	49562 (100%)
1-word tone units (with prominence only)	37410 (66.14%)	17408 (30.78%)	1745 (3.09%)	56563 (100%)	42403 (86.39%)	5068 (10.33%)	1611 (3.28%)	49082 (100%)
2-word tone units	27632 (68.03%)	11627 (28.63%)	1359 (3.35%)	40618 (100%)	26218 (87.38%)	2832 (9.44%)	954 (3.18%)	30004 (100%)
3-word tone units	21176 (68.39%)	8988 (29.03%)	801 (2.59%)	30965 (100%)	18904 (86.99%)	2080 (9.57%)	746 (3.43%)	21730 (100%)
4-word tone units	14131 (65.38%)	6925 (32.04%)	558 (2.58%)	21614 (100%)	12257 (85.55%)	1580 (11.03%)	490 (3.42%)	14327 (100%)
5-word tone units	8735 (62.16%)	4957 (35.28%)	360 (2.56%)	14052 (100%)	7366 (83.34%)	1110 (12.56%)	363 (4.11%)	8838 (100%)
6-word tone units	5102 (58.83%)	3382 (38.99%)	191 (2.2%)	8673 (100.02%)	4351 (80.5%)	819 (15.15%)	235 (4.35%)	5405 (100%)
7-word tone units	2887 (55.74%)	2177 (42.04%)	115 (2.22%)	5179 (100%)	2425 (78.35%)	524 (16.93%)	145 (4.68%)	3095 (100%)
8-word tone units	1509 (53.15%)	1264 (44.52%)	66 (2.32%)	2839 (100%)	1285 (75.68%)	328 (19.32%)	85 (5.01%)	1698 (100%)
9-word tone units	794 (51.09%)	723 (46.53%)	37 (2.38%)	1554 (100%)	626 (72.29%)	166 (19.17%)	75 (8.66%)	866 (100%)

Tone Unit { }	HKC Males	NES Males	Other Speakers Males	All Males	HKC Females	NES Females	Other Speakers Females	All Females
10-word	411	405	12	828	332	105	34	471
tone units	(49.64%)	(48.91%)	(1.45%)	(100%)	(70.49%)	(22.29%)	(7.22%)	(100%)
11-word	194	194	13	401	167	58	18	243
tone units	(48.38%)	(48.38%)	(3.24%)	(100%)	(68.72%)	(23.87%)	(7.41%)	(100%)
12-word	82	109	8	199	66	35	4	105
tone units	(41.21%)	(54.77%)	(4.02%)	(100%)	(62.86%)	(33.33%)	(3.81%)	(100%)
13-word	55	58	3	116	23	11	5	39
tone units	(47.41%)	(50%)	(2.59%)	(100%)	(58.97%)	(28.21%)	(12.82%)	(100%)
14-word	22	27	2	51	9	6	4	19
tone units	(43.14%)	(52.94%)	(3.92%)	(100%)	(47.37%)	(31.58%)	(21.05%)	(100%)
15-word	7	10	1	18	3	6	0	9
tone units	(38.89%)	(55.56%)	(5.56%)	(100%)	(33.33%)	(66.67%)	(0%)	(100%)
16-word	2	5	0	7	1	2	1	4
tone units	(28.57%)	(71.43%)	(0%)	(100%)	(25%)	(50%)	(25%)	(100%)
17-word	1	4	0	5	0	2	1	3
tone units	(20%)	(80%)	(0%)	(100%)	(0%)	(66.67%)	(33.33%)	(100%)
18-word	1	1	0	2	0	0	0	0
tone units	(50%)	(50%)	(0%)	(100%)	(0%)	(0%)	(0%)	(0%)

Table 47 Tone Units – Academic sub-corpus – gender

Tone Unit {}	HKC Males	NES Males	Other Speakers Males	All Males	HKC Females	NES Females	Other Speakers Females	All Females
All tone units	34934 (85.05%)	6140 (14.95%)	0 (0%)	41074 (100%)	30841 (87.38%)	2199 (6.23%)	2256 (6.39%)	35296 (100%)
1-word tone units (ALL)	12774 (92.22%)	1078 (7.78%)	0 (0%)	13852 (100%)	11445 (88.78%)	753 (5.84%)	694 (5.38%)	12892 (100%)
1-word tone units (with prominence only)	12482 (92.23%)	1051 (7.77%)	0 (0%)	13533 (100%)	11278 (88.73%)	745 (5.86%)	688 (5.41%)	12711 (100%)
2-word tone units	8179 (88.71%)	1041 (11.29%)	0 (0%)	9220 (100%)	6871 (90.68%)	334 (4.41%)	372 (4.91%)	7577 (100%)
3-word tone units	5576 (84.51%)	1022 (15.49%)	0 (0%)	6598 (100%)	4763 (88.76%)	262 (4.88%)	341 (6.35%)	5366 (100%)
4-word tone units	3585 (79.05%)	950 (20.95%)	0 (0%)	4535 (100%)	3016 (86.62%)	231 (6.63%)	235 (6.75%)	3482 (100%)
5-word tone units	2157 (74.66%)	732 (25.34%)	0 (0%)	2889 (100%)	1936 (83.38%)	194 (8.35%)	192 (8.27%)	2322 (100%)
6-word tone units	1187 (69.78%)	514 (30.22%)	0 (0%)	1701 (100%)	1190 (80.9%)	138 (9.38%)	143 (9.72%)	1471 (100%)
7-word tone units	654 (65.01%)	352 (34.99%)	0 (0%)	1006 (100%)	723 (79.54%)	92 (10.12%)	94 (10.34%)	909 (100%)
8-word tone units	317 (58.92%)	221 (41.08%)	0 (0%)	538 (100%)	381 (76.35%)	66 (13.23%)	52 (10.42%)	499 (100%)
9-word tone units	151 (56.34%)	117 (43.66%)	0 (0%)	268 (100%)	163 (62.45%)	44 (16.86%)	54 (20.69%)	261 (100%)

Tone Unit { }	HKC Males	NES Males	Other Speakers Males	All Males	HKC Females	NES Females	Other Speakers Females	All Females
10-word tone units	71 (58.2%)	51 (41.8%)	0 (0%)	122 (100%)	95 (61.29%)	35 (22.58%)	25 (16.13%)	155 (100%)
11-word tone units	38 (61.29%)	24 (38.71%)	0 (0%)	62 (100%)	41 (63.08%)	13 (20%)	11 (16.92%)	65 (100%)
12-word tone units	16 (53.33%)	14 (46.67%)	0 (0%)	30 (100%)	19 (67.86%)	7 (25%)	2 (7.14%)	28 (100%)
13-word tone units	7 (38.89%)	11 (61.11%)	0 (0%)	18 (100%)	5 (38.46%)	5 (38.46%)	3 (23.08%)	13 (100%)
14-word tone units	1 (16.67%)	5 (83.33%)	0 (0%)	6 (100%)	1 (16.67%)	1 (16.67%)	4 (66.67%)	6 (100%)
15-word tone units	0 (0%)	0 (0%)	0 (0%)	0 (0%)	0 (0%)	1 (100%)	0 (0%)	1 (100%)
16-word tone units	0 (0%)	1 (100%)	1 (100%)	1 (100%)	0 (0%)	1 (100%)	0 (0%)	1 (100%)
17-word tone units	0 (0%)	0 (0%)	0 (0%)	0 (0%)	0 (0%)	0 (0%)	1 (100%)	1 (100%)
18-word tone units	0 (0%)	0 (0%)	0 (0%)	0 (0%)	0 (0%)	0 (0%)	0 (0%)	0 (0%)

Table 48 Tone Units – Business sub-corpus – gender

Tone Unit { }	HKC Males	NES Males	Other Speakers Males	All Males	HKC Females	NES Females	Other Speakers Females	All Females
All tone units	19399 (48.88%)	19230 (48.45%)	1058 (2.67%)	39687 (100%)	44726 (93.41%)	3080 (6.43%)	75 (0.16%)	47881 (100%)
1-word tone units (ALL)	5360 (46.63%)	5858 (50.96%)	277 (2.41%)	11495 (100%)	17010 (93.58%)	1136 (6.25%)	31 (0.17%)	18177 (100%)
1-word tone units (with prominence only)	5302 (46.64%)	5790 (50.93%)	276 (2.43%)	11368 (100%)	16875 (93.56%)	1130 (6.27%)	31 (0.17%)	18036 (100%)
2-word tone units	4093 (51.19%)	3721 (46.54%)	182 (2.28%)	7996 (100%)	9569 (94.31%)	562 (5.54%)	15 (0.15%)	10146 (100%)
3-word tone units	3295 (51.95%)	2903 (45.77%)	145 (2.29%)	6343 (100%)	6846 (94.14%)	415 (5.71%)	11 (0.15%)	7272 (100%)
4-word tone units	2439 (51.26%)	2188 (45.99%)	131 (2.75%)	4758 (100%)	4624 (93.74%)	302 (6.12%)	7 (0.14%)	4933 (100%)
5-word tone units	1594 (48.44%)	1608 (48.86%)	89 (2.7%)	3291 (100%)	2771 (93.43%)	189 (6.37%)	6 (0.2%)	2966 (100%)
6-word tone units	1019 (45.86%)	1128 (50.77%)	75 (3.38%)	2222 (100%)	1642 (91.27%)	155 (8.62%)	2 (0.11%)	1799 (100%)
7-word tone units	621 (44.97%)	709 (51.34%)	51 (3.69%)	1381 (100%)	934 (90.15%)	101 (9.75%)	1 (0.1%)	1036 (100%)
8-word tone units	316 (42.65%)	394 (53.17%)	31 (4.18%)	741 (100%)	495 (87.77%)	69 (12.23%)	0 (0%)	564 (100%)
9-word tone units	196 (42.33%)	249 (53.78%)	18 (3.89%)	463 (100%)	234 (88.3%)	30 (11.32%)	1 (0.38%)	265 (100%)

Tone Unit {}	HKC Males	NES Males	Other Speakers Males	All Males	HKC Females	NES Females	Other Speakers Females	All Females
10-word tone units	105 (38.32%)	160 (58.39%)	9 (3.28%)	274 (100%)	121 (89.63%)	14 (10.37%)	0 (0%)	135 (100%)
11-word tone units	54 (38.57%)	79 (56.43%)	7 (5%)	140 (100%)	71 (81.61%)	16 (18.39%)	0 (0%)	87 (100%)
12-word tone units	23 (33.82%)	41 (60.29%)	4 (5.88%)	68 (100%)	28 (73.68%)	10 (26.32%)	0 (0%)	38 (100%)
13-word tone units	20 (46.51%)	20 (46.51%)	3 (6.98%)	43 (100%)	9 (75%)	3 (25%)	0 (0%)	12 (100%)
14-word tone units	9 (47.37%)	8 (42.11%)	2 (10.53%)	19 (100%)	5 (71.43%)	2 (28.57%)	0 (0%)	7 (100%)
15-word tone units	2 (33.33%)	3 (50%)	1 (16.67%)	6 (100%)	2 (50%)	2 (50%)	0 (0%)	4 (100%)
16-word tone units	2 (33.33%)	4 (66.67%)	0 (0%)	6 (100%)	0 (0%)	1 (50%)	0 (0%)	1 (100%)
17-word tone units	1 (50%)	1 (50%)	0 (0%)	2 (100%)	0 (0%)	1 (100%)	0 (0%)	1 (100%)
18-word tone units	1 (100%)	0 (0%)	0 (0%)	1 (100%)	0 (0%)	0 (0%)	0 (0%)	0 (0%)

Table 49 Tone Units – Conversation sub-corpus – gender

Tone Unit {}	HKC Males	NES Males	Other Speakers Males	All Males	HKC Females	NES Females	Other Speakers Females	All Females
All tone units	18565 (36.73%)	28143 (55.69%)	3834 (7.59%)	50539 (100.01%)	25275 (70.88%)	8954 (25.11%)	1429 (4.01%)	35657 (100%)
1-word tone units (ALL)	6988 (39.45%)	9348 (52.78%)	1376 (7.77%)	17712 (100%)	10383 (74.82%)	3044 (21.94%)	450 (3.24%)	13877 (100%)
1-word tone units (with prominence only)	6929 (39.41%)	9295 (52.86%)	1359 (7.73%)	17583 (100%)	10320 (74.87%)	3018 (21.89%)	446 (3.24%)	13784 (100%)
2-word tone units	4306 (38.94%)	5691 (51.46%)	1062 (9.6%)	11059 (100%)	5583 (73.32%)	1776 (23.32%)	256 (3.36%)	7615 (100%)
3-word tone units	2832 (37.8%)	4098 (54.7%)	562 (7.5%)	7492 (100%)	3752 (71.49%)	1277 (24.33%)	219 (4.17%)	5248 (100%)
4-word tone units	1812 (35.01%)	3007 (58.11%)	356 (6.88%)	5175 (100%)	2343 (68.07%)	944 (27.43%)	155 (4.5%)	3442 (100%)
5-word tone units	1151 (32.8%)	2134 (60.82%)	224 (6.38%)	3509 (100%)	1319 (62.96%)	648 (30.93%)	129 (6.16%)	2095 (100%)
6-word tone units	579 (27.72%)	1423 (68.12%)	89 (4.26%)	2089 (100.1%)	797 (59.66%)	463 (34.66%)	76 (5.69%)	1336 (100%)
7-word tone units	338 (25.92%)	913 (70.02%)	53 (4.06%)	1304 (100%)	428 (55.44%)	297 (38.47%)	46 (5.96%)	772 (100%)
8-word tone units	196 (26.42%)	520 (70.08%)	27 (3.64%)	742 (100.13%)	227 (53.29%)	169 (39.67%)	30 (7.04%)	426 (100%)
9-word tone units	93 (23.85%)	282 (72.31%)	15 (3.85%)	390 (100%)	111 (52.61%)	80 (37.91%)	20 (9.48%)	211 (100%)

Tone Unit { }	HKC Males	NES Males	Other Speakers Males	All Males	HKC Females	NES Females	Other Speakers Females	All Females
10-word tone units	44 (21.26%)	160 (77.29%)	3 (1.45%)	207 (100%)	64 (52.46%)	49 (40.16%)	9 (7.38%)	122 (100%)
11-word tone units	22 (21.36%)	75 (72.82%)	6 (5.83%)	103 (100%)	33 (54.1%)	22 (36.07%)	6 (9.84%)	61 (100%)
12-word tone units	6 (11.11%)	47 (87.04%)	1 (1.85%)	54 (100%)	11 (36.67%)	17 (56.67%)	2 (6.67%)	30 (100%)
13-word tone units	9 (27.27%)	24 (72.73%)	0 (0%)	33 (100%)	6 (54.55%)	3 (27.27%)	2 (18.18%)	11 (100%)
14-word tone units	4 (23.53%)	13 (76.47%)	0 (0%)	17 (100%)	2 (66.67%)	1 (33.33%)	0 (0%)	3 (100%)
15-word tone units	0 (0%)	6 (100%)	0 (0%)	6 (100%)	0 (0%)	3 (100%)	0 (0%)	3 (100%)
16-word tone units	0 (0%)	0 (0%)	0 (0%)	0 (0%)	0 (0%)	0 (0%)	1 (100%)	1 (100%)
17-word tone units	0 (0%)	3 (100%)	0 (0%)	3 (100%)	0 (0%)	1 (100%)	0 (0%)	1 (100%)
18-word tone units	0 (0%)	1 (100%)	0 (0%)	1 (100%)	0 (0%)	0 (0%)	0 (0%)	0 (0%)

Table 50 Tone Units – Public sub-corpus – gender

Tone Unit {}	HKC Males	NES Males	Other Speakers Males	All Males	HKC Females	NES Females	Other Speakers Females	All Females
All tone units	48727 (89.03%)	5510 (10.07%)	497 (0.91%)	54734 (100%)	16814 (89.9%)	802 (4.29%)	1088 (5.82%)	18703 (100%)
1-word tone units (ALL)	12906 (90.14%)	1298 (9.07%)	113 (0.79%)	14317 (100%)	3990 (86.44%)	177 (3.83%)	449 (9.73%)	4616 (100%)
1-word tone units (with prominence only)	12697 (90.18%)	1272 (9.03%)	110 (0.78%)	14079 (100%)	3930 (86.35%)	175 (3.85%)	446 (9.8%)	4551 (100%)
2-word tone units	11054 (89.56%)	1174 (9.51%)	115 (0.93%)	12343 (100%)	4195 (89.91%)	160 (3.43%)	311 (6.67%)	4666 (100%)
3-word tone units	9473 (89.94%)	965 (9.16%)	94 (0.89%)	10532 (100%)	3543 (92.17%)	126 (3.28%)	175 (4.55%)	3844 (100%)
4-word tone units	6295 (88.09%)	780 (10.92%)	71 (0.99%)	7146 (100%)	2274 (92.06%)	103 (4.17%)	93 (3.77%)	2470 (100%)
5-word tone units	3833 (87.85%)	483 (11.07%)	47 (1.08%)	4363 (100%)	1340 (92.1%)	79 (5.43%)	36 (2.47%)	1455 (100%)
6-word tone units	2317 (87.07%)	317 (11.91%)	27 (1.01%)	2661 (100%)	722 (90.36%)	63 (7.88%)	14 (1.75%)	799 (100%)
7-word tone units	1274 (85.62%)	203 (13.64%)	11 (0.74%)	1488 (100%)	340 (89.95%)	34 (8.99%)	4 (1.06%)	378 (100%)
8-word tone units	681 (83.25%)	129 (15.77%)	8 (0.98%)	818 (100%)	182 (87.08%)	24 (11.48%)	3 (1.44%)	209 (100%)
9-word tone units	354 (81.76%)	75 (17.32%)	4 (0.92%)	433 (100%)	118 (91.47%)	12 (9.3%)	0 (0%)	129 (100%)

Tone Unit { }	HKC Males	NES Males	Other Speakers Males	All Males	HKC Females	NES Females	Other Speakers Females	All Females
10-word tone units	191 (84.89%)	34 (15.11%)	0 (0%)	225 (100%)	52 (88.14%)	7 (11.86%)	0 (0%)	59 (100%)
11-word tone units	80 (83.33%)	16 (16.67%)	0 (0%)	96 (100%)	22 (73.33%)	7 (23.33%)	1 (3.33%)	30 (100%)
12-word tone units	37 (78.72%)	7 (14.89%)	3 (6.38%)	47 (100%)	8 (88.89%)	1 (11.11%)	0 (0%)	9 (100%)
13-word tone units	19 (89.36%)	3 (13.64%)	0 (0%)	22 (100%)	3 (100%)	0 (0%)	0 (0%)	3 (100%)
14-word tone units	8 (88.89%)	1 (11.11%)	0 (0%)	9 (100%)	1 (100%)	2 (66.67%)	0 (0%)	3 (100%)
15-word tone units	5 (83.33%)	1 (16.67%)	0 (0%)	6 (100%)	1 (100%)	0 (0%)	0 (0%)	1 (100%)
16-word tone units	0 (0%)	0 (0%)	0 (0%)	0 (0%)	1 (100%)	0 (0%)	0 (0%)	1 (100%)
17-word tone units	0 (0%)	0 (0%)	0 (0%)	0 (0%)	0 (0%)	0 (0%)	0 (0%)	0 (0%)
18-word tone units	0 (0%)	0 (0%)	0 (0%)	0 (0%)	0 (0%)	0 (0%)	0 (0%)	0 (0%)

Quantitative data

Prominence

Table 1 Prominences – HKCSE (prosodic) – L1

Tone Unit {}	HKC	NES	Other Speakers	Unidentified Speakers	All Speakers
1 Prominence in a tone unit	153725 (74.45%)	45933 (22.24%)	6743 (3.27%)	95 (0.05%)	206493 (100%)
2 Prominences in a tone unit	60926 (74.34%)	18696 (22.81%)	2312 (2.82%)	19 (0.02%)	81958 (100%)
3 Prominences in a tone unit	15715 (71.78%)	5604 (25.6%)	575 (2.63%)	1 (0%)	21892 (100%)
4 Prominences in a tone unit	3428 (69.86%)	1327 (27.04%)	152 (3.1%)	0 (0%)	4907 (100%)

Table 2 Prominences – HKCSE (prosodic) – gender

Tone Unit {}	HKC Males	NES Males	Other Speakers Males	All Males	HKC Females	NES Females	Other Speakers Females	All Females
1 Prominence in a tone unit	76193 (65.63%)	36183 (31.17%)	3727 (3.21%)	116101 (100%)	77533 (85.86%)	9750 (10.8%)	3016 (3.34%)	90298 (100%)
2 Prominences in a tone unit	32500 (66.6%)	15182 (31.11%)	1115 (2.28%)	48797 (100%)	28425 (85.77%)	3514 (10.6%)	1197 (3.61%)	33140 (100%)
3 Prominences in a tone unit	8384 (63.64%)	4607 (34.97%)	183 (1.39%)	13175 (100%)	7333 (84.09%)	997 (11.43%)	392 (4.5%)	8720 (100%)
4 Prominences in a tone unit	1785 (60.37%)	1127 (38.11%)	45 (1.52%)	2957 (100%)	1643 (84.3%)	200 (10.26%)	107 (5.49%)	1949 (100%)

Table 3 One Prominence in a tone unit – L1

1 Prominence in a tone unit	HKC	NES	Other Speakers	Unidentified Speakers	All Speakers
HKCSE (Prosodic)	153725 (74.45%)	45933 (22.24%)	6743 (3.27%)	95 (0.05%)	206493 (100%)
A- corpus	41674 (88.92%)	3953 (8.43%)	1237 (2.64%)	2 (0%)	46865 (100%)
B- corpus	41875 (74.08%)	13978 (24.73%)	662 (1.17%)	12 (0.02%)	56527 (100%)
C- corpus	30811 (52.2%)	24420 (41.37%)	3716 (6.3%)	81 (0.14%)	59026 (100%)
P- corpus	39365 (89.31%)	3582 (8.13%)	1128 (2.56%)	0 (0%)	44075 (100%)

Table 4 One Prominence in a tone unit – gender

1 Prominence in a tone unit	HKC Males	NES Males	Other speakers Males	All Males (M)	HKC Females	NES Females	Other Speakers Females	All Females (F)
HKCSE (Prosodic)	76193 (65.63%)	36183 (31.17%)	3727 (3.21%)	116101 (100%)	77533 (85.86%)	9750 (10.8%)	3016 (3.34%)	90298 (100%)
A- corpus	22392 (89.58%)	2605 (10.42%)	0 (0%)	24997 (100%)	19282 (88.18%)	1348 (6.16%)	1237 (5.66%)	21867 (100%)
B- corpus	11674 (48.25%)	11914 (49.24%)	608 (2.51%)	24196 (100%)	30201 (93.45%)	2064 (6.39%)	54 (0.17%)	32319 (100%)
C- corpus	12970 (37.83%)	18505 (53.98%)	2810 (8.2%)	34284 (100%)	17841 (72.34%)	5915 (23.99%)	906 (3.67%)	24661 (100%)
P- corpus	29157 (89.37%)	3159 (9.68%)	309 (0.95%)	32624 (100%)	10209 (89.15%)	423 (3.69%)	819 (7.15%)	11451 (100%)

Table 5 Two Prominences in a tone unit – L1

2 Prominences in a tone unit	HKC	NES	Other Speakers	Unidentified Speakers	All Speakers
HKCSE (Prosodic)	60926 (74.34%)	18696 (22.81%)	2312 (2.82%)	19 (0.02%)	81958 (100%)
A- corpus	16938 (83.63%)	2715 (13.4%)	598 (2.95%)	1 (0%)	20254 (100%)
B- corpus	15487 (72.92%)	5480 (25.8%)	271 (1.28%)	2 (0.01%)	21239 (100%)
C- corpus	9162 (48.49%)	8624 (45.64%)	1091 (5.77%)	16 (0.08%)	18896 (100%)
P- corpus	19339 (89.66%)	1877 (8.7%)	352 (1.63%)	0 (0%)	21569 (100%)

Table 6 Two Prominences in a tone unit – gender

2 Prominences in a tone unit	HKC Males	NES Males	Other speakers Males	All Males (M)	HKC Females	NES Females	Other Speakers Females	All Females (F)
HKCSE (Prosodic)	32500 (66.6%)	15182 (31.11%)	1115 (2.28%)	48797 (100%)	28425 (85.77%)	3514 (10.6%)	1197 (3.61%)	33140 (100%)
A- corpus	9051 (80.79%)	2152 (19.21%)	0 (0%)	11203 (100%)	7886 (87.17%)	563 (6.22%)	598 (6.61%)	9047 (100%)
B- corpus	5232 (50.54%)	4864 (46.99%)	256 (2.47%)	10352 (100%)	10255 (94.2%)	616 (5.66%)	15 (0.14%)	10886 (100%)
C- corpus	3908 (34.93%)	6553 (58.57%)	729 (6.52%)	11189 (100%)	5254 (68.33%)	2071 (26.93%)	362 (4.71%)	7689 (100%)
P- corpus	14309 (89.14%)	1613 (10.05%)	130 (0.81%)	16053 (100%)	5030 (91.16%)	264 (4.78%)	222 (4.02%)	5518 (100%)

Table 7 Three Prominences in a tone unit – L1

3 Prominences in a tone unit	HKC	NES	Other Speakers	Unidentified Speakers	All Speakers
HKCSE (Prosodic)	15715 (71.78%)	5604 (25.6%)	575 (2.63%)	1 (0%)	21892 (100%)
A- corpus	4643 (76.1%)	1187 (19.46%)	272 (4.46%)	0 (0%)	6101 (100%)
B- corpus	4090 (71.37%)	1572 (27.43%)	70 (1.22%)	0 (0%)	5731 (100%)
C- corpus	2156 (47.3%)	2232 (48.97%)	170 (3.73%)	1 (0.02%)	4558 (100%)
P- corpus	4826 (87.71%)	613 (11.14%)	63 (1.15%)	0 (0%)	5502 (100%)

Table 8 Three Prominences in a tone unit – gender

3 Prominences in a tone unit	HKC Males	NES Males	Other speakers Males	All Males (M)	HKC Females	NES Females	Other Speakers Females	All Females (F)
HKCSE (Prosodic)	8384 (63.64%)	4607 (34.97%)	183 (1.39%)	13175 (100%)	7333 (84.09%)	997 (11.43%)	392 (4.5%)	8720 (100%)
A- corpus	2237 (68.96%)	1007 (31.04%)	0 (0%)	3244 (100%)	2408 (84.2%)	180 (6.29%)	272 (9.51%)	2860 (100%)
B- corpus	1538 (51.49%)	1380 (46.2%)	69 (2.31%)	2987 (100%)	2552 (92.97%)	192 (6.99%)	1 (0.04%)	2745 (100%)
C- corpus	945 (34.82%)	1687 (62.16%)	81 (2.98%)	2714 (100%)	1211 (65.67%)	545 (29.56%)	89 (4.83%)	1844 (100%)
P- corpus	3664 (86.62%)	533 (12.6%)	33 (0.78%)	4230 (100%)	1162 (91.42%)	80 (6.29%)	30 (2.36%)	1271 (100%)

Table 9 Four Prominences in a tone unit – L1

4 Prominences in a tone unit	HKC	NES	Other Speakers	Unidentified Speakers	All Speakers
HKCSE (Prosodic)	3428 (69.86%)	1327 (27.04%)	152 (3.1%)	0 (0%)	4907 (100%)
A- corpus	1118 (73.02%)	338 (22.08%)	75 (4.9%)	0 (0%)	1531 (100%)
B- corpus	849 (66.85%)	402 (31.65%)	17 (1.34%)	0 (0%)	1270 (100%)
C- corpus	444 (47.08%)	456 (48.36%)	44 (4.67%)	0 (0%)	943 (100%)
P- corpus	1017 (87.45%)	131 (11.26%)	16 (1.38%)	0 (0%)	1163 (100%)

Table 10 Four Prominences in a tone unit – gender

4 Prominences in a tone unit	HKC Males	NES Males	Other speakers Males	All Males (M)	HKC Females	NES Females	Other Speakers Females	All Females (F)
HKCSE (Prosodic)	1785 (60.37%)	1127 (38.11%)	45 (1.52%)	2957 (100%)	1643 (84.3%)	200 (10.26%)	107 (5.49%)	1949 (100%)
A- corpus	466 (61.07%)	297 (38.93%)	0 (0%)	763 (100%)	652 (84.9%)	41 (5.34%)	75 (9.77%)	768 (100%)
B- corpus	328 (46.72%)	357 (50.85%)	17 (2.42%)	702 (100%)	521 (92.05%)	45 (7.95%)	0 (0%)	566 (100%)
C- corpus	193 (33.92%)	359 (63.09%)	17 (2.99%)	569 (100%)	251 (66.93%)	97 (25.87%)	27 (7.2%)	375 (100%)
P- corpus	798 (86.46%)	114 (12.35%)	11 (1.19%)	923 (100%)	219 (91.25%)	17 (7.08%)	5 (2.08%)	240 (100%)

Table 11 Words with more than one prominent syllable – HKCSE (prosodic) – L1

Prominence	HKC	NES	Other Speakers	Unidentified Speakers	All Speakers
All	337981	106236	13870	150	458212
	(73.76%)	(23.18%)	(3.03%)	(0.03%)	(100%)
1 word 2 prominences	830	169	27	0	1026
	(80.9%)	(16.47%)	(2.63%)	(0%)	(100%)
1 word 3 prominences	3	0	0	0	3
	(100%)	(0%)	(0%)	(0%)	(100%)

Table 12 Words with more than one prominent syllable – Academic sub-corpus – L1

Prominence	HKC	NES	Other Speakers	Unidentified Speakers	All Speakers
All	94289	14324	3594	5	112209
	(84.03%)	(12.77%)	(3.2%)	(0%)	(100%)
1 word 2 prominences	365	30	4	0	399
	(91.48%)	(7.52%)	(1%)	(0%)	(100%)
1 word 3 prominences	1	0	0	0	1
	(100%)	(0%)	(0%)	(0%)	(100%)

Table 13 Words with more than one prominent syllable – Business sub-corpus – L1

Prominence	HKC	NES	Other Speakers	Unidentified Speakers	All Speakers
All	89102	31501	1530	24	122134
	(72.95%)	(25.79%)	(1.25%)	(0.02%)	(100%)
1 word 2 prominences	142	51	0	0	193
	(73.58%)	(26.42%)	(0%)	(0%)	(100%)
1 word 3 prominences	1	0	0	0	1
	(100%)	(0%)	(0%)	(0%)	(100%)

Table 14 Words with more than one prominent syllable – Conversation sub-corpus – L1

Prominence	HKC	NES	Other Speakers	Unidentified Speakers	All Speakers
All	57734 (50.12%)	50674 (43.99%)	6655 (5.78%)	121 (0.11%)	115185 (100%)
1 word 2 prominences	81 (50.94%)	60 (37.74%)	18 (11.32%)	0 (0%)	159 (100%)
1 word 3 prominences	1 (100%)	0 (0%)	0 (0%)	0 (0%)	1 (100%)

Table 15 Words with more than one prominent syllable – Public sub-corpus – L1

Prominence	HKC	NES	Other Speakers	Unidentified Speakers	All Speakers
All	96896 (89.15%)	9737 (8.96%)	2091 (1.92%)	0 (0%)	108684 (100%)
1 word 2 prominences	242 (88%)	28 (10.18%)	5 (1.82%)	0 (0%)	275 (100%)
1 word 3 prominences	0 (0%)	0 (0%)	0 (0%)	0 (0%)	0 (0%)

Table 16 Words with more than one prominent syllable – HKCSE (prosodic) – gender

Prominence	HKC Males	NES Males	Other Speakers Males	All Males	HKC Females	NES Females	Other Speakers Females	All Females
All	174324 (65.4%)	85452 (32.06%)	6782 (2.54%)	266541 (100%)	163666 (85.45%)	20793 (10.86%)	7097 (3.71%)	191538 (100%)
1 word 2 prominences	509 (76.43%)	139 (20.87%)	18 (2.7%)	666 (100%)	321 (89.17%)	30 (8.33%)	9 (2.5%)	360 (100%)
1 word 3 prominences	2 (100%)	0 (0%)	0 (0%)	2 (100%)	1 (100%)	0 (0%)	0 (0%)	1 (100%)

Table 17 Words with more than one prominent syllable – Academic sub-corpus – gender

Prominence	HKC Males	NES Males	Other Speakers Males	All Males	HKC Females	NES Females	Other Speakers Females	All Females
All	49270 (81.58%)	11127 (18.42%)	0 (0%)	60396 (100%)	45020 (86.89%)	3198 (6.17%)	3594 (6.94%)	51810 (100%)
1 word 2 prominences	243 (91.01%)	24 (8.99%)	0 (0%)	267 (100%)	122 (92.42%)	6 (4.55%)	4 (3.03%)	132 (100%)
1 word 3 prominences	1 (100%)	0 (0%)	0 (0%)	1 (100%)	0 (0%)	0 (0%)	0 (0%)	0 (0%)

Table 18 Words with more than one prominent syllable – Business sub-corpus – gender

Prominence	HKC Males	NES Males	Other Speakers Males	All Males	HKC Females	NES Females	Other Speakers Females	All Females
All	28306 (49.57%)	27374 (47.94%)	1440 (2.52%)	57104 (100%)	60804 (93.51%)	4135 (6.36%)	98 (0.15%)	65021 (100%)
1 word 2 prominences	41 (45.56%)	49 (54.44%)	0 (0%)	90 (100%)	101 (98.06%)	2 (1.94%)	0 (0%)	103 (100%)
1 word 3 prominences	0 (0%)	0 (0%)	0 (0%)	0 (0%)	1 (100%)	0 (0%)	0 (0%)	1 (100%)

Table 19 Words with more than one prominent syllable – Conversation sub-corpus – gender

Prominence	HKC Males	NES Males	Other Speakers Males	All Males	HKC Females	NES Females	Other Speakers Females	All Females
All	24561 (36.3%)	38478 (56.87%)	4625 (6.84%)	67665 (100%)	33173 (69.99%)	12196 (25.73%)	2030 (4.28%)	47399 (100%)
1 word 2 prominences	32 (36.78%)	40 (45.98%)	15 (17.24%)	87 (100%)	49 (68.06%)	20 (27.78%)	3 (4.17%)	72 (100%)
1 word 3 prominences	1 (100%)	0 (0%)	0 (0%)	1 (100%)	0 (0%)	0 (0%)	0 (0%)	0 (0%)

Table 20 Words with more than one prominent syllable – Public sub-corpus – gender

Prominence	HKC Males	NES Males	Other Speakers Males	All Males	HKC Females	NES Females	Other Speakers Females	All Females
All	72187 (88.71%)	8473 (10.41%)	716 (0.88%)	81376 (100%)	24669 (90.34%)	1264 (4.63%)	1375 (5.04%)	27308 (100%)
1 word 2 prominences	193 (86.94%)	26 (11.71%)	3 (1.35%)	222 (100%)	49 (92.45%)	2 (3.77%)	2 (3.77%)	53 (100%)
1 word 3 prominences	0 (0%)	0 (0%)	0 (0%)	0 (0%)	0 (0%)	0 (0%)	0 (0%)	0 (0%)

Table 21 All – L1

All	HKC	NES	Other Speakers	Unidentified Speakers	All Speakers
HKCSE (Prosodic)	337981 (73.76%)	106236 (23.18%)	13870 (3.03%)	150 (0.03%)	458212 (100%)
A- corpus	94289 (84.03%)	14324 (12.77%)	3594 (3.2%)	5 (0%)	112209 (100%)
B- corpus	89102 (72.95%)	31501 (25.79%)	1530 (1.25%)	24 (0.02%)	122134 (100%)
C- corpus	57734 (50.12%)	50674 (43.99%)	6655 (5.78%)	121 (0.11%)	115185 (100%)
P- corpus	96896 (89.15%)	9737 (8.96%)	2091 (1.92%)	0 (0%)	108684 (100%)

Table 22 All – gender

All	HKC Males	NES Males	Other speakers Males	All Males (M)	HKC Females	NES Females	Other Speakers Females	All Females (F)
HKCSE (Prosodic)	174324 (65.4%)	85452 (32.06%)	6782 (2.54%)	266541 (100%)	163666 (85.45%)	20793 (10.86%)	7097 (3.71%)	191538 (100%)
A- corpus	49270 (81.58%)	11127 (18.42%)	0 (0%)	60396 (100%)	45020 (86.89%)	3198 (6.17%)	3594 (6.94%)	51810 (100%)
B- corpus	28306 (49.57%)	27374 (47.94%)	1440 (2.52%)	57104 (100%)	60804 (93.51%)	4135 (6.36%)	98 (0.15%)	65021 (100%)
C- corpus	24561 (36.3%)	38478 (56.87%)	4625 (6.84%)	67665 (100%)	33173 (69.99%)	12196 (25.73%)	2030 (4.28%)	47399 (100%)
P- corpus	72187 (88.71%)	8473 (10.41%)	716 (0.88%)	81376 (100%)	24669 (90.34%)	1264 (4.63%)	1375 (5.04%)	27308 (100%)

Table 23　One word two prominences – L1

1 word 2 prominences	HKC	NES	Other Speakers	Unidentified Speakers	All Speakers
HKCSE (Prosodic)	830 (80.9%)	169 (16.47%)	27 (2.63%)	0 (0%)	1026 (100%)
A- corpus	365 (91.48%)	30 (7.52%)	4 (1%)	0 (0%)	399 (100%)
B- corpus	142 (73.58%)	51 (26.42%)	0 (0%)	0 (0%)	193 (100%)
C- corpus	81 (50.94%)	60 (37.74%)	18 (11.32%)	0 (0%)	159 (100%)
P- corpus	242 (88%)	28 (10.18%)	5 (1.82%)	0 (0%)	275 (100%)

Table 24　One word two prominences – gender

1 word 2 prominences	HKC Males	NES Males	Other speakers Males	All Males (M)	HKC Females	NES Females	Other Speakers Females	All Females (F)
HKCSE (Prosodic)	509 (76.43%)	139 (20.87%)	18 (2.7%)	666 (100%)	321 (89.17%)	30 (8.33%)	9 (2.5%)	360 (100%)
A- corpus	243 (91.01%)	24 (8.99%)	0 (0%)	267 (100%)	122 (92.42%)	6 (4.55%)	4 (3.03%)	132 (100%)
B- corpus	41 (45.56%)	49 (54.44%)	0 (0%)	90 (100%)	101 (98.06%)	2 (1.94%)	0 (0%)	103 (100%)
C- corpus	32 (36.78%)	40 (45.98%)	15 (17.24%)	87 (100%)	49 (68.06%)	20 (27.78%)	3 (4.17%)	72 (100%)
P- corpus	193 (86.94%)	26 (11.71%)	3 (1.35%)	222 (100%)	49 (92.45%)	2 (3.77%)	2 (3.77%)	53 (100%)

Table 25 One word three prominences – L1

1 word 3 prominences	HKC	NES	Other Speakers	Unidentified Speakers	All Speakers
HKCSE (Prosodic)	3 (100%)	0 (0%)	0 (0%)	0 (0%)	3 (100%)
A- corpus	1 (100%)	0 (0%)	0 (0%)	0 (0%)	1 (100%)
B- corpus	1 (100%)	0 (0%)	0 (0%)	0 (0%)	1 (100%)
C- corpus	1 (100%)	0 (0%)	0 (0%)	0 (0%)	1 (100%)
P- corpus	0 (0%)	0 (0%)	0 (0%)	0 (0%)	0 (0%)

Table 26 One word three prominences – gender

1 word 3 prominences	HKC Males	NES Males	Other speakers Males	All Males (M)	HKC Females	NES Females	Other Speakers Females	All Females (F)
HKCSE (Prosodic)	2 (100%)	0 (0%)	0 (0%)	2 (100%)	1 (100%)	0 (0%)	0 (0%)	1 (100%)
A- corpus	1 (100%)	0 (0%)	0 (0%)	1 (100%)	0 (0%)	0 (0%)	0 (0%)	0 (0%)
B- corpus	0 (0%)	0 (0%)	0 (0%)	0 (0%)	1 (100%)	0 (0%)	0 (0%)	1 (100%)
C- corpus	1 (100%)	0 (0%)	0 (0%)	1 (100%)	0 (0%)	0 (0%)	0 (0%)	0 (0%)
P- corpus	0 (0%)	0 (0%)	0 (0%)	0 (0%)	0 (0%)	0 (0%)	0 (0%)	0 (0%)

Quantitative data

Tones

Table 1 Tones – HKCSE (prosodic) – L1

Tone	HKC	NES	Other Speakers	Unidentified Speakers	All Speakers
Rising /	13548	4664	514	16	18742
	(72.29%)	(24.89%)	(2.74%)	(0.09%)	(100%)
Falling \	88851	32571	4295	52	125769
	(70.65%)	(25.9%)	(3.41%)	(0.04%)	(100%)
Rise-Fall /\	40	9	4	0	53
	(75.47%)	(16.98%)	(7.55%)	(0%)	(100%)
Fall-Rise \/	7065	2888	168	2	10123
	(69.79%)	(28.53%)	(1.66%)	(0.02%)	(100%)
Level =	118013	28254	4259	30	150556
	(78.38%)	(18.77%)	(2.83%)	(0.02%)	(100%)
Unclassifiable	11765	5672	997	34	18460
	(63.73%)	(30.73%)	(5.4%)	(0.18%)	(100%)
Total	239282	74058	10237	134	323703
	(73.92%)	(22.88%)	(3.16%)	(0.04%)	(100%)

Table 2 Tones – Academic sub-corpus– L1

Tone	HKC	NES	Other Speakers	Unidentified Speakers	All Speakers
Rising /	2664 (71.38%)	819 (21.95%)	249 (6.67%)	0 (0%)	3732 (100%)
Falling \	23544 (83.97%)	3312 (11.81%)	1179 (4.21%)	2 (0.01%)	28037 (100%)
Rise-Fall /\	2 (28.57%)	2 (28.57%)	3 (42.86%)	0 (0%)	7 (100%)
Fall-Rise \/	1928 (71.28%)	689 (25.47%)	88 (3.25%)	0 (0%)	2705 (100%)
Level =	35936 (89.99%)	3334 (8.35%)	662 (1.66%)	1 (0%)	39933 (100%)
Unclassifiable	1703 (86.62%)	193 (9.82%)	75 (3.81%)	7 (0.36%)	1966 (100%)
Total	65777 (86.12%)	8349 (10.93%)	2256 (2.95%)	10 (0.01%)	76380 (100%)

Table 3 Tones Business sub-corpus– L1

Tone	HKC	NES	Other Speakers	Unidentified Speakers	All Speakers
Rising /	3783	1251	26	0	5060
	(74.76%)	(24.72%)	(0.51%)	(0%)	(100%)
Falling \	24368	9680	501	5	34554
	(70.52%)	(28.01%)	(1.45%)	(0.01%)	(100%)
Rise-Fall /\	2	1	0	0	3
	(66.67%)	(33.33%)	(0%)	(0%)	(100%)
Fall-Rise \/	1761	510	10	1	2282
	(77.17%)	(22.35%)	(0.44%)	(0.04%)	(100%)
Level =	32009	9834	458	6	42307
	(75.66%)	(23.24%)	(1.08%)	(0.01%)	(100%)
Unclassifiable	2201	1034	995	4	3376
	(65.2%)	(30.63%)	(29.47%)	(0.12%)	(100%)
Total	64124	22310	1133	16	87582
	(73.22%)	(25.47%)	(1.29%)	(0.02%)	(100%)

Table 4 Tones – Conversation sub-corpus– L1

Tone	HKC	NES	Other Speakers	Unidentified Speakers	All Speakers
Rising /	3774	2475	222	16	6487
	(58.18%)	(38.15%)	(3.42%)	(0.25%)	(100%)
Falling \	17108	17267	2003	45	36423
	(46.97%)	(47.41%)	(5.5%)	(0.12%)	(100%)
Rise-Fall / \	34	6	1	0	41
	(82.93%)	(14.63%)	(2.44%)	(0%)	(100%)
Fall-Rise \ /	1190	1512	67	1	2770
	(42.96%)	(54.58%)	(2.42%)	(0.04%)	(100%)
Level =	16848	11639	2250	23	30760
	(54.77%)	(37.84%)	(7.31%)	(0.07%)	(100%)
Unclassifiable	4886	4198	720	23	9823
	(49.74%)	(42.74%)	(7.33%)	(0.23%)	(100%)
Total	43840	37097	5263	108	86304
	(50.8%)	(42.98%)	(6.1%)	(0.13%)	(100%)

Table 5 Tones – Public sub-corpus– L1

Tone	HKC	NES	Other Speakers	Unidentified Speakers	All Speakers
Rising /	3327	119	17	0	3463
	(96.07%)	(3.44%)	(0.49%)	(0%)	(100%)
Falling \	23831	2312	612	0	26755
	(89.07%)	(8.64%)	(2.29%)	(0%)	(100%)
Rise-Fall /\	2	0	0	0	2
	(100%)	(0%)	(0%)	(0%)	(100%)
Fall-Rise \/	2186	177	3	0	2366
	(92.39%)	(7.48%)	(0.13%)	(0%)	(100%)
Level =	33220	3447	889	0	37556
	(88.45%)	(9.18%)	(2.37%)	(0%)	(100%)
Unclassifiable	2975	257	64	0	3295
	(90.29%)	(7.8%)	(1.94%)	(0%)	(100%)
Total	65541	6312	1585	0	73437
	(89.25%)	(8.6%)	(2.16%)	(0%)	(100%)

Table 6 Tones – HKCSE (prosodic) – gender

Tone	HKC Males	NES Males	Other Speakers Males	All Males	HKC Females	NES Females	Other Speakers Females	All Females
Rising /	6984 (64.79%)	3682 (34.16%)	113 (1.05%)	10779 (100%)	6564 (82.6%)	982 (12.36%)	401 (5.05%)	7947 (100%)
Falling \	43124 (60.85%)	25653 (36.2%)	2092 (2.95%)	70869 (100%)	45727 (83.37%)	6918 (12.61%)	2203 (4.02%)	54848 (100%)
Rise-Fall /\	25 (83.33%)	4 (13.33%)	1 (3.33%)	30 (100%)	15 (65.22%)	5 (21.74%)	3 (13.04%)	23 (100%)
Fall-Rise \/	3626 (59.71%)	2397 (39.47%)	50 (0.82%)	6073 (100%)	3439 (84.96%)	491 (12.13%)	118 (2.92%)	4048 (100%)
Level =	61850 (71.05%)	22782 (26.17%)	2417 (2.78%)	87049 (100%)	56163 (88.48%)	5472 (8.62%)	1842 (2.9%)	63477 (100%)
Unclassifiable	6016 (53.55%)	4505 (40.1%)	716 (6.37%)	11234 (100%)	5748 (79.9%)	1167 (16.22%)	281 (3.91%)	7194 (100%)
Total	121625 (65.38%)	59023 (31.73%)	5389 (2.9%)	186034 (100%)	117656 (85.54%)	15035 (10.93%)	4848 (3.52%)	137537 (100%)

Table 7 Tones – Academic sub-corpus – gender

Tone	HKC Males	NES Males	Other Speakers Males	All Males	HKC Females	NES Females	Other Speakers Females	All Females
Rising /	1593 (71.72%)	628 (28.28%)	0 (0%)	2221 (100%)	1071 (70.88%)	191 (12.64%)	249 (16.48%)	1511 (100%)
Falling \	12080 (83.33%)	2416 (16.67%)	0 (0%)	14496 (100%)	11464 (84.67%)	896 (6.62%)	1179 (8.71%)	13539 (100%)
Rise-Fall /\	1 (50%)	1 (50%)	0 (0%)	2 (100%)	1 (20%)	1 (20%)	3 (60%)	5 (100%)
Fall-Rise \/	1124 (65.39%)	595 (34.61%)	0 (0%)	1719 (100%)	804 (81.54%)	94 (9.53%)	88 (8.92%)	986 (100%)
Level =	19248 (89%)	2378 (11%)	0 (0%)	21626 (100%)	6688 (91.16%)	956 (5.22%)	662 (3.62%)	18306 (100%)
Unclassifiable	888 (87.92%)	122 (12.08%)	0 (0%)	1010 (100%)	813 (85.67%)	61 (6.43%)	75 (7.9%)	949 (100%)
Total	34934 (85.05%)	6140 (14.95%)	0 (0%)	41074 (100%)	30841 (87.38%)	2199 (6.23%)	2256 (6.39%)	35296 (100%)

Table 8 Tones – Business sub-corpus – gender

Tone	HKC Males	NES Males	Other Speakers Males	All Males	HKC Females	NES Females	Other Speakers Females	All Females
Rising /	887 (47.51%)	958 (51.31%)	22 (1.18%)	1867 (100%)	2896 (90.7%)	293 (9.18%)	4 (0.13%)	3193 (100%)
Falling \	6742 (43.42%)	8305 (53.49%)	479 (3.09%)	15526 (100%)	17626 (92.66%)	1375 (7.23%)	22 (0.12%)	19023 (100%)
Rise-Fall /\	0 (0%)	1 (100%)	0 (0%)	1 (100%)	2 (100%)	0 (0%)	0 (0%)	2 (100%)
Fall-Rise \/	474 (51.97%)	429 (47.04%)	9 (0.99%)	912 (100%)	1287 (94.01%)	81 (5.92%)	1 (0.07%)	1369 (100%)
Level =	10598 (53.85%)	8659 (44%)	422 (2.14%)	19679 (100%)	21411 (94.65%)	1175 (5.19%)	36 (0.16%)	22622 (100%)
Unclassifiable	698 (41.01%)	878 (51.59%)	126 (7.4%)	1702 (100%)	1504 (89.95%)	156 (9.33%)	12 (0.72%)	1672 (100%)
Total	19399 (48.88%)	19230 (48.45%)	1058 (2.67%)	39687 (100%)	44726 (93.41%)	3080 (6.43%)	75 (0.16%)	47881 (100%)

Table 9 Tones – Conversation sub-corpus – gender

Tone	HKC Males	NES Males	Other Speakers Males	All Males	HKC Females	NES Females	Other Speakers Females	All Females
Rising /	1491 (41.8%)	1986 (55.68%)	90 (2.52%)	3567 (100%)	2283 (78.62%)	489 (16.84%)	132 (4.55%)	2904 (100%)
Falling \	7124 (33.12%)	12966 (60.28%)	1419 (6.6%)	21509 (100%)	9984 (67.15%)	4301 (28.93%)	584 (3.93%)	14869 (100%)
Rise-Fall /\	22 (88%)	2 (8%)	1 (4%)	25 (100%)	12 (75%)	4 (25%)	0 (0%)	16 (100%)
Fall-Rise \/	565 (31.18%)	1209 (66.72%)	38 (2.1%)	1812 (100%)	625 (65.31%)	303 (31.66%)	29 (3.03%)	957 (100%)
Level =	7376 (41.41%)	8700 (48.85%)	1734 (9.74%)	17810 (100%)	9472 (73.27%)	2939 (22.74%)	516 (3.99%)	12927 (100%)
Unclassifiable	1987 (34.16%)	3280 (56.4%)	552 (9.49%)	5816 (100%)	2899 (72.77%)	918 (23.04%)	168 (4.22%)	3984 (100%)
Total	18565 (36.73%)	28143 (55.69%)	3834 (7.59%)	50539 (100%)	25275 (70.88%)	8954 (25.11%)	1429 (4.01%)	35657 (100%)

Table 10 Tones – Public sub-corpus – gender

Tone	HKC Males	NES Males	Other Speakers Males	All Males	HKC Females	NES Females	Other Speakers Females	All Females
Rising /	3013 (96.45%)	110 (3.52%)	1 (0.03%)	3124 (100%)	314 (92.63%)	9 (2.65%)	16 (4.72%)	339 (100%)
Falling \	17178 (88.83%)	1966 (10.17%)	194 (1%)	19338 (100%)	6653 (89.7%)	346 (4.66%)	418 (5.64%)	7417 (100%)
Rise-Fall /\	2 (100%)	0 (0%)	0 (0%)	2 (100%)	0 (0%)	0 (0%)	0 (0%)	0 (0%)
Fall-Rise \/	1463 (89.75%)	164 (10.06%)	3 (0.18%)	1630 (100%)	723 (98.23%)	13 (1.77%)	0 (0%)	736 (100%)
Level =	24628 (88.16%)	3045 (10.9%)	261 (0.93%)	27934 (100%)	8592 (89.3%)	402 (4.18%)	628 (6.53%)	9622 (100%)
Unclassifiable	2443 (90.28%)	225 (8.31%)	38 (1.4%)	2706 (100%)	532 (90.32%)	32 (5.43%)	26 (4.41%)	589 (100%)
Total	48727 (89.03%)	5510 (10.07%)	497 (0.91%)	54734 (100%)	16814 (89.9%)	802 (4.29%)	1088 (5.82%)	18703 (100%)

Table 11 Rise Tone (/) – L1

Rise (/)	HKC	NES	Other Speakers	Unidentified Speakers	All Speakers
HKCSE (Prosodic)	13548 (72.29%)	4664 (24.89%)	514 (2.74%)	16 (0.09%)	18742 (100%)
A- corpus	2664 (71.38%)	819 (21.95%)	249 (6.67%)	0 (0%)	3732 (100%)
B- corpus	3783 (74.76%)	1251 (24.72%)	26 (0.51%)	0 (0%)	5060 (100%)
C- corpus	3774 (58.18%)	2475 (38.15%)	222 (3.42%)	16 (0.25%)	6487 (100%)
P- corpus	3327 (96.07%)	119 (3.44%)	17 (0.49%)	0 (0%)	3463 (100%)

Table 12 Rise Tone (/) – gender

Rise (/)	HKC Males	NES Males	Other speakers Males	All Males (M)	HKC Females	NES Females	Other Speakers Females	All Females (F)
HKCSE (Prosodic)	6984 (64.79%)	3682 (34.16%)	113 (1.05%)	10779 (100%)	6564 (82.6%)	982 (12.36%)	401 (5.05%)	7947 (100%)
A- corpus	1593 (71.72%)	628 (28.28%)	0 (0%)	2221 (100%)	1071 (70.88%)	191 (12.64%)	249 (16.48%)	1511 (100%)
B- corpus	887 (47.51%)	958 (51.31%)	22 (1.18%)	1867 (100%)	2896 (90.7%)	293 (9.18%)	4 (0.13%)	3193 (100%)
C- corpus	1491 (41.8%)	1986 (55.68%)	90 (2.52%)	3567 (100%)	2283 (78.62%)	489 (16.84%)	132 (4.55%)	2904 (100%)
P- corpus	3013 (96.45%)	110 (3.52%)	1 (0.03%)	3124 (100%)	314 (92.63%)	9 (2.65%)	16 (4.72%)	339 (100%)

Table 13 Falling Tone (\ ) – L1

Falling (\ )	HKC	NES	Other Speakers	Unidentified Speakers	All Speakers
HKCSE (Prosodic)	88851 (70.65%)	32571 (25.9%)	4295 (3.41%)	52 (0.04%)	125769 (100%)
A- corpus	23544 (83.97%)	3312 (11.81%)	1179 (4.21%)	2 (0.01%)	28037 (100%)
B- corpus	24368 (70.52%)	9680 (28.01%)	501 (1.45%)	5 (0.01%)	34554 (100%)
C- corpus	17108 (46.97%)	17267 (47.41%)	2003 (5.5%)	45 (0.12%)	36423 (100%)
P- corpus	23831 (89.07%)	2312 (8.64%)	612 (2.29%)	0 (0%)	26755 (100%)

Table 14 Falling Tone (\ ) – gender

Falling (\ )	HKC Males	NES Males	Other speakers Males	All Males (M)	HKC Females	NES Females	Other Speakers Females	All Females (F)
HKCSE (Prosodic)	43124 (60.85%)	25653 (36.2%)	2092 (2.95%)	70869 (100%)	45727 (83.37%)	6918 (12.61%)	2203 (4.02%)	54848 (100%)
A- corpus	12080 (83.33%)	2416 (16.67%)	0 (0%)	14496 (100%)	11464 (84.67%)	896 (6.62%)	1179 (8.71%)	13539 (100%)
B- corpus	6742 (43.42%)	8305 (53.49%)	479 (3.09%)	15526 (100%)	17626 (92.66%)	1375 (7.23%)	22 (0.12%)	19023 (100%)
C- corpus	7124 (33.12%)	12966 (60.28%)	1419 (6.6%)	21509 (100%)	9984 (67.15%)	4301 (28.93%)	584 (3.93%)	14869 (100%)
P- corpus	17178 (88.83%)	1966 (10.17%)	194 (1%)	19338 (100%)	6653 (89.7%)	346 (4.66%)	418 (5.64%)	7417 (100%)

Table 15 Rise-Fall Tone (/\ ) – L1

Rise-Fall (/\)	HKC	NES	Other Speakers	Unidentified Speakers	All Speakers
HKCSE (Prosodic)	40 (75.47%)	9 (16.98%)	4 (7.55%)	0 (0%)	53 (100%)
A- corpus	2 (28.57%)	2 (28.57%)	3 (42.86%)	0 (0%)	7 (100%)
B- corpus	2 (66.67%)	1 (33.33%)	0 (0%)	0 (0%)	3 (100%)
C- corpus	34 (82.93%)	6 (14.63%)	1 (2.44%)	0 (0%)	41 (100%)
P- corpus	2 (100%)	0 (0%)	0 (0%)	0 (0%)	2 (100%)

Table 16 Rise-Fall Tone (/\ ) – gender

Rise-Fall (/\)	HKC Males	NES Males	Other speakers Males	All Males (M)	HKC Females	NES Females	Other Speakers Females	All Females (F)
HKCSE (Prosodic)	25 (83.33%)	4 (13.33%)	1 (3.33%)	30 (100%)	15 (65.22%)	5 (21.74%)	3 (13.04%)	23 (100%)
A- corpus	1 (50%)	1 (50%)	0 (0%)	2 (100%)	1 (20%)	1 (20%)	3 (60%)	5 (100%)
B- corpus	0 (0%)	1 (100%)	0 (0%)	1 (100%)	2 (100%)	0 (0%)	0 (0%)	2 (100%)
C- corpus	22 (88%)	2 (8%)	1 (4%)	25 (100%)	12 (75%)	4 (25%)	0 (0%)	16 (100%)
P- corpus	2 (100%)	0 (0%)	0 (0%)	2 (100%)	0 (0%)	0 (0%)	0 (0%)	0 (0%)

Table 17 Fall-Rise Tone (\/) – L1

Fall-Rise (\/)	HKC	NES	Other Speakers	Unidentified Speakers	All Speakers
HKCSE (Prosodic)	7065	2888	168	2	10123
	(69.79%)	(28.53%)	(1.66%)	(0.02%)	(100%)
A- corpus	1928	689	88	0	2705
	(71.28%)	(25.47%)	(3.25%)	(0%)	(100%)
B- corpus	1761	510	10	1	2282
	(77.17%)	(22.35%)	(0.44%)	(0.04%)	(100%)
C- corpus	1190	1512	67	1	2770
	(42.96%)	(54.58%)	(2.42%)	(0.04%)	(100%)
P- corpus	2186	177	3	0	2366
	(92.39%)	(7.48%)	(0.13%)	(0%)	(100%)

Table 18 Fall-Rise Tone (\ /) – gender

Fall-Rise (\ /)	HKC Males	NES Males	Other speakers Males	All Males (M)	HKC Females	NES Females	Other Speakers Females	All Females (F)
HKCSE (Prosodic)	3626 (59.71%)	2397 (39.47%)	50 (0.82%)	6073 (100%)	3439 (84.96%)	491 (12.13%)	118 (2.92%)	4048 (100%)
A- corpus	1124 (65.39%)	595 (34.61%)	0 (0%)	1719 (100%)	804 (81.54%)	94 (9.53%)	88 (8.92%)	986 (100%)
B- corpus	474 (51.97%)	429 (47.04%)	9 (0.99%)	912 (100%)	1287 (94.01%)	81 (5.92%)	1 (0.07%)	1369 (100%)
C- corpus	565 (31.18%)	1209 (66.72%)	38 (2.1%)	1812 (100%)	625 (65.31%)	303 (31.66%)	29 (3.03%)	957 (100%)
P- corpus	1463 (89.75%)	164 (10.06%)	3 (0.18%)	1630 (100%)	723 (98.23%)	13 (1.77%)	0 (0%)	736 (100%)

Table 19 Level Tone (=) – L1

Level (=)	HKC	NES	Other Speakers	Unidentified Speakers	All Speakers
HKCSE (Prosodic)	118013 (78.38%)	28254 (18.77%)	4259 (2.83%)	30 (0.02%)	150556 (100%)
A- corpus	35936 (89.99%)	3334 (8.35%)	662 (1.66%)	1 (0%)	39933 (100%)
B- corpus	32009 (75.66%)	9834 (23.24%)	458 (1.08%)	6 (0.01%)	42307 (100%)
C- corpus	16848 (54.77%)	11639 (37.84%)	2250 (7.31%)	23 (0.07%)	30760 (100%)
P- corpus	33220 (88.45%)	3447 (9.18%)	889 (2.37%)	0 (0%)	37556 (100%)

Table 20 Level Tone (=) – gender

Level (=)	HKC Males	NES Males	Other speakers Males	All Males (M)	HKC Females	NES Females	Other Speakers Females	All Females (F)
HKCSE (Prosodic)	61850 (71.05%)	22782 (26.17%)	2417 (2.78%)	87049 (100%)	56163 (88.48%)	5472 (8.62%)	1842 (2.9%)	63477 (100%)
A- corpus	19248 (89%)	2378 (11%)	0 (0%)	21626 (100%)	16688 (91.16%)	956 (5.22%)	662 (3.62%)	18306 (100%)
B- corpus	10598 (53.85%)	8659 (44%)	422 (2.14%)	19679 (100%)	21411 (94.65%)	1175 (5.19%)	36 (0.16%)	22622 (100%)
C- corpus	7376 (41.41%)	8700 (48.85%)	1734 (9.74%)	17810 (100%)	9472 (73.27%)	2939 (22.74%)	516 (3.99%)	12927 (100%)
P- corpus	24628 (88.16%)	3045 (10.9%)	261 (0.93%)	27934 (100%)	8592 (89.3%)	402 (4.18%)	628 (6.53%)	9622 (100%)

Table 21 Unclassifiable – L1

Unclassifiable	HKC	NES	Other Speakers	Unidentified Speakers	All Speakers
HKCSE (Prosodic)	11765 (63.73%)	5672 (30.73%)	997 (5.4%)	34 (0.18%)	18460 (100%)
A- corpus	1703 (86.62%)	193 (9.82%)	75 (3.81%)	7 (0.36%)	1966 (100%)
B- corpus	2201 (65.2%)	1034 (30.63%)	995 (29.47%)	4 (0.12%)	3376 (100%)
C- corpus	4886 (49.74%)	4198 (42.74%)	720 (7.33%)	23 (0.23%)	9823 (100%)
P- corpus	2975 (90.29%)	257 (7.8%)	64 (1.94%)	0 (0%)	3295 (100%)

Table 22 Unclassifiable – gender

Unclassifiable	HKC Males	NES Males	Other speakers Males	All Males (M)	HKC Females	NES Females	Other Speakers Females	All Females (F)
HKCSE (Prosodic)	6016 (53.55%)	4505 (40.1%)	716 (6.37%)	11234 (100%)	5748 (79.9%)	1167 (16.22%)	281 (3.91%)	7194 (100%)
A- corpus	888 (87.92%)	122 (12.08%)	0 (0%)	1010 (100%)	813 (85.67%)	61 (6.43%)	75 (7.9%)	949 (100%)
B- corpus	698 (41.01%)	878 (51.59%)	126 (7.4%)	1702 (100%)	1504 (89.95%)	156 (9.33%)	12 (0.72%)	1672 (100%)
C- corpus	1987 (34.16%)	3280 (56.4%)	552 (9.49%)	5816 (100%)	2899 (72.77%)	918 (23.04%)	168 (4.22%)	3984 (100%)
P- corpus	2443 (90.28%)	225 (8.31%)	38 (1.4%)	2706 (100%)	532 (90.32%)	32 (5.43%)	26 (4.41%)	589 (100%)

Table 23 Total – L1

Total	HKC	NES	Other Speakers	Unidentified Speakers	All Speakers
HKCSE (Prosodic)	239282 (73.92%)	74058 (22.88%)	10237 (3.16%)	134 (0.04%)	323703 (100%)
A- corpus	65777 (86.12%)	8349 (10.93%)	2256 (2.95%)	10 (0.01%)	76380 (100%)
B- corpus	64124 (73.22%)	22310 (25.47%)	1133 (1.29%)	16 (0.02%)	87582 (100%)
C- corpus	43840 (50.8%)	37097 (42.98%)	5263 (6.1%)	108 (0.13%)	86304 (100%)
P- corpus	65541 (89.25%)	6312 (8.6%)	1585 (2.16%)	0 (0%)	73437 (100%)

Table 24 Total – gender

Total	HKC Males	NES Males	Other speakers Males	All Males (M)	HKC Females	NES Females	Other Speakers Females	All Females (F)
HKCSE (Prosodic)	121625 (65.38%)	59023 (31.73%)	5389 (2.9%)	186034 (100%)	117656 (85.54%)	15035 (10.93%)	4848 (3.52%)	137537 (100%)
A- corpus	34934 (85.05%)	6140 (14.95%)	0 (0%)	41074 (100%)	30841 (87.38%)	2199 (6.23%)	2256 (6.39%)	35296 (100%)
B- corpus	19399 (48.88%)	19230 (48.45%)	1058 (2.67%)	39687 (100%)	44726 (93.41%)	3080 (6.43%)	75 (0.16%)	47881 (100%)
C- corpus	18565 (36.73%)	28143 (55.69%)	3834 (7.59%)	50539 (100.01%)	25275 (70.88%)	8954 (25.11%)	1429 (4.01%)	35657 (100%)
P- corpus	48727 (89.03%)	5510 (10.07%)	497 (0.91%)	54734 (100%)	16814 (89.9%)	802 (4.29%)	1088 (5.82%)	18703 (100%)

Quantitative data

Key and termination

Table 1 Key – HKCSE (prosodic) – L1

Key (only)	HKC	NES	Other Speakers	Unidentified Speakers	All Speakers
High [∧]	7528 (75.33%)	2214 (22.16%)	251 (2.51%)	0 (0%)	9993 (100%)
Mid [ ]	71311 (73.45%)	23009 (23.7%)	2752 (2.83%)	18 (0.02%)	97087 (100%)
Low [_]	173 (56.17%)	125 (40.58%)	10 (3.25%)	0 (0%)	308 (100%)
All [***]	79012 (73.58%)	25348 (23.6%)	3013 (2.81%)	18 (0.02%)	107388 (100%)

Table 2 Key – Academic sub-corpus – L1

Key (only)	HKC	NES	Other Speakers	Unidentified Speakers	All Speakers
High [∧]	1656 (75.89%)	418 (19.16%)	108 (4.95%)	0 (0%)	2182 (100%)
Mid [ ]	20600 (81.75%)	3762 (14.93%)	836 (3.32%)	1 (0%)	25198 (100%)
Low [_]	29 (67.44%)	8 (18.6%)	6 (13.95%)	0 (0%)	43 (100%)
All [***]	22285 (81.26%)	4188 (15.27%)	950 (3.46%)	1 (0%)	27423 (100%)

Table 3 Key – Business sub-corpus – L1

Key (only)	HKC	NES	Other Speakers	Unidentified Speakers	All Speakers
High [^]	2140	661	27	0	2828
	(75.67%)	(23.37%)	(0.95%)	(0%)	(100%)
Mid [ ]	18131	6691	341	2	25164
	(72.05%)	(26.59%)	(1.36%)	(0.01%)	(100%)
Low [_]	53	42	0	0	95
	(55.79%)	(44.21%)	(0%)	(0%)	(100%)
All [***]	20324	7394	368	2	28087
	(72.36%)	(26.33%)	(1.31%)	(0.01%)	(100%)

Table 4 Key – Conversation sub-corpus – L1

Key (only)	HKC	NES	Other Speakers	Unidentified Speakers	All Speakers
High [^]	881	879	85	0	1845
	(47.75%)	(47.64%)	(4.61%)	(0%)	(100%)
Mid [ ]	10671	10245	1184	15	22115
	(48.25%)	(46.33%)	(5.35%)	(0.07%)	(100%)
Low [_]	41	68	4	0	113
	(36.28%)	(60.18%)	(3.54%)	(0%)	(100%)
All [***]	11593	11192	1273	15	24073
	(48.16%)	(46.49%)	(5.29%)	(0.06%)	(100%)

Table 5 Key – Public sub-corpus– L1

Key (only)	HKC	NES	Other Speakers	Unidentified Speakers	All Speakers
High [∧]	2851 (90.85%)	256 (8.16%)	31 (0.99%)	0 (0%)	3138 (100%)
Mid [ ]	21909 (89.02%)	2311 (9.39%)	391 (1.59%)	0 (0%)	24610 (100%)
Low [_]	50 (87.72%)	7 (12.28%)	0 (0%)	0 (0%)	57 (100%)
All [***]	24810 (89.23%)	2574 (9.26%)	422 (1.52%)	0 (0%)	27805 (100%)

Table 6 Key – HKCSE (prosodic) – gender

Key (only)	HKC Males	NES Males	Other Speakers Males	All Males	HKC Females	NES Females	Other Speakers Females	All Females
High [∧]	4134 (68.17%)	1832 (30.21%)	98 (1.62%)	6064 (100%)	3394 (86.38%)	382 (9.72%)	153 (3.89%)	3929 (100%)
Mid [ ]	37802 (65.46%)	18730 (32.43%)	1219 (2.11%)	57751 (100%)	33509 (85.22%)	4279 (10.88%)	1533 (3.9%)	39321 (100%)
Low [_]	101 (49.51%)	100 (49.02%)	3 (1.47%)	204 (100%)	72 (69.23%)	25 (24.04%)	7 (6.73%)	104 (100%)
All [***]	42037 (65.66%)	20662 (32.27%)	1320 (2.06%)	64019 (100%)	36975 (85.29%)	4686 (10.81%)	1693 (3.91%)	43354 (100%)

Table 7 Key – Academic sub-corpus – gender

Key (only)	HKC Males	NES Males	Other Speakers Males	All Males	HKC Females	NES Females	Other Speakers Females	All Females
High [^]	873 (71.73%)	344 (28.27%)	0 (0%)	1217 (100%)	783 (81.14%)	74 (7.67%)	108 (11.19%)	965 (100%)
Mid [ ]	10596 (77.61%)	3057 (22.39%)	0 (0%)	13653 (100%)	10004 (86.65%)	705 (6.11%)	836 (7.24%)	11545 (100%)
Low [_]	14 (73.68%)	5 (26.32%)	0 (0%)	19 (100%)	15 (62.5%)	3 (12.5%)	6 (25%)	24 (100%)
All [***]	11483 (77.12%)	3406 (22.88%)	0 (0%)	14889 (100%)	10802 (86.18%)	782 (6.24%)	950 (7.58%)	12534 (100%)

Table 8 Key – Business sub-corpus – gender

Key (only)	HKC Males	NES Males	Other Speakers Males	All Males	HKC Females	NES Females	Other Speakers Females	All Females
High [^]	765 (54.88%)	603 (43.26%)	26 (1.87%)	1394 (100%)	1375 (95.89%)	58 (4.04%)	1 (0.07%)	1434 (100%)
Mid [ ]	6291 (50.3%)	5892 (47.11%)	325 (2.6%)	12508 (100%)	11840 (93.56%)	799 (6.31%)	16 (0.13%)	12655 (100%)
Low [_]	20 (34.48%)	38 (65.52%)	0 (0%)	58 (100%)	33 (89.19%)	4 (10.81%)	0 (0%)	37 (100%)
All [***]	7076 (50.69%)	6533 (46.8%)	351 (2.51%)	13960 (100%)	13248 (93.78%)	861 (6.1%)	17 (0.12%)	14126 (100%)

Table 9 Key – Conversation sub-corpus – gender

Key (only)	HKC Males	NES Males	Other Speakers Males	All Males	HKC Females	NES Females	Other Speakers Females	All Females
High [^]	358 (33.24%)	661 (61.37%)	58 (5.39%)	1077 (100%)	523 (68.1%)	218 (28.39%)	27 (3.52%)	768 (100%)
Mid [ ]	4594 (35%)	7793 (59.38%)	738 (5.62%)	13125 (100%)	6077 (67.71%)	2452 (27.32%)	446 (4.97%)	8975 (100%)
Low [_]	23 (29.87%)	51 (66.23%)	3 (3.9%)	77 (100%)	18 (50%)	17 (47.22%)	1 (2.78%)	36 (100%)
All [***]	4975 (34.84%)	8505 (59.56%)	799 (5.6%)	14279 (100%)	6618 (67.68%)	2687 (27.48%)	474 (4.85%)	9779 (100%)

Table 10 Key – Public sub-corpus – gender

Key (only)	HKC Males	NES Males	Other Speakers Males	All Males	HKC Females	NES Females	Other Speakers Females	All Females
High [^]	2138 (89.98%)	224 (9.43%)	14 (0.59%)	2376 (100%)	713 (93.57%)	32 (4.2%)	17 (2.23%)	762 (100%)
Mid [ ]	16321 (88.39%)	1988 (10.77%)	156 (0.84%)	18465 (100%)	5588 (90.92%)	323 (5.26%)	235 (3.82%)	6146 (100%)
Low [_]	44 (88%)	6 (12%)	0 (0%)	50 (100%)	6 (85.71%)	1 (14.29%)	0 (0%)	7 (100%)
All [***]	18503 (88.57%)	2218 (10.62%)	170 (0.81%)	20891 (100%)	6307 (91.21%)	356 (5.15%)	252 (3.64%)	6915 (100%)

Table 11 High Key [^] – L1

High [^]	HKC	NES	Other Speakers	Unidentified Speakers	All Speakers
HKCSE (Prosodic)	7528 (75.33%)	2214 (22.16%)	251 (2.51%)	0 (0%)	9993 (100%)
A- corpus	1656 (75.89%)	418 (19.16%)	108 (4.95%)	0 (0%)	2182 (100%)
B- corpus	2140 (75.67%)	661 (23.37%)	27 (0.95%)	0 (0%)	2828 (100%)
C- corpus	881 (47.75%)	879 (47.64%)	85 (4.61%)	0 (0%)	1845 (100%)
P- corpus	2851 (90.85%)	256 (8.16%)	31 (0.99%)	0 (0%)	3138 (100%)

Table 12 High Key [^] – gender

High [^]	HKC Males	NES Males	Other speakers Males	All Males (M)	HKC Females	NES Females	Other Speakers Females	All Females (F)
HKCSE (Prosodic)	4134 (68.17%)	1832 (30.21%)	98 (1.62%)	6064 (100%)	3394 (86.38%)	382 (9.72%)	153 (3.89%)	3929 (100%)
A- corpus	873 (71.73%)	344 (28.27%)	0 (0%)	1217 (100%)	783 (81.14%)	74 (7.67%)	108 (11.19%)	965 (100%)
B- corpus	765 (54.88%)	603 (43.26%)	26 (1.87%)	1394 (100%)	1375 (95.89%)	58 (4.04%)	1 (0.07%)	1434 (100%)
C- corpus	358 (33.24%)	661 (61.37%)	58 (5.39%)	1077 (100%)	523 (68.1%)	218 (28.39%)	27 (3.52%)	768 (100%)
P- corpus	2138 (89.98%)	224 (9.43%)	14 (0.59%)	2376 (100%)	713 (93.57%)	32 (4.2%)	17 (2.23%)	762 (100%)

Table 13 Mid Key [ ] – L1

Mid [ ]	HKC	NES	Other Speakers	Unidentified Speakers	All Speakers
HKCSE (Prosodic)	71311 (73.45%)	23009 (23.7%)	2752 (2.83%)	18 (0.02%)	97087 (100%)
A- corpus	20600 (81.75%)	3762 (14.93%)	836 (3.32%)	1 (0%)	25198 (100%)
B- corpus	18131 (72.05%)	6691 (26.59%)	341 (1.36%)	2 (0.01%)	25164 (100%)
C- corpus	10671 (48.25%)	10245 (46.33%)	1184 (5.35%)	15 (0.07%)	22115 (100%)
P- corpus	21909 (89.02%)	2311 (9.39%)	391 (1.59%)	0 (0%)	24610 (100%)

Table 14 Mid Key [ ] – gender

Mid [ ]	HKC Males	NES Males	Other speakers Males	All Males (M)	HKC Females	NES Females	Other Speakers Females	All Females (F)
HKCSE (Prosodic)	37802 (65.46%)	18730 (32.43%)	1219 (2.11%)	57751 (100%)	33509 (85.22%)	4279 (10.88%)	1533 (3.9%)	39321 (100%)
A- corpus	10596 (77.61%)	3057 (22.39%)	0 (0%)	13653 (100%)	10004 (86.65%)	705 (6.11%)	836 (7.24%)	11545 (100%)
B- corpus	6291 (50.3%)	5892 (47.11%)	325 (2.6%)	12508 (100%)	11840 (93.56%)	799 (6.31%)	16 (0.13%)	12655 (100%)
C- corpus	4594 (35%)	7793 (59.38%)	738 (5.62%)	13125 (100%)	6077 (67.71%)	2452 (27.32%)	446 (4.97%)	8975 (100%)
P- corpus	16321 (88.39%)	1988 (10.77%)	156 (0.84%)	18465 (100%)	5588 (90.92%)	323 (5.26%)	235 (3.82%)	6146 (100%)

Table 15 Low Key [_] – L1

Low [_]	HKC	NES	Other Speakers	Unidentified Speakers	All Speakers
HKCSE (Prosodic)	173 (56.17%)	125 (40.58%)	10 (3.25%)	0 (0%)	308 (100%)
A- corpus	29 (67.44%)	8 (18.6%)	6 (13.95%)	0 (0%)	43 (100%)
B- corpus	53 (55.79%)	42 (44.21%)	0 (0%)	0 (0%)	95 (100%)
C- corpus	41 (36.28%)	68 (60.18%)	4 (3.54%)	0 (0%)	113 (100%)
P- corpus	50 (87.72%)	7 (12.28%)	0 (0%)	0 (0%)	57 (100%)

Table 16 Low Key [_] – gender

Low [_]	HKC Males	NES Males	Other speakers Males	All Males (M)	HKC Females	NES Females	Other Speakers Females	All Females (F)
HKCSE (Prosodic)	101 (49.51%)	100 (49.02%)	3 (1.47%)	204 (100%)	72 (69.23%)	25 (24.04%)	7 (6.73%)	104 (100%)
A- corpus	14 (73.68%)	5 (26.32%)	0 (0%)	19 (100%)	15 (62.5%)	3 (12.5%)	6 (25%)	24 (100%)
B- corpus	20 (34.48%)	38 (65.52%)	0 (0%)	58 (100%)	33 (89.19%)	4 (10.81%)	0 (0%)	37 (100%)
C- corpus	23 (29.87%)	51 (66.23%)	3 (3.9%)	77 (100%)	18 (50%)	17 (47.22%)	1 (2.78%)	36 (100%)
P- corpus	44 (88%)	6 (12%)	0 (0%)	50 (100%)	6 (85.71%)	1 (14.29%)	0 (0%)	7 (100%)

Table 17 All Key [***] – L1

All [***]	HKC	NES	Other Speakers	Unidentified Speakers	All Speakers
HKCSE (Prosodic)	79012 (73.58%)	25348 (23.6%)	3013 (2.81%)	18 (0.02%)	107388 (100%)
A- corpus	22285 (81.26%)	4188 (15.27%)	950 (3.46%)	1 (0%)	27423 (100%)
B- corpus	20324 (72.36%)	7394 (26.33%)	368 (1.31%)	2 (0.01%)	28087 (100%)
C- corpus	11593 (48.16%)	11192 (46.49%)	1273 (5.29%)	15 (0.06%)	24073 (100%)
P- corpus	24810 (89.23%)	2574 (9.26%)	422 (1.52%)	0 (0%)	27805 (100%)

Table 18 All Key [***] – gender

All [***]	HKC Males	NES Males	Other speakers Males	All Males (M)	HKC Females	NES Females	Other Speakers Females	All Females (F)
HKCSE (Prosodic)	42037 (65.66%)	20662 (32.27%)	1320 (2.06%)	64019 (100%)	36975 (85.29%)	4686 (10.81%)	1693 (3.91%)	43354 (100%)
A- corpus	11483 (77.12%)	3406 (22.88%)	0 (0%)	14889 (100%)	10802 (86.18%)	782 (6.24%)	950 (7.58%)	12534 (100%)
B- corpus	7076 (50.69%)	6533 (46.8%)	351 (2.51%)	13960 (100%)	13248 (93.78%)	861 (6.1%)	17 (0.12%)	14126 (100%)
C- corpus	4975 (34.84%)	8505 (59.56%)	799 (5.6%)	14279 (100%)	6618 (67.68%)	2687 (27.48%)	474 (4.85%)	9779 (100%)
P- corpus	18503 (88.57%)	2218 (10.62%)	170 (0.81%)	20891 (100%)	6307 (91.21%)	356 (5.15%)	252 (3.64%)	6915 (100%)

Table 19 Termination (only) – HKCSE (prosodic) – L1

Termination (only)	HKC	NES	Other Speakers	Unidentified Speakers	All Speakers
High <^ >	7767 (66.46%)	3611 (30.9%)	304 (2.6%)	5 (0.04%)	11687 (100%)
Mid < >	69037 (74.6%)	20965 (22.65%)	2528 (2.73%)	17 (0.02%)	92542 (100%)
Low <_ >	2487 (67.22%)	1006 (27.19%)	208 (5.62%)	0 (0%)	3700 (100%)
All < *** >	79291 (73.47%)	25582 (23.7%)	3040 (2.82%)	22 (0.02%)	107929 (100%)

Table 20 Termination (only) – Academic sub-corpus – L1

Termination (only)	HKC	NES	Other Speakers	Unidentified Speakers	All Speakers
High <^ >	1498 (64.6%)	746 (32.17%)	75 (3.23%)	0 (0%)	2319 (100%)
Mid < >	20327 (83.28%)	3316 (13.59%)	766 (3.14%)	1 (0%)	24409 (100%)
Low <_ >	489 (67.26%)	128 (17.61%)	110 (15.13%)	0 (0%)	727 (100%)
All < *** >	22314 (81.27%)	4190 (15.26%)	951 (3.46%)	1 (0%)	27455 (100%)

Table 21 Termination (only) – Business sub-corpus – L1

Termination (only)	HKC	NES	Other Speakers	Unidentified Speakers	All Speakers
High <^>	1899 (67.15%)	886 (31.33%)	43 (1.52%)	0 (0%)	2828 (100%)
Mid <>	17873 (73.44%)	6158 (25.3%)	306 (1.26%)	2 (0.01%)	24337 (100%)
Low <_>	660 (59.78%)	427 (38.68%)	18 (1.63%)	0 (0%)	1104 (100%)
All <***>	20432 (72.28%)	7471 (26.43%)	367 (1.3%)	2 (0.01%)	28269 (100%)

Table 22 Termination (only) – Conversation sub-corpus – L1

Termination (only)	HKC	NES	Other Speakers	Unidentified Speakers	All Speakers
High <^>	1029 (37.68%)	1571 (57.52%)	126 (4.61%)	5 (0.18%)	2731 (100%)
Mid <>	10452 (49.76%)	9429 (44.89%)	1111 (5.29%)	14 (0.07%)	21005 (100%)
Low <_>	233 (36.81%)	339 (53.55%)	61 (9.64%)	0 (0%)	633 (100%)
All <***>	11714 (48.07%)	11339 (46.53%)	1298 (5.33%)	19 (0.08%)	24369 (100%)

Table 23 Termination (only) – Public sub-corpus – L1

Termination (only)	HKC	NES	Other Speakers	Unidentified Speakers	All Speakers
High <^ >	3341 (87.71%)	408 (10.71%)	60 (1.58%)	0 (0%)	3809 (100%)
Mid < >	20398 (89.5%)	2062 (9.05%)	345 (1.51%)	0 (0%)	22791 (100%)
Low <_ >	1106 (89.48%)	112 (9.06%)	19 (1.54%)	0 (0%)	1236 (100%)
All < *** >	24845 (89.25%)	2582 (9.28%)	424 (1.52%)	0 (0%)	27836 (100%)

Table 24 Termination (only) – HKCSE (prosodic) – gender

Termination (only)	HKC Males	NES Males	Other Speakers Males	All Males	HKC Females	NES Females	Other Speakers Females	All Females
High <^ >	4585 (58.39%)	3135 (39.92%)	133 (1.69%)	7853 (100%)	3182 (83.1%)	476 (12.43%)	171 (4.47%)	3829 (100%)
Mid < >	36025 (66.63%)	16899 (31.26%)	1142 (2.11%)	54066 (100%)	33012 (85.83%)	4066 (10.57%)	1386 (3.6%)	38464 (100%)
Low <_ >	1536 (63.52%)	820 (33.91%)	62 (2.56%)	2418 (100%)	951 (74.12%)	186 (14.5%)	146 (11.38%)	1283 (100%)
All < *** >	42146 (65.51%)	20854 (32.41%)	1337 (2.08%)	64337 (100%)	37145 (85.24%)	4728 (10.85%)	1703 (3.91%)	43576 (100%)

Table 25 Termination (only) – Academic sub-corpus – gender

Termination (only)	HKC Males	NES Males	Other Speakers Males	All Males	HKC Females	NES Females	Other Speakers Females	All Females
High <^ >	1018 (59.92%)	681 (40.08%)	0 (0%)	1699 (100%)	480 (77.42%)	65 (10.48%)	75 (12.1%)	620 (100%)
Mid < >	10228 (79.49%)	2639 (20.51%)	0 (0%)	12867 (100%)	10099 (87.5%)	677 (5.87%)	766 (6.64%)	11542 (100%)
Low <_ >	259 (73.79%)	92 (26.21%)	0 (0%)	351 (100%)	230 (61.17%)	36 (9.57%)	110 (29.26%)	376 (100%)
All < *** >	11505 (77.13%)	3412 (22.87%)	0 (0%)	14917 (100%)	10809 (86.21%)	778 (6.21%)	951 (7.58%)	12538 (100%)

Table 26 Termination (only) – Business sub-corpus – gender

Termination (only)	HKC Males	NES Males	Other Speakers Males	All Males	HKC Females	NES Females	Other Speakers Females	All Females
High <^ >	572 (40.2%)	808 (56.78%)	43 (3.02%)	1423 (100%)	1327 (94.45%)	78 (5.55%)	0 (0%)	1405 (100%)
Mid < >	6210 (52.19%)	5400 (45.38%)	289 (2.43%)	11899 (100%)	11663 (93.77%)	758 (6.09%)	17 (0.14%)	12438 (100%)
Low <_ >	312 (43.39%)	389 (54.1%)	18 (2.5%)	719 (100%)	348 (90.16%)	38 (9.84%)	0 (0%)	386 (100%)
All < *** >	7094 (50.52%)	6597 (46.98%)	350 (2.49%)	14041 (100%)	13338 (93.74%)	874 (6.14%)	17 (0.12%)	14229 (100%)

Table 27 Termination (only) – Conversation sub-corpus – gender

Termination (only)	HKC Males	NES Males	Other Speakers Males	All Males	HKC Females	NES Females	Other Speakers Females	All Females
High <^ >	535 (28.28%)	1291 (68.23%)	66 (3.49%)	1892 (100%)	494 (59.23%)	280 (33.57%)	60 (7.19%)	834 (100%)
Mid < >	4369 (35.93%)	7079 (58.21%)	713 (5.86%)	12161 (100%)	6083 (68.88%)	2350 (26.61%)	398 (4.51%)	8831 (100%)
Low <_ >	117 (28.75%)	252 (61.92%)	38 (9.34%)	407 (100%)	116 (51.33%)	87 (38.5%)	23 (10.18%)	226 (100%)
All < *** >	5021 (34.72%)	8622 (59.63%)	817 (5.65%)	14460 (100%)	6693 (67.67%)	2717 (27.47%)	481 (4.86%)	9891 (100%)

Table 28 Termination (only) – Public sub-corpus – gender

Termination (only)	HKC Males	NES Males	Other Speakers Males	All Males	HKC Females	NES Females	Other Speakers Females	All Females
High <^ >	2460 (86.65%)	355 (12.5%)	24 (0.85%)	2839 (100%)	881 (90.82%)	53 (5.46%)	36 (3.71%)	970 (100%)
Mid < >	15218 (88.79%)	1781 (10.39%)	140 (0.82%)	17139 (100%)	5167 (91.4%)	281 (4.97%)	205 (3.63%)	5653 (100%)
Low <_ >	848 (90.12%)	87 (9.25%)	6 (0.64%)	941 (100%)	257 (87.12%)	25 (8.47%)	13 (4.41%)	295 (100%)
All < *** >	18526 (88.56%)	2223 (10.63%)	170 (0.81%)	20919 (100%)	6305 (91.14%)	359 (5.19%)	254 (3.67%)	6918 (100%)

Table 29 High Termination <^> – L1

High <^>	HKC	NES	Other Speakers	Unidentified Speakers	All Speakers
HKCSE (Prosodic)	7767 (66.46%)	3611 (30.9%)	304 (2.6%)	5 (0.04%)	11687 (100%)
A- corpus	1498 (64.6%)	746 (32.17%)	75 (3.23%)	0 (0%)	2319 (100%)
B- corpus	1899 (67.15%)	886 (31.33%)	43 (1.52%)	0 (0%)	2828 (100%)
C- corpus	1029 (37.68%)	1571 (57.52%)	126 (4.61%)	5 (0.18%)	2731 (100%)
P- corpus	3341 (87.71%)	408 (10.71%)	60 (1.58%)	0 (0%)	3809 (100%)

Table 30 High Termination <^> – gender

High <^>	HKC Males	NES Males	Other speakers Males	All Males (M)	HKC Females	NES Females	Other Speakers Females	All Females (F)
HKCSE (Prosodic)	4585 (58.39%)	3135 (39.92%)	133 (1.69%)	7853 (100%)	3182 (83.1%)	476 (12.43%)	171 (4.47%)	3829 (100%)
A- corpus	1018 (59.92%)	681 (40.08%)	0 (0%)	1699 (100%)	480 (77.42%)	65 (10.48%)	75 (12.1%)	620 (100%)
B- corpus	572 (40.2%)	808 (56.78%)	43 (3.02%)	1423 (100%)	1327 (94.45%)	78 (5.55%)	0 (0%)	1405 (100%)
C- corpus	535 (28.28%)	1291 (68.23%)	66 (3.49%)	1892 (100%)	494 (59.23%)	280 (33.57%)	60 (7.19%)	834 (100%)
P- corpus	2460 (86.65%)	355 (12.5%)	24 (0.85%)	2839 (100%)	881 (90.82%)	53 (5.46%)	36 (3.71%)	970 (100%)

Table 31 Mid Termination < > – L1

Mid < >	HKC	NES	Other Speakers	Unidentified Speakers	All Speakers
HKCSE (Prosodic)	69037 (74.6%)	20965 (22.65%)	2528 (2.73%)	17 (0.02%)	92542 (100%)
A- corpus	20327 (83.28%)	3316 (13.59%)	766 (3.14%)	1 (0%)	24409 (100%)
B- corpus	17873 (73.44%)	6158 (25.3%)	306 (1.26%)	2 (0.01%)	24337 (100%)
C- corpus	10452 (49.76%)	9429 (44.89%)	1111 (5.29%)	14 (0.07%)	21005 (100%)
P- corpus	20398 (89.5%)	2062 (9.05%)	345 (1.51%)	0 (0%)	22791 (100%)

Table 32 Mid Termination < > – gender

Mid < >	HKC Males	NES Males	Other speakers Males	All Males (M)	HKC Females	NES Females	Other Speakers Females	All Females (F)
HKCSE (Prosodic)	36025 (66.63%)	16899 (31.26%)	1142 (2.11%)	54066 (100%)	33012 (85.83%)	4066 (10.57%)	1386 (3.6%)	38464 (100%)
A- corpus	10228 (79.49%)	2639 (20.51%)	0 (0%)	12867 (100%)	10099 (87.5%)	677 (5.87%)	766 (6.64%)	11542 (100%)
B- corpus	6210 (52.19%)	5400 (45.38%)	289 (2.43%)	11899 (100%)	11663 (93.77%)	758 (6.09%)	17 (0.14%)	12438 (100%)
C- corpus	4369 (35.93%)	7079 (58.21%)	713 (5.86%)	12161 (100%)	6083 (68.88%)	2350 (26.61%)	398 (4.51%)	8831 (100%)
P- corpus	15218 (88.79%)	1781 (10.39%)	140 (0.82%)	17139 (100%)	5167 (91.4%)	281 (4.97%)	205 (3.63%)	5653 (100%)

Table 33 Low Termination <_> – L1

Low <_>	HKC	NES	Other Speakers	Unidentified Speakers	All Speakers
HKCSE (Prosodic)	2487 (67.22%)	1006 (27.19%)	208 (5.62%)	0 (0%)	3700 (100%)
A- corpus	489 (67.26%)	128 (17.61%)	110 (15.13%)	0 (0%)	727 (100%)
B- corpus	660 (59.78%)	427 (38.68%)	18 (1.63%)	0 (0%)	1104 (100%)
C- corpus	233 (36.81%)	339 (53.55%)	61 (9.64%)	0 (0%)	633 (100%)
P- corpus	1106 (89.48%)	112 (9.06%)	19 (1.54%)	0 (0%)	1236 (100%)

Table 34 Low Termination <_> – gender

Low <_>	HKC Males	NES Males	Other speakers Males	All Males (M)	HKC Females	NES Females	Other Speakers Females	All Females (F)
HKCSE (Prosodic)	1536 (63.52%)	820 (33.91%)	62 (2.56%)	2418 (100%)	951 (74.12%)	186 (14.5%)	146 (11.38%)	1283 (100%)
A- corpus	259 (73.79%)	92 (26.21%)	0 (0%)	351 (100%)	230 (61.17%)	36 (9.57%)	110 (29.26%)	376 (100%)
B- corpus	312 (43.39%)	389 (54.1%)	18 (2.5%)	719 (100%)	348 (90.16%)	38 (9.84%)	0 (0%)	386 (100%)
C- corpus	117 (28.75%)	252 (61.92%)	38 (9.34%)	407 (100%)	116 (51.33%)	87 (38.5%)	23 (10.18%)	226 (100%)
P- corpus	848 (90.12%)	87 (9.25%)	6 (0.64%)	941 (100%)	257 (87.12%)	25 (8.47%)	13 (4.41%)	295 (100%)

Table 35 All Termination <***> – L1

All <***>	HKC	NES	Other Speakers	Unidentified Speakers	All Speakers
HKCSE (Prosodic)	79291 (73.47%)	25582 (23.7%)	3040 (2.82%)	22 (0.02%)	107929 (100%)
A- corpus	22314 (81.27%)	4190 (15.26%)	951 (3.46%)	1 (0%)	27455 (100%)
B- corpus	20432 (72.28%)	7471 (26.43%)	367 (1.3%)	2 (0.01%)	28269 (100%)
C- corpus	11714 (48.07%)	11339 (46.53%)	1298 (5.33%)	19 (0.08%)	24369 (100%)
P- corpus	24845 (89.25%)	2582 (9.28%)	424 (1.52%)	0 (0%)	27836 (100%)

Table 36 All Termination <***> – gender

All <***>	HKC Males	NES Males	Other speakers Males	All Males (M)	HKC Females	NES Females	Other Speakers Females	All Females (F)
HKCSE (Prosodic)	42146 (65.51%)	20854 (32.41%)	1337 (2.08%)	64337 (100%)	37145 (85.24%)	4728 (10.85%)	1703 (3.91%)	43576 (100%)
A- corpus	11505 (77.13%)	3412 (22.87%)	0 (0%)	14917 (100%)	10809 (86.21%)	778 (6.21%)	951 (7.58%)	12538 (100%)
B- corpus	7094 (50.52%)	6597 (46.98%)	350 (2.49%)	14041 (100%)	13338 (93.74%)	874 (6.14%)	17 (0.12%)	14229 (100%)
C- corpus	5021 (34.72%)	8622 (59.63%)	817 (5.65%)	14460 (100%)	6693 (67.67%)	2717 (27.47%)	481 (4.86%)	9891 (100%)
P- corpus	18526 (88.56%)	2223 (10.63%)	170 (0.81%)	20919 (100%)	6305 (91.14%)	359 (5.19%)	254 (3.67%)	6918 (100%)

Table 37 Key + Termination – HKCSE (prosodic) – L1

Key + Termination	HKC	NES	Other Speakers	Unidentified Speakers	All Speakers
High [< ^.. >]	15670 (72.33%)	5339 (24.64%)	646 (2.98%)	9 (0.04%)	21666 (100%)
Mid [< >]	131986 (74.99%)	38145 (21.67%)	5779 (3.28%)	89 (0.05%)	176001 (100%)
Low [< _.. >]	8181 (69.82%)	3106 (26.51%)	428 (3.65%)	2 (0.02%)	11718 (100%)
All [< *** >]	155837 (74.43%)	46590 (22.25%)	6853 (3.27%)	100 (0.05%)	209385 (100%)

Table 38 Key + Termination – Academic sub-corpus – L1

Key + Termination	HKC	NES	Other Speakers	Unidentified Speakers	All Speakers
High [< ^.. >]	3371 (84.44%)	453 (11.35%)	168 (4.21%)	0 (0%)	3992 (100%)
Mid [< >]	37064 (89.58%)	3351 (8.1%)	954 (2.28%)	4 (0.01%)	41375 (100%)
Low [< _.. >]	1986 (84.91%)	221 (9.45%)	132 (5.64%)	0 (0%)	2339 (100%)
All [< *** >]	42421 (88.92%)	4025 (8.44%)	1254 (2.63%)	4 (0.01%)	47706 (100%)

Table 39 Key + Termination – Business sub-corpus – L1

Key + Termination	HKC	NES	Other Speakers	Unidentified Speakers	All Speakers
High [< ^.. >]	4014	1448	53	1	5518
	(72.74%)	(26.24%)	(0.96%)	(0.02%)	(100%)
Mid [< >]	35949	11715	596	10	48269
	(74.48%)	(24.27%)	(1.23%)	(0.02%)	(100%)
Low [< _.. >]	2403	977	26	1	3408
	(70.51%)	(28.67%)	(0.76%)	(0.03%)	(100%)
All [< ★★★ >]	42366	14140	675	12	57195
	(74.07%)	(24.72%)	(1.18%)	(0.02%)	(100%)

Table 40 Key + Termination – Conversation sub-corpus – L1

Key + Termination	HKC	NES	Other Speakers	Unidentified Speakers	All Speakers
High [< ^.. >]	3048	2918	301	8	6275
	(48.57%)	(46.5%)	(4.8%)	(0.13%)	(100%)
Mid [< >]	26364	20154	3280	75	49873
	(52.86%)	(40.41%)	(6.58%)	(0.15%)	(100%)
Low [< _.. >]	1730	1708	204	1	3643
	(47.49%)	(46.88%)	(5.6%)	(0.03%)	(100%)
All [< ★★★ >]	31142	24780	3785	84	59791
	(52.08%)	(41.44%)	(6.33%)	(0.14%)	(100%)

Table 41 Key + Termination – Public sub-corpus– L1

Key + Termination	HKC	NES	Other Speakers	Unidentified Speakers	All Speakers
High [< ^..>]	5238 (89.07%)	520 (8.84%)	124 (2.11%)	0 (0%)	5881 (100%)
Mid [<>]	32614 (89.39%)	2925 (8.02%)	949 (2.6%)	0 (0%)	36484 (100%)
Low [<_..>]	2064 (88.66%)	200 (8.59%)	66 (2.84%)	0 (0%)	2328 (100%)
All [<***>]	39916 (89.31%)	3645 (8.16%)	1139 (2.55%)	0 (0%)	44693 (100%)

Table 42 Key + Termination – HKCSE (prosodic) – gender

Key + Termination	HKC Males	NES Males	Other Speakers Males	All Males	HKC Females	NES Females	Other Speakers Females	All Females
High [< ^..>]	8454 (65%)	4271 (32.84%)	282 (2.17%)	13007 (100%)	7216 (83.44%)	1068 (12.35%)	364 (4.21%)	8648 (100%)
Mid [<>]	64480 (65.98%)	29935 (30.63%)	3312 (3.39%)	97727 (100%)	67506 (86.34%)	8210 (10.5%)	2467 (3.16%)	78183 (100%)
Low [<_..>]	4459 (62.46%)	2479 (34.72%)	201 (2.82%)	7139 (100%)	3722 (81.34%)	627 (13.7%)	227 (4.96%)	4576 (100%)
All [<***>]	77393 (65.66%)	36685 (31.12%)	3795 (3.22%)	117873 (100%)	78444 (85.82%)	9905 (10.84%)	3058 (3.35%)	91407 (100%)

Table 43 Key + Termination – Academic sub-corpus – gender

Key + Termination	HKC Males	NES Males	Other Speakers Males	All Males	HKC Females	NES Females	Other Speakers Females	All Females
High [< ^.. >]	2157 (87.08%)	320 (12.92%)	0 (0%)	2477 (100%)	1214 (80.13%)	133 (8.78%)	168 (11.09%)	1515 (100%)
Mid [<>]	19563 (89.84%)	2212 (10.16%)	0 (0%)	21775 (100%)	17501 (89.32%)	1139 (5.81%)	954 (4.87%)	19594 (100%)
Low [<_..>]	1119 (89.74%)	128 (10.26%)	0 (0%)	1247 (100%)	867 (79.4%)	93 (8.52%)	132 (12.09%)	1092 (100%)
All [<*** >]	22839 (89.57%)	2660 (10.43%)	0 (0%)	25499 (100%)	19582 (88.2%)	1365 (6.15%)	1254 (5.65%)	22201 (100%)

Table 44 Key + Termination – Business sub-corpus – gender

Key + Termination	HKC Males	NES Males	Other Speakers Males	All Males	HKC Females	NES Females	Other Speakers Females	All Females
High [< ^.. >]	1139 (46.6%)	1254 (51.31%)	51 (2.09%)	2444 (100%)	2875 (93.62%)	194 (6.32%)	2 (0.07%)	3071 (100%)
Mid [<>]	9969 (48.76%)	9932 (48.58%)	545 (2.67%)	20446 (100%)	25980 (93.41%)	1783 (6.41%)	51 (0.18%)	27814 (100%)
Low [<_..>]	759 (46.17%)	860 (52.31%)	25 (1.52%)	1644 (100%)	1644 (93.3%)	117 (6.64%)	1 (0.06%)	1762 (100%)
All [<*** >]	11867 (48.37%)	12046 (49.1%)	621 (2.53%)	24534 (100%)	30499 (93.42%)	2094 (6.41%)	54 (0.17%)	32647 (100%)

Table 45 Key + Termination – Conversation sub-corpus – gender

Key + Termination	HKC Males	NES Males	Other Speakers Males	All Males	HKC Females	NES Females	Other Speakers Females	All Females
High [<^..>]	1350 (35.88%)	2233 (59.34%)	180 (4.78%)	3763 (100%)	1698 (67.81%)	685 (27.36%)	121 (4.83%)	2504 (100%)
Mid [<>]	10862 (37.98%)	15212 (53.19%)	2523 (8.82%)	28597 (100%)	15502 (73.12%)	4942 (23.31%)	757 (3.57%)	21201 (100%)
Low [<_..>]	909 (38.11%)	1319 (55.3%)	157 (6.58%)	2385 (100%)	821 (65.31%)	389 (30.95%)	47 (3.74%)	1257 (100%)
All [<***>]	13121 (37.76%)	18764 (54%)	2860 (8.23%)	34745 (100%)	18021 (72.19%)	6016 (24.1%)	925 (3.71%)	24962 (100%)

Table 46 Key + Termination – Public sub-corpus – gender

Key + Termination	HKC Males	NES Males	Other Speakers Males	All Males	HKC Females	NES Females	Other Speakers Females	All Females
High [<^..>]	3808 (88.09%)	464 (10.73%)	51 (1.18%)	4323 (100%)	1429 (91.72%)	56 (3.59%)	73 (4.69%)	1558 (100%)
Mid [<>]	24086 (89.51%)	2579 (9.58%)	244 (0.91%)	26909 (100%)	8523 (89.02%)	346 (3.61%)	705 (7.36%)	9574 (100%)
Low [<_..>]	1672 (89.75%)	172 (9.23%)	19 (1.02%)	1863 (100%)	390 (83.87%)	28 (6.02%)	47 (10.11%)	465 (100%)
All [<***>]	29566 (89.34%)	3215 (9.71%)	314 (0.95%)	33095 (100%)	10342 (89.18%)	430 (3.71%)	825 (7.11%)	11597 (100%)

Table 47 High Key + Termination [< ^.. >] – L1

High [<^..>]	HKC	NES	Other Speakers	Unidentified Speakers	All Speakers
HKCSE (Prosodic)	15670 (72.33%)	5339 (24.64%)	646 (2.98%)	9 (0.04%)	21666 (100%)
A- corpus	3371 (84.44%)	453 (11.35%)	168 (4.21%)	0 (0%)	3992 (100%)
B- corpus	4014 (72.74%)	1448 (26.24%)	53 (0.96%)	1 (0.02%)	5518 (100%)
C- corpus	3048 (48.57%)	2918 (46.5%)	301 (4.8%)	8 (0.13%)	6275 (100%)
P- corpus	5238 (89.07%)	520 (8.84%)	124 (2.11%)	0 (0%)	5881 (100%)

Table 48 High Key + Termination [< ^.. >] – gender

High [<^..>]	HKC Males	NES Males	Other speakers Males	All Males (M)	HKC Females	NES Females	Other Speakers Females	All Females (F)
HKCSE (Prosodic)	8454 (65%)	4271 (32.84%)	282 (2.17%)	13007 (100%)	7216 (83.44%)	1068 (12.35%)	364 (4.21%)	8648 (100%)
A- corpus	2157 (87.08%)	320 (12.92%)	0 (0%)	2477 (100%)	1214 (80.13%)	133 (8.78%)	168 (11.09%)	1515 (100%)
B- corpus	1139 (46.6%)	1254 (51.31%)	51 (2.09%)	2444 (100%)	2875 (93.62%)	194 (6.32%)	2 (0.07%)	3071 (100%)
C- corpus	1350 (35.88%)	2233 (59.34%)	180 (4.78%)	3763 (100%)	1698 (67.81%)	685 (27.36%)	121 (4.83%)	2504 (100%)
P- corpus	3808 (88.09%)	464 (10.73%)	51 (1.18%)	4323 (100%)	1429 (91.72%)	56 (3.59%)	73 (4.69%)	1558 (100%)

Table 49 Mid Key + Termination [< >] – L1

Mid [<>]	HKC	NES	Other Speakers	Unidentified Speakers	All Speakers
HKCSE (Prosodic)	131986 (74.99%)	38145 (21.67%)	5779 (3.28%)	89 (0.05%)	176001 (100%)
A- corpus	36064 (87.16%)	3351 (8.1%)	954 (2.31%)	4 (0.01%)	41375 (97.58%)
B- corpus	35949 (74.48%)	11715 (24.27%)	596 (1.23%)	10 (0.02%)	48269 (100%)
C- corpus	26364 (52.86%)	20154 (40.41%)	3280 (6.58%)	75 (0.15%)	49873 (100%)
P- corpus	32614 (89.39%)	2925 (8.02%)	949 (2.6%)	0 (0%)	36484 (100%)

Table 50 Mid Key with Termination [< >] – gender

Mid [<>]	HKC Males	NES Males	Other speakers Males	All Males (M)	HKC Females	NES Females	Other Speakers Females	All Females (F)
HKCSE (Prosodic)	64480 (65.98%)	29935 (30.63%)	3312 (3.39%)	97727 (100%)	67506 (86.34%)	8210 (10.5%)	2467 (3.16%)	78183 (100%)
A- corpus	19563 (89.84%)	2212 (10.16%)	0 (0%)	21775 (100%)	17501 (89.32%)	1139 (5.81%)	954 (4.87%)	19594 (100%)
B- corpus	9969 (48.76%)	9932 (48.58%)	545 (2.67%)	20446 (100%)	25980 (93.41%)	1783 (6.41%)	51 (0.18%)	27814 (100%)
C- corpus	10862 (37.98%)	15212 (53.19%)	2523 (8.82%)	28597 (100%)	15502 (73.12%)	4942 (23.31%)	757 (3.57%)	21201 (100%)
P- corpus	24086 (89.51%)	2579 (9.58%)	244 (0.91%)	26909 (100%)	8523 (89.02%)	346 (3.61%)	705 (7.36%)	9574 (100%)

Table 51 Low Key + Termination [< _...>] – L1

Low [<_...>]	HKC	NES	Other Speakers	Unidentified Speakers	All Speakers
HKCSE (Prosodic)	8181 (69.82%)	3106 (26.51%)	428 (3.65%)	2 (0.02%)	11718 (100%)
A- corpus	1986 (84.91%)	221 (9.45%)	132 (5.64%)	0 (0%)	2339 (100%)
B- corpus	2403 (70.51%)	977 (28.67%)	26 (0.76%)	1 (0.03%)	3408 (100%)
C- corpus	1730 (47.49%)	1708 (46.88%)	204 (5.6%)	1 (0.03%)	3643 (100%)
P- corpus	2064 (88.66%)	200 (8.59%)	66 (2.84%)	0 (0%)	2328 (100%)

Table 52 Low Key + Termination [< _...>] - gender

Low [<_...>]	HKC Males	NES Males	Other speakers Males	All Males (M)	HKC Females	NES Females	Other Speakers Females	All Females (F)
HKCSE (Prosodic)	4459 (62.46%)	2479 (34.72%)	201 (2.82%)	7139 (100%)	3722 (81.34%)	627 (13.7%)	227 (4.96%)	4576 (100%)
A- corpus	1119 (89.74%)	128 (10.26%)	0 (0%)	1247 (100%)	867 (79.4%)	93 (8.52%)	132 (12.09%)	1092 (100%)
B- corpus	759 (46.17%)	860 (52.31%)	25 (1.52%)	1644 (100%)	1644 (93.3%)	117 (6.64%)	1 (0.06%)	1762 (100%)
C- corpus	909 (38.11%)	1319 (55.3%)	157 (6.58%)	2385 (100%)	821 (65.31%)	389 (30.95%)	47 (3.74%)	1257 (100%)
P- corpus	1672 (89.75%)	172 (9.23%)	19 (1.02%)	1863 (100%)	390 (83.87%)	28 (6.02%)	47 (10.11%)	465 (100%)

Table 53 All Key + Termination [<*** >] – L1

All [<*** >]	HKC	NES	Other Speakers	Unidentified Speakers	All Speakers
HKCSE (Prosodic)	155837 (74.43%)	46590 (22.25%)	6853 (3.27%)	100 (0.05%)	209385 (100%)
A- corpus	42421 (88.92%)	4025 (8.44%)	1254 (2.63%)	4 (0.01%)	47706 (100%)
B- corpus	42366 (74.07%)	14140 (24.72%)	675 (1.18%)	12 (0.02%)	57195 (100%)
C- corpus	31142 (52.08%)	24780 (41.44%)	3785 (6.33%)	84 (0.14%)	59791 (100%)
P- corpus	39916 (89.31%)	3645 (8.16%)	1139 (2.55%)	0 (0%)	44693 (100%)

Table 54 All Key + Termination [<*** >] – gender

All [<*** >]	HKC Males	NES Males	Other speakers Males	All Males (M)	HKC Females	NES Females	Other Speakers Females	All Females (F)
HKCSE (Prosodic)	77393 (65.66%)	36685 (31.12%)	3795 (3.22%)	117873 (100%)	78444 (85.82%)	9905 (10.84%)	3058 (3.35%)	91407 (100%)
A- corpus	22839 (89.57%)	2660 (10.43%)	0 (0%)	25499 (100%)	19582 (88.2%)	1365 (6.15%)	1254 (5.65%)	22201 (100%)
B- corpus	11867 (48.37%)	12046 (49.1%)	621 (2.53%)	24534 (100%)	30499 (93.42%)	2094 (6.41%)	54 (0.17%)	32647 (100%)
C- corpus	13121 (37.76%)	18764 (54%)	2860 (8.23%)	34745 (100%)	18021 (72.19%)	6016 (24.1%)	925 (3.71%)	24962 (100%)
P- corpus	29566 (89.34%)	3215 (9.71%)	314 (0.95%)	33095 (100%)	10342 (89.18%)	430 (3.71%)	825 (7.11%)	11597 (100%)

Author index

Subject index

In the series *Studies in Corpus Linguistics (SCL)* the following titles have been published thus far or are scheduled for publication:

5 **GHADESSY, Mohsen, Alex HENRY and Robert L. ROSEBERRY (eds.):** Small Corpus Studies and ELT. Theory and practice. 2001. xxiv, 420 pp.

4 **HUNSTON, Susan and Gill FRANCIS:** Pattern Grammar. A corpus-driven approach to the lexical grammar of English. 2000. xiv, 288 pp.

3 **BOTLEY, Simon Philip and Tony McENERY (eds.):** Corpus-based and Computational Approaches to Discourse Anaphora. 2000. vi, 258 pp.

2 **PARTINGTON, Alan:** Patterns and Meanings. Using corpora for English language research and teaching. 1998. x, 158 pp.

1 **PEARSON, Jennifer:** Terms in Context. 1998. xii, 246 pp.